Catherine Jane Sands
306 South Ruby St.
Ellensburg, Washington
98926
925-4241

OLD WORLD ARCHAEOLOGY:
Foundations of Civilization

Readings from
**SCIENTIFIC
AMERICAN**

OLD WORLD ARCHAEOLOGY:

Foundations of Civilization

with introductions by
C. C. Lamberg-Karlovsky
Harvard University

W. H. Freeman and Company
San Francisco

Some of the SCIENTIFIC AMERICAN articles
in *Old World Archaeology: Foundations of
Civilization* are available as separate Offprints.
For a complete list of more than 900 articles now
available as Offprints, write to W. H. Freeman
and Company, 660 Market Street, San Francisco,
California 94104.

Printed in the United States of America

Library of Congress Catalog Card Number: 72–1961

Standard Book Number: 0–7167–0860–4 (cloth)
0–7167–0859–0 (paper)

98765432

PREFACE

Today, in a world that sees an ever-increasing number of social problems, which are only partly due to an increasing polarization of the "have" and the "have-not" nations, I am often asked what relevance archaeology has to the present world. Of what relevance is it to know what happened 3,000 years ago, let alone 300,000 years ago? To an archaeologist, its relevance is almost commonplace. No one today needs to be reminded of the lack of perspective in a typical European or American view of history, which excises from its own past whatever is unflattering and emphasizes out of all proportion its own relevance to universal history. Our moral, aesthetic, scientific, and practical interests today urgently call for an anthropological view of our own history, an effort to see in perspective not only our nation but the entirety of our civilization. We must never, as Arnold Toynbee has reminded us, allow transient economic and political power to obscure the fact that Western Civilization is only one of the many civilizations that have existed, only one of the handful that now exist. Archaeology surely helps us take a genuinely world view of man and his past history. It helps us see the literate, history-recording civilizations as branches from a common trunk that is rooted in prehistoric antiquity. Only if we take such a view will the assumed superiority of any one nation be placed in perspective, be revealed as arrogance. Only so can we understand the truly cousinly relationship of all cultures and civilizations, both past and present. A view of history adequate to modern times must take into account the entirety of man's life on earth, and we must remember that over 99 percent of this life has, in fact, been prehistoric.

Frequently archaeology is still considered to be the collecting of curios, from a long and forgotten past, that will end up on exhibit in some museum. Indeed, this earlier archaeological function expanded our appreciation of man's aesthetic diversity. Today, however, the archaeologist asks "how" and "why": what processes in the past were involved in man's transition from hunter and gatherer to village dweller, and eventually to settler in that most unusual of man's experiments, the city? By understanding such processes, we have come to appreciate better the almost infinite variability of man's responses to manipulations of, and control over his environment. We can guide our decisions today by considering that spectrum of past decisions, by noting which ones under certain circumstances led to failure and which ones led to success. Without such understanding of the past, we would be the worse off today, for the practical lessons gained from the past can often be applied to make more likely a successful future. It would be far too optimistic, however, to say that eventually the historical sciences, of which archaeology is one, will provide us with the rigor of prediction.

The papers gathered here provide us with glimpses of more than 500,000 years of man's cultural evolution, and of the rise and fall of his past civilizations, which can remind us of our own transience. We need continually to remind ourselves that archaeology has revealed a prehistory that is far from "dead": it is still very much with us. Only a few hundred generations ago all peoples were prehistoric; a sizable percentage of the countries constituting the United Nations were prehistoric down to modern times. The archaeological recovery of prehistoric cultures has helped us understand the processes involved in the transition from a nonliterate, "primitive" society to an urban complex. Comprehension of this transition in the past can help man today to understand, and even participate in, present transformations more effectively.

Much remains yet to be accomplished. Entire areas of the globe are archaeologically unknown, and many problems have hardly been broached. Today archaeology benefits from a renewed interest by universities, even a public popularity. Only by the combined efforts of prehistoric archaeologists, cultural anthropologists, and the broad range of natural scientists who today work in conjunction with them can we reach the universal understanding necessary to coexistence in the modern world.

C. C. Lamberg-Karlovsky
Cambridge, Mass.
Jan. 3, 1972

CONTENTS

IV. RECENT PERSPECTIVES AND PROBLEMS

Note on cross-references: References to articles included in this book are noted by the title of the article and the page on which it begins; references to articles that are available as Offprints, but are not included here, are noted by the article's title and Offprint number; references to articles published by SCIENTIFIC AMERICAN, but which are not available as Offprints, are noted by the title of the article and the month and year of its publication.

OLD WORLD ARCHAEOLOGY:
Foundations of Civilization

I

PALEOLITHIC HUNTERS AND GATHERERS

I

PALEOLITHIC HUNTERS AND GATHERERS

INTRODUCTION

The Old Stone Age constitutes well over 99 per cent of man's past. Its study is inextricably interwoven with man's organic evolution, from the small primate of over 2 million years ago to modern man long before the end of the Old Stone Age some 12,000 years ago. Paleolithic archaeology is above all characterized by the very close collaboration of the archaeologist with the biologist, detailing human evolution; the geologist, who works out geological time-scales by studies of glacial advances and retreats, pluvials, etc.; the pedologist and palynologist, who study the soils and pollen in order to reconstruct the ancient habitat; the petrologist, who studies and identifies the rocks and minerals from which early man fabricated his tools; and the paleontologist, who studies the fossil animal remains to determine the ecology of man's early environment and his eating habits. The paleolithic archaeologist has perhaps the longest tradition within archaeology of a close and continued collaboration with the natural sciences.

The articles in this section review three important paleolithic sites of three different continents: Shanidar in Western Asia, Terre Amata in France, and Isimila in Africa. The remarkable accomplishments of the Paleolithic artist are reviewed by Leroi-Ghourhan, and a synthesis of the Solutrean culture of some 17,000 years ago is presented by Philip Smith. It is of necessity a minimal introduction to the wealth of information available on the earliest tool-using cultures of the Old World, which stretch from China to Europe and cover a time-span of almost two million years. I can provide here only a short background to these articles, and urge the interested reader to turn to an excellent recent review of the Paleolithic, that of Francoise Bordes (1968).[1]

The earliest well-dated stone industries manufactured by "man" (almost two million years ago, dated by potassium-argon) come from the Lower Pleistocene deposits at Olduvai Gorge in Tanzania, which yielded traces of an early primate believed to be of a type ancestral to man (Leakey, 1968). The debris excavated from the floor of this site consists of natural stones brought there from a considerable distance (perhaps these were used as structural supports for a shelter), primitive stone tools, together with the waste flakes resulting from their manufacture, and animal bones all intentionally fractured to extract the marrow. These early ape-men, in contrast to surviving apes today, were already carniverous: hunters preying on birds, fish, and

---

1. References given in this form are to books listed at the end of the Introduction.

reptiles, and even on larger mammals. We know nothing of their hunting techniques. At this stage our evidence is so meager that almost all must be conjecture when we speak of their social organization, hunting technology, and so on. The most important single tool in the earliest man's tool kit was a simple chopping tool, manufactured by striking off a few flakes from a stone pebble — often from both sides of the pebble to form a pointed axe-like tool. Stone industries of this general type have been found in Lower Pleistocene deposits in Algeria, Tanzania, and Morocco, and most recently have been reported from a site discovered in western Hungary. It is far too early to say whether or not East Africa will maintain its present position as the cradle of mankind's earliest physical evolution and the focus of his earliest stone industries. Perhaps further research will show that this development took place over extensive areas, and that individual advances in techniques of tool manufacture occurred in many different centers.

The Middle Pleistocene (400,000–100,000) witnessed notable advances, both in the physical evolution of man and in his tool-making capacity. Within this time span, toward the start of the Middle Pleistocene, *Homo erectus* (Pithecanthropus) made his first appearance. He was most surely a hominid with a markedly larger brain and new traditions in stone-tool manufacture, characterized above all by the manufacture of bifacial hand-axes. The best-documented finds of *Homo erectus* are in the Far East, at Choukoutien, near Pekin, China, though his remains have also been reported from Olduvai Gorge, Algeria, and Java. Pekin Man, as the finds from Choukoutien are referred to, was largely a meat eater, and a manipulator of fire (among the earliest evidence of the control of fire), who hunted with pointed wooden spears and stripped his kills with crude stone tools. Beyond question, it was as hunters and predators that the earliest men achieved their new status in the biological world. The pebble and flake tools of Pekin Man have broad similarities, with expected regional differences, to Middle Pleistocene finds in different parts of the Eurasian land mass, from the Clactonian culture of southeastern England, the Soan of the Punjab and the Anyathian of Burma, to the Pajitanian of Java. In all these areas, the hand-axe continued to be the principal tool. When one examines a stratified site, such as Olduvai Gorge, it is possible to detect, through time, a broad evolutionary development in the manufacture of this tool type, which became ever-increasingly more efficient. Progressively improved skill and control over the flint enabled Paleolithic man to turn out shapelier axes, better suited to the task, while using decreasing amounts of flint.

The first half of the Late Pleistocene (100,000–50,000) saw the physical evolution of Neanderthal man and his ever-increasing cultural complexity. Physical anthropologists have long argued, and the controversy continues today, over whether Neanderthal man belongs to the modern family of man, *Homo sapiens*. Most physical anthropologists would classify him as *Homo sapiens neanderthalensis*. The tool kit of Neanderthal man became more varied and complex, particularly throughout southern Europe, North Africa, and southwestern Asia. Several distinct industrial traditions appear throughout this area—testimony to the increasing rate of regional development and specialization. One such industry takes its name from Levallois, a site near Paris, where tools were manufactured from a block of flint prepared in such a way that flakes could be struck from one face, ready to use as they were chipped from the core. Another widespread tradition, first identified in the cave of Le Moustier (Dordogne, France), involved the striking of flakes from disc cores and the production from the flakes of points or side scrapers. Both of the above techniques of stone-tool manufacture have been recorded, with variations, over a large area (see the articles by Solecki and by Howell), most notably North Africa, southwestern Asia, and particularly Palestine, where they are referred to conveniently as Levalloiso-Mousterian tool industries. Neanderthal man was advancing not only in the production of his material culture but also in his biological capacity as a "thinker"—a carrier of a distinctive and unique culture that he was capable of transmitting to subsequent generations. Pekin Man cracked open the skulls of his own in order to extract their brains (of course, we don't know whether he was merely satisfying a physical appetite or was perhaps, by analogy with Melanesian practice, engaging in a ritual cannibalism).

Neanderthal man was surely of a different nature than his possible evolutionary progenitor, *Homo erectus*. It is he that appears to have initiated the practice of careful burial and concern for the dead. Ralph Solecki, in his excavations at Shanidar Cave (see his article in this section) had the good fortune to excavate a number of Neanderthal skeletons. One burial was obviously an intentional internment: analysis of pollen found around the grave suggested an unusual percentage of pollen from a variety of flowers. The interpretation seems clear: Neanderthal man, in burying his dead, placed or planted about the body quantities of flowers! On the terrace in front of the Mount Carmel cave in Palestine, a regular cemetery of ten Neanderthals was uncovered. One of the dead was wounded in the thigh, apparently by a wooden spear; we are left to speculate about the cause of the wound (accident? fight?). The Mount Carmel burials all had their legs drawn up to the body. A female Neanderthal at La Ferrassie, France, was so tightly flexed that she may have been bound by thongs, a practice that might reflect the desire of the living to keep the dead permanently away and immovable. Throughout this long period, we have little information on Neanderthal's adaptive responses to his changing environment, characterized by the periodic retreats and advances of the European ice sheets, which in turn affected the climate over even wider areas.

Articles in this section also detail the latter half of the Late Pleistocene, beginning around 50,000 years ago. Developments throughout this time period were of prime importance to the history of mankind. It is difficult for us to appreciate the enormous advances made and equally difficult for us to appreciate the enormous time-scale on which these advances were made. If we take a generation to be 25 years, then it was but 80 generations ago that Jesus walked the earth, 160 generations ago that the Sumerians thrived in Mesopotamia (see the article by Kramer, page 145), 680 generations ago that the people of the Solutrean culture occupied southern France, and over 1,300 generations ago that Neanderthal man inhabited Shanidar Cave. It is, thus, well over a thousand generations ago that saw the final emergence of modern man, his expansion over the entirety of the Earth's surface (save Australia, the Arctic, and Antarctica), and his differentiation into the varied races of man. Neanderthal man had by that time achieved the cranial capacity of modern man (*ca.* 1,200 c.c.), which is almost double that of the earlier *Homo erectus*. Modern man differs from Neanderthal man only in his lighter jaw, more pointed chin, smaller teeth, and less prominent brow-ridges.

Geographically, the Late Pleistocene was marked by a great expansion in the area of human settlement. Radiocarbon dates attest to the fact that 12,000 years ago both the New World and Australasia were occupied; in fact, the New World as much as 5,000 years prior to that. By their invasion of the New World, the Stone Age hunters opened a new and exciting chapter in the cultural history of mankind. It is interesting to note that the world as a whole was colonized by man while he was still a hunter and gatherer. Over the whole world, new flint industries appeared, based on the production, by specialized techniques, of blades with parallel flakes, one of the highest elaborations of which appeared in the Solutrean culture of France (see the article by Smith in this section).

The papers in this section discuss the tangible remains of paleolithic man's technology, and his marvelous aesthetic accomplishments in the caves of France. By contrasting the different articles, one can realize the great degree of cultural and biological variation in man's long evolution. One can see, in the superb reconstruction of what is clearly the earliest house yet excavated, at Terre Amata, France, some 300,000 years ago, that man's tools and homes had already separated this creature from the rest of the animal kingdom. How unfortunate for the archaeologist that actual physical remains of the builders were not found in association with this cultural complex; however, we may assume that they were advanced *Homo erectus* or perhaps even Neanderthal. It is an inescapable fact that the archaeologist rarely finds the association that he would like; and even when he does, we are still left to speculate about religious beliefs, kinship systems, and so on. Neanderthal's survival depended, no doubt, on his greatest biological asset, that which separated him from the rest of the animal kingdom: his brain.

Today we are faced with a revolution in our understanding and appreciation of the accomplishments of Paleolithic man. Evidence that his thought processes were already complex tens of thousands of years ago has recently been advanced by Alexander Marshack. Not content to accept as random the intentionally produced marks and patterns incised on bone and stone, Marshack undertook a microscopic analysis of them. He found them to have a mathematical replication in certain sets and classes. An intensive analysis led him to conclude that they were systematic notations, intended to record a calendrical system. Thus, we can today appreciate in our ancestors of some 1,000 generations ago their great intellectual conquest of time, by means of their ability to predict the calendrical cycle of seasons. In recognizing this, we come closer to appreciating and identifying with this previously misunderstood "savage brute" of the past who in one way or another remains with us to the present.

REFERENCES

F. Bordes. 1968. *The Old Stone Age*. World Universal Library.
L. S. B. Leakey. 1965. *Olduvai Gorge, 1951–1961*, vol. I. Cambridge University Press.

1

THE IDEA OF MAN'S ANTIQUITY

GLYN E. DANIEL
November 1959

Digging near the Bavarian city of Bayreuth in 1771, Johann Friedrich Esper found human bones at the same level as the remains of extinct animals. He was more startled than elated by his find, because it confronted him with a disturbing anachronism in the then-accepted timetable of the world's history. In the preceding century Archbishop Ussher had worked out this chronology from the complicated genealogies of *Genesis;* he concluded that the world and man had been created in 4004 B.C. Six millennia took in everything, and man was only a trifle younger than time itself. In this view of human history there was no inkling that sources other than written ones existed. The antiquaries of the time were concerned with describing monuments and cataloguing

portable relics; they had no idea that history lay in the soil, much less any notion of how to wrest it from its grave. Samuel Johnson spoke for the pre-archaeological scholar when he declared: "All that is really known of the ancient state of Britain is contained in a few pages. . . . We can know no more than what old writers have told us."

Except for a few pagan myths, the old writers did not suggest that there were men before Man. Geology in Esper's and Johnson's time was little more than an elaboration of the Biblical story of Creation and the Flood. In accordance with that tradition it was easy, and not without logic, to explain fossils and river gravels in terms of the Flood, or sometimes of several floods. This was catastrophist or diluvialist geology. There

was, to be sure, some talk of animals antedating 4004 B.C., but their fossils were believed to be the remains of creatures discarded by the Creator before his culminating creation: the world of Genesis. But with the creation of Adam, according to the doctrine, further creation ceased. Opposed to this account were the antediluvians—the near-heretics who held that man may have lived before Adam. This was the danger apprehended by Esper, and it caused him to ask: "Did [the bones] belong to a Druid or to an Antediluvian or to a mortal man of more recent time? I dare not presume without sufficient reason these members to be of the same age as the other animal petrifactions. They must have got there by chance."

The "sufficient reason" Esper asked

FLINT TOOL FROM HOXNE IN SUFFOLK is typical of the discoveries that caused speculation about man's antiquity. This hand-axe, dated according to the stratum in which it was found and the workmanship it displays, belongs to the Lower Paleolithic of about half a million years ago. The illustration appeared in 1800 in *Archeologia*, a publication of the Society of Antiquaries of London.

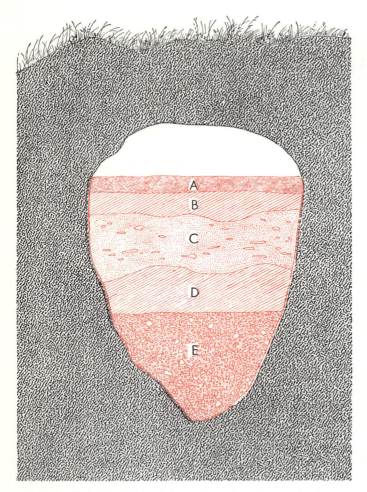
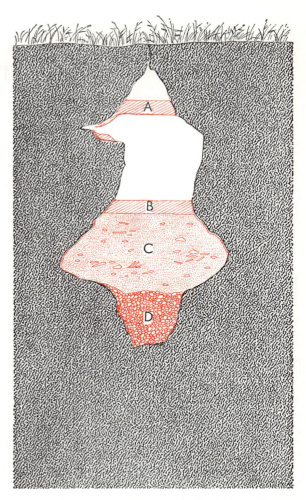

DEVON CAVES IN ENGLAND figured prominently in establishing the antiquity of man. Kent's Cavern (*left*) was the earlier find. Under surface layer (A) lay a stalagmite stratum (B) which sealed the cave earth (C) containing human artifacts amid the remains of extinct animals. Layers D and E are stalagmite and breccia. The floor of the 600-foot long Brixham Cave (*right*) had once been at A, but when excavated in 1858 the stalagmite at B was the cave floor. In the six feet of cave earth (C) were remains similar to those found in Kent's Cavern. Level D is gravel bed. Both the caves measure more than 20 feet from roof to gravel-bed bottom.

for was soon to be forthcoming. James Hutton, in his *Theory of the Earth*, published in 1785, offered the first persuasive alternative to cataclysmic geology. He suggested that the stratification of rocks was due not to floods and other supernatural calamities but to processes still going on in seas and rivers and lakes. He wrote: "No processes are to be employed that are not natural to the globe, no action to be admitted except those of which we know the principle." Hutton's reasoning was carried forward by William Smith—"Strata" Smith as he was called—who assigned relative ages to rocks according to their fossil contents, and who argued for an orderly, noncatastrophic deposition of strata over a long period of time—much longer than 6,000 years.

But the climate of opinion was still catastrophist. In 1797, just 26 years after Esper's discovery, John Frere, a gentleman of Suffolk, sent to the Secretary of the Society of Antiquaries of London some hand-axes and other implements of flint found at Hoxne, near Diss. In his accompanying letter he wrote: "If [these] weapons of war, fabricated and used by a people who had not the use of metals . . . are not particularly objects of curiosity in themselves, they must, I think, be considered in that light from the situation in which they are found, [which] may tempt us to refer them to a very remote period indeed; even beyond that of the present world."

They were indeed to be referred "to a very remote period": modern archaeologists would place them in the Lower Paleolithic of perhaps half a million years ago. But at the time no one took Frere's speculations seriously.

William Buckland, Reader in Geology at Oxford and later Dean of Westminster, perhaps typified catastrophist thinking. In 1823 he published his great book *Reliquiae Diluvianae, or Observations on the Organic Remains contained in Caves, Fissures and Diluvial Gravel, and on Other Geological Phenomena attesting the Action of an Universal Deluge*. Buckland himself had found evidence of the antiquity of man, but he refused to believe it. He had excavated Goat's Hole Cave near Paviland in South Wales and amid Upper Paleolithic implements had found the skeleton of a young man. (He believed it to be that of a young woman, and it is still referred to as the Red Lady of Paviland.) But he insisted that the skeleton was "clearly not coeval with the antediluvian bones of the extinct species" of animals. He made similar discoveries in the caves of the Mendip Hills of southwestern England but again refused to believe they were antediluvian. He argued instead that the caves had "been used either as a place of sepulture in early times or resorted to for refuge by the wretches that perished in it, when the country was suffering under one of our numerous military operations. . . . The state of the bones affords indication of very high antiquity but there is no reason for not considering them post-Diluvian."

When a Roman Catholic priest, Father MacEnery, discovered some flint implements at Kent's Cavern near Torquay in Devon, he wrote of them to Buckland. Buckland reacted characteristically. The flints had been found amid the stratified remains of rhinoceros and other animals under the unbroken, stalagmite-sealed floor of the cave. Buckland avoided the implications of this sealed evidence and offered another ingenious and tortured explanation that preserved catastrophist doctrine. He told MacEnery that ancient Britons must have camped in the cave; they had probably scooped out ovens in the stalagmite and in that way the flint implements had got below. Thus, according to Buckland, the association of the flints with the skeletal remains of extinct animals was only apparent. It was all very reasonable, except that, as MacEnery noted, there were no such ovens in the cave. But Buckland was insistent, and out of deference to his views MacEnery did not publish his evidence.

At about this time, however, the National Museum in Copenhagen had been opened to the public with its antiquities arranged in three ages: Stone, Bronze and Iron. This classification was the work of Christian Jurgenson Thomsen, director of the Museum, and he set forth its underlying idea in a treatise that served as a guidebook to the display. His three-age system has been described very properly as "the cornerstone of modern archaeology"; it helped to secure recognition for the view that the human species had come through a long prehistory. (The word "prehistory" did not appear in print until 1851, when Daniel Wilson used it in *The Archaeology and Prehistoric Annals of Scotland*.)

The 1830's were eventful for the emerging new science of archaeology. In 1833 Sir Charles Lyell published his *Principles of Geology*, a powerful contribution to the cause of the fluvialists, as the supporters of Hutton and Smith were called. This book was in its way as important as Darwin's *Origin of Species*. Lyell took the many fragmentary observations and insights of the fluvialists and organized them into a coherent system. He stated the principle of uniformitarianism: the central geological idea that strata could only be interpreted correctly by assuming that the agencies that formed them had operated at a uniform rate and in a uniform way, just as they work in the present. Lyell's great book was a staggering blow to catastrophist geology. But though the discoveries of Esper and Frere were thus rationalized, and the work of Hutton and Smith endorsed, this was not yet sufficient to swing general opinion behind belief in the true antiquity of man. More evidence was needed to shatter the old view and establish the new one; it soon came from Devon and northern France.

Boucher de Perthes was a customs official at Abbeville in the north of France. He had become interested in archaeology when he encountered neolithic artifacts and bones—"Celtic" remains as they were called—brought up by the dredging of the Somme Canal. His interest grew as more remains of "diluvial" man and animals were found in the quarries of nearby Manchecourt and Moulin-Quignon. By 1838, some five or six years after Lyell's *Principles* had appeared, de Perthes set forth his views in a five-volume work entitled *De la création: essai sur l'origine et la progression des êtres*. At about the same time he was exhibiting *haches diluviennes*, roughly chipped hand-axes, before the Société Imperiale d'Emulation de la Somme in Abbeville and at the Institut de Paris.

He was received with the same coldness suffered by his fellows in England, and like them he was regarded as a crank. "At the very mention of the words 'axe' and 'diluvium,'" he once remarked, "I observe a smile on the face of those to whom I speak. It is the workmen who help me, not the geologists." But de Perthes worked on and accumulated more evidence. The association he observed of human artifacts and extinct animals in the Somme gravels was compelling and no longer to be explained by the diluvial theory. In 1847 he published the first part of a three-volume work entitled *Antiquités celtiques et antédiluviennes*. The very title of the work indicates the effect his researches had on his thinking: the *haches diluviennes* were now *haches antédiluviennes*.

In England, meanwhile, the new archaeology had found other champions. William Pengelly, a schoolmaster, reworked MacEnery's cavern in Kent and,

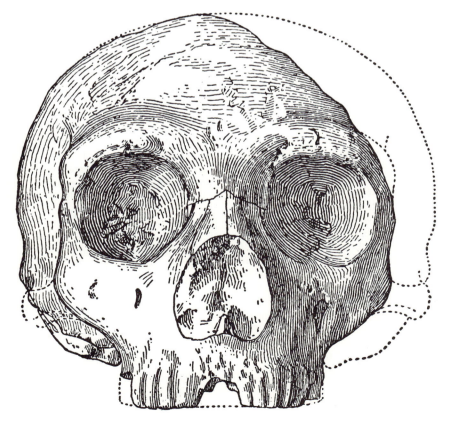

SKULL OF NEANDERTHAL WOMAN was found in Forbes Quarry at Gibraltar in 1848. First believed to be a new species, Neanderthal was later seen to be a human variant. Missing portions of skull are outlined in this drawing from Hugo Obermaier's *Fossil Man in Spain*.

viewing the evidence there in terms of Lyell's uniformitarianism, saw it as proof of man's antiquity. But he realized that objections could be raised because the cavern had been disturbed by other workers. He found an entirely new site in an undisturbed cave across the bay in Devon above Brixham Harbour—Windmill Hill Cave. To supervise his excavations here he enlisted a committee of distinguished geologists in London. Pengelly, carrying out the actual digging, worked from July, 1858, to the next summer. It was a successful year. On the floor of the cave "lay a sheet of stalagmite from three to eight inches thick having within it and on it relics of lion, hyena, bear, mammoth, rhinoceros and reindeer." Below the floor Pengelly found flint tools.

The Brixham discoveries were compelling. Sir Charles Lyell said of them: "The facts recently brought to light during the systematic investigation of the Brixham Cave must, I think, have prepared you to admit that scepticism in regard to the cave evidence in favour of the antiquity of man had previously been pushed to an extreme."

The revolution was nearing a crisis: within the immediately foreseeable future man's history was to reach back beyond Archbishop Ussher's 6,000 years. The catastrophist theory was once and for all to be discarded and with it the Biblical notion that the world and man represented unalterable acts of special creation.

In 1858, while Pengelly was digging in the Brixham cave, the Scottish geologist Hugh Falconer visited Boucher de Perthes at Abbeville. De Perthes' evidence of man's antiquity immediately convinced Falconer. When he returned to London, he persuaded the geologist Joseph Prestwich and the antiquary John Evans to go and see the finds of Abbeville for themselves. As Evans was leaving for France, he wrote of the widely separated events that were revising men's beliefs: "Think of their finding flint axes and arrowheads at Abbeville in conjunction with the bones of elephants and rhinoceroses 40 feet below the surface in a bed of drift. In this bone cave in Devon now being excavated . . . they say they have found flint arrowheads among the bones and the same is reported of a cave in Sicily. I can hardly believe it. It will make my ancient Britons quite modern if man is carried back in England to the days when elephants, rhinoceroses, hippopotamuses and tigers were also inhabitants of the country."

Evans then records what happened when they got to France. De Perthes showed them his collection of flint axes and implements "found among the beds of gravel, . . . the remains of a race of men who existed at the time when the deluge or whatever was the origin of these gravel beds took place. One of the most remarkable features of the case is that nearly all . . . of the animals whose bones are found in the same beds as the axes are extinct. There is the mammoth, the rhinoceros, the urus, . . . etc." Then they arrive at the actual gravel pits: "Sure enough, the edge of an axe was visible in an entirely undisturbed bed of gravel and eleven feet from the surface. We had a photographer with us to take a view of it so as to corroborate our testimony."

The evidence at Abbeville convinced Evans and Prestwich as it had convinced Falconer, and this, with Pengelly's work at Windmill Hill Cave, brought the whole matter to a head. When they got back to London, Prestwich read a paper to the Royal Society in which he said: "It was not until I had myself witnessed the conditions under which these flint implements had been found at Brixham that I became fully impressed with the validity of the doubts thrown upon the previously prevailing opinions with respect to such remains in caves." That famous meeting of the Royal Society was on May 26, 1859, and of it John Evans wrote: "There were a good many geological nobs there: Sir Charles Lyell, Murchison, Huxley, Morris, Dr. Perry, Faraday, Wheatstone, Babbage, etc. . . . Our assertions as to the finding of the weapons seemed to be believed."

A week later Evans read a paper on the same subject to the Society of Antiquaries of London. In his account of this meeting he remarked: "I think I was generally believed in."

In August Sir Charles Lyell himself went to see the evidence of the Abbeville pits. He too was convinced, and a month later, in his presidential address to Section C of the British Association for the Advancement of Science, with Prince Albert presiding, he said: "I am fully prepared to corroborate the conclusions recently laid before the Royal Society by Mr. Prestwich." The battle was over; the great antiquity of man was an established fact. Victorian thought had to adjust itself not only to organic evolution but also to the antiquity of man; 4004 B.C. was forgotten.

It is perhaps strange that Charles Darwin himself was not at first impressed by the findings of de Perthes. Later in life he confessed: "I am ashamed to think that I concluded the whole was rubbish. Yet [de Perthes] has done for man something like what Agassiz did for glaciers." Perhaps Darwin held back because he did not want to involve his theory of evolution, at least at the outset, in anything so controversial as the ancestry of man. In the first edition of the *Origin of Species* he refused to discuss the relationship of evolution to man, and made only one cryptic statement on the general thesis of his book: "Light will be thrown on the origin of man and his history." In later editions this sentence was modified to: "Much light will be thrown. . . ."

But Darwin threw no light, not at any rate until 1871, when he published his views on the relation between man and general evolutionary theory in his *Descent of Man*. But this was eight years after T. H. Huxley's *Evidence as to Man's Place in Nature* had been published, and a dozen years after the climactic events of 1859. Thus whatever contribution Darwin made to the discovery of the antiquity of man, it was indirect and unwitting. It consisted entirely in the new way of thinking that he exemplified: uniformitarianism and evolution. The doctrine of evolution had man evolving from a prehuman ancestor; obviously there must somewhere be evidence of his passage from savagery through barbarism to civilization. The roughly chipped tools from Devon and the Somme now were more than credible, they were essential. People now had to accept the discoveries of de Perthes and Pengelly, where only a generation or two before, when the immutability of the species and catastrophist diluvialism were the dominant ideas, such discoveries had been scorned or ignored. Thus though Darwinism did not create prehistoric archaeology, it did give a great impetus to its acceptance and study; it helped set the stage for the acceptance of the idea of man's antiquity.

But even after the idea seemed well established, many students of the mid-century discoveries had misgivings about them. There was one particularly troublesome point: Men had left their axes but no trace of their physical selves, no bones. "Find us human remains in the diluvium," some of de Perthes' countrymen said to him, "and we will believe you." For de Perthes it was a sad challenge; this was 1863 and he was an old man of 75. Unable to dig for himself, he offered a 200-franc reward to the first quarryman to find human remains. With four months' wages as the prize, the quarrymen could not leave it to honest luck. Soon after the offer was made, they "found" human remains; first a human tooth; five days later a human jaw.

Boucher de Perthes was vindicated, and his French colleagues were at last satisfied. But the drama had not played out. Some British archaeologists had long suspected that de Perthes' gravel pits were being salted, and they proved that the jaw and several hand-axes had been inserted into the gravel faces by some of his workmen. It was a cruel blow.

Fortunately the case did not hang by so meager a thread. There was genuine skeletal evidence of man's antiquity. Two years before the 1859 pronouncements about the antiquity of man, the long bones and skullcap of a manlike being had been discovered in a limestone cave in the ravine of Neanderthal near the Rhenish city of Düsseldorf.

Hermann Schaaffhausen, who first described these remains, noted the large size, low forehead and enormous browridges of the skullcap. He believed that the Neanderthal skeleton belonged to "a barbarous and savage race," and he regarded it "as the most ancient memorial of the early inhabitants of Europe."

There was still more evidence. A female cranium had been found nine years before that, in 1848, during blasting operations in the Forbes Quarry at Gibraltar. The significance of the relic was not realized at the time, but at this juncture, in 1859, George Busk read a paper on it before a meeting of the British Association. The ebullient Falconer, who had persuaded Evans and Prestwich to visit de Perthes six years before, again apprehended the importance of a crucial find. He perceived

that here was a new species of man; he proposed to name it *Homo calpicus*, after Calpe, the ancient name for Gibraltar. He wrote his suggestion to Busk, referring somewhat redundantly to his "Grand, Priscan, Pithecoid, Agrioblematous, Platycnemic, wild *Homo calpicus* of Gibraltar." It was only later realized that this "grand, primitive, manlike, wild-eyed, flat-headed, wild Calpic man of Gibraltar" was not one of a new species but a member of that curious human variant, Neanderthal man.

And so by 1859 all the evidence for proper recognition of the antiquity of man was available: artifacts from the Somme and south Devon and fossils from Neanderthal and Gibraltar. The century since then has been given to building on that premise, to filling in its outlines with new evidence of man's physical and cultural evolution.

RED DEER STAG (*above*) appears on a cave wall at Lascaux, a French Paleolithic site discovered in 1940. Both the stag and the two abstract signs below it, a rectangle and a row of dots, were painted on the rock surface with a manganese pigment; the stag is about five feet high. The painting was made some 15,000 years ago.

SPOTTED HORSE (*below*) dominates a cave wall at Pech-Merle, another French Paleolithic site. A hand seen in negative outline indicates the scale of the painting, which, like the stag, belongs to the early Magdalenian period of European prehistory. Abstract signs include many dots and a grill-like red rectangle by the hand.

2

THE EVOLUTION OF PALEOLITHIC ART

ANDRÉ LEROI-GOURHAN
February 1968

The earliest forms of art, at least among those art forms that can be dated with any certainty, were created in Europe between 30,000 and 10,000 B.C. They belong to a time before the oldest civilizations and the earliest agriculture—the Upper Paleolithic period at the end of the last continental glaciation. Paleolithic art has manifested itself in two principal forms: engraved or sculptured objects found by the thousands in excavations from the Urals to the Atlantic, and the awe-inspiring decorations of more than 100 caves in France and Spain. It has now been studied for nearly a century, and such caves as Lascaux and Altamira have become as well known as the most famous art works of historic times.

Until recently studies of Paleolithic art were focused largely on its aesthetic and magico-religious significance. Today attention has turned to the relations among such art forms—to their classification in terms of time and space. As a result we can now begin to perceive how Paleolithic art evolved from its appearance in Aurignacian times to its inexplicable disappearance in Magdalenian times 20,000 years later.

Can an art that embraced all Europe for such a mighty span truly be considered a single art? Should we perhaps speak of prehistoric arts, as we speak of the arts of Africa? The analogy provides the answer to our question: The living arts of Africa south of the Sahara, with all their nuances, are clearly subdivisions of one wholly African art. They cannot be confused with the art of any other region. In the same sense Paleolithic art also constitutes a single episode in art history. Such is the unanimous opinion of its students. This view is based on the continuity that Paleolithic art exhibits in region after region over a span of 20

millenniums. Greek art or Christian art is so identified because its images continuously translate its ideologies. In the same way the term "Paleolithic art" serves to relate various techniques of representation that have undergone changes over a long period of time to a body of figurative themes that has remained remarkably constant. Indeed, consistency is one of the first facts that strikes the student of Paleolithic art. In painting, engraving and sculpture on rock walls or in ivory, reindeer antler, bone and stone, and in the most diverse styles, Paleolithic artists repeatedly depict the same inventory of animals in comparable attitudes. Once this unity is recognized, it only remains for the student to seek ways of arranging the art's temporal and spatial subdivisions in a systematic manner.

The Problem of Chronology

The task of temporal subdivision is by no means an easy one. To understand its difficulties, let us imagine an art historian who must arrange in their correct chronological order 1,000 statues belonging to every epoch from 500 B.C. to A.D. 1900. Imagine further that his only points of reference are five or six of the statues that are by chance correctly dated. The prehistorian's position is the same—or worse. The large majority of the Paleolithic period's small sculptures (which we classify as "portable art" to distinguish them from "wall art," the paintings, engravings and sculptures of the caves and rock-shelters) were discovered at the beginning of this century, a time when precision in the excavation of stratified sites was far from absolute. As a result there are very few instances in which associations are established between excavated works of art and imple-

ments such as scrapers and projectile points that have been firmly dated on the basis of stratigraphy. Even in the few cases where such dating is possible, the style of the object is not always so clear-cut as to allow strong conclusions. Finally, the thousands of wall paintings and engravings created during the period are not stratified at all. If the earth floors of their caves contain the remains of more than one Paleolithic culture, it is difficult to decide to which of these culture periods the art should be assigned. For all these reasons classifying Paleolithic art is a task considerably harder than the classification of prehistoric man's other material remains.

The work of the Abbé Breuil over more than half a century provides the principal source of traditional views concerning the evolution of Paleolithic art. This pioneer prehistorian undertook a prodigious labor of inventory and classification with the limited means available in his day. Except for a few instances in which specific dating was possible, his method of establishing the relative chronology of wall art rested on three assumptions. The first was simply that when two wall paintings are superimposed, the one underneath must be the older. The second, based on the probability that the caves where wall art is found were inhabited continuously for many centuries, was that one should find examples of work from many periods among the decorations. The third assumption was that, since the animal and human forms depicted in the caves were executed individually for magical purposes, there is no order in their arrangement. It follows from this last assumption that such works are not necessarily contemporaneous and that they are not, when taken together, evidence of any organized body of thought.

14

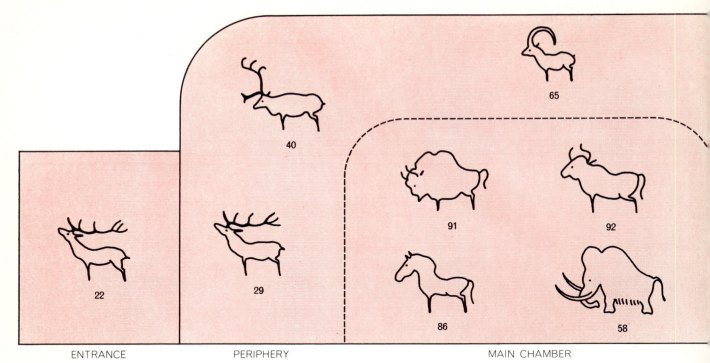

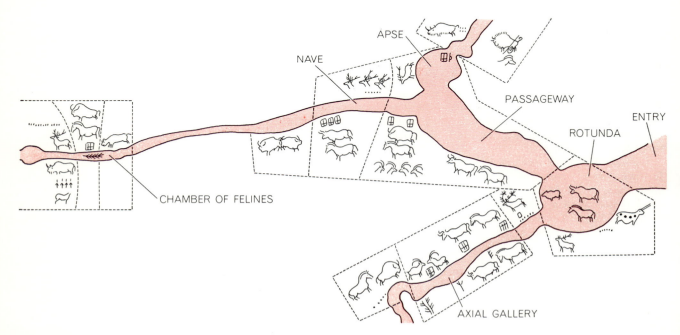

ENTRANCE   PERIPHERY   MAIN CHAMBER

METHODICAL ARRANGEMENT of the animal depictions at various Paleolithic sites was revealed by the author's survey of 62 caves. The diagram shows an idealized cave with an entrance, a main chamber and its periphery and, finally, a back passage to a deep inner area. Numbers below each animal figure show the percent of depictions of that animal present in that part of all the

From this viewpoint (which is still held by some prehistorians) wall art represents the gradual accumulation of isolated pictures, each created by the need of the moment. When one stands before the great wall paintings of Lascaux in France or Altamira in Spain, however,

it is hard to imagine how the random accumulation of isolated subjects could possibly have led to an assemblage that impresses the most naïve viewer with its overall balance. Doubts on this score are what inspired Annette Laming-Emperaire to publish her important study of

1962: *The Meaning of Paleolithic Wall Art*. There she vigorously challenges the traditional theories. My own work has been motivated by a similar conviction and is based on the following postulate. If, rather than working haphazardly, the men of the Paleolithic consciously—or

LASCAUX CAVE, a famous Paleolithic site in France, is shown in plan view; more than 300 feet separate the cave's deepest recess *(left)* from the entrance *(right)*. The broken lines enclosing the

groups of depictions suggest how the cave's many decorated areas were originally subdivided. The stag and the two abstract signs just inside the Axial Gallery are reproduced in color on page 12.

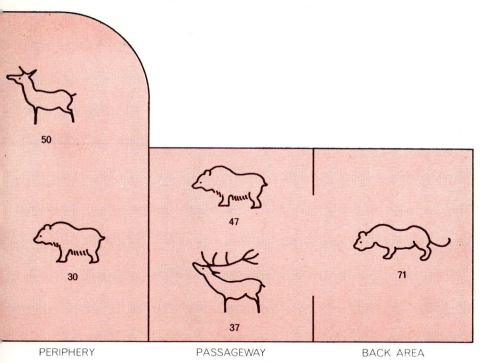

PERIPHERY   PASSAGEWAY   BACK AREA

caves surveyed. More than 90 percent of all bison and wild-ox paintings appear in main chambers, as do most horse paintings. Most stag paintings are located elsewhere: nearly 40 percent are in inner areas, 22 percent are in entrances and 29 percent are in peripheral areas.

even unconsciously—introduced order into the way their pictures are positioned, then an analysis of where various animal paintings are located in a sizable number of caves (say 50 or more out of the 100-odd sites) should reveal what general scheme, if any, the artists had in mind.

To test this postulate I have reviewed the topography of some 60 caves, established the position of more than 2,000 individual animal pictures in them and tabulated the results. The following related facts can be perceived: (1) If one defines "central position" either as the middle of a painted panel or as the most prominent chamber within a cave, it is in this position that more than 85 percent of all pictures of bison, wild oxen and horses are found. (2) The next most prominent animals—deer, ibex and mammoth—appear in positions other than a central one. (3) Three other species— rhinoceros, lion and bear—are found only in the deepest parts of the cave, or far from the central position [see bottom illustration on page 19].

A similar analysis can be made of the subjects other than animals that are depicted in Paleolithic art: representations of humans, male and female, and signs that are more or less abstract. More than 80 percent of all the female figures—and of the symbols that I call "wide" abstract signs, which are evidently related to fe-

male figures—are found in the same central places where bison and wild oxen are depicted. Other symbols designated "narrow" signs are in the same areas where the remaining animal figures are found; that is to say, nearly 70 percent of them are in positions that are peripheral.

This is not the place to consider what such patterns may be able to tell us about the religious beliefs of Paleolithic man. For anyone who is trying to establish a chronology of Paleolithic art, however, the orderliness of these arrays has its own significance. First, one is led to the conclusion that in most of the wall art in most of the caves the separate elements belong to a single period, and that later works were executed in other parts of the cave. Even in those caves where the wall art clearly represents the accumulation of several periods, the later works repeat the elements and order of the earlier ones. Second, in any single assemblage of pictures the wide abstract signs are all much the same, whereas in caves that contain a number of separate picture groups the wide signs differ from group to group. The existence of these differences suggests that the wide signs can serve as chronological guideposts, or at the very least as guides to the relations between the various styles in which the animal figures are executed. Thus, regardless of any hypotheses concerning

prehistoric religion, the fact that there is order in Paleolithic man's art provides a basis for investigating its evolution.

Discovering Points in Time

All such problems of chronology would have vanished long ago if only one of two things had happened. Each Paleolithic site could have yielded stratified sequences of buried sculptures and the style of the material from each stratum could have shown it to be unmistakably contemporaneous with one after another of the cave's displays of wall art. Alternatively, the examples of the wall art in a number of caves could all have been executed in a single style, and the artifacts excavated from the floors of the same caves could all have been attributed to a single interval of time. In actuality very few examples of wall art can be firmly attributed to a specific period during the many millenniums in which prehistoric art flourished. Still, the few examples that do exist provide us with some degree of chronological framework.

As a starting point, there are no known examples of representational art before the Aurignacian period, beginning about 30,000 B.C. There are, however, firmly dated pieces of Aurignacian sculpture. They are found, for example, in the Aurignacian strata of two sites in the Dordogne valley of France: the Cellier rock-shelter and La Ferassie. They are crudely engraved figures of animals and wide and narrow signs.

Our next bench mark in time is found in strata of Solutrean age (about 15,000 B.C.) at the Roc de Sers site in the Charente valley of France: a low-relief frieze rendered in a vigorous style. It depicts horses, bison, ibexes and men. The date is firmly established because the rock of the frieze had fallen from its original position and was discovered lying face down between two strata containing Solutrean artifacts.

A third bench mark is provided by a number of engraved stone plaques discovered in strata of Upper Magdalenian age (about 10,000 B.C.) in the caves of Teyjat in the Dordogne. The animals depicted on the plaques are the same as those in the Roc de Sers frieze, but they are executed in a more detailed, almost photographic style. The final bench mark, denoting the end of Paleolithic art, is also found in the Dordogne. At Villepin engraved pebbles from strata dating to the very end of the Magdalenian period (about 8000 B.C.) display sketchy, often barely identifiable animal figures.

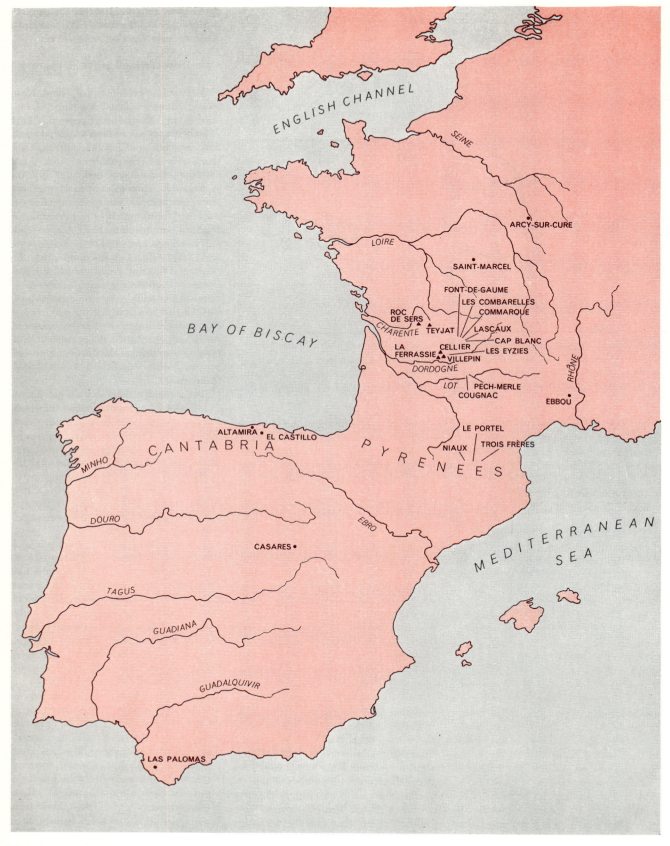

ENGLISH CHANNEL

SEINE

ARCY-SUR-CURE

LOIRE

SAINT-MARCEL

FONT-DE-GAUME

LES COMBARELLES

COMMARQUE

ROC DE SERS   TEYJAT   LASCAUX

CHARENTE   CAP BLANC

LA FERRASSIE   CELLIER   LES EYZIES

VILLEPIN

DORDOGNE

LOT   PECH-MERLE

COUGNAC

BAY OF BISCAY

EBBOU

RHÔNE

LE PORTEL

NIAUX   TROIS FRÈRES

ALTAMIRA   EL CASTILLO

CANTABRIA   P Y R E N E E S

MINHO

DOURO

EBRO

MEDITERRANEAN SEA

CASARES

TAGUS

GUADIANA

GUADALQUIVIR

LAS PALOMAS

HEARTLAND of Paleolithic cave art was western Europe south of the Loire River. Sites mentioned by the author in the valleys of the Charente, the Dordogne and the Lot and in the foothills of the French Pyrenees are shown, as are some with cave art in Canta-brian, central and southern Spain, in France north of the Charente and in the Rhône valley. Cave art has also been found at three sites in Italy and Sicily. Five Charente-Dordogne sites marked with triangles contained sculpture in strata with well-established dates.

Four points in time, all found in the same Dordogne-Charente region, scarcely suffice to establish a chronology for all Europe. Fortunately a number of less exact bench marks are available in France, Spain and Italy. Although these bench marks can be fixed no more exactly than around the start, the middle and the end of the Upper Paleolithic, they are in general accord with the Dordogne-Charente reference points and allow us not only to recognize the entire period's major chronological subdivisions but also to perceive a new and very important fact. Up to now it has been thought that the portable art and the wall art of the Upper Paleolithic evolved in a strictly parallel manner, and that one could find pictures characteristic of each of the period's subdivisions in the caves. It is now apparent that, on the contrary, wall art was extremely rare or even nonexistent early in the Upper Paleolithic, that most of it belongs to a middle phase during which the portable art becomes less abundant, and that portable art catches up with wall art once more in the period's final phase.

The Evolution of Abstract Signs

Students of Paleolithic art have always been intrigued by certain abstract signs that appear in wall art almost from its beginning to its end, although not so commonly as pictures of animals. In the opinion of some investigators some of the signs represent huts or tents; other signs are interpreted as representing weapons and traps, shields and even primitive heraldic designs. It would seem, however, that only a few signs out of the hundreds known can be explained by their resemblance to actual objects. If instead of selecting a few such examples one makes an inclusive inventory of all the things found in wall art that do not obviously portray animals, a rather different picture emerges. One can even group such representations into general categories.

One category is men and women, sometimes pictured whole and sometimes reduced to a head or torso. To this category can be added numerous realistic representations of the male and female sexual organs, which evidently have the same significance as the fuller figures. The existence of these drawings has suggested to some scholars that a fertility cult existed in Paleolithic times. This is hard to disprove, but given the fact that the male and female representations are as often separate as they are together, they would appear to be at best quite abstract fertility symbols.

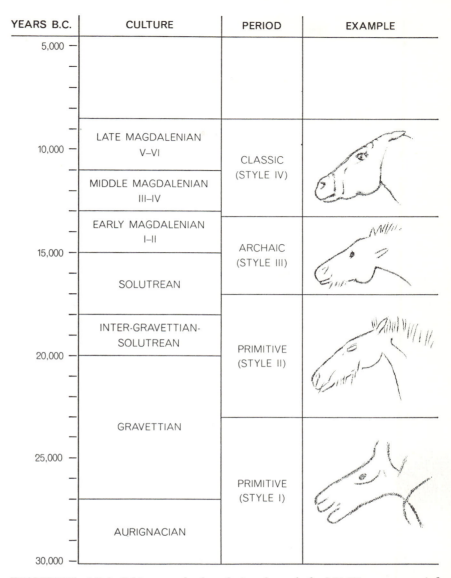

YEARS B.C.	CULTURE	PERIOD	EXAMPLE
5,000			
10,000	LATE MAGDALENIAN V–VI	CLASSIC (STYLE IV)	
	MIDDLE MAGDALENIAN III–IV		
15,000	EARLY MAGDALENIAN I–II	ARCHAIC (STYLE III)	
	SOLUTREAN		
20,000	INTER-GRAVETTIAN-SOLUTREAN	PRIMITIVE (STYLE II)	
25,000	GRAVETTIAN	PRIMITIVE (STYLE I)	
30,000	AURIGNACIAN		

EVOLUTION of Paleolithic art took place during the era's final 20,000 years, a period known as the Upper Paleolithic. The first examples are dated around 30,000 B.C., when the Aurignacian culture makes its appearance. They were crude outlines cut into rock (*bottom figure is unidentified; the others portray horses*). This Style I work, as it is classified by the author, and later work in Style II comprise the primitive period. The best-known cave art was produced during the archaic (Style III) and the classic (Style IV) periods.

By far the largest number of signs belong to one or the other of the two groups I have mentioned: the wide and narrow signs. The wide signs include rectangles, triangles, ovals and shield shapes. Most of them clearly belong to the category of human representations; they are quite realistic depictions of the female sexual organ. The narrow signs include short strokes, rows of dots and barbed lines. Some of them clearly suggest male sexual organs, although they are extremely stylized. For that matter, the entire inventory of abstract signs could well be nothing but animal and human figures rendered symbolically.

These abstract signs are strikingly di-

verse in both time and space. One kind of rectangle, for example, accompanies animal figures that themselves have a number of stylistic features in common: the rectangle appears in the Dordogne, in the nearby Lot valley and in Cantabria, beyond the Pyrenees in Spain. This enables us to assign all the cave art in which the rectangle appears to the same time period. At the same time how abstract decoration is used to embellish each rectangle varies sufficiently from cave to cave to establish the fact that the art of Lascaux in the Dordogne, of Pech-Merle in the Lot valley and of Altamira in Spain each belongs to a distinct ancient province. Such a distinction

18

FOUR QUADRUPEDS, three of them bison, show how styles evolved. Work in Style I (*bottom engraving, cross section at right*) seldom depicted entire animals as here; both line and workmanship are rough. Style II technique (*second from bottom, cross section at left*) remains primitive but forms are more powerful. In Style III (*painting second from top*) line and color have been mastered although anatomical details are unperfected. The work in Style IV (*top painting*) shows both anatomical fidelity and a sense of movement.

cannot be made with equal precision when one must base one's judgment on the style in which the animals are depicted. As a matter of fact, signs remote from realism are a better mirror of local influences than animal portraits are. I have therefore based my use of abstract signs on a twofold principle: first, that as generalized forms they are contemporaneous and, second, that in their details they reveal regional influences.

As in the pictures of animals, the abstract signs do not establish much in the way of precise chronology. Most of the sites where they are found contain nothing that can be rigorously dated. Nonetheless, they make it possible to establish a sequence that is about as reliable as the one based on animal figures. For example, the oldest known abstract signs appear about 30,000 B.C., in Aurignacian times. The wide signs are realistically feminine; the narrow ones are either realistically masculine or are stylized into a series of strokes or dots. In Solutrean times, roughly from 20,000 to 15,000 B.C., full figures of men and women seem to predominate; the style of the latter is familiar to us from the numerous "Venus figurines" that have been found in both western and eastern Europe. The transition between Solutrean and early Magdalenian times (between 15,000 and 13,000 B.C.) is a period of rectangular signs, followed closely by bracket-shaped ones. At this point regional differences in abstract signs make their classification difficult, although a revival in the popularity of small sculptures provides a precise means of determining the chronological position of other animal representations. During the Magdalenian proper, from 13,000 to 9000 B.C., the most important group of abstract signs are "key-shaped" ones, derived from the representation of a woman in profile [*see illustration on page 20*]. In the Dordogne and the Lot Valley it is possible to trace the evolution from early to middle Magdalenian by means of the key-shaped signs. Thereafter these signs become increasingly stylized, both in space (as one moves south) and in time (as the end of the Magdalenian approaches).

Key-shaped signs are by no means the only abstractions of this period. Here a variety of influences appear to have crisscrossed in space and time. At Les Eyzies in the Dordogne, for example, roof-shaped signs (which apparently evolved out of the bracket-shaped ones) seem to take the place of the key shapes. Another trend in symbolism is marked by the appearance of what some scholars have assumed are representations of

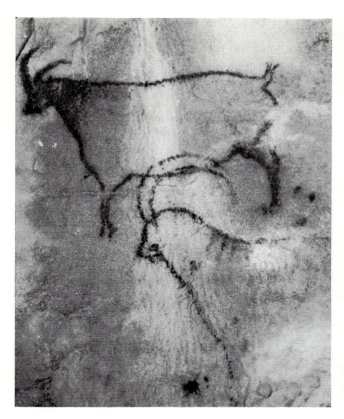

PAINTED IBEXES of the archaic period, a female (*top*) and a male, were done in red ocher at Cougnac, a Lot valley site in France. Painting, engraving and combinations of both are known.

ENGRAVED IBEX, also executed during the archaic period, is one of scores of animal figures cut into the cave walls at Ebbou, a Rhône valley site in France that contains engravings exclusively.

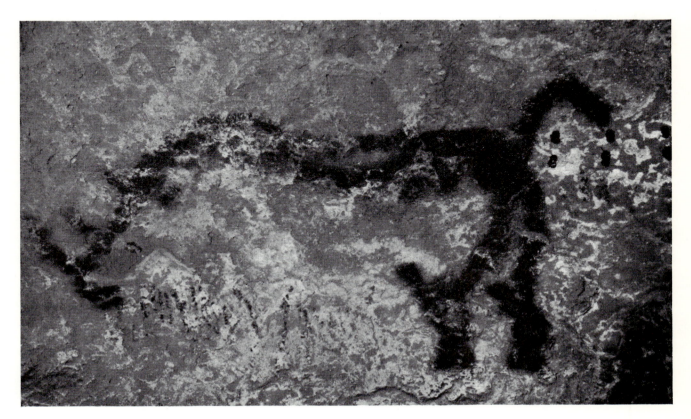

PAINTED RHINOCEROS, one of the animals typically found in the back areas of caves, occupies a niche opening off the main chamber at Lascaux. The work, in manganese, is transitional between Style III and Style IV. Dots by the tail form an abstract sign.

wounds on the bodies of animals. Both symbolic wounds and realistic representations of the female sexual organ are found in a comparable setting in a large number of caves. Since the realistic female representations of the Magdalenian are executed differently from the earliest female representations, it seems likely that the "wounds" are a different kind of female symbol.

The Time Scale

By putting together all three classes of evidence—from excavations, from the study of reasonably well-dated wall art and from the evolution of human figures and abstract signs—a chronological framework can be erected that begins to approximate reality. The most attractive of all Paleolithic art works, the animal pictures, remain the most difficult to interpret directly. The reason is that any analysis of their evolution is founded on criteria of style, and judgments of style are primarily subjective. When details that allow objective evaluation are scanty, only the most general conclusions are possible. What appears to be an important criterion may reflect nothing more than a regional characteristic or the relative skill of the artist.

In spite of such qualifications, it can be said that the evidence in general allows us to discern the emergence of three great periods of Paleolithic art during the 20,000 years from the Aurignacian to the end of the Magdalenian.

They are, first, a primitive period, then an archaic period (in the same sense that one speaks of archaic Greek art: a well-developed body of art rapidly approaching maturity) and finally a classic period. Where the conditions are most favorable, as in the Dordogne-Charente region, we can point to the succession of four styles in the course of the three major periods. These I have designated Styles I and II (in the primitive period), Style III (in the archaic) and Style IV (in the classic). Even finer subdivisions are possible: the wall art of Lascaux and Pech-Merle, for example, is divisible into early and late Style III, and elsewhere Style IV shows similar early and late stages.

What are the characteristics of each period and style? Style I embraces history's oldest examples of representational art, examples that are precisely dated to the Aurignacian period by virtue of the fact that they are found in association with Aurignacian tools. The Aurignacian sculptures of Cellier and La Ferassie are Style I. As I noted earlier, the representations of animals from this time are very crude; sometimes the whole body is shown but more often the rendering is limited to a head or a forequarter. The inventory of animals includes the horse, the bison, the wild ox, the ibex and the rhinoceros—in other words, the main cast of characters found throughout Paleolithic art. The representations include realistic depictions of the female sexual organ as well as such male symbols as lines and rows of dots.

A long interval, extending from 25,000 to 18,000 B.C. and thus from the late Aurignacian through Gravettian times to early Solutrean ones, is the setting for Style II. In a chronology based on the evolution of techniques this 7,000-year interval is a confused period. One can assume that a number of cultures succeeded one another, but it is hard to equate the changes in one region with those in another. In any case, this was the period in which Paleolithic art attained its greatest geographical range, from the Atlantic coast on the west to the valley of the Don on the east. It is also the period in which the first wall art appears: paintings and engravings executed on the walls of open rock-shelters or on those cave walls that were illuminated by daylight.

The animal forms of Style II are powerful, but the technique of rendering remains quite primitive. The stereotyped curved line representing the neck and back and the line representing the belly are drawn first; the details characteristic of each animal species are then roughly connected to the generalized torsos and are often left unfinished. The abstract signs that are included in the wall art remain close to realism and generally consist of ovals and series of strokes. In the realm of small sculptures the numerous female figurines of this period, usually made of stone or of mammoth ivory, all have much the same shape. The trunk is corpulent and rendered in some detail but the extremities and the

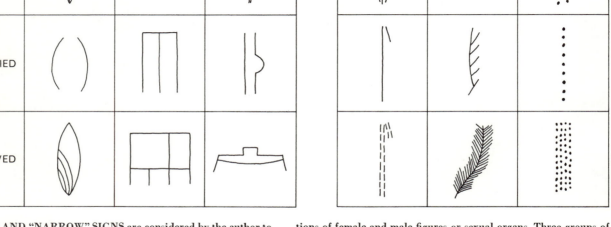

"WIDE" AND "NARROW" SIGNS are considered by the author to be symbolic of the sexes and to have evolved from earlier depictions of female and male figures or sexual organs. Three groups of symbols are shown for each sex, in normal and more abstract forms.

head are stylized and often quite reduced in size.

Style III, which is typical of the entire archaic period, finds its most elo-
quent expression in the great frieze of
the Roc de Sers in Charente, in the
equally impressive murals at Lascaux
and in some of the Spanish cave paintings. The representations of animals re-
tain a primitive flavor: the bodies are
bulky and the small heads and hooves
are joined to the bodies without much
care for detail or proportion. Line, however, is now handled with great sen-
sitivity, and the control of painting and
sculptural technique is complete. The in-
terplay of manganese blacks and ocher
reds and yellows in the paintings and the
use of color accents on the low reliefs reflect a mastery of both mediums. Representations of humans are scarce and do
not compare in quality with the animal
pictures. On the other hand, the abstract
signs characteristic of Style III, which
are rectangular or bracket-shaped, show
such a diversity of embellishment that
they have been compared to heraldic
coats of arms.

Chronologically the style of the archaic period occupies the interval between 18,000 and 13,000 B.C., thus including the late Solutrean and the early
Magdalenian. The evolution of animal
portrayal can be traced through all five
millenniums. At Lascaux and at Pech-
Merle, for example, one can differenti-
ate between early Style III animal paintings that are still close to Style II and
late Style III paintings that already
verge on Style IV.

In western Europe small sculptures
are notably rare during the archaic period; of the few works in the category of
portable art most are engraved plaques.
In eastern Europe, on the other hand,
there is no Style III wall art at all but
there is a trove of animal and human
figurines. Such regional differences probably correspond to ethnic ones. Thus one
can readily distinguish between an eastern domain (from what is now Czechoslovakia to the U.S.S.R. west of the
Urals) and a western one. Although we
are a long way from knowing all the
schools of Style III in the western domain, variations in rectangular signs and
associated animal figures enable us to detect shades of difference between works
from the Dordogne, the Lot valley, the
central Pyrenees, Cantabria and the
Rhône valley.

The whole of the Magdalenian proper,
from 13,000 to 9000 B.C., provides the
stage for the classic period of Paleolithic
art and Style IV. Outside of western

THE TWO SEXES are represented by this array of wide and narrow signs painted on
the wall of a cave at El Castillo in Cantabrian Spain during the archaic period. The em-
bellished rectangles belong to one of five groups of female symbols recognized by the author and the rows of dots to one of four male groups (see *illustration on opposite page*).

"WOUNDED" BISON, painted during the classic period at Niaux in the French Pyrenees,
is interpreted by the author as neither a hunting scene nor a sorcerer's spell but instead
as a combination of animal figure and abstract female sign found only in Style IV. Female
signs are usually found with bison and wild-ox pictures in the caves' central chambers.

CRUDELY OUTLINED HEAD of an animal from the earliest Aurignacian stratum at the Cellier rock-shelter in the Dordogne valley is typical of the art of the primitive period.

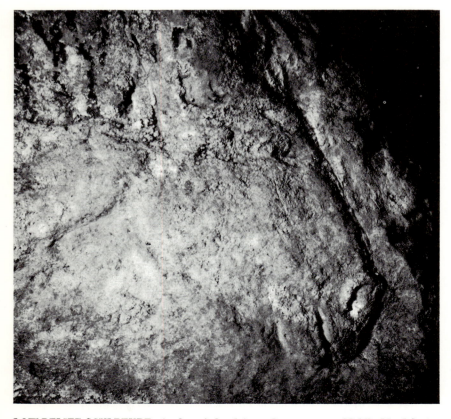

LOW-RELIEF SCULPTURE of a horse's head from Commarque, a Middle Magdalenian cave site in the Dordogne, shows the sophistication of classic period art, 15,000 years later.

Europe, Style IV is not particularly well represented at present, but within that area it is rich in wall art and especially rich in portable art. Small sculptures were widely disseminated in western Europe during the classic period. Toward the end of the period, when an increasingly mild climate allowed occupation of the northern and mountainous areas of Europe, examples of portable art reached the areas of Switzerland, Germany and even Britain. Wall art also extended its boundaries, appearing in Italy for the first time.

The wealth of classic small sculptures makes possible many comparisons between them and Style IV wall paintings that illuminate the main features of the period's art evolution. One result is that a distinction can be made between early and late Style IV animal pictures. In the early period faint traces of the archaic models still remain; regardless of the correctness of their proportions, the animals give the appearance of being suspended in midair. Body contours are filled in with incised lines or splashes of color that convey the texture of the coat. This surface modeling is present in figures found from Spain to the Loire valley in France; each animal species—horse, bison, ibex, reindeer and the like—is rendered by means of the same conventions from one end of this region to the other. In late Style IV representations the rendering of texture is less clear and many animals are presented in simple outline. It is now that anatomical fidelity and a sense of movement reach their peak. If the final art of the Paleolithic lacks the rather solemn grandeur of Lascaux, it nonetheless possesses an extraordinary vitality.

Most of the best-known examples of cave art are either early or late Style IV. These include the wall paintings at Font-de-Gaume, Les Combarelles and Cap Blanc in the Dordogne, the paintings at Le Portel, Trois-Frères and Niaux in the Pyrenees, the great painted ceiling at Altamira and paintings in several other cave sites in Biscay, Cantabria and Asturias. Because Style IV animal pictures are handled in a remarkably uniform manner all the way from Spain to central Europe, regional subdivisions are much harder to establish in the classic period than in the archaic one. Indeed, the uniformity of the classic period suggests not only the existence of contacts between various regional populations but also the existence of a firmly based cosmopolitan artistic tradition. One subdivision that can be detected is a single cohesive Franco-Cantabrian body of early Style IV art; it extends from the Loire valley to the Pyrenees and Asturias and is reflected in the rendering of females in profile and in associated abstract key-shaped signs. The distribution of small Style IV sculptures demonstrates a connection between the Pyrenees-Loire region and areas to the north and east as far as Germany.

What are the main developments during the huge span in which Paleolithic art flourished? At the foot of the evolutionary path a master plan already existed even though techniques were virtually unformed; this was the primitive period. In the extended period of refinement in technique that followed, the key developments involve the delineation of those characteristics that distinguish one species of animal from another; this was the archaic period. Finally both technique and delineation were progressively united in a more and

more realistic portrayal of shape and movement; this was the classic period. Then it is all gone, much as the mammoth and the woolly rhinoceros disappeared from the same region. The ideological line uniting an artistic tradition of 20,000 years comes to an end.

Obviously both the long lifetime of Paleolithic art and its disappearance are topics that will occupy generations of investigators. Today, although we know only a fraction of what remains to be learned, we have made some progress. It might be said that historians of Paleolithic art have reached a level of precision comparable to the level achieved by historians of Christian art when they were at last able to fix the date of some object within a century or two. They could be justly criticized for a lack of precision, but they had achieved a clear view of the path along which Christian art had evolved.

ANATOMICAL FIDELITY is characteristic of Style IV work, produced during the classic period of Paleolithic art. The deftly rendered outline of a wild-ox cow's head is one of the animal engravings in the cave at Teyjat, an Upper Magdalenian site in the Dordogne valley.

3

THE SOLUTREAN CULTURE

PHILIP E. L. SMITH
August 1964

During the last advances and the final retreat of the Pleistocene ice sheets in Europe, between 32,000 and 10,000 years ago, the most vigorous cultures of the Old Stone Age flourished. The hunting peoples of this Upper Paleolithic period enjoyed an abundance of cold-climate game: migrating reindeer by the thousands, herds of horses and wild cattle, and such giants of the subarctic zone as the mammoth and the woolly rhinoceros. The well-fed hunters made these same animals the subjects of sculpture, in the round or in relief, of fine-line engraving on bone, antler and ivory, and of richly colored cave paintings such as those found at Altamira in Spain and Lascaux in France.

Prehistorians generally divide the Upper Paleolithic culture of western Europe into four major components. The two earliest of these, called the Perigordian and the Aurignacian, were roughly contemporary; the distinction between them is based primarily on differences in their assemblages of stone tools and weapons. In western Europe both of these cultural traditions were succeeded some 21,000 years ago by a new array of distinctive stone implements that are assigned to the Solutrean culture. About 17,000 years ago, in turn, the last phase of the Solutrean gave way to the Magdalenian culture, whose members produced many of the most notable examples of Upper Paleolithic art. Finally, as the ice sheets began their last retreat, Magdalenian artifacts disappeared and in southwestern France a comparatively impoverished successor culture, the Azilian, marked the end of an era [see illustration on page 27].

These cultural successions have been interpreted in a number of ways.

Thinking in terms of the many waves of migration and conquest that have passed over Europe during historical times, some students argue that each distinctive assemblage of Upper Paleolithic artifacts represents a fresh influx of people from Asia or Africa. Other students point to the enormous time span of the Upper Paleolithic: roughly five times longer than all recorded history. These scholars do not discount the possibility that ideas were imported into western Europe, but they prefer to attribute most of the cultural changes in the region to cultural evolution within a relatively stable population.

It might be less difficult to determine which, if either, of these hypotheses is best supported by the evidence if the history of archaeological research in Europe had been different. For much of its 100-year history the collection of archaeological evidence in some countries has been in the hands not only of scholars but also of amateur antiquarians and professional looters. One result is that few Upper Paleolithic sites have been excavated under controlled conditions. This means that the stratigraphic positions, and thus the age and associations, of many of the period's most significant artifacts have been lost forever.

France is western Europe's greatest Upper Paleolithic treasure-house and the department of Dordogne, in southwestern France, is the country's richest single depository. Thanks to stringent government regulations, looters can no longer mine the limestone caves and shelters in the valleys of the Dordogne and Vézère rivers. During the years since World War II a number of promising sites have been scientifically ex-

cavated. Some are still in the process of long-term excavation; an example is the Pataud rock-shelter near the village of Les Eyzies, where a group from Harvard University has been working for eight years. In the 1950's another rock-shelter at Les Eyzies was reinvestigated by François Bordes of the University of Bordeaux. Known as Laugerie-Haute, it had been shown to be rich in Upper Paleolithic artifacts by the noted French prehistorian Denis Peyrony in the 1920's. More than half of the site was still untouched in the 1950's; the strata containing Upper Paleolithic remains were 10 meters thick in some places, with Solutrean layers occupying more than a meter of this depth.

I worked at Laugerie-Haute with Bordes in 1957. In 1959 he asked me to investigate the site's Solutrean levels to see if some of the problems concerning this comparatively short-lived but remarkable culture could be cleared up by recovering new samples of Solutrean artifacts from a precisely calibrated stratigraphic sequence.

Peyrony's studies of the 1920's were not the first conducted at Laugerie-Haute. A century ago, in 1863, two pioneer prehistorians began a series of now classic investigations at a number of sites in the vicinity of Les Eyzies. One was Édouard Lartet, a French paleontologist whose interests had turned to the new field of archaeology; the other was a British businessman, Henry Christy. Before they were done at such sites as La Madeleine (from which the Magdalenian culture takes its name), the Gorge d'Enfer and Laugerie-Haute the two investigators had discovered the first evidence of prehistoric art—the figure of a mammoth engraved on bone—and had given the name "Reindeer Age" to what we rec-

PAIR OF WILD CATTLE, attributed to a Solutrean sculptor, was rendered in bas-relief on the surface of a limestone outcropping on the Dronne River in southwestern France. This Upper Paleolithic work of art was found at a site called Fourneau du Diable.

26

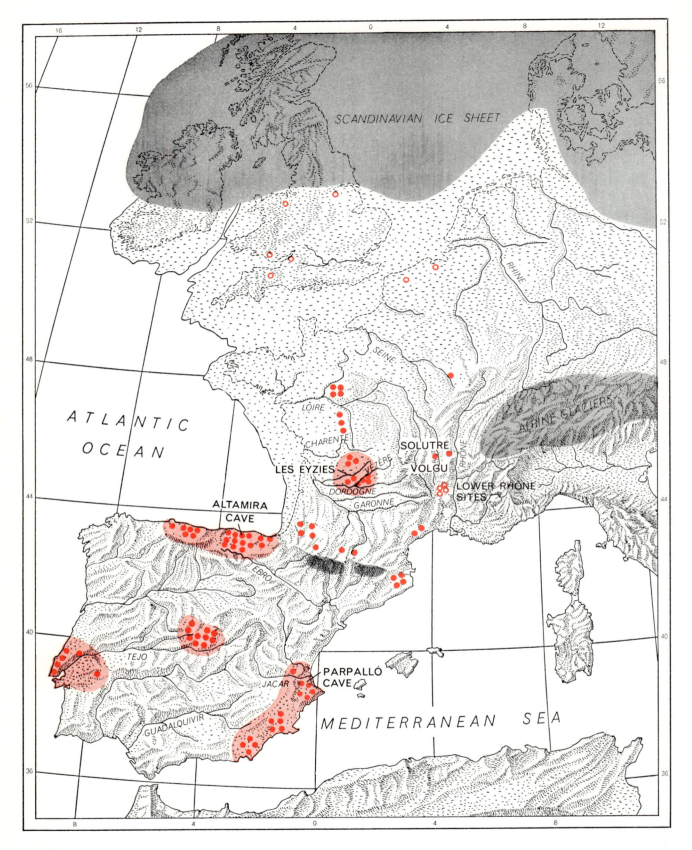

WESTERN EUROPE some 20,000 years ago had approximately today's Mediterranean coastline, but neither the English Channel nor the North Sea existed. Glaciers were extensive in the Alps and the Pyrenees, and the great Scandinavian ice sheet covered most of Ireland and all of Scotland and the Baltic. The third advance of the Würm glaciation was just ending and the weather was cold. Solid dots locate sites where Solutrean materials have been discovered. The five major areas (*light color*) are the classic Solutrean region of the Dordogne in southwestern France and four outlying Iberian regions. The open dots in the lower Rhône valley identify sites from which the earliest Solutrean techniques seem to have dispersed. The other open dots locate sites of less certain affinity.

ognize today as the whole of the Upper Paleolithic. In addition, at Laugerie-Haute they excavated examples of three distinctive Solutrean flint tools: the laurel-leaf blade, the willow-leaf blade and the shouldered point [*see illustration on page 29*].

Lartet and Christy recognized that the exquisite flat flaking of these artifacts was unique, and they christened them the "industry of Laugerie-Haute." This might be the name of the Solutrean culture today except for the fact that other important Upper Paleolithic finds were made at nearby Laugerie-Basse. To avoid confusion prehistorians named the Laugerie-Haute industry after Solutré, a site in eastern France where the same distinctive stone tools were found a few years later.

There were several questions that new excavations at Laugerie-Haute could help to answer. One was that even after 100 years there is little real agreement among prehistorians as to what the Solutrean industry really represents. Some believe, as they do of other Upper Paleolithic cultures, that the Solutrean is merely the grafting of a few foreign ideas onto already existing traditions. Others visualize an invasion of western Europe by groups armed with superior weapons who absorbed or eliminated the earlier inhabitants until they in turn were absorbed or eliminated by the people of the later Magdalenian culture. Finally, still other prehistorians deny both of these hypotheses and assert that the Solutrean culture evolved indigenously in western Europe from one or another of the immediately preceding traditions.

In the past there has been a tendency to overemphasize the exotic and spectacular among Solutrean artifacts, particularly the leaf-shaped blades and the elegantly made projectile points, and to ignore the rest of the Solutrean tool kit: ordinary implements such as burins for engraving and incising, scrapers, perforators and other such tools. Whether special tools were made locally or were introduced from outside is the kind of question that can be answered only by statistical analysis. For this, it is not enough merely to distinguish the major "periods" of a culture. For example, the period named *Solutréen inférieur* in France (and here called early Solutrean) shows five distinct strata at Laugerie-Haute. Careful dissection of these microlayers—each of which may correspond to a separate human occupation of the site—is a prerequisite for sound statistical conclusions.

I began my work in April, 1959, with

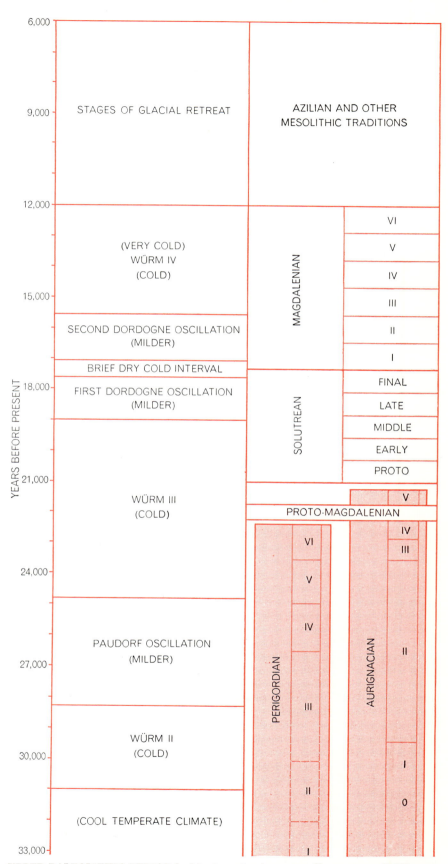

UPPER PALEOLITHIC PERIOD had its inception in western Europe some 32,000 years ago, at a time of retreating ice. The first Solutrean-style tools appeared 11,000 years later, near the end of a cold period. During the next 4,000 years Solutrean culture dominated southwestern France and offshoots appeared in the Iberian Peninsula. It was succeeded some 17,000 years ago by the final Upper Paleolithic culture: the art-rich Magdalenian.

the following questions in mind. Is the Solutrean a continuum with each phase evolving indigenously into the next, or does each phase reflect new stimuli from elsewhere? What clues do the earliest Solutrean levels provide to even earlier ancestral periods? And what was happening at the end of Solutrean times just before the Solutrean culture was replaced by the Magdalenian?

The Laugerie-Haute rock-shelter stretches for about 50 meters under the limestone cliffs bordering the Vézère River. Today the house of the curator of the Museum of Prehistory at Les Eyzies is built directly over the mid-

LAUREL-LEAF BLADE is an example of the remarkable capacity for working in stone that characterizes Solutrean culture.

dle of the site, so that excavating is restricted to the east and west ends. The shelter was inhabited for several thousand years before Solutrean times by people using Perigordian, proto-Magdalenian and Aurignacian tools. After the final Aurignacian occupation there was a short interval during a period of very cold climate when the site and perhaps the whole region was deserted.

This hiatus at Laugerie-Haute is marked by a thick layer of limestone fragments that had fallen from the roof and sides of the shelter. The layer contains no trace of human occupation. Lying directly on this sterile rubble in one small area of the site is a stratum that can be considered proto-Solutrean. The artifacts possess many of the characteristics of later Solutrean assemblages but in a rudimentary form. Very fine, flat flaking is evident on certain flint tools, and a large number of flint blades show the secondary flaking that is called retouching.

Of particular importance are the tools known as unifacial points. These are blades of flint with one surface fully or partially retouched by flat flaking and with the base often chipped to a narrower width as if for mounting on a shaft or handle. The exact use to which these unifacial points were put is unknown. The important thing is that in this proto-Solutrean stratum they are already present but in a form that is heavier and thicker than that in later levels.

There is no doubt that this bottom layer is the earliest evidence of the Solutrean industry in the Les Eyzies region. It probably dates back to somewhere between 21,000 and 22,000 years ago. The proto-Solutrean occupation at Laugerie-Haute seems to have been no more than a brief encampment by a visiting group. The only other site in southwestern France that has yielded a similar assemblage of tools is some 30 kilometers away at Badegoule.

Above this lowest Solutrean stratum there is another short hiatus and then a sequence of five levels, all of which can be classed as early Solutrean. Charcoal from one of these levels gave a radiocarbon date of 18,700 B.C. The discovery of these five strata has allowed a finer subdivision of the early Solutrean than was hitherto possible. The period proves to have evolved by stages from a rather archaic assemblage not much different from proto-Solutrean at the bottom to an uppermost level that is on the point of transforming itself into middle Solutrean. The character-

istic unifacial points become finer and more carefully retouched until, in the final early Solutrean level, the more archaic types disappear and the retouching invades much of the opposite face of the blade. The statistical distribution of other tool types similarly approaches the values typical of the middle Solutrean.

The next strata at Laugerie-Haute belong to the middle Solutrean and consist of at least four layers. In the earliest of these the only real difference from the final early Solutrean lies in the timid appearance of a very few laurel-leaf blades. These elegant implements make up scarcely 3 percent of the total flint inventory, but their appearance may be said to have been heralded by the increasing popularity of bifacial workmanship on the unifacial points in the immediately preceding strata.

In the next three middle-Solutrean levels these laurel leaves increase in numbers and variety and the unifacial points decline proportionately. Flat retouching now becomes an extremely popular flintworking technique. In succeeding strata the Solutrean craftsmen show an amazing flair for experimenting with the forms of the laurel leaves. Some are tiny and delicate; others are long and thick. Many are long and slender, and the retouching consists of fine parallel flaking. Some have such thin cross sections that it is difficult to imagine how they could have served any utilitarian purpose. Indeed, they may have been showpieces and luxury items. This same extravagance is reflected in many bizarre bifacial tools that exhibit notches, stems and asymmetrical shapes [see illustration on page 31].

A count of the laurel-leaf blades found in successive Solutrean levels at Laugerie-Haute shows them to have been scarce at the lowest levels of the middle Solutrean, then increasingly abundant and finally constituting a fourth of all stone tools by the end of that period [see illustration on opposite page]. It has already been noted that a lengthy evolution of bifacial retouching techniques preceded the first appearance of the laurel leaves. Both facts favor the conclusion that these seemingly exotic tools are the result of local evolution rather than an explosive invasion of either new peoples or new ideas.

It is not known exactly how long the middle Solutrean lasted—probably not more than 1,000 years at the most—but in its uppermost strata there is evidence that new ideas were being introduced or pioneered. Very small flint blades appear, their backs blunted by retouching, perhaps to make them fit into slots in wooden or bone shafts. Equally tiny scrapers are found. Another introduction or invention at the end of this period is the "single-shouldered" point [*see illustration at right*]. Thus, much as in the transition from the early to the middle Solutrean, the top levels of the middle Solutrean grade almost imperceptibly into the next division, the late Solutrean.

At Laugerie-Haute there are four strata that can be assigned to the late Solutrean. One key artifact that marks these layers is an increasingly sophisticated version of the single-shouldered point, which grows longer and shows more elaborate bifacial retouching from layer to layer. In contrast, the unifacial point of the proto-Solutrean and early Solutrean levels has now almost disappeared. The laurel leaves continue, and although they diminish in number and size they exhibit increasingly fine workmanship. Meanwhile a new kind of blade—the willow leaf, with rounded ends and delicate retouching on one face only—is found.

In the middle strata of the late Solutrean at Laugerie-Haute a very practical invention makes its first known appearance: the eyed needle made of bone. This seems to have been a Solutrean innovation; although bone needles are common in the Magdalenian strata that follow, none have been found in earlier Upper Paleolithic levels. The needle eyes are sometimes quite small, and it is a safe supposition that these implements were used for fine stitching or to produce fitted clothing.

Toward the end of the Solutrean period a curious change is evident. In contrast with the thick and rich deposits of earlier age, the sites of human occupation both at Laugerie-Haute and elsewhere in France become thin, restricted in area and impoverished in tools. There seems good reason to suppose that by this time the population of the Dordogne was composed of much smaller or more nomadic bands than before. These bands may even have been single families. Certainly they remained at each site for a shorter time. This phenomenon may be related to the unusually mild climate in the late Solutrean, which may have made the game animals scarcer.

A recent analysis of the strata at Laugerie-Haute has shown that at the

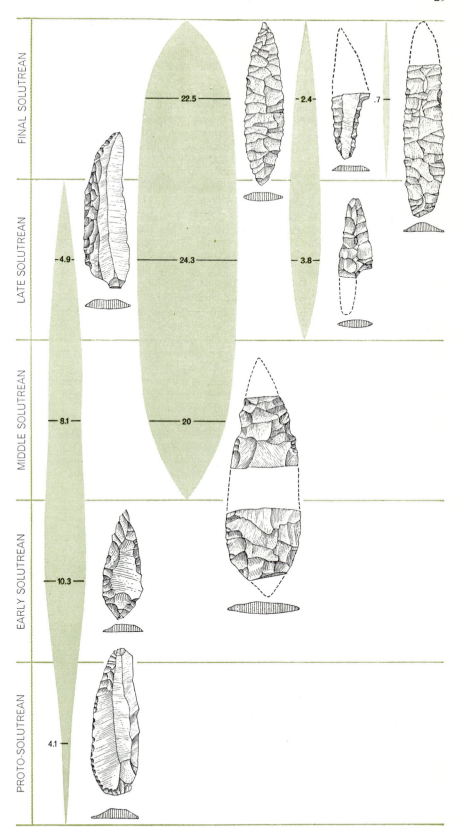

FOUR KEY STONE TOOLS appeared during successive Solutrean periods. Unifacial points (flaked on one surface only) are found at Laugerie-Haute from proto-Solutrean through late Solutrean times. They total 10.3 percent of all tools found in the early Solutrean period. Next to appear are laurel-leaf blades, which account for a fourth of all late Solutrean tools found at Laugerie-Haute. The shouldered point is unknown before the late Solutrean. Last of all to appear at Laugerie-Haute are the exquisitely flaked willow-leaf blades. These number less than 1 percent of the tool inventory in the final Solutrean period.

very end of the Solutrean a cold, dry spell struck southern France. This climatic change was brief: it lasted only into the earliest Magdalenian times. It is not yet possible to say whether the preceding mild period, the cold snap or a combination of both was responsible for the disappearance of the Solutrean culture from the Dordogne. In other regions the Solutrean may have lasted longer, but at Laugerie-Haute it was suddenly succeeded by an early Magdalenian industry.

There are as yet no radiocarbon dates for the end of the Solutrean at Laugerie-Haute, but somewhere around 17,000 years ago is probably not far off. Elsewhere, perhaps, there were contacts of some kind between the final Solutrean and the early Magdalenian; the Magdalenian industry not only possesses eyed needles but also shares with the Solutrean the production of carved stone bas-reliefs. There was no such contact at Laugerie-Haute, however. The rock-shelter had already been deserted before the 5,000 years of Magdalenian occupation began.

During the middle and late Solutrean the population of southwestern France was expanding into surrounding areas. A factor in these migrations may have been the mild climate of the period. To judge by widespread finds, some groups equipped with Solutrean techniques not only occupied sites near the Pyrenees but also spilled over into Spain. The Spanish Solutrean is in some ways distinct from the French, marked by characteristic versions of bifacial blades and stemmed and barbed points.

The expansion was not exclusively to the south; middle Solutrean industries are also found in central France, north of the Loire and almost into Brittany. The Solutrean of this period apparently never reached the Paris basin or the open lands of Belgium and Britain, which was then attached to the Continent. One thriving colony far to the east, however, was the site of Solutré itself in the Rhône valley not far from Lyons. The curious thing about this open-air site, which was discovered in 1866, is that it is the only scene of Solutrean occupation in all that region; if other occupation sites exist, they have yet to be found. In 1873 an isolated cache of 17 very large laurel-leaf blades was found by canal diggers at Volgu, about 50 kilometers west of Solutré, but this hoard was not associated with an occupation site.

After nearly a century of digging at Solutré, there is still no clear knowledge of the length of time the site was occupied or how it ties in chronologically with the Solutrean of other regions. Yet it is clear that Solutré was by no means the scene of a brief encampment far from some home base. It is a large occupation area that shows two thick and quite separate levels: a middle Solutrean (which corresponds roughly to the middle Solutrean of the Dordogne region) and a later stage. These later strata do not contain the shouldered points, willow-leaf blades or eyed needles typical of the Dordogne; instead they show a local specialization in laurel-leaf blades. Certainly this famous site deserves further investigation.

Combining the specific knowledge gained at Laugerie-Haute with more general information about the Solutrean obtained elsewhere, what can be said in summary about this short-lived Upper Paleolithic culture? First and most important is the fact that the Solutrean does not differ fundamentally from other hunting cultures of western Europe. Almost all Upper Paleolithic peoples were skilled hunters adapted to a rigorous cold environment and living in rock shelters, caves and open-air settlements. They had many kinds of stone implements in common, some of them "secondary" tools intended for fashioning other artifacts in bone, antler, ivory and wood. The ordinary Solutrean tool kit—stone, bone and antler—was not particularly different from that of other hunters. The Solutrean

SITE OF SOLUTRÉ, near Lyons in eastern France, gave the distinctive Upper Paleolithic culture its name. Most Solutrean sites are located in rock-shelters. Solutré, however, was an open-air encampment below a steep precipice. It contains two distinct levels. The earliest one resembles the middle Solutrean of the Dordogne, but the later level shows a local specialization in big blade tools.

subsistence pattern was founded, as was that of the other cultures, on the hunting of large game animals. At Laugerie-Haute more than 90 percent of the animal bones in Solutrean strata belong to reindeer, but horses, wild cattle, ibex and occasionally mammoth and musk-ox were also prey. The bones of salmon and other fishes are sometimes found; at one Solutrean site in Spain hares were the principal game.

Like most other Upper Paleolithic cultures, the Solutrean left an abundance of personal decorations. There are bone and ivory pendants, beads and bracelets: long bone pins with notches may possibly have been used in hair arrangement. Red, yellow and black pigments, found in some sites, could indicate the custom of body or face painting.

For many years it was thought that the Solutrean culture was unlike other Upper Paleolithic cultures of western Europe because it was almost without art. In due course Solutrean decorative work in bone and antler was recognized, but the experts still denied the culture either paintings or sculpture. Then the discovery of Solutrean stone friezes and bas-reliefs added sculpture to the cultural repertoire [*see illustration on page 25*]. Finally, in the 1930's the discovery of paintings on plaques of stone buried in Solutrean strata at the cave of Parpalló in eastern Spain filled the final gap in the artistic inventory. Moreover, associated with early Solutrean remains in the lower valley of the Rhône are paintings and engravings on cave walls that show mammoths, bears and horses in a distinctive style. A case might also be made for viewing the remarkable Solutrean work in flint as a product of some basic Upper Paleolithic artistic drive. In some Solutrean sites, particularly the later ones, the number of such specialized decorative artifacts as laurel leaves and willow leaves reaches amazing proportions—sometimes approaching 50 percent of all stone implements.

How, then, does the Solutrean differ from the other Upper Paleolithic traditions in western Europe? In the first place, its geographical range is surprisingly limited compared with such cultures as the Aurignacian that preceded it or the Magdalenian that followed it. This fact may be related to the culture's relatively short lifetime—a matter of little more than 4,000 years. Negative evidence is perhaps less persuasive, yet the absence of the "Venuses"—female figurines—that are char-

VIRTUOSO FLAKING characterizes four unusual Solutrean tools (*reproduced full-size*). The large bifacial blade (*lower left*) has its base chipped into a neat semicircle. The point (*upper left*) shows two such basal semicircles. At center a small laurel-leaf blade has been given a stemmed base. What use the asymmetrical form (*right*) served is conjectural.

acteristic of other Upper Paleolithic traditions may indicate a distinctive set of Solutrean beliefs or values. The lack of deliberate burials may point in the same direction.

But it is in flintworking techniques that the Solutrean is unique. The passion for fine, flat retouching extended beyond specialized blades and points to many commonplace tools. Moreover, the Solutrean abounds in artifacts not only of flint but also of fine-grained and brightly colored quartzes, jaspers and other fancy stones. Finally, wherever the Solutrean is found there are, in spite of variations due to time or place, quantitative and morphological consistencies in these stone tools. The

proportion of the specialized blades and points is high; the proportion of burins and ordinary blades is low; the proportion of scrapers and perforators is in between. It is this statistical consistency, together with an emphasis on fine retouching and imaginative forms, that gives the Solutrean its distinctive "personality."

Where did the Solutrean culture originate? One school of prehistorians believed it was born in Hungary, where large bifacial flints resembling the laurel-leaf blades have been found, and then expanded across Central Europe to develop into the classic Solutrean of France and Spain. Another school has suggested that its origins lie in a North

African stone-tool industry: the Aterian, which possesses not only bifacial blades but also tanged points that resemble those of the late Solutrean in eastern Spain. The same flaw mars both arguments; each implies that when the Solutrean culture first reached France, it already possessed laurel-leaf blades. The two earliest Solutrean periods in France have no laurel leaves and yet they are fully set in the Solutrean tradition. Therefore few prehistorians any longer believe that there are links between the Solutrean and cultures of eastern Europe or North Africa.

What about the possibility of an indigenous evolution of Solutrean culture from some preceding tradition in western Europe itself? Spain can be ruled out as a birthplace; the earliest levels known there contain an already well-developed middle Solutrean apparently derived from France. As for France itself, some interesting suggestions have come out of the ground in recent years.

The proto-Solutrean at Laugerie-Haute and at two other French sites is the earliest Solutrean identified so far. Any postulated ancestral Solutrean should therefore show certain affinities with proto-Solutrean. In the past decade some curious industries have been found in the lower valley of the Rhône, which is in eastern France. They are earlier in date than the Solutrean of the Dordogne. There are unifacially retouched blades and flakes very reminiscent of the proto-Solutrean; many of the other implements could fit well enough into an early Solutrean tool kit. Ancestral Solutrean may therefore have crystallized in the lower Rhône valley and then branched out, in the form of the proto-Solutrean culture, not only to southwestern France but also to the north. There the site of Le Trilobite in the Yonne valley has yielded suggestions of proto-Solutrean culture. Other possible traces of proto-Solutrean remains are found in northern France, in Belgium and even in Britain.

Why it was that the main Solutrean development took place only in southwestern France remains an unanswered question that only further fieldwork can solve. One fact, however, now seems established: It is no longer necessary to go outside western Europe or indeed outside France itself to locate the birthplace of the Solutrean culture.

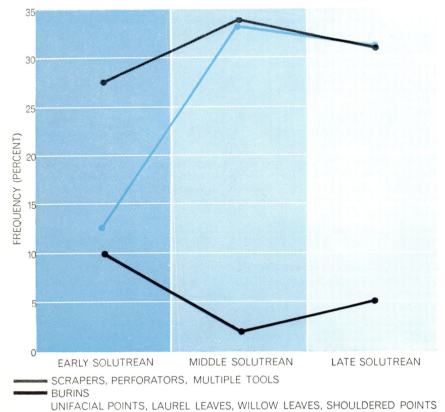

SCRAPERS, PERFORATORS, MULTIPLE TOOLS
BURINS
UNIFACIAL POINTS, LAUREL LEAVES, WILLOW LEAVES, SHOULDERED POINTS

CONSISTENCY of the Solutrean culture is evident in the quantities of different types of tool. During three successive periods the engraving and chiseling tools called burins never exceeded 10 percent of the stone-tool inventory at Laugerie-Haute. The number of scrapers, perforators and multiple tools at the site, in turn, remained consistently at a higher level. Only the four typically Solutrean blade tools showed a significant quantitative increase.

4

A PALEOLITHIC CAMP AT NICE

HENRY DE LUMLEY
May 1969

A Paleolithic site uncovered recently in the south of France contains traces of the earliest-known architecture: huts that were built some 300,000 years ago. The structures were evidently made by nomadic hunters who visited the Mediterranean shore briefly each year. They left behind artifacts and animal bones that, together with the plant pollen found at the site, yield a remarkably detailed picture of the occupants' activities during their annual sojourn by the sea. Because the discovery of the site and its excavation were unusual, I shall give a brief account of both before describing the new evidence the site provides concerning human life during this very early period of prehistory.

The city of Nice, in southeastern France, stands on a basement formation of limestone and marl. The bedrock is covered by layers of sand, clay and soil that mark the glacial oscillations of the ice age. During the construction of a shipyard some years ago certain glacial strata were exposed to view and attracted the attention of several scholars. In one sandy layer in 1959 Georges Iaworsky of the Monaco Museum of Prehistoric Anthropology found a few stone tools of typical Paleolithic workmanship. Two years later in another sandy section he found a tool of the early Paleolithic type known as Acheulean. Acheulean tools take their name from St. Acheul, a site in France where examples were first discovered, but since then Acheulean implements have been found at many other sites in Europe and in Asia and Africa. It had originally seemed that the sands had been deposited in the warm period between the glaciations called the Riss and the Würm, but Iaworsky pointed out that the age of the Acheulean tool indicated that these deposits were much older.

Then, in the course of foundation work during October, 1965, bulldozers cut a series of terraces into the sloping grounds of the Château de Rosemont, on the shoulder of Mont Boron in the eastern part of the city. The area of excavation, near the corner of Boulevard Carnot and an alley romantically named Terra Amata (beloved land), was scarcely 300 yards from Nice's commercial harbor and not far from the shipyard where Iaworsky and others, myself included, had studied the glacial strata. As the excavation proceeded the bulldozers exposed an extensive sandy deposit containing more Paleolithic implements. The significance of the discovery was quickly realized, and the builders agreed to halt operations temporarily. With the help of the French Ministry of Culture, a major archaeological salvage effort was mounted.

Starting on January 28, 1966, and continuing without interruption until July 5 more than 300 workers, including young students of archaeology from the universities and a number of enthusiastic amateurs, devoted a total of nearly 40,000 man-hours to the excavation of the Terra Amata site. The excavated area covered 144 square yards; in the course of investigating the 21 separate living floors found within the area the workers gradually removed a total of 270 cubic yards of fill, using no tools except trowels and brushes. The digging brought to light nearly 35,000 objects, and the location of each object was recorded on one or another of 1,200 charts. In addition, casts were made of 108 square yards of living floor and the progress of the work was documented in some 9,000 photographs.

In stratigraphic terms the deposits at Terra Amata begin at the surface with a layer of reddish clay that is nine feet thick in places and contains potsherds of the Roman period. Below the clay is a series of strata indicative of glacial advances during the Würm, Riss and Mindel periods and the warmer periods that intervened. The site embraces three fossil beaches, all belonging to the latter part of the Mindel glaciation. The youngest beach, marked by a dune and a sandbar, proved to be the site of human habitation.

When the youngest beach was deposited, the level of the Mediterranean was 85 feet higher than it is today. Soon after the beach was formed the sea level dropped somewhat, exposing the sandbar and allowing the wind to build a small dune inland. The hunters must have visited the area during or soon after a major period of erosion that occurred next. The evidence of their presence is found on or in the sands but not in the reddish-brown soil that later covered the eroded sand surface. Numerous shells of land snails, found at the base of the reddish soil, indicate a period of temperate climate.

The landscape of Terra Amata at the time of the hunters' visits differed in a number of respects from today's. The backdrop of the Alps, dominated by Mont Chauve, was much the same, but the sea covered most of the plain of Nice and even penetrated a short distance into what is now the valley of the Paillon River. The climate, though temperate, was somewhat brisker and more humid than the one we know. Pollen studies, undertaken by Jacques-Louis de Beaulieu of the pollen-analysis laboratory at the University of Aix-Marseilles, indicate that fir and Norway pine on the alpine heights grew farther down the slopes than is now the case, and that heather, sea pine, Aleppo pine and holm oak covered Mont Boron and its coastal neighbors.

In the limestone of Mont Boron's western slope the sea had cut a small cove opening to the south. Within the cove a sandy, pebble-strewn beach extended down to the sea, sheltered from the north and east winds. A small spring to one side provided a source of fresh water. A few seashore plants—grasses, horsetails, short-stemmed plantain and various shrubs—grew in the cove. The stream from the spring held water lilies of the genus *Euryale,* which, as De Beaulieu notes, can be found only in Asia today. All things considered, it appears that nothing was lacking even 300 millenniums ago to make Terra Amata a beloved land.

The superimposed living floors at Terra Amata are located in three separate areas. Four are on the section of beach that had formed the sandbar until the sea level dropped; six are on the beach seaward of the bar, and 11 are on the dune inland. The huts that were built on the living floors all had the same shape: an elongated oval. They ranged from 26 to 49 feet in length and from 13 to nearly 20 feet in width. Their outline can be traced with two kinds of evidence. The first is the imprint of a series of stakes, averaging some three inches in diameter, that were driven into the sand to form the walls of the hut. The second is a line of stones, paralleling the stake imprints, that apparently served to brace the walls. One of the earliest of the huts is perfectly outlined by an oval of stones, some as much as a foot in diameter and some even stacked one on the other. The living floor within the oval consisted of a thick bed of organic matter and ash.

The palisade of stakes that formed the walls was not the huts' only structural element. There are also visible the imprints left by a number of stout posts, each about a foot in diameter. These supports were set in place down the long axis of the hut. Evidence of how the palisade and the center posts were integrated to form the roof of the hut has not survived.

A basic feature of each hut is a hearth placed at the center. These fireplaces are either pebble-paved surface areas or shallow pits, a foot or two in diameter, scooped out of the sand. A little wall, made by piling up cobbles or pebbles, stands at the northwest side of each hearth. These walls were evidently windscreens to protect the fire against drafts, particularly from the northwest wind that is the prevailing one at Nice to this day.

The fact that the hunters built windscreens for their hearths makes it clear that their huts were not draft-free. This suggests that many of the palisade stakes may have been no more than leafy branches. Certainly nothing more permanent was required. As we shall see, the huts were occupied very briefly. As we shall also see, the time of the annual visit can be narrowed down to the end of spring and the beginning of summer, a season when such a building material would have been readily available.

In the huts on the dune the hearths were apparently designed for small fires. If one can judge from the larger amounts of charcoal and ash, the hearths in the huts closer to the sea must have accommodated much bigger fires. It is worth noting that the hearths at Terra Amata, together with those at one other site in Europe, are the oldest yet discovered anywhere in the world. The hearths that

OVAL HUTS, ranging from 26 to 49 feet in length and from 13 to 20 feet in width, were built at Terra Amata by visiting hunters. A reconstruction shows that the hut walls were made of stakes, about three inches in diameter, set as a palisade in the sand and braced on the outside by a ring of stones. Some larger posts were set up along the huts' long axes, but how these and the walls were joined to make roofs is unknown; the form shown is conjectural. The huts' hearths were protected from drafts by a small pebble windscreen.

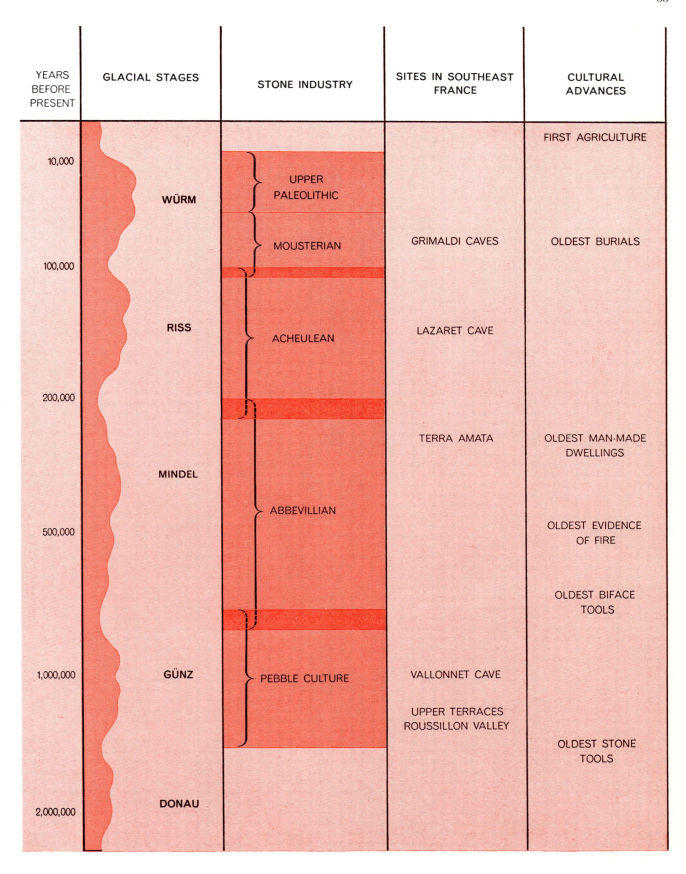

YEARS BEFORE PRESENT	GLACIAL STAGES	STONE INDUSTRY	SITES IN SOUTHEAST FRANCE	CULTURAL ADVANCES
				FIRST AGRICULTURE
10,000	WÜRM	UPPER PALEOLITHIC		
		MOUSTERIAN	GRIMALDI CAVES	OLDEST BURIALS
100,000	RISS	ACHEULEAN	LAZARET CAVE	
200,000			TERRA AMATA	OLDEST MAN-MADE DWELLINGS
	MINDEL	ABBEVILLIAN		
500,000				OLDEST EVIDENCE OF FIRE
				OLDEST BIFACE TOOLS
1,000,000	GÜNZ	PEBBLE CULTURE	VALLONNET CAVE	
			UPPER TERRACES ROUSSILLON VALLEY	
				OLDEST STONE TOOLS
2,000,000	DONAU			

CHRONOLOGICAL POSITION of Terra Amata in prehistory is indicated on this chart, which shows (*left to right*) the time, given in thousands of years before the present, of the major glacial advances and retreats in Europe, the successive stone industries of the Paleolithic period, sites in southeastern France where the industries have been found and early man's progress in technology.

FLOOR OF A HUT at Terra Amata is one of several brought to light by the excavators, revealing the ancient debris left behind by the occupants. The whole pebbles are raw material for tools; the chips and flakes, toolmakers' waste. The antler is from a stag.

equal them in age were found by László Vértes in strata of Mindel age at Vértesszölös in Hungary. Like some of the hearths at Terra Amata, those at the Hungarian site are shallow pits a foot or two in diameter.

Also from Vértesszölös comes a significant early human fossil: the occipital bone of a skull that has been assigned to modern man. No such human remains were found in our excavation at Terra Amata, but we came on two indirect sources of information about the site's inhabitants. One is the imprint of a right foot, 9½ inches long, preserved in the sand of the dune. Calculating a human being's height from the length of the foot is an uncertain procedure. If, however, one uses the formula applied to Neanderthal footprints found in the grotto of Toirano in Italy, the individual whose footprint was found at Terra Amata may have been five feet one inch tall.

Our other indirect source of information consists of fossilized human feces found in the vicinity of the huts. De Beaulieu's analysis of their pollen content shows that all of it comes from plants, such as *Genista*, that shed their pollen at the end of spring or the beginning of summer. This is the finding that enables us to state the precise time of year when the hunters came to Terra Amata.

How did the visitors occupy themselves during their stay? The evidence shows that they gathered a little seafood, manufactured stone tools and hunted in the nearby countryside. The animal bones unearthed at Terra Amata include the remains of birds, turtles and at least eight species of mammals. Although the visitors did not ignore small game such as rabbits and rodents, the majority of the bones represent larger animals. They are, in order of their abundance, the stag *Cervus elaphus*, the extinct elephant *Elephas meridionalis*, the wild boar (*Sus scrofa*), the ibex (*Capra ibex*), Merk's rhinoceros (*Dicerothinus merki*) and finally the wild ox *Bos primigenius*. Although the hunters showed a preference for big game, they generally selected as prey not the adults but the young of each species, doubtless because they were easier to bring down.

The visitors did not systematically exploit the food resources available in the Mediterranean. Nevertheless, they were not entirely ignorant of seafood. A few shells of oysters, mussels and limpets at the site show that they gathered shellfish; fishbones and fish vertebrae indicate that on occasion the hunters also fished.

The large majority of all the artifacts found at Terra Amata are stone tools. They represent two different but closely related stone industries. Both appear to be contemporary with the earliest "biface" industries of the Paleolithic period (so named because many of the tools are made out of stone "cores" that are shaped by chipping flakes from both faces rather than from one face only). They bear certain resemblances to the tools of an early Paleolithic biface industry named the Abbevillian (after the site in France where they were first discovered) and to the Acheulean biface industry, which is somewhat more advanced. On balance, both Terra Amata industries should probably be characterized as early Acheulean.

The more primitive of the two Terra Amata industries is represented by the tools found in the huts closest to the sea. Mainly pebble tools, they include many pieces of the type designated choppers, a few of the type called chopping tools and some crude bifaces made by detaching flakes from one end of an oval cobble but leaving a smooth, unflaked "heel" at the other end. Among the other tools found in the seaside huts are cleavers, scrapers, projectile points of a kind known in France as *pointes de Tayac*

REPRESENTATIVE TOOLS unearthed at Terra Amata include a pebble (*middle*) that has been flaked on one of its faces to form a pick, another stone tool (*left*), flaked on both faces but with one end left smooth, and a bone fragment (*right*) pointed to make an awl.

FIRE PIT (*right*) was protected from drafts and from the prevailing northwest wind in particular by a windscreen built of cobbles and pebbles, seen partially preserved at left.

TOOLMAKER'S ATELIER occupies one section of a hut. It is easily identified by the debris of tool manufacture that surrounds the bare patch of floor where the toolmaker sat.

and pebble tools flaked on one face only.

The stone industry represented by the tools found in the huts on the dune is more advanced, although it too includes choppers, chopping tools and cobble bifaces with a smooth heel. There are no single-faced pebble tools or cleavers on the dune, however, and tools made from flakes rather than from cores are relatively numerous. The tools made from flakes include those designated scrapers with abrupt retouch, end scrapers with toothed edges and flakes of the kind named Clactonian (after the English site Clacton-on-Sea). Some of the Clactonian flakes have been notched on one edge; others have been made into perforators by chipping out two notches side by side so that a point of stone protrudes. Projectile points from the dunes include, in addition to *pointes de Tayac*, some that are triangular in cross section and others of a kind known in France as *pointes de Quinson*.

Some of the tools found at Terra Amata were probably made on the spot. The hut floors show evidence of tool manufacturing, and the toolmaker needed only to walk along the beach to find workable pebbles and cobbles of flint, quartzite, limestone and other rock. The toolmaker's place inside the huts is easily recognized: a patch of living floor is surrounded by the litter of tool manufacture. The bare patches are where the toolmakers sat, sometimes on animal skins that have left a recognizable impression.

Not all the stone debris represents the waste from finished work. In one instance the excavators found a cobble from which a single chip had been struck. Nearby was a chip that fitted the scar perfectly. In another toolmaker's atelier several flakes had been removed from a cobble by a series of successive blows. Both the core and the flakes were found, and it was possible for us to reassemble the cobble. Scarcely a flake was missing; evidently the toolmaker did not put either the core or the flakes to use.

At least one of the projectile points unearthed at Terra Amata could not have been produced locally. The stone from which it is made is a volcanic rock of a kind found only in the area of Estérel, southwest of Cannes and some 30 miles from Nice. This discovery allows us to conclude that these summer visitors' travels covered at least that much territory in the south of France, although we cannot be sure how much more widely they may have roamed.

A few tools made of bone have been

found at Terra Amata. One leg bone of an elephant has a hammered point at one end. Another bone has a point that was probably hardened in a fire (a technique used today by some primitive peoples to harden the tips of wooden spears). A third bone fragment has one end smoothed by wear; still another may have served as an awl, and some fragments of bone may have been used as scrapers.

As for other kinds of artifacts, there are traces of only two. On the dune a spherical imprint in the sand, filled with a whitish substance, may be the impression left by a wooden bowl. Some pieces of red ocher found at the site obviously belonged to the visitors: the ends are worn smooth by wear. They recall the red ocher found at sites belonging to the much later Mousterian period, which François Bordes of the University of Bordeaux suggests were used for body-painting.

Let us see if the pattern of the hunters' annual visits to Terra Amata can be reconstructed. We know from the pollen evidence that they arrived in the late spring or early summer, and we can assume that they chose the sheltered cove as their camping ground as much because of its supply of fresh water as for any other reason. On arrival they set up their huts, built their hearths and windscreens, hunted for a day or two, gathered some seafood, rested by their fires, made a few tools and then departed. How do we know that their stay was so short? First, the living floors show no sign of the compaction that would characterize a longer occupation. Second, we have independent evidence that the huts collapsed soon after they were built. A freshly chipped stone tool that is left in the sun will quickly become bleached on the exposed side whereas the bottom side retains its original coloring. Many of the tools on the living floors at Terra Amata are bleached in this way. For the implements to be exposed to the full force of the Mediterranean summer sun the huts must have fallen apart soon after they were abandoned.

In the fall the winds covered the living floors, the leveled palisades and the rest of the camp debris with a layer of sand perhaps two inches deep. The rains then spread out the sand and packed it down, so that when the hunters returned to the cove the following year the evidence of their earlier stay had been almost obliterated. Only a few objects, such as the windscreens for the hearths, still protruded from the sand. The visi-

tors then built new huts, often digging the hearth pit exactly where the preceding year's had been and rekindling their fires on the ashes of the previous season. After a day or two of hunting, gathering seafood and making tools the annual visit was ended. The 11 living floors on the dune at Terra Amata are so precisely superimposed that they almost certainly represent 11 consecutive yearly visits, probably involving many of the same individuals.

There is no older evidence of man-

made structures than that at Terra Amata. Until this site was excavated the record for antiquity was held by the traces of construction discovered at Latamne, an open-air site in Syria, by J. Desmond Clark of the University of California at Berkeley. An early Acheulean site, Latamne is believed to be as old as the Mindel-Riss interglacial period. Terra Amata, which evidently was inhabited at the end of the Mindel glacial period, is therefore even earlier.

The evidence indicating that the hunt-

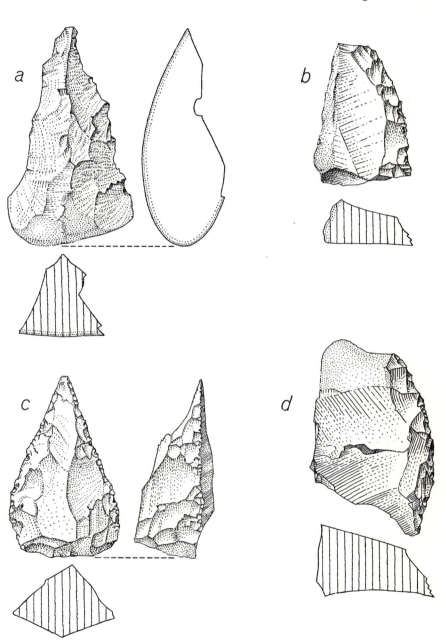

LESS PRIMITIVE TOOLS were found in the huts on the dune at Terra Amata. There were no cleavers or single-faced pebble tools and many more of the tools were made from flakes rather than from cores. Tools common to both areas are *pointes de Tayac* (*a*) and flakes made into simple scrapers (*b*), choppers, chopping tools and bifaces like those on the opposite page. Flakes were also made into projectile points (*c*) and more elaborate scrapers (*d*).

40

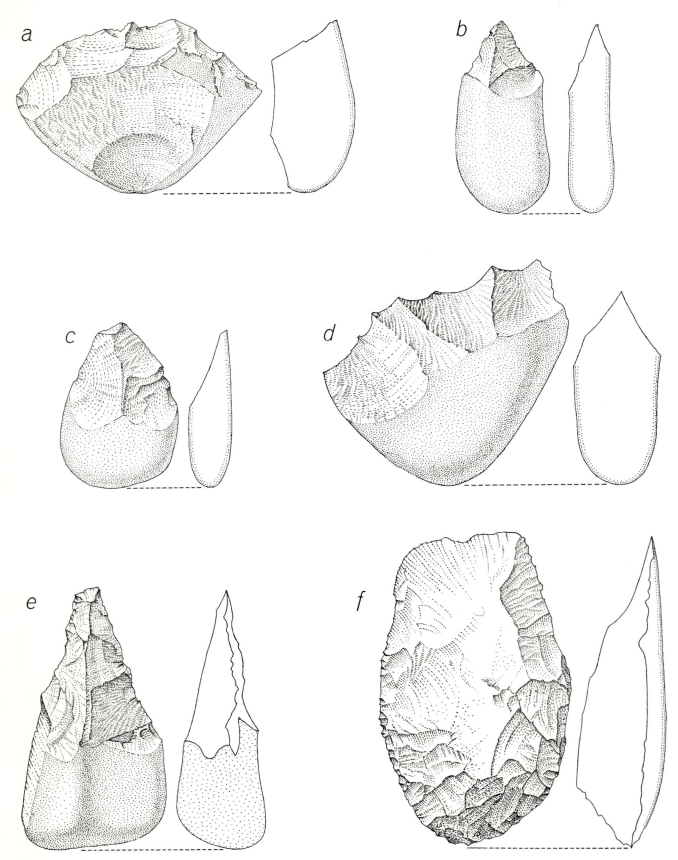

a

b

c

d

e

f

GROUP OF PRIMITIVE TOOLS was found in association with the huts closest to the sea at Terra Amata. They include choppers (*a*) and picks (*b,c*), made from pebbles that are flaked on one face only; chopping tools (*d*) that are flaked on both faces; crude bi-faces (*e*), made by detaching flakes from one end of a cobble but leaving an unflaked "heel" at the opposite end; cleavers (*f*), and two other kinds of stone artifacts (*illustrated on preceding page*): scrapers and projectile points of a kind known as *pointes de Tayac.*

ers came to Terra Amata at about the same time year after year, together with the likelihood that the dune huts sheltered some of the same individuals for more than a decade, suggests that the visitors possessed stable and even complex social institutions. It is thus appropriate to conclude with the words of the French historian Camille Jullian, written soon after the Terra Amata living floors had been exposed. "The hearth," Jullian wrote, "is a place for gathering together around a fire that warms, that sheds light and gives comfort. The toolmaker's seat is where one man carefully pursues a work that is useful to many. The men here may well be nomadic hunters, but before the chase begins they need periods of preparation and afterward long moments of repose beside the hearth. The family, the tribe will arise from these customs, and I ask myself if they have not already been born."

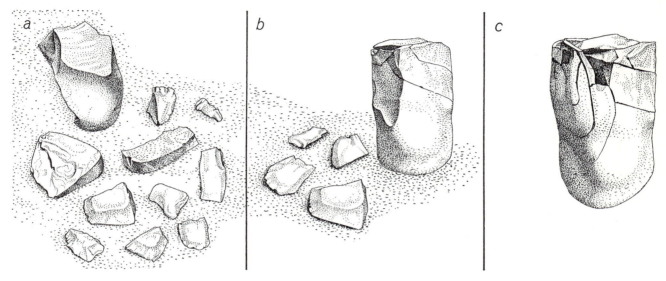

UNUTILIZED RAW MATERIAL was found in one Terra Amata toolmaker's atelier. Near the shattered half of a large cobble lay most of the fragments that had been struck from it (a). They could be reassembled (b) so that the cobble was almost whole again (c).

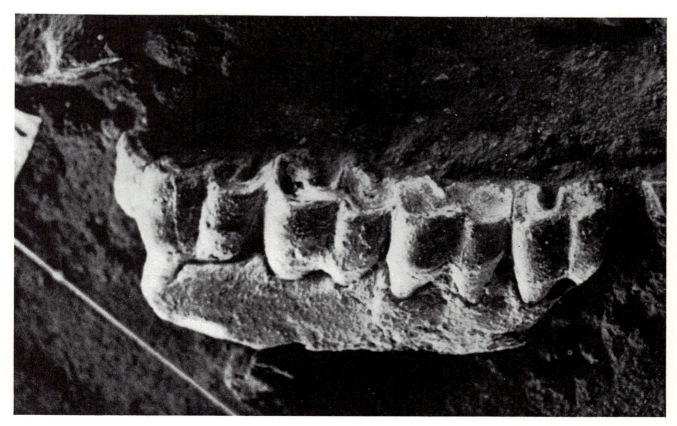

ANIMAL BONE, photographed *in situ* near one corner of an excavation unit, is a fragment of rhinoceros mandible, complete with teeth. The visitors preferred large mammals to other game. Along with rhinoceros they hunted stag, elephant, boar, ibex and wild ox.

MOUTH OF SHANIDAR CAVE is an opening in the flank of Baradost Mountain, some 250 miles from Baghdad. The cave is 130 feet deep; its mouth is 26 feet high and 82 feet wide. From November to April it is inhabited by Kurdish goatherds (*see photograph below*).

FLOOR OF SHANIDAR CAVE is covered with simple shelters for its Kurdish inhabitants and corrals for their animals. In this photograph Kurdish workmen have just begun the excavation of the earthen floor of the cave. Bedrock was reached at a depth of 45 feet.

5

SHANIDAR CAVE

RALPH S. SOLECKI
November 1957

In a mountainside in the Zagros Mountains of northern Iraq is a human dwelling place known as "The Big Cave of Shanidar." It is a high-vaulted natural cave about the size of four tennis courts—capacious enough to house a considerable band of people. The cave has a warm southern exposure and is well protected from winter winds. Nearby are springs and a stream to supply water. Remnants of wild game and the few stands of still-undisturbed virgin forest on the hillsides testify that the place has long had a fertile and livable climate. Today the Cave of Shanidar is inhabited by a clan of Kurdish goatherds and their animals. It is not hard to imagine that men have lived in this commodious, sun-warmed shelter for generation after generation. Out of scientific curiosity we have dug into the floor of the cave, and found to our delight that this conjecture is a feeble understatement. The inhabitation of the Shanidar Cave apparently goes back at least 100,000 years! Remains unearthed from deep beneath its trampled floor give evidence that Neanderthal man once lived here, and that the cave has been a home of man more or less continuously for something like 3,000 generations.

Needless to say, the Shanidar Cave has become one of our most important and fruitful sites for tracing the early history of mankind. Rarely do archaeologists have a chance to see so clear a succession of man's development over so long a period as we have in the layers that make the pages of the story of Shanidar. The story is not lessened in interest by the fact that Shanidar Cave is close to the birthplace of the first great civilizations in Mesopotamia [see "The Sumerians," by Samuel Noah Kramer, beginning on page 145].

Mesopotamia itself is a poor place to look for the Stone Age cultures that preceded its ancient civilizations. A hunting and foraging people would have found little food in its marshes and deserts; moreover, it would be difficult to discover or to date any of their camp sites in this sea-flooded and river-washed plain. Archaeologists have long realized that the best chance of finding Stone Age human remains lay in the foothills and mountains north of the Tigris and Euphrates. In 1928 a small party led by Dorothy Garrod of the University of Cambridge found such remains in two caves near a town called Suleimaniyah in the Zagros foothills [see map on next page]. There were no other serious excavations until Robert Braidwood of the University of Chicago began his explorations of Stone Age sites in the same vicinity in 1950 [see the article "From Cave to Village," by Robert J. Braidwood, beginning on page 67]. Braidwood discovered evidences of the beginnings of human agriculture and village settlements. But the dream of archaeologists looking into man's distant past is to find a site where the stages of his development are piled layer upon layer so that we can get a consecutive, slow-motion picture, so to speak.

In 1951, while working in Iraq with a University of Michigan expedition, I heard about Shanidar Cave and decided to stay on, after the expedition went home, to do some exploratory digging in the cave. These first soundings were so promising that I returned in 1953, and again in 1956, for two more full seasons of excavation. The investigations have been conducted on behalf of the Iraq Directorate-General of Antiquities and the Smithsonian Institution, with support from several other organizations.

The Zagros Mountains resemble the highlands of Scotland; their foothills look like the hills of the U. S. Southwest. Shanidar Cave is in a mountain called Baradost, overlooking Shanidar Valley. From the cave mouth one can see the Greater Zab River, a tributary of the Tigris. The cave, now some 2,500 feet above sea level, was dissolved out of the mountain's limestone rock, originally laid down by an ancient sea. It has a flat earthen floor, about 11,700 square feet in area, and a high ceiling (45 feet at the highest point) blackened with a centuries-old deposit of soot. The Kurdish goatherds and their families, who live in the cave all winter from November to April, have built individual brush huts inside it, each with a small fireplace, and corrals for goats, chickens, cows and horses [see drawing on page 45]. The Kurds are a proud, self-sufficient, but backward people. They make fire with flint and steel and grind wheat by hand with circular stones. The women cut hay in the mountain meadows with short iron sickles and toil barefooted up a mountain trail with goatskins to fetch water from the springs. Compared with modern Baghdad, only 250 miles away, the present dwellers in Shanidar Cave could just as well be living in the days of the Assyrian herdsmen 2,500 years ago.

It was from this level of culture, then, that we began our digging journey into man's early history. We marked off a small area in the center of the cave and started our slow, careful excavation down through the floor. In three seasons of work we have cut through the full depth of the cave's earthen accumulations, down to bedrock at 45 feet, and have sifted about a tenth of the total bulk of its deposits. The excavations have yielded a rich record of human

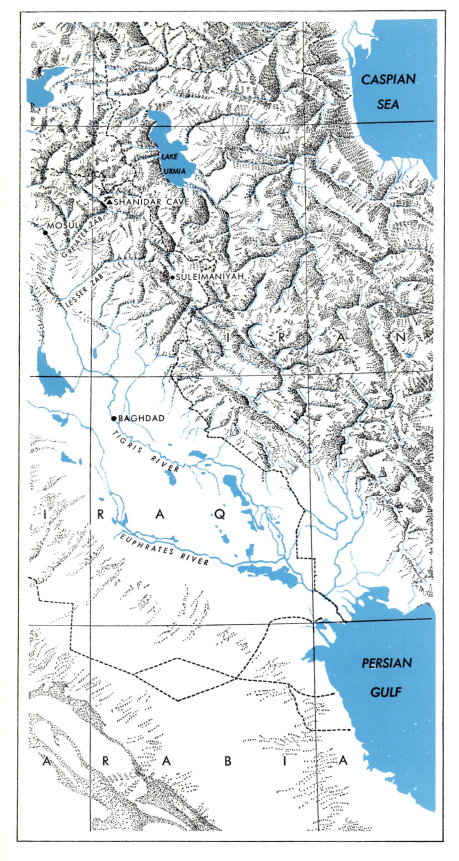

CAVE IS LOCATED on this map of the region north of the Persian Gulf. Suleimaniyah is the site of earlier cave excavations by Dorothy Garrod of the University of Cambridge.

occupation—ancient hearths, tools, animal bones, even Neanderthal skeletons—going back some 100,000 years.

We found four main layers, distinguishable by soil color and the types of artifacts they contained. Each corresponded to a recognizable stage of man's development. I shall first review briefly the general contents of these layers, which are identified, according to an archaeological convention, by the letters A to D from the top down [see drawing on page 46].

Layer A, averaging about five feet thick, is a black, greasy soil, compacted by many generations of feet. It dates from the present back to some time in the Neolithic (New Stone) Age, perhaps 7,000 years ago. This layer covers the revolutionary period in man's way of life when he emerged from mere hunting to food gathering, agriculture and animal herding. Throughout Layer A we found ash beds of communal fires, bones of domesticated animals and domestic tools such as stone mortars (which the Kurds still use for cracking nuts). The circular millstones with which they still grind wheat showed up only in the upper part of Layer A; apparently these are a comparatively recent development. About a foot below the surface we found some primitive clay tobacco bowls—mute evidence that the tobacco habit came to this part of Asia about 300 years ago. A little farther down was a bit of burnished pottery similar to the kind known as "Uruk" ware, named for the city of Erech in ancient Mesopotamia. This pottery dates from the time of the invention of cuneiform writing in Sumer.

Layer B, just below A, is a fairly thin, brown-stained deposit which, according to carbon-14 measurements, dates back to the Middle Stone Age, about 12,000 years ago. It contains the primitive artifacts of a people who knew neither agriculture nor animal domestication nor pottery making. There is no sign that they even collected edible nuts. Apparently snails made up a considerable part of their diet, for there are heaps of snail shells strewn about. Animal bones are relatively scarce in this layer: there are no domestic animals and few wild ones. Possibly it was a period of game scarcity in Shanidar Valley.

Nonetheless the prehistoric people of Layer B seem to have thrived and even to have had some leisure. They made exquisitely chipped projectile points, and bone awls which must have been used for sewing or lacing. What is more, there are engraved pieces of slate, and also fragments of well-rubbed coloring stones which suggest that these people may have made paintings or decorations.

Below Layer B we come to a gap of some 17,000 years during which the cave apparently was not occupied. The next layer, C, dates from about 29,000 to more than 34,000 years ago, according to radiocarbon measurements of charcoal in its firebeds. Near the top of the layer are many boulders, which probably fell from the ceiling during an

earthquake and may well have discouraged residence in the cave. The soil layer itself, a yellowish deposit about eight feet thick with the remains of many fires, bespeaks a long occupation by the late Paleolithic (Old Stone Age) people who had lived in the cave in this period.

Now these people are an anomaly in the Iraq region. Their flint tools—so-called "blade tools"—were like the implements of a late Paleolithic culture in Europe known as the Aurignacian (which used to be identified with Cro-

Magnon man). But no such culture has been found anywhere in Iraq except at Shanidar, although other sites in the area have yielded earlier and later cultures. To the distinctive culture of Layer C we therefore gave the name "Baradostian," after the name of the mountain on which Shanidar Cave is located.

The people of Layer C, like their counterparts in Europe and elsewhere, must have been good woodworkers, for their deposits contain many flint wood-working tools, including scrapers and

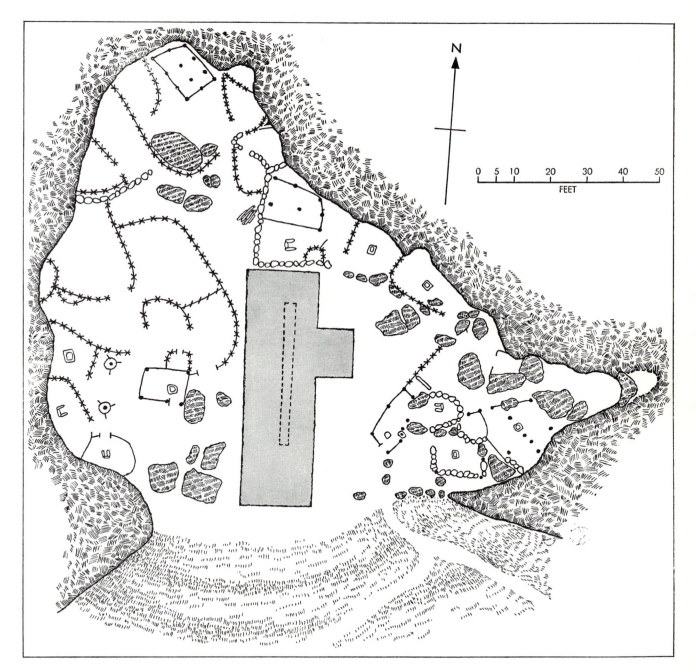

EXCAVATION IS LOCATED by the gray area on this map of the cave. The broken line in the gray area, and its extension toward the mouth of the cave, is the outline of a test trench dug in 1951. The floor of the cave is littered with rocks from the ceiling.

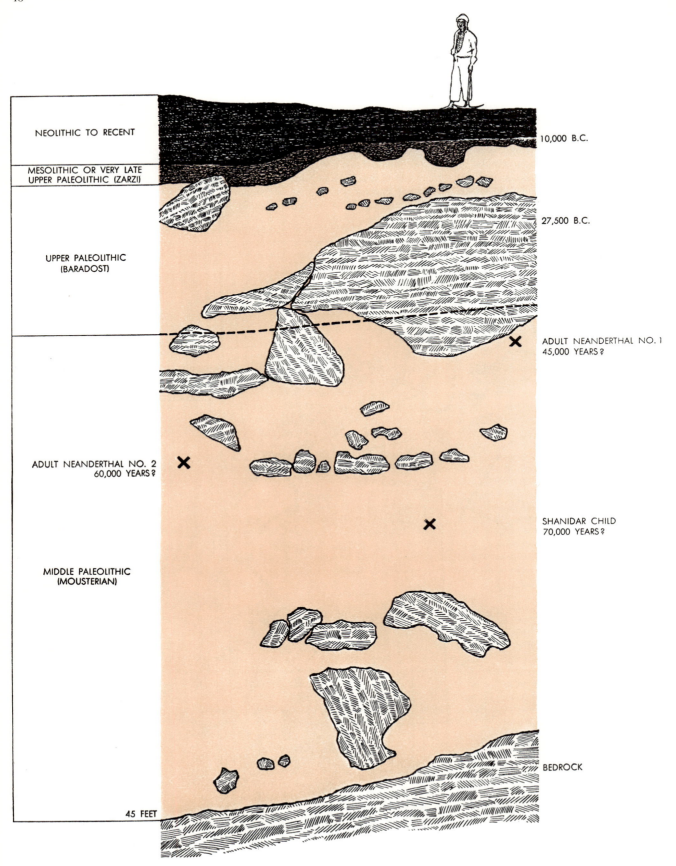

NEOLITHIC TO RECENT

10,000 B.C.

MESOLITHIC OR VERY LATE
UPPER PALEOLITHIC (ZARZI)

27,500 B.C.

UPPER PALEOLITHIC
(BARADOST)

ADULT NEANDERTHAL NO. 1
45,000 YEARS?

ADULT NEANDERTHAL NO. 2
60,000 YEARS?

SHANIDAR CHILD
70,000 YEARS?

MIDDLE PALEOLITHIC
(MOUSTERIAN)

BEDROCK

45 FEET

LAYERS IN THE FLOOR of the cave are indicated on this cross section. At the top (Neolithic to Recent) is Layer A; second from the top (Mesolithic or Very Late Upper Paleolithic), Layer B; third from the top (Upper Paleolithic), Layer C; fourth from the top (Middle Paleolithic), Layer D. The location of the Neanderthal finds are marked by crosses. The rocks fell from roof of the cave.

gravers. Of course none of their wood products has survived in the soil of the cave, but we know from the reports of ancient explorers that Stone Age peoples were capable of a wonderful wood technology.

In Layer D of the cave, a 29-foot-thick series of deposits extending from about 16 feet below the surface to bedrock at 45 feet, we arrived at a distinct break in the human line. The peoples above were presumably all *Homo sapiens:* here, some 45,000 years ago and earlier, we discover the extinct *Homo neanderthalensis.* Not only do we recognize his crude tools, but by incredibly good luck the Shanidar Cave yields up no fewer than three skeletons of Neanderthal man, including the first Neanderthal infant!

First, a brief word about his artifacts, of which, naturally, there are not many. The flint implements of Neanderthal man are called Mousterian, after a site in France where typical ones were found. Like those unearthed elsewhere, the Neanderthal tools in Shanidar Cave are simple flakes of flint with one worked face, struck to form a cutting edge or a point. Apparently Neanderthal man was smart enough to make the most of his material, because every flint core we found had been hacked down to the last flake that could be extracted from it.

We have no clue to what clothing he wore, but he must have wrapped himself in some sort of covering, for this was a cold period in the history of Shanidar Cave—the height of the last Ice Age. In Layer D there is a dark, eight-foot stratum with an especially heavy concentration of fire remains, probably representing a period when the cave was continually occupied because of the cold outside. Apparently the occupants kept a constant fire going, for warmth and to repel wild animals. The period was not only cold but also very wet: there is a layer of stalagmitic lime—drippings from the ceiling—which marks the only era of appreciable dampness in the history of this cave.

Although the cave afforded protection from the miserable climate, it was not without its hazards to the Neanderthal occupants. From time to time there were terrific rockfalls from the ceiling, probably caused by earthquakes. We found firebeds and an animal buried under such falls, and the skeletons of both of the Neanderthal adults lay crushed under boulders which may have crashed down and killed them.

Neanderthal man has been found in a number of places in Europe, but he is a rarity in Asia. Shanidar Cave is only the fifth site in Asia where his bones have turned up. (The nearest to Shanidar is Mount Carmel in Palestine.) This alone gives the skeletons in our cave extraordinary interest, for we may learn something about man's evolution by comparing these skeletons with Neanderthals elsewhere. And added to this is the fact that one of the Shanidar finds is a year-old baby, the only infant Neanderthal yet unearthed.

The three skeletons lay at three different levels, separated by thousands of years [*drawing on opposite page*]. The most recent, and best preserved because its bones were least crushed by rocks and the overburden, is that of an adult estimated to have lived in the cave about 45,000 years ago. A rockfall shattered some of its bones badly, but the skeleton is fairly complete, and much of the skull is intact. The second adult skeleton was found about 23 feet below the surface and is believed to be about 60,000 to 65,000 years old. It was considerably more damaged than the first: a rockfall crushed not only its bones but also its skull. The child lay at a still lower level, perhaps 70,000 years old. Its skeleton was found doubled up, with the legs tucked under the chin and the arms folded close to the body. Most of the fragile skeleton, including the head, was crushed under the earth overburden, and only its teeth and the hand and foot bones are in good condition.

Every frequenter of museums is familiar with the classic picture of Neanderthal man of Europe: the low, sloping forehead, the bulging brow ridges, the massive, prognathous jaw, the receding chin, the worn teeth. Our best-preserved specimen, the Shanidar 45,000-year-old, is generally faithful to this picture. He was what anthropologists call a "conservative" type—almost fully Neanderthaloid, with few suggestions of progress toward the features of *Homo sapiens.* But he does show one feature which is more human than Neanderthaloid: his brow bulge is not one continuous ridge running across the forehead but has a depression in the middle between the eyes, and it flares at the sides. This skeleton is about five feet three inches long—the typical height of Neanderthal man. Two of the front teeth are missing, and he evidently lost them while he was alive, because there is some replacement of tissue in the jawbone where they were rooted. The teeth of both of our Neanderthal adults show heavy wear: they were worn quite flat.

It will take time to analyze the skeletons, to relate them to the Neanderthals of Europe and of other sites in Asia, to discover whether the three Neanderthals of different eras at Shanidar differ from one another, to reconstruct their posture and other attributes and to read any clues they may offer to the evolution of early man in the Middle East. It is possible that the still unexcavated part of Shanidar Cave will yield more skeletons; indeed, we have found two human skeletons from the Neolithic Period and one from the time of Mohammed.

Meanwhile the priceless hoard of remains in Shanidar Cave is being studied by archaeologists, physical anthropologists, zoologists, geologists, climatologists and other specialists. With the combined insights of all these investigators we can hope to translate the scraps of evidence into a comprehensive account of the peoples who lived in the cave and of how they wrested a living from nature in various times and conditions. The Kurdish families who still live at Shanidar are, of course, a vivid and illuminating part of the picture. Stone Age archaeology would be a vague and frustrated science were it not for the assistance that anthropologists and their living subjects are able to give in enriching the meaning of artifacts. As a prehistorian once put it, in anthropology "one catches one's archaeology alive." We see an excellent illustration of what this may mean when we look at the remarkable products made by "primitive" tribes with seemingly crude and limited tools. An archaeologist unearthing a prehistoric wood-scraper made of stone or a shell has no idea of what its users manufactured with it, for the wood objects have long since decayed. But when we discover what living aborigines have done with similar tools, we begin to realize that prehistoric man may well have been far more resourceful, and capable of more exquisite workmanship, than his tools suggest.

We still know comparatively little about the history of the Big Cave of Shanidar. But standing before the deep cut that we have sliced into its floor, we can see the general outlines of that history. We see Neanderthal man crouching over a fire nearly 100,000 years ago, and looking out from the cave mouth at a valley landscape not too different from the one today. He goes forth to hunt tortoises, wild goats and wild pigs (which still roam the valley but are now untouched by the Kurds because of a religious taboo). Apparently he does not try to catch the swift deer or tackle the dangerous bear, wolf or leopard (at least their bones are practically absent in the deposits of Shanidar Cave). The splintered bones of his game show that he cracked open the bones to suck out every bit of marrow.

For tens of thousands of years Neanderthal man hangs on at the cave, surviving the Ice Age, rockfalls and unremitting rains. Although he is a backward type, he lingers on in this mountain fastness for thousands of years after physically more "progressive" Neanderthals have died out in Palestine, only

600 miles away. Century after century his life continues with a monotonous sameness; even his flint tools do not change. Eventually he is succeeded by *Homo sapiens*. Now the curve of culture begins to rise gradually: the new men improve their hunting weapons, fashion tools for woodworking and sit around a communal fire. Thousands of years later the inhabitants of the cave have advanced to finely chipped tools, sewing and painting. But the curve of progress still clings low on the horizon. Then, some 7,000 years ago (only yesterday in the long history of the cave), the curve suddenly begins to shoot up with

a burst of power. The people of Shanidar Cave learn to domesticate animals, till the soil, grind wheat, make pottery, spin thread. They remain, however, an isolated, pastoral people, in spite of the successive Sumerian, Babylonian, Assyrian and Persian civilizations that rise and fall in nearby Mesopotamia.

So the story of Shanidar Cave ends just a little beyond the Stone Age. Soon, it seems, its story will come to a final end, because the Iraq Government plans to build a dam on the Greater Zab which will flood Shanidar Valley and cut off access to the cave. Fortunately it was discovered in time to tell us its history.

NEANDERTHAL SKELETONS were exposed by an extension of earlier soundings made in the spring of 1957. The first adult Neanderthal to be discovered is at lower right. The arrow on the rear wall points to the location of the second adult Neanderthal.

6

ISIMILA: A PALEOLITHIC SITE IN AFRICA

F. CLARK HOWELL
October 1961

The prehistorian who studies the earlier part of the Old Stone Age is attempting to reconstruct the habits and behavior of peoples dead for more than 75,000 years. In going about the task he is not encumbered by an over-supply of evidence: the total inventory comprises a few fragments of human skeletons; some bones of the animals that the early hunters killed (and vice versa); pieces of wooden implements, preserved through rare accidents; and large numbers of the chipped stones with which man then carved, scraped and battered out his living.

If one is to extract much valid information about the way of life these artifacts represent, one must examine them in the settings in which they were used—in "archaeological context." For a long time, when Europe was the main theater of archaeological exploration, stone tools dating from the early Paleolithic period were not seen this way. Abandoned at the exposed sites where their makers· had lived (men did not become cave dwellers until rather late in the Old Stone Age), the tools were subsequently disturbed and even transported over considerable distances during the glaciations of the Pleistocene epoch. During the past 30 years or so much research on early man has been conducted in the unglaciated landscape of central Africa. A number of undisturbed, open living sites have been turned up. One of these, at Isimila in southern Tanganyika, has provided an assortment of Paleolithic tools in archaeological context. Together with my colleagues Maxine R. Kleindienst and Glen H. Cole, I have spent a considerable part of the past several years excavating and analyzing the material. It has provided valuable new insights into the activities of early man.

A number of the undisturbed sites are situated in or are adjacent to the Great Rift Valley of eastern central Africa. These include Kariandusi and Olorgesailie in Kenya and Olduvai Gorge in northern Tanganyika. Olduvai Gorge presents the longest known sequence of Pleistocene living sites. There L. S. B. Leakey of the Coryndon Museum in Nairobi has recently discovered remains of the oldest known toolmakers, dating back some 1,750,000 years. The Isimila site is situated not in the Rift Valley but in the Iringa highlands of southern Tanganyika, and the tools there are not nearly so old. They belong to the style of manufacture known as Acheulean, after the place in northern France where an abundance of such tools has been found. Current estimates place the beginning of the Acheulean industry about 300,000 years ago, in the middle of the Pleistocene, and the end about 75,000 years ago, toward the end of the last interglacial period. Judging by the geological formations represented there, Isimila seems to have been inhabited for only a few thousand years near the end of the long span of the Acheulean period.

The geological history of the site was traced for us by Edward G. Haldemann and Ray Pickering of the Department of Geological Survey of Tanganyika. Millions of years ago the place was a major river valley. Then a series of upward and downward geological movements transformed the landscape, leaving the old valley as a small trough at an

EXCAVATION SITE was dotted with tools and rubble, exposed by erosion of Isimila beds. Nine living sites were excavated in three upper levels. One was excavated in fourth.

AERIAL VIEW of Isimila, looking northeast, shows main areas of sheet erosion. Trenches at middle right are excavation H20 in Level 4, the only bed containing fossil animal bones.

elevation of 5,400 feet, drained only by a small stream. During a period of increased rainfall in the middle of the Pleistocene the surrounding hills were covered with trees. Later the climate became drier and scrub vegetation replaced the woodland. Soil slipped and washed down from the deforested hills, choking the outlet of the basin and damming up an elongated body of water. This was alternately a marsh and a shallow pond, sometimes with an overflow. A steady deposition of silt in this basin eventually filled it to a depth of more than 60 feet with alternating beds of fine clay and coarser sandy sediment. The whole silting process seems to have required a few thousand years at most, and during this time early Stone Age hunters camped around the water hole.

There are five distinct beds of coarse sediment. Recent erosion has bared a good part of the upper three, and we have excavated them extensively. They contain an extraordinary number of living areas, all of them littered with tools. Indeed, it is hardly possible to walk over the site in any direction without stepping over quantities of finished and partly finished tools and waste chips. Since these upper layers are quite acid, no bone (except for a single hippopotamus tooth) has been found in them. In the fourth layer, however, we found bones of a number of animals, representing both extinct and still existing species. The skeleton of a hippopotamus, with the head and legs missing, looks very much as though it had been slaughtered or scavenged by human beings. The lower layers also yielded tools, but very few living areas to provide context.

With artifacts scattered so liberally through the three upper layers, the delimitation of a living area is somewhat arbitrary. In certain places, however, the pieces lie at the bottom of the sandy bed, on the surface of the underlying clay or within an inch or two of it. Horizontally they are densely distributed in a central region, becoming sparser with distance from the center. Although the boundaries may be uncertain, it seems quite clear that these assemblages mark out a site occupied for some time.

Nine living areas have been extensively excavated in the upper three levels, and one in the fourth bed has been partially exposed. The existence of several occupation areas on each level provides the first opportunity to compare different assemblages of tools known to be roughly contemporaneous. At other sites it has been possible only to compare them with those from different strata. Con-

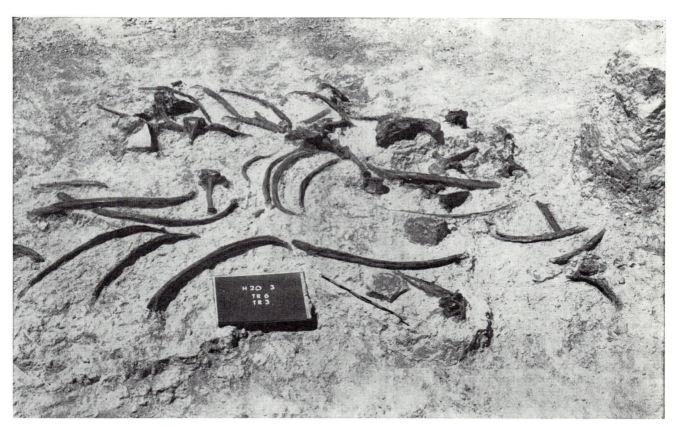

HIPPOPOTAMUS BONES found in Level 4 form skeleton lacking head and extremities. The animal may have been slaughtered or scavenged by early man. This level contained fossil animal bones, of both extinct and extant species. No human bones were found.

HAND AXES found on Level 1 were resting on edge, as their users left them. Only one other Paleolithic site in Africa yielded tools resting in this position. It has been suggested that implements left lying thus were used for a specialized purpose, as yet unknown.

sequently the work at Isimila is forcing a revision of some widely held notions about the earlier Old Stone Age.

Our method of studying the occupation site was simple enough in principle but tedious and exacting in practice. After carefully excavating an area, we examined, classified and tabulated each one of the hundreds of tools that were exposed, as well as the numerous bits of rubble and waste chips. From these counts we were able to prepare charts showing the relative frequency of each type of object at each place [see illustration on pages 54 and 55].

Of what use is all this detail? In part the answer is still uncertain. When the same sort of analysis has been carried out at other sites, a comparison of the data may bring out new facts and relations. At Isimila alone, however, there was enough diversity to provide an entirely new idea of the full range of the Acheulean tool complex and to reveal an unsuspected degree of specialization.

Before proceeding to a description of what we found, a word about the different kinds of tool is in order. Unlike earlier toolmakers, the Acheulean craftsmen did not merely trim up likely looking stones that were ready to hand. They knew how to strike flakes from boulders or large stones and then fashion the blanks into a wide variety of standardized shapes. The kinds of rock with which they worked—mylonite (a strongly coherent rock containing fine mineral grains), granite, quartz and quartzite—show that they had mastered the most intractable raw materials.

The stone artifacts at Isimila fall into several classes. These include large and small shaped tools, pieces that were modified or slightly trimmed, pieces that were used but not trimmed and waste products. Within these classes various types of tool can be recognized and differentiated on the basis of the kind and the treatment of edges, the nature of the secondary trimming and so on. The tool types also exhibit different shapes or forms, and these vary between assemblages from the same site as well as between those from different sites. The large shaped tools with sharp cutting edges are usually made of mylonite and occasionally of quartz or quartzite. According to their shape and type of edge they are designated as hand axes, cleavers, knives, flake scrapers and "discoids" [see illustration on page 57]. The list of the blunter large pieces—generally of granite, quartz or quartzite—includes picks, core scrapers, choppers and "spheroids." Small tools are most often quartz, and their worked edges are frequently notched or otherwise shaped for scraping or perhaps for piercing.

Although many of the names suggest that the purposes for which the different tools were used are known, this is not at all true. In some cases, however, the most common guesses seem fairly plausible. It appears likely that the large blunt tools, which were always made of particularly durable varieties of stone, were meant for heavy duty. The small tools may have been used for working wood.

The hand ax was formerly thought to be an all-purpose tool, used for cutting, skinning, digging and so on, but the evidence from the undisturbed living sites at Isimila and elsewhere contradicts this notion. The sharp edges of the hand axes and some of the other large tools suggest beyond doubt that they were used only on soft substances. Recently some authorities have suggested that certain of the large sharp pieces were used for skinning and dismembering thick-skinned animals.

There is no proof for any of these hypotheses. Some of the evidence is distinctly mysterious. For example, both at Isimila and at another East African site several hand axes were found resting on one edge. Were they merely stuck in the ground after their users had finished their work or does their position indicate some specialized application? With further research such questions may be answered. Meanwhile the list of names serves to describe an assortment of well-defined tool types, whatever their purpose. The conventional labels furnish the prehistorian with an essential system of classification.

Among the various living areas at Isimila we could distinguish three distinct types of tool assemblage. The first type, represented in six places, has been traditionally regarded as the typical Acheulean tool kit. It consists mostly (up to 70 per cent and in one case even more) of large, sharp-edged tools—notably hand axes, cleavers and knives. The rest of the collection is divided about equally into large blunt tools and small flake tools. There are few waste products. The second type, of which there are two examples, is just the reverse:

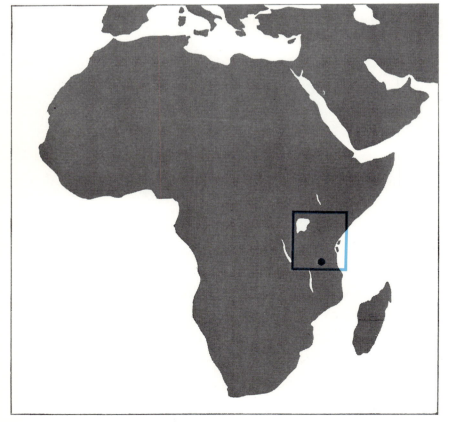

LOCATION OF ISIMILA is shown by the blue dot at right of center on this map of Africa. Most of the continent escaped glaciation during the ice age and still preserves some of the open-air sites at which early man camped in the period before he began to inhabit caves.

small tools predominate (40 to 60 per cent). Here there are few large cutting-edged tools and a fairly large quantity of waste products.

Both of these general categories have been observed in other Paleolithic sites in East Africa. The third type is new. Found at one place in the third level,

it contains a few small tools and a few large cutting-edged ones, the latter of an unusual shape. About half of the total is made up of large, heavy-duty tools—principally picks, core scrapers and choppers.

Before the excavations at Isimila were undertaken, different styles of individual

tools and different tool kits had always been found at separate sites, or in separate levels of the same site. Therefore they were usually held to reflect the passage of time and changes in culture or technology. Some authorities have attributed the first two types of tool kit we found at Isimila to distinct "cultures"

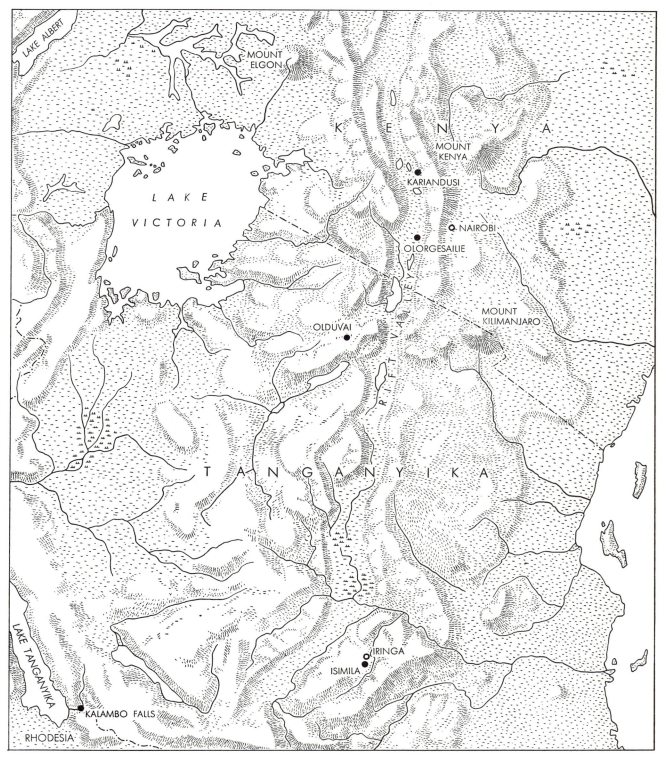

RIFT VALLEY AREA holds most of the human occupation sites recently excavated in eastern Central Africa. Shown here as black dots, from Kenya in the north to Rhodesia in the south, are Kariandusi, Olorgesailie, Olduvai Gorge, Isimila and Kalambo Falls.

with different ecological adjustments and subsistence patterns. There has even been talk of two different species of man.

The results at Isimila make such interpretations highly questionable. The place was occupied for a relatively short time. Yet a wide variety of tools and tool kits appears at different places within a single level. It seems most likely that in this case differences in tool kits reflect different activities. Members of the same group may well have been simultaneously performing different tasks requiring different tools.

On the other hand, variations in in-dividual styles in similar assemblages also found at Isimila may mean that more than one band of early men occupied the site at about the same time. For example, in one living area most of the hand axes are shaped like spearheads, in another most are egg-shaped. In one tool kit the sides of many of the cleavers con-verge; in a similar one they are largely parallel. Miss Kleindienst has discovered regional differences in the workmanship of certain tools at a number of East Af-rican Acheulean sites. Perhaps groups from different localities may have con-centrated at the same campsite together. Stylistic variations had been known in

the tools of hunters and gatherers of the present day and of Neolithic times, but it was interesting to find them so much earlier.

Similarly, there are differences in ma-terials from one occupation site to an-other even in the same level. In some locations the full range of raw materials is represented; in others, only one or two varieties. The mylonite used for large cutting-edged tools also varies from site to site in color, hardness and flaking qualities. To some extent the variation may simply reflect the sources that were available at a given time. But it could also mean that the toolmakers selected

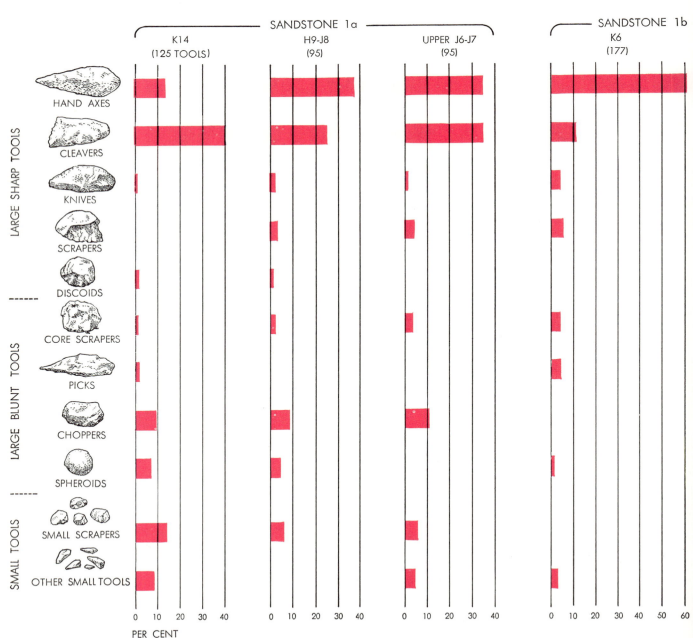

TOOL ASSEMBLAGES at nine sites in the three upper levels of the Isimila beds are shown in this chart based on an analysis by Maxine R. Kleindienst. At six sites (K14, H9-J8, Upper J6-J7, K6, J12, K19) large sharp tools predominate. At two (Lower K18, Low-er J6-J7) small tools are numerous. At one (Lower H15) large blunt tools form the majority. This assemblage is unique for this

their materials from a number of exposed deposits, choosing the kinds best suited to the pieces they were working on. Conceivably different bands may even have enjoyed exclusive rights of exploitation to sources they had discovered. This would account for differences between the varieties of stone used at different sites in the same level.

The pattern of stone rubble found at different locations varies with the type of tool kit and tells its own story. Where there are small tools there is usually a good deal of rubble, most of it chips of the tool material. Evidently

these pieces were fashioned at the living sites where they were used. In the case of large tools, on the other hand, the living areas contain relatively few waste products of the same materials. Such waste as is there looks as though it was the product of minimal reworking or sharpening. Most of the tools were evidently made elsewhere.

One factory site has been uncovered at Isimila. The frequencies of both tools and waste products there are quite unlike those at any living place. The workshop contains few finished, or even semifinished, large tools. There are some roughed-out specimens and some fresh

blanks. Most of the inventory consists of large flakes of mylonite struck off in shaping the blocks of raw material from which the blanks were subsequently produced.

Certain of the living areas contain a puzzling distribution of stone pieces: a good many large tools and, as usual, little or no factory waste products but a large amount of extraneous rubble. In these places the inhabitants must have deliberately amassed stone rubble. What they wanted it for we have no idea, but there is little doubt that they went out and collected it. Other open sites in East Africa as well as some caves in Europe

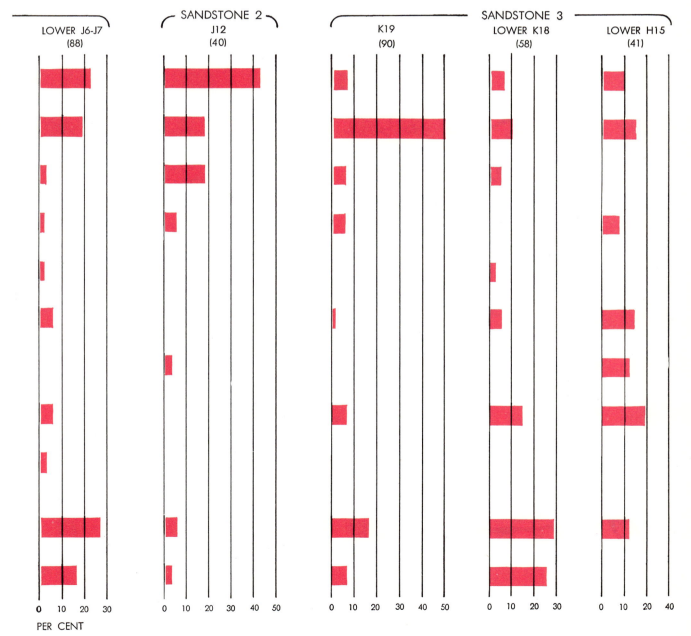

LOWER J6-J7 (88)   SANDSTONE 2 J12 (40)   K19 (90)   SANDSTONE 3 LOWER K18 (58)   LOWER H15 (41)

PER CENT

period in East Africa. It had been thought that each kit represented a different time or culture. But all kits are present on Level 3, at roughly contemporaneous sites. It may be that they were made by the same people and each was used for a different task. At all sites except one (Lower J6-J7) a few tools are omitted from the count. These were broken and too damaged to be identified by name.

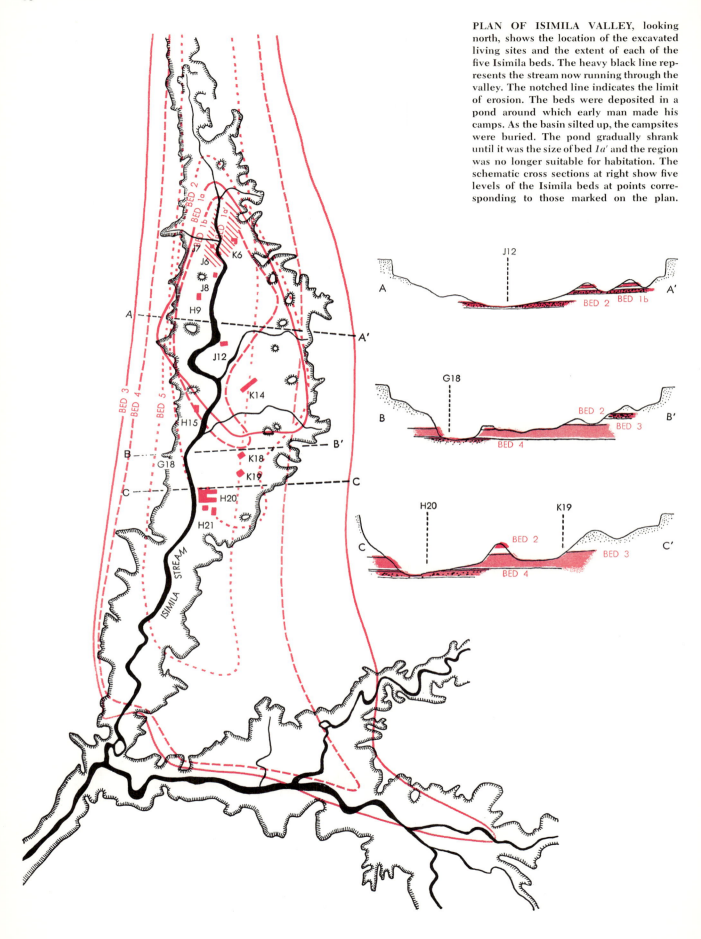

PLAN OF ISIMILA VALLEY, looking north, shows the location of the excavated living sites and the extent of each of the five Isimila beds. The heavy black line represents the stream now running through the valley. The notched line indicates the limit of erosion. The beds were deposited in a pond around which early man made his camps. As the basin silted up, the campsites were buried. The pond gradually shrank until it was the size of bed *1a'* and the region was no longer suitable for habitation. The schematic cross sections at right show five levels of the Isimila beds at points corresponding to those marked on the plan.

STONE TOOLS at Isimila were made some 75,000 years ago. Their diversity in size, shape and material suggests each type had its own use. Shown here, from top left to bottom right, are: two hand axes, two cleavers, knife, scraper, "discoid," pick, core scraper, chopper and "spheroid." The hand axes are 11 inches long. Chopper and spheroid are made of quartz; all others, of the mineral mylonite.

reveal evidence of the same activity.

At Isimila we found no wood or any evidence of fire. Both have been uncovered at other Acheulean sites, however. Pieces of wood preserved at Kalambo Falls in Rhodesia and at three European deposits—in Germany, Spain and England—indicate that men in the earlier Old Stone Age made wooden implements and weapons, including hardwood spears and what are probably clubs and throwing sticks. Charred wood, charcoal and ash at Kalambo Falls and in two African caves testify to the use of fire during the latter part of the Acheulean period.

From the recent work at Isimila, as well as at other undisturbed open-air sites, a much fuller picture of the life of Paleolithic man has begun to emerge. It shows a more varied and specialized technology and perhaps a higher degree of social organization than had been envisaged before. As always, the new information suggests still further questions: How large were the groups that camped at the open-air sites? Were there several different families in the same band? Were there different bands? How long did the people stay? Days? Weeks? Did they come back several times a year?

The very profusion of the remains at Isimila constitutes a puzzle in itself. What did the people want with all those tools? To be sure, the objects are not hard to make; a skilled prehistorian can turn one out in a few minutes. It is likely that the cutting-edged tools were discarded and replaced as soon as they lost their edge. Even so, the quantity seems out of proportion to any conceivable need.

Not all the problems may be solvable. But further studies of evidence in the archaeological context of the earlier Old Stone Age cannot fail to enlarge our understanding of man's place in nature.

II

NEOLITHIC VILLAGERS AND FARMERS

Philosophical and anthropological speculations on the origins of food production—the use of domesticated plants and animals as the primary basis of subsistence—began several hundred years ago. It may come as a surprise, however, that only since the late 1940s has the how and why of the transition from hunter and gatherer to food producer been empirically studied by means of the analysis of archaeological materials gained from excavations. Throughout the eighteenth and nineteenth centuries, cultural-evolutionary schemes of universal history were formulated and accepted as explanations of man's cultural evolution. These evolutionary schemes postulated man's earliest societies as based on a hunting and gathering economy. This was believed to have been followed by a later stage characterized by the invention of agriculture and/or pastoralism. The economic revolution brought about by the domestication of plants and animals was believed to have allowed man for the first time to settle in permanent villages. Only after establishment of these permanent villages did craft specialization, social stratification, division of labor, i.e., urbanization and civilized life (civilization), actually begin. All this was mere speculation: hypotheses were formulated, arguments of detail discussed, in the writings of eighteenth- and nineteenth-century natural philosophers, but no one chose to test these ideas by actual fieldwork. These untested cultural-evolutionary models, which saw man pass through a series of "stages," (1) hunting and gathering, (2) domestication of plants and animals, (3) urban civilization, received their most concise formulation in the works of the British archaeologist V. G. Childe (1952). Childe introduced the term Neolithic Revolution to describe the origin of food production and its consequences. For Childe, the time during which the food-producing revolution took place was one of major climatic change. He postulated that with the retreat of European ice sheets, during post-Pleistocene times, *ca.* 10,000 B.C., the summer rains that watered North Africa and Arabia shifted to Europe, resulting in the desiccation of much of the Near East, save for a few oases. Childe argued that such desiccation provided the essential stimulus toward adopting a food-producing economy. The enforced concentration along banks of streams, and in oases, of both men and animals entailed an intensive readaptation for survival, which, through the new enforced juxtaposition of animals, plants, and man in restricted areas, promoted a new symbiosis that led directly toward domestication. Childe thus provided an environmentally deterministic model that replaced the older cultural-evolutionary one by introducing a changing environment as the causal factor of the "Neolithic Revolution." Before the development of the radiocarbon technique of dating (see Part IV), it was hypothesized that this "revolution" took place somewhere in the Near East around 5000 B.C. Today, as readings here point out, we may add at least 2,500 years to that date.

For the past 25 years, the majority of fieldwork in the Near East has been devoted to testing the hypotheses outlined by Childe. In

1948 the Oriental Institute of the University of Chicago began excavations at Qalat Jarmo in the Kurdish foothills of Iraq. The excavations were directed by Robert J. Braidwood, the author of the first two articles in this section. At this point, and for the first time, the actual testing of hypotheses about the origins of, and processes that led to, food production began. Professor Braidwood (1960) believed the causes of the move toward the development of agriculture to be entirely cultural. He rejected Childe's argument of extreme climatic changes in the Near East (at the end of the Pleistocene) as causally related to the origins of agriculture. Braidwood further argued (1) there had been similar climatic changes in earlier interglacial periods that had not led toward the development of an agricultural economy, and (2) there was nothing in the nature of the environment at the end of the Pleistocene that predetermined a shift in human adaptation from hunting and gathering to agriculture. To Professor Braidwood, the development of an agricultural way of life "occurred as the culmination of the ever-increasing cultural differentiation and specialization of human communities" (see his second article). Braidwood's research design necessitated the close collaboration of zoologists, botanists, meteorologists, geologists, and even metallurgists to discover both the nature of climatic change, if any, and the processes that led toward animal and plant domestication. This first major interdisciplinary approach to solving an archaeological problem has today become the standard practice in archaeological staffing of field excavations.

The papers selected here both trace the changing ideas on the origins of food production and present the substantive evidence on which they rest. From Braidwood's original position of the early 1950's, we have progressed a long way toward a new understanding of the "Neolithic Revolution." Braidwood originally believed that this revolution took place in a "nuclear zone"; the hilly flanks of the Zagros Mountains, which constitute the northern flank of the fertile crescent in Iraq. Here were to be found the naturally distributed wild varieties of plants and animals that had the potentiality for domestication. From this "nuclear zone" the ideas and techniques of domestication, Braidwood argues, would be diffused to other parts of the world, together with an entire complex of traits characteristic of the village farming pattern, including sedentism, ceramic manufacture, and architectural elaborations. The excavations at Jarmo and Jericho were among the very first to elucidate the complexity of the Neolithic Revolution. It came as a great surprise when it was found in the early 1950s that both sites had been permanently settled, with domesticated plants and animals, by at least 6500 B.C. The situation is recognized today as being by no means as simple as Childe had earlier hypothesized, or even as Braidwood's early evidence and interpretations from Jarmo made it seem. Braidwood's most recent excavation has been at Cayonu, in southeastern Turkey, a site he continues excavating today (see his first article in this section). At Cayonu, the excavators found, in a context of *ca.* 7000 B.C., evidence of the use of native copper in the form of cold-hammered pins, a technology usually conceived of as practiced far later in the early bronze age. Recent excavations have also made us aware of the existence, as early as 6500 B.C., of an exchange network in obsidian, from which man struck flakes to make razor sharp tools (see Rodden's article). The nuclear zone in the Near East has vastly expanded, to include such distant sites in the Near East as Beidha in Trans-Jordan (Kirkbride, 1966), Djeitun in Soviet Turkmenistan (Masson, 1971), Aq Kupruk in Afghanistan, and Ali Kosh in southwestern Iran (Hole, 1969). It may fairly be said that neither Jarmo nor Jericho are exceptions on the Neolithic distribution map. To date archaeologists have excavated well over two dozen sites that predate 6000 B.C.; several dozen more have been recorded but not excavated. These sites present much diversity in their settlement organization, economic subsistence pattern, and social organization. In fact, we have come to understand that agriculture was not even a prerequisite for settled life. A number of sites, Mureybit in Syria (van Loon, 1968) and contemporary sites of *ca.* 7000 B.C. in Palestine (Perrot, 1969), are without any evidence for the use of domesticated animals or plants, yet represent permanent settlement, no doubt based on the intensive use of such natural resources as fish, game, and wild cereals.

The nature and degree of climatic change in certain areas of the Near East, after 10,000 B.C., has become better understood, though it remains far from clear. It is generally agreed that after 10,000 B.C. climatic shifts did occur but were too minor to have seriously altered man's environment (Wright, 1968).

Perhaps one archaeological site, above all other Neolithic communities excavated, has given us an understanding of their great complexity: Catal Huyuk. At Catal Huyuk, *ca.* 6000 B.C., we are faced not with a small rural village but with what Mellaart has fairly called a "city," with elaborate architectural features, a native copper metallurgy, sculpture, luxury items traded from afar, and other indications of the existence of a social organization far more elaborate than our previous evolutionary conceptions for this time period. The cause of this florescence at Catal Huyuk continues to elude us; perhaps it is unique only to the archaeological record, perhaps such "cities" were plentiful at that time—but this is the only one excavated. The meaning behind the art eludes us, as does the function of the elaborate buildings, but Mellaart suggests some plausible explanations in the final article in this section. Catal Huyuk has given us an idea of the complexity of man's early social organization and technological achievements; the excavation of other sites continues to push back our time horizons for the Neolithic period. Recent work at Ganj Dareh in northwestern Iran, excavated by Philip Smith (see his article, "Solutrean Culture," page 24) evidences architectural permanency and domestication of goats before 8000 B.C.

Recently, even the primacy of the Neolithic Revolution and the restrictive aspect of such a concept, has been challenged by discoveries in southeastern Asia. Archaeologists working at Spirit Cave in northeastern Thailand have recovered evidence that nuts and perhaps even tubers had been domesticated by 9000 B.C. (Solheim, 1970). It thus becomes possible that there were several Neolithic Revolutions, independent of each other, in the Old World. It seems unlikely that the simple diffusionist model that saw agricultural domestication spreading from the Near East throughout the Old World will stand the test of time. Another area that has yielded recent evidence of early domestication, perhaps independent of the Near East, is the Sudan. Here a number of sites that have been excavated yielded stone mortars and grinders used for the preparation of cereals. We cannot yet be sure whether in the Sudan, *ca.* 10,000 B.C., they were manipulating wild cereals or were in the process of domesticating them.

The excavations at Nea Nikomedia in Greece (see Solecki's "Shanidar Cave," page 43) were among the very first to be undertaken outside the Near Eastern "nuclear area." Professor Solecki, who conducted the investigation, believes that the site mirrors the economic and social organization evident on Near Eastern sites of *ca.* 6000 B.C. Nea Nikomedia is one of the most important European Neolithic sites, and is often cited as evidence that the Neolithic "way of life" was diffused from the Near East into Europe. With this one can agree, for surely diffusion and independent invention are not mutually exclusive phenomenon; both may well provide specific explanations in different cases.

Since the 1950s our underrstanding of the Neolithic has greatly expanded. It would have astounded Childe to hear archaeologists discuss Neolithic *cities*, metallurgy, settled communities without agriculture, an absence of major climatic changes, and even the absence of a single nuclear zone from which the "Revolution" spread. But even though we have a whole new corpus of evidence bearing on the origins of agriculture, we still have before us the question of "how" and "why" the Neolithic Revolution came about. We have the descriptive evidence for it, but that does not explain how it happened. Archaeologists increasingly address themselves to such questions of process (Binford, 1968; Flannery, 1969). At least three major factors appear to have played a role in the shift from hunting and gathering to food production: (1) demographic stresses, (2) proper environment, (3) a distinctive level and type of exploitative technology.

Demographic stresses could well have resulted from population growth, developing from a need for an increased food supply in areas with limited resources: new resources would have to be procured, and one way to do so would be raising and taming of plants and animals. The environment in which we might expect the Neolithic Revolution to have occurred would be one offering a wide variety of indigenous plant and animal resources. Such plant and animal resources would have to be of types that would provide stable supplies on which hunters and gatherers could depend while initially manipulating a wider variety of resources. Finally, the level of technology could simply be of any type, and at a level that would permit edible animals or plants to be exploited in a systematic manner. If one finds that these demographic, environmental, and cultural elements are present, the potential for a gradual, indigenous shift to food production is clearly possible. It may be premature to claim that these elements sufficiently explain the Neolithic Revolution, but it is apparent that all are necessary and interlock to form a single complex process. Certainly, as the following pages indicate, we have added immeasurably to our understanding of what Childe termed man's most profound revolution, the shift from hunting and gathering to a food-producing technology.

REFERENCES

Binford, L. 1968. Post Pleistocene Adaptations. In S. R. and L. R. Binford, eds., *New Perspectives in Archeology.* Aldine.

Braidwood, R. J., and B. Howe. 1960. *Prehistoric Investigations in Iraqui Kurdistan.* Studies in Ancient Oriental Civilizations, no. 31. University of Chicago Press.

Childe, V. G. 1952. *New Light on the Ancient Near East.* Routledge and Kegan Paul.

Flannery, K. 1969. Origins and Ecological Effects of Early Domestication in Iran and the Near East. In P. J. Ucko and G. W. Dimbleby, eds., *The Domestication and Exploitation of Plants and Animals.* Aldine.

Hole, F., K. V. Flannery, and J. A. Neely. 1969. *Prehistory and Human Ecology of the Deh Luran Plain.* Memoirs of the Museum of Anthropology, no. 1. University of Michigan.

Kirkbride, D. 1966. Five Seasons at the Pre-Pottery Neolithic Village of Beidha, in Jordan. *Palestine Exploration Quarterly,* Jan.-June, pp. 8–72.

Van Loon, M. 1968. The Oriental Institute Excavations at Mureybit, Syria. *Journal of Near Eastern Studies,* vol. 27, no. 4.

Masson, V. 1971. *Excavations at Djeitun.* [In Russian] Materialni i issledovange arkeologiya i CCP, no. 180. Leningrad.

Perrot, J. 1969. La Prehistoire Palestiniene. In *Dictionaire Supplement de la Bible,* vol. VIII. Paris: Letouyeg and Ave.

Solheim, W. G. III. 1970. *Reworking Southeast Asia Prehistory.* Social Science Research Institute, Publ. 34. University of Hawaii.

Wright, H. E., Jr. 1968. Natural Environment of Early Food Production North of Mesopotamia. *Science,* vol. 161, pp. 334–338.

MASONRY excavated at Jarmo had provided the foundation for houses made of *touf*, or pressed mud. These remains are in one of Jarmo's upper architectural levels. Earlier houses had been built without foundations.

BRACELETS worn by the people of Jarmo were made of stone. Numerous fragments of these have been found.

TOOLS were also made of stone. Shown here are several stone axes and adzes found at the site of the village.

7

FROM CAVE TO VILLAGE

ROBERT J. BRAIDWOOD
October 1952

THUS FAR in human history there have been two principal economic revolutions. One is the Industrial Revolution, which began 175 years ago and which, to judge by the stresses of our period, is still far from complete. The other is the food-producing revolution—the invention of agriculture and animal husbandry—which began in prehistoric times. Although there is no contemporary written record of this earlier revolution, its material remains may be read by the prehistoric archaeologist. This article is concerned with some meaningful remains of the food-producing revolution uncovered by a recent expedition of the Oriental Institute of the University of Chicago to the Near East.

For 500,000 years before the food-producing revolution small groups of men lived mostly in caves. They were obliged to spend almost all of their time in the quest for food; they hunted, fished and gathered a few edible wild plants. After the revolution larger groups of men lived in villages. Tilling the soil and tending the animals gave them enough food, and thus enough leisure, to develop specialized skills. It is easiest for the archaeologist to comprehend the economic and technological features of such a profound development, but it must have embraced all the other aspects of culture: social, political, religious, moral and esthetic. To say that the economic and technological aspects came before the others would be rather like asking the conundrum: "Which came first, the chicken or the egg?"

WHERE did the food-producing revolution occur? There is overwhelming evidence that the first experiments in food production and village life were made in the Near East. Similar experiments in China and India surely came later, and quite possibly were due to Near Eastern influence. The beginnings of food production in the New World were independent, but still later.

The Near East also appears to have been the natural habitat of the plants and animals that were later domesticated to provide the basis for the agriculture and animal husbandry of the western Old World. One might assume that these species grew, as did the earliest civilizations, on the classic plains of the Tigris and the Euphrates and the Nile—the region that the great historian James H. Breasted called "The Fertile Crescent." Actually it now seems that they and the first villages were native to the hills that flank this region. These hilly grasslands were independent of irrigation; in them the winter rains of any normal year assure a spring crop even today. Thus it would appear that as the revolution progressed the basic food plants and animals were brought to the Fertile Crescent from the hills.

But exactly when and how did the food-producing revolution come about? In 1947, when we began to organize our expedition at the Oriental Institute, we held the following view of Near Eastern prehistory. The remains of preagricultural cave dwellers had been found in Palestine and Egypt, and to a lesser extent in Syria, Lebanon and Iraq. The latest of these cultures, the Natufian of Palestine, differed from the others only in that its people had domesticated the dog and devised a flint sickle, apparently for the collection of a wild food plant. Then there was an abrupt break in the historical sequence. The next remains are those of villages in full flower: established settlements with architecture, pottery and weaving—a vastly larger Sears, Roebuck catalogue than that of the cave dwellers.

In Iraq, for example, the latest remnants of the preagricultural people had been found in the cave of Zarzi; they were represented by tools of chipped flint. Next came the village materials of Hassuna, whose people first camped around hearths in the open and later built mud houses, made several different kinds of pottery and altogether lived a full peasant existence. After Hassuna followed an uninterrupted succession of excavated cultural materials, in which

were presently seen the settlement of the Mesopotamian plain, the building of towns and temples, the invention of writing and the founding of city-states. Between the cave of Zarzi and the village of Hassuna there was clearly a large gap in culture and time. In this gap occurred the food-producing revolution.

We chose to seek evidence of the revolution in Iraq, where the sequence of villages after the gap had been thoroughly worked out, where the world's earliest civilization later developed and where the Government Directorate-General of Antiquities was cordial and cooperative. Early in 1947 Dr. Naji-al-Asil, the Director-General, had sent us a list of promising sites, and in the fall of that year three of us departed for Iraq. From March to May of 1948 we excavated the remains of a village south of the great modern oil-producing town of Kirkuk. These remains resembled those of Hassuna, but we were unable to find anything more primitive. In May and June we spent a month digging at another site that had been listed by the Director-General. This was Qalat Jarmo, 30 miles east of Kirkuk in the Kurdish hills. Our test soundings showed that Jarmo was surely part of what we were after.

A large-scale prehistoric excavation is expensive, and its financing is not easy. It took us two years to get back to Iraq. We reopened our excavation at Jarmo in the fall of 1950, and, with the exception of time lost to winter rains, continued to dig until the spring of 1951.

THE village of Jarmo lay on the crest of a hill overlooking a deep *wadi*, or gully. It covered an area of at least three acres. It was inhabited for a moderately long time; the debris of its life is 25 feet deep. When we dug into the debris, we discovered that it was made up of perhaps 12 different levels, each represented by a change in architecture.

The people of Jarmo lived in houses made of what the modern Iraqi calls *touf*: pressed mud. At any one time there

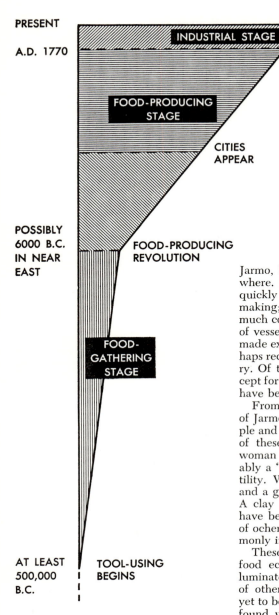

PRESENT
A.D. 1770

INDUSTRIAL STAGE

STEAM ENGINE INVENTED

FOOD-PRODUCING
STAGE

CITIES
APPEAR

POSSIBLY
6000 B.C.
IN NEAR
EAST

FOOD-PRODUCING
REVOLUTION

FOOD-
GATHERING
STAGE

AT LEAST
500,000
B.C.

TOOL-USING
BEGINS

CHART shows place of the food-producing revolution in human history.

were about 30 of these structures, sheltering perhaps 200 people. In the uppermost levels of the debris the touf walls rested on foundations of stone. The houses had mud floors, often packed over a layer of reeds. Each house was equipped with an oven; in one case we found a fairly intact oven vault, with its fire door opening into an adjoining room. Another feature of the houses, especially those in the lower levels of the debris, was a basin that was baked into the floor; this was apparently used as a permanent receptacle.

In the five uppermost levels of Jarmo we found portable pottery vessels. The earliest fragments of pottery are few in number, but have painted and burnished exteriors. Their advanced workmanship suggests that they were not made at

Jarmo, but were brought in from elsewhere. However, the people of Jarmo quickly adopted the notion of pottery making; the resulting product was a much coarser and very poorly fired type of vessel. Throughout their history they made excellent vessels of stone, and perhaps receptacles of skin, wood or basketry. Of the latter we found no trace except for impressions in the mud that may have been made by mats or baskets.

From the beginning the inhabitants of Jarmo made little clay figures of people and animals. The most characteristic of these represents a seated pregnant woman with rather fat buttocks—probably a "mother goddess" symbol of fertility. We also found beads, pendants and a great variety of marble bracelets. A clay stamp with a spiral motif may have been used to apply a tattoo mark of ocher paint—red ocher occurred commonly in the debris.

These things give us little clue to the food economy of Jarmo. This was illuminated, however, by a vast number of other remains, most of which have yet to be analyzed in the laboratory. We found weights for digging sticks, hoe-like celts, flint sickle-blades and a wide variety of milling stones. Bone was abundantly employed in the manufacture of hafts, awls, needles, blades and spoons. We also discovered several pits that were probably used for the storage of grain. Perhaps the most important evidence of all was animal bones and the impressions left in the mud by cereal grains.

One of our collaborators, Hans Helbaek of the Danish National Museum, has already shown that the people of Jarmo grew at least two varieties of wheat and a legume. Fredrik Barth of the University of Oslo, who was with us in the field, classified the bones of pigs, cattle, dogs, sheeplike goats and a relative of the horse, as well as those of wild animals. Barth found that the proportion of sheep-goat bones was very high, and that the teeth of these animals indicated that almost all of them had

been yearlings—a selection that does not suggest hunting.

All of these things indicate that Jarmo is the earliest village site yet uncovered in the Near East. One of our keenest hopes was to determine its actual age by means of the radiocarbon method, in which organic substances such as charcoal, shell or burnt bone can be dated by their radioactivity. Even in 1948 we had brought snail shells from Jarmo to the Institute of Nuclear Studies at the University of Chicago, where Willard Libby and his associates developed the radiocarbon method. To these shells Libby's laboratory assigned an age of 4757 B.C. ± 320 years. Libby was reluctant to accept this as a firm date because shell is less reliable than charcoal for radiocarbon purposes. During the past summer, however, he has run tests on two samples of charcoal from Jarmo, one taken from exactly the same site as the shell. The ages of these charcoal samples are 4654 B.C. ± 330 years and 4743 B.C. ± 360 years. In other words, the shell and charcoal dates corroborate one another with a surprising degree of accuracy. This not only suggests the validity of shell dates, but also leaves little doubt that Jarmo began to flourish around 4750 B.C.

Our own date for Jarmo, reckoned by fitting its remains into the accepted "relative" chronology of Near Eastern archaeology, had been 6000 B.C. We suspect that as the possibility for errors is reduced in the still experimental radiocarbon instrumental procedure, and as more samples from the Near East are tested, it will be necessary to bring the whole sequence of Near Eastern prehistoric dates forward in time.

ON BEHALF of the American Schools of Oriental Research we began in March of 1951 to explore the region around Jarmo for even earlier settlements. We first selected Karim Shahir, a two-acre site on a hill two miles up the wadi that runs past Jarmo. Karim Shahir has only one archaeological level; architecturally it consists only of an incomprehensible scatter of stones, each about the size of a human fist. These had been definitely carried to the site, but we could make no architectural sense of them. There was no trace of either stone or pottery vessels. We did find a storage pit, fragments of stone mills and a fair number of chipped and ground stone-hoes—all of which suggest an incipient agriculture.

At Karim Shahir we gathered a great many of the tiny stone blades that the archaeologist calls microliths. We had also found microliths at Jarmo, but there was an important distinction between those of the two sites. All of the Karim Shahir microliths were made of flint; some of those at Jarmo were of the volcanic glass obsidian. The lack of obsid-

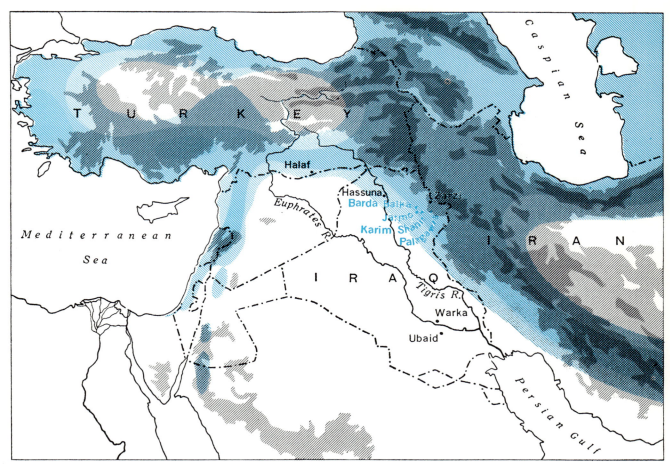

MAP of the Near East shows the location of the sites described in this article. Lighter gray shading denotes land higher than 3,000 feet; darker gray shading, land higher than 6,000 feet. Blue shading indicates rainfall.

ECONOMY	HISTORICAL CHARACTERISTICS	PERIOD IN IRAQ
		2000 B.C.
	Civilization: Fully efficient food production, cities, formal political state, formal laws, formal projects and works, classes and hierarchies, writing, monumentality in art.	AKKADIAN
		EARLY DYNASTIC
		3000 B.C.
FOOD-PRODUCING	*Era of Incipient Urbanization:* New social and political aspects of culture crystallize.	PROTO-LITERATE
	Era of Established Peasant Efficiency: Market towns, temples, expansion into river valleys.	WARKA
		UBAID
	Era of Primary Peasant Efficiency: Permanent villages, pottery, metal, weaving.	HALAF
		HASSUNA
		JARMO
	Incipient Agriculture and Animal Domestication.	KARIM SHAHIR
		PALEGAWRA
FOOD-GATHERING	*Era of Cave-dwelling Hunters, Fishermen and Food-collectors:* Cultural unit probably small mobile band.	ZARZI
		BARDA BALKA

DIAGRAM locates the sites shown on the map at the top of this page in time and in cultural development. The names of the sites excavated by the expedition, and the historical gap that is filled by them, are in blue.

ian at Karim Shahir is an example of the difference between the two settlements. The closest known sources of obsidian are several hundred miles away in Turkey; it must have been imported to Jarmo. Thus Jarmo represents a new era in which trade has begun. Karim Shahir is only on the verge of that era.

In every way Karim Shahir seems to represent the cultural stage just before Jarmo: a time when men were probably making their first experiments with agriculture and animal domestication—as well as with that most significant consequence of deliberate food production, village life. We purposely do not call Karim Shahir a village; the deposit there was very thin and it is possible that its population was only seasonal.

From Karim Shahir we extended our exploration in time by investigating the cave of Palegawra, some 15 miles east of Jarmo. Judging by the bones we found in the cave, its occupants were successful hunters of wild horses, deer, goats, gazelles, sheep and pigs. They made long stone blades and minute microlithic tools which must have been mounted, perhaps as harpoons or arrow points. But we found no evidence of agriculture or animal husbandry.

Finally we inspected one still earlier site called Barda Balka. Here the remains indicated men who made flint and limestone hand-axes, pebble-tools and scrapers. They lived a catch-as-catch-can existence, along with extinct elephants and rhinoceroses, in a landscape that must have been very different from the now almost treeless countryside. Although Barda Balka shed no light on our central problem, it provided an archaeological and geological check point for the early cave materials of Iraq.

As of now the account cannot be any more complete than this. It is clear, however, that we have bracketed the gap in knowledge between the terminal cave-stage and the established village stage in Iraq. Our work adds four new phases to the known sequence of prehistory in a "nuclear" area of cultural activity, but I do not suspect that we have completely closed the gap. Nevertheless, when the reports are all in and the full story can be written, there will be a new understanding of a range of time and of cultural activities which were of vast consequence to human history. The people of Jarmo were adjusting themselves to a completely new way of life, just as we are adjusting ourselves to the consequences of such things as the steam engine. What they learned about living in a revolution may be of more than academic interest to us in our troubled times.

8

THE AGRICULTURAL REVOLUTION

ROBERT J. BRAIDWOOD
September 1960

Tool-making was initiated by pre-*sapiens* man. The first comparable achievement of our species was the agricultural revolution. No doubt a small human population could have persisted on the sustenance secured by the hunting and food-gathering technology that had been handed down and slowly improved upon over the 500 to 1,000 millennia of pre-human and pre-*sapiens* experience. With the domestication of plants and animals, however, vast new dimensions for cultural evolution suddenly became possible. The achievement of an effective food-producing technology did not, perhaps, predetermine subsequent developments, but they followed swiftly: the first urban societies in a few thousand years and contemporary industrial civilization in less than 10,000 years.

The first successful experiment in food production took place in southwestern Asia, on the hilly flanks of the "fertile crescent." Later experiments in agriculture occurred (possibly independently) in China and (certainly independently) in the New World. The multiple occurrence of the agricultural revolution suggests that it was a highly probable outcome of the prior cultural evolution of mankind and a peculiar combination of environmental circumstances. It is in the record of culture, therefore, that the origin of agriculture must be sought.

About 250,000 years ago wide-wandering bands of ancient men began to make remarkably standardized stone hand-axes and flake tools which archeologists have found throughout a vast area of the African and western Eurasian continents, from London to Capetown to Madras. Cultures producing somewhat different tools spread over all of eastern Asia. Apparently the creators of these artifacts employed general, non-specialized techniques in gathering and preparing food. As time went on, the record shows, specialization set in within these major traditions, or "genera," of tools, giving rise to roughly regional "species" of tool types. By about 75,000 years ago the tools became sufficiently specialized to suggest that they corresponded to the conditions of food-getting in broad regional environments. As technological competence increased, it became possible to extract more food from a given environment; or, to put the matter the other way around, increased "living into" a given environment stimulated technological adaptation to it.

Perhaps 50,000 years ago the mod-

AIR VIEW OF JARMO shows 3.2-acre site and surroundings. About one third of original area has eroded away. Archeologists dug the square holes in effort to trace village plan.

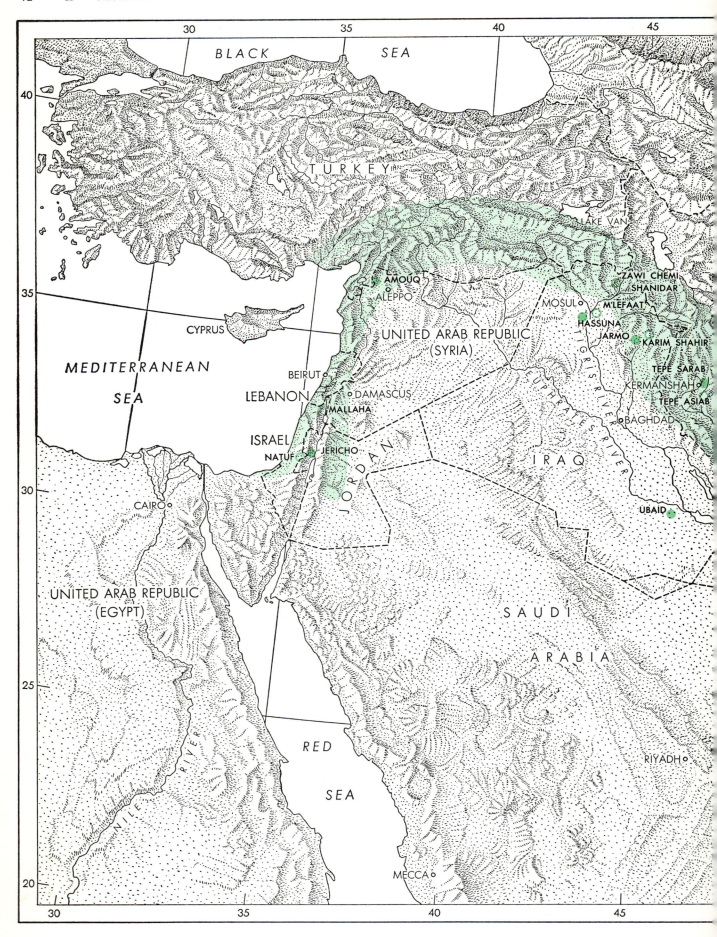

BLACK   SEA

TURKEY

LAKE VAN

MEDITERRANEAN

SEA

CYPRUS

AMOUQ
ALEPPO

ZAWI CHEMI
SHANIDAR

MOSUL
M'LEFAAT

UNITED ARAB REPUBLIC
(SYRIA)

HASSUNA
JARMO   KARIM SHAHIR

BEIRUT

TEPE SARAB
KERMANSHAH
TEPE ASIAB

LEBANON   DAMASCUS

MALLAHA

BAGHDAD

ISRAEL

NATUF   JERICHO

JORDAN

IRAQ

CAIRO

UBAID

UNITED ARAB REPUBLIC
(EGYPT)

SAUDI

ARABIA

NILE   RIVER

RED

SEA

RIYADH

MECCA

ern physical type of man appeared. The record shows concurrently the first appearance of a new genera of tools: the blade tools which incorporate a qualitatively higher degree of usefulness and skill in fabrication. The new type of man using the new tools substituted more systematic food-collection and organized hunting of large beasts for the simple gathering and scavenging of his predecessors. As time passed, the human population increased and men were able to adjust themselves to environmental niches as diverse as the tropical jungle and the arctic tundra. By perhaps 30,000 years ago they spread to the New World. The successful adaptation of human communities to their different environments brought on still greater cultural complexity and differentiation. Finally, between 11,000 and 9,000 years ago some of these communities arrived at the threshold of food production.

In certain regions scattered throughout the world this period (the Mesolithic in northwestern Europe and the Archaic in North America) was characterized by intensified food-collection: the archeological record of the era is the first that abounds in the remains of small, fleet animals, of water birds and fish, of snails and mussels. In a few places signs of plant foods have been preserved, or at least we archeologists have learned to pay attention to them. All of these remains show that human groups had learned to live into their environment to a high degree, achieving an intimate familiarity with every element in it. Most of the peoples of this era of intensified food-collecting changed just enough so that they did not need to change. There are today still a few relict groups of intensified food-collectors—the Eskimos, for example—and there were many more only a century or two ago. But on the grassy and forested uplands bordering the fertile crescent a real change was under way. Here in a climate that provided generous winter and spring rainfall, the intensified food-collectors had been accumulating a rich lore of experience with wild wheat, barley and other food plants, as well as with wild dogs,

HILLS FLANKING fertile crescent, where agricultural revolution occurred, are indicated in color. Hatched areas are probably parts of this "nuclear" zone of food-producing revolution. Sites discussed in this article are indicated by large circles. Open circles are prefarming sites; solid circles indicate that food production was known there.

goats, sheep, pigs, cattle and horses. It was here that man first began to control the production of his food.

Not long ago the proponents of environmental determinism argued that the agricultural revolution was a response to the great changes in climate which accompanied the retreat of the last glaciation about 10,000 years ago. However, the climate had altered in equally dramatic fashion on other occasions in the past 75,000 years, and the potentially domesticable plants and animals were surely available to the bands of food-gatherers who lived in southwestern Asia and similar habitats in various parts of the globe. Moreover, recent studies have revealed that the climate did not change radically where farming began in the hills that flank the fertile crescent. Environmental determinists have also argued from the "theory of propinquity" that the isolation of men along with appropriate plants and animals in desert oases started the process of domestication. Kathleen M. Kenyon of the University of London, for example, advances the lowland oasis of Jericho as a primary site of the agricultural revolution [see the article "Ancient Jericho," by Kathleen M. Kenyon, beginning on page 89].

In my opinion there is no need to complicate the story with extraneous "causes." The food-producing revolution seems to have occurred as the culmination of the ever increasing cultural differentiation and specialization of human communities. Around 8000 B.C. the inhabitants of the hills around the fertile crescent had come to know their habitat so well that they were beginning to domesticate the plants and animals they had been collecting and hunting. At slightly later times human cultures reached the corresponding level in Central America and perhaps in the Andes, in southeastern Asia and in China. From these "nuclear" zones cultural diffusion spread the new way of life to the rest of the world.

In order to study the agricultural revolution in southwestern Asia I have since 1948 led several expeditions, sponsored by the Oriental Institute of the University of Chicago, to the hills of Kurdistan north of the fertile crescent in Iraq and Iran. The work of these expeditions has been enriched by the collaboration of botanists, zoologists and geologists, who have alerted the archeologists among us to entirely new kinds of evidence. So much remains to be done, however, that we can describe in only a tentative and quite incomplete fashion how food production began. In part, I must freely admit, my reconstruction depends upon extrapolation backward from what I know had been achieved soon after 9,000 years ago in southwestern Asia.

The earliest clues come from sites of the so-called Natufian culture in Palestine, from the Kurdistan site of Zawi Chemi Shanidar, recently excavated by Ralph S. Solecki of the Smithsonian Institution, from our older excavations at Karim Shahir and M'lefaat in Iraq, and from our current excavations at Tepe Asiab in Iran [see map on preceding two pages]. In these places men appear to have moved out of caves, although perhaps not for the first time, to live in at least semipermanent communities. Flint sickle-blades occur in such Natufian locations as Mallaha, and both the Palestine and Kurdistan sites have yielded milling and pounding stones—strong indications that the people reaped and ground wild cereals and other plant foods. The artifacts do not necessarily establish the existence of anything more than intensified or specialized food-collecting. But these people were at home in a landscape in which the grains grew wild, and they may have begun to cultivate them in open meadows. Excavations of later village-farming communities, which have definitely been identified as such, reveal versions of the same artifacts that are only slightly more developed than those from Karim Shahir and other earlier sites. We are constantly finding additional evidence that will eventually make the picture clearer. For example, just this spring at Tepe Asiab we found many coprolites (fossilized excrement) that appear to be of human origin. They contain abundant impressions of plant and animal foods, and when analyzed in the laboratory they promise to be a gold mine of clues to the diet of the Tepe

SICKLE BLADES FROM JARMO are made of chipped flint. They are shown here approximately actual size. When used for harvest-ing grain, several were mounted in a haft of wood or bone. Other Jarmo flint tools show little advance over those found at earlier sites.

Asiab people. The nature of these "antiquities" suggests how the study of the agricultural revolution differs from the archeology of ancient cities and tombs.

The two earliest indisputable village-farming communities we have so far excavated were apparently inhabited between 7000 and 6500 B.C. They are on the inward slopes of the Zagros mountain crescent in Kurdistan. We have been digging at Jarmo in Iraq since 1948 [see the article "From Cave to Village," by Robert J. Braidwood, beginning on page 67], and we started our investigations at Tepe Sarab in Iran only last spring. We think there are many sites of the same age in the hilly-flanks zone, but these two are the only ones we have so far been able to excavate. Work should also be done in this zone in southern Turkey, but the present interpretation of the Turkish antiquities law discourages our type of "problem-oriented" research, in which the investigator must take most of the ancient materials back to his laboratory. I believe that these northern parts of the basins of the Tigris and Euphrates rivers and the Cilician area of Turkey will one day yield valuable information.

Although Jarmo and Tepe Sarab are 120 miles apart and in different drainage systems, they contain artifacts that are remarkably alike. Tepe Sarab may have been occupied only seasonally, but Jarmo was a permanent, year-round settlement with about two dozen mud-walled houses that were repaired and rebuilt frequently, creating about a dozen distinct levels of occupancy. We have identified there the remains of two-row barley (cultivated barley today has six rows of grains on a spike) and two forms of domesticated wheat. Goats and dogs, and possibly sheep, were domesticated. The bones of wild animals, quantities of snail shells and acorns and pistachio nuts indicate that the people still hunted and collected a substantial amount of food. They enjoyed a varied, adequate and well-balanced diet which was possibly superior to that of the people living in the same area today. The teeth of the Jarmo people show even milling and no marginal enamel fractures. Thanks apparently to the use of querns and rubbing stones and stone mortars and pestles, there were no coarse particles in the diet that would cause excessive dental erosion. We have calculated that approximately 150 people lived in Jarmo. The archeological evidence from the area indicates a population density of 27 people per square mile, about the same as today. Deforestation, soil deteriora-

JARMO WHEAT made imprint upon clay. Cast of imprint (*left*) resembles spikelet of present-day wild wheat *Triticum dicoccoides* (*right*). Specimens are enlarged seven times.

tion and erosion, the results of 10,000 years of human habitation, tend to offset whatever advantages of modern tools and techniques are available to the present population.

Stone vessels of fine craftsmanship appear throughout all levels at Jarmo, but portable, locally made pottery vessels occur only in the uppermost levels. A few impressions on dried mud indicate that the people possessed woven baskets or rugs. The chipped flint tools of Jarmo and Tepe Sarab, in both normal and microlithic sizes, are direct and not very distant descendants of those at Karim Shahir and the earlier communities. But the two farming villages exhibit a geo-

metric increase in the variety of materials of other types in the archeological catalogue. Great numbers of little clay figurines of animals and pregnant women (the "fertility goddesses") hint at the growing nonutilitarian dimensions of life. In both communities the people for the first time had tools of obsidian, a volcanic glass with a cutting edge much sharper and harder than stone. The obsidian suggests commerce, because the nearest source is at Lake Van in Turkey, some 200 miles from Jarmo. The sites have also yielded decorative shells that could have come only from the Persian Gulf.

For an explanation of how plants and animals might have been domesticated

KERNELS OF JARMO WHEAT were carbonized in fires of ancient village. They resemble kernels of wild wheat growing in area today. They are enlarged approximately four times.

between the time of Karim Shahir and of Jarmo, we have turned to our colleagues in the biological sciences. As the first botanist on our archeological team, Hans Helbaek of the Danish National Museum has studied the carbonized remains of plants and the imprints of grains, seeds and other plant parts on baked clay and adobe at Jarmo and other sites. He believes that the first farmers, who grew both wheat and barley, could

only have lived in the highlands around the fertile crescent, because that is the only place where both plants grew wild. The region is the endemic home of wild wheat. Wild barley, on the other hand, is widely scattered from central Asia to the Atlantic, but no early agriculture was based upon barley alone.

Helbaek surmises that from the beginning man was unintentionally breeding the kind of crop plants he needed.

Wild grasses have to scatter their seeds over a large area, and consequently the seed-holding spike of wild wheat and barley becomes brittle when the plant ripens. The grains thus drop off easily. A few wild plants, however, exhibit a recessive gene that produces tough spikes that do not become brittle. The grains hang on, and these plants do not reproduce well in nature. A man harvesting wild wheat and barley would necessarily reap plants with tough spikes and intact heads. When he finally did sow seeds, he would naturally have on hand a large proportion of grains from tough-spike plants—exactly the kind he needed for farming. Helbaek points out that early farmers must soon have found it advantageous to move the wheat down from the mountain slopes, from 2,000 to 4,300 feet above sea level (where it occurs in nature), to more level ground near a reliable water supply and other accommodations for human habitation. Still, the plant had to be kept in an area with adequate winter and spring rainfall. The piedmont of the fertile crescent provides even today precisely these conditions. Since the environment there differs from the native one, wheat plants with mutations and recessive characteristics, as well as hybrids and other freaks, that were ill adapted to the uplands would have had a chance to survive. Those that increased the adaptation of wheat to the new environment would have made valuable contributions to the gene pool. Domesticated wheat, having lost the ability to disperse its seeds, became totally dependent upon man. In turn, as Helbaek emphasizes, man became the servant of his plants, since much of his routine of life now depended upon the steady and ample supply of vegetable food from his fields.

The traces and impressions of the grains at Jarmo indicate that the process of domestication was already advanced at that place and time, even though human selection of the best seed had not yet been carried far. Carbonized field peas, lentils and vetchling have also been found at Jarmo, but it is not certain that these plants were under cultivation.

Apparently farming and a settled community life were cultural prerequisites for the domestication of animals. Charles A. Reed, zoologist from the University of Illinois, has participated in the Oriental Institute expeditions to Iraq and Iran and has studied animal skeletons we have excavated. He believes that animal domestication first occurred in this area, because wild goats, sheep, cattle, pigs, horses, asses and dogs were all present

CARBONIZED BARLEY KERNELS from Jarmo, enlarged four times, are from two-row grain. The internodes attached to kernels at right indicate tough spikes of cultivated barley.

there, and settled agricultural communities had already been established. The wild goat (*Capra hircus aegagrus*, or pasang) and sheep (*Ovis orientalis*), as well as the wild ass (onager) still persist in the highlands of southwestern Asia. Whether the dog was the offspring of a hypothetical wild dog, of the pariah dog or of the wolf is still uncertain, but it was undoubtedly the first animal to be domesticated. Reed has not been able to identify any dog remains at Jarmo, but doglike figurines, with tails upcurled, show almost certainly that dogs were established in the domestic scene. The first food animal to be domesticated was the goat; the shape of goat horns found at Jarmo departs sufficiently from that of the wild animal to certify generations of domestic breeding. On the other hand, the scarcity of remains of cattle at Jarmo indicates that these animals had not yet been domesticated; the wild cattle in the vicinity were probably too fierce to submit to captivity.

No one who has seriously considered the question believes that food needs motivated the first steps in the domestication of animals. The human proclivity for keeping pets suggests itself as a much simpler and more plausible explanation. Very young animals living in the environment may have attached themselves to people as a result of "imprinting," which is the tendency of the animal to follow the first living thing it sees and hears during a critically impressionable period in its infancy [see " 'Imprinting' in Animals," by Eckhard H. Hess; SCIENTIFIC AMERICAN Offprint 416].

Young animals were undoubtedly also captured for use as decoys on the hunt. Some young animals may have had human wet nurses—a practice in some primitive tribes even today. After goats were domesticated, their milk would have been available for orphaned wild calves, colts and other creatures. Adult wild animals, particularly goats and sheep, which sometimes approach human beings in search of food, might also have been tamed.

Reed defines the domesticated animal as one whose reproduction is controlled by man. In his view the animals that were domesticated were already physiologically and psychologically preadapted to being tamed without loss of their ability to reproduce. The individual animals that bred well in captivity would have contributed heavily to the' gene pool of each succeeding generation. When the nucleus of a herd was established, man would have automatically selected against the aggressive and un-

CLAY FIGURES from Sarab, shown half size, include boar's head (*top*), what seems to be lion (*upper left*), two-headed beast (*upper right*), sheep (*bottom left*) and boar.

"FERTILITY GODDESS" or "Venus" from Tepe Sarab is clay figure shown actual size. Artist emphasized parts of body suggesting fertility. Grooves in leg indicate musculature.

STONE PALETTES from Jarmo show that the men who lived there were highly skilled in working stone. The site has also yielded many beautifully shaped stone bowls and mortars.

JARMO IN IRAQI KURDISTAN is the site of the earliest village-farming community yet discovered. This photograph of an upper level of excavation shows foundation and paving stones. Site was occupied for perhaps 300 years somewhere around 6750 B.C.

EXCAVATION AT KARIM SHAHIR contained confused scatter of rocks brought there by ancient men and disturbed by modern plowing. This prefarming site had no clear evidence of permanent houses, but did have skillfully chipped flints and other artifacts.

manageable individuals, eventually producing a race of submissive creatures. This type of unplanned breeding no doubt long preceded the purposeful artificial selection that created different breeds within domesticated species. It is apparent that goats, sheep and cattle were first husbanded as producers of meat and hides; wild cattle give little milk, and wild sheep are not woolly but hairy. Only much later did the milk- and wool-producing strains emerge.

As the agricultural revolution began to spread, the trend toward ever increasing specialization of the intensified food-collecting way of life began to reverse itself. The new techniques were capable of wide application, given suitable adaptation, in diverse environments. Archeological remains at Hassuna, a site near the Tigris River somewhat later than Jarmo, show that the people were exchanging ideas on the manufacture of pottery and of flint and obsidian projectile points with people in the region of the Amouq in Syro-Cilicia. The basic elements of the food-producing complex —wheat, barley, sheep, goats and probably cattle—in this period moved west beyond the bounds of their native habitat to occupy the whole eastern end of the Mediterranean. They also traveled as far east as Anau, east of the Caspian Sea. Localized cultural differences still existed, but people were adopting and adapting more and more cultural traits from other areas. Eventually the new way of life traveled to the Aegean and beyond into Europe, moving slowly up such great river valley systems as the Dnieper, the Danube and the Rhone, as well as along the coasts. The intensified food-gatherers of Europe accepted the new way of life, but, as V. Gordon Childe has pointed out, they "were not slavish imitators: they adapted the gifts from the East . . . into a new and organic whole capable of developing on its own original lines." Among other things, the Europeans appear to have domesticated rye and oats that were first imported to the European continent as weed plants contaminating the seed of wheat and barley. In the comparable diffusion of agriculture from Central America, some of the peoples to the north appear to have rejected the new ways, at least temporarily.

By about 5000 B.C. the village-farming way of life seems to have been fingering down the valleys toward the alluvial bottom lands of the Tigris and Euphrates. Robert M. Adams believes that there may have been people living in the lowlands who were expert in collecting food from the rivers. They would have

POTTERY MADE AT JARMO, in contrast to the stonework, is simple. It is handmade, vegetable-tempered, buff or orange-buff in color. It shows considerable technical competence.

taken up the idea of farming from people who came down from the higher areas. In the bottom lands a very different climate, seasonal flooding of the land and small-scale irrigation led agriculture through a significant new technological transformation. By about 4000 B.C. the people of southern Mesopotamia had achieved such increases in productivity that their farms were beginning to support an urban civilization. The ancient site at Ubaid is typical of this period [see the article "The Origin of Cities," by Robert M. Adams, beginning on page 137].

Thus in 3,000 or 4,000 years the life of man had changed more radically than in all of the preceding 250,000 years. Before the agricultural revolution most men must have spent their waking moments seeking their next meal, except when they could gorge following a great kill. As man learned to produce food, instead of gathering, hunting or collecting it, and to store it in the grain bin and on the hoof, he was compelled as well as enabled to settle in larger communities. With human energy released for a whole spectrum of new activities, there came the development of specialized

nonagricultural crafts. It is no accident that such innovations as the discovery of the basic mechanical principles, weaving, the plow, the wheel and metallurgy soon appeared.

No prehistorian worth his salt may end or begin such a discussion without acknowledging the present incompleteness of the archeological record. There is the disintegration of the perishable materials that were primary substances of technology at every stage. There is the factor of chance in archeological discovery, of vast areas of the world still incompletely explored archeologically, and of inadequate field techniques and interpretations by excavators. There are the vagaries of establishing a reliable chronology, of the whimsical degree to which "geobiochemical" contamination seems to have affected our radioactive-carbon age determinations. There is the fact that studies of human paleo-environments by qualified natural historians are only now becoming available. Writing in the field, in the midst of an exciting season of excavation, I would not be surprised if the picture I have presented here needs to be altered somewhat by the time that this article has appeared in print.

9

OBSIDIAN AND THE ORIGINS OF TRADE

J. E. DIXON, J. R. CANN AND COLIN RENFREW
March 1968

The transition from hunting to farming, which started mankind on the road to civilization, presents a number of interesting questions for investigators, not the least of which is the extent of communication among early human settlements. Archaeological explorations in recent years have unearthed the sites of prehistoric villages that were widely scattered in southwestern Asia and around the Mediterranean. The earliest communities—for example Jarmo in what is now Iraq and Jericho in Jordan—apparently were settled some 10,-000 years ago [see the article "The Agricultural Revolution," by Robert J. Braidwood, beginning on page 71]. One might suppose the primeval villages, separated by hundreds of miles and often by mountains or water, were isolated developments, not even aware of one another's existence. There have been reasons to suspect, however, that this was not the case, and we have now found definitive evidence that the prehistoric communities throughout the Near East and the Mediterranean region were in active communication.

What kinds of evidence of communication between geographically separated peoples might one look for? Obviously in the case of prehistoric peoples the only materials available for study are the remains of the objects they made or used. In the search for signs of possible contact between two cultures archaeologists have generally depended on a comparative examination of the artifacts. If the two cultures show strong similarities in knowledge or technique—say in the method of working flint or the style of pottery—this is taken to signify mutual contact and perhaps actual trade in objects. At best, however, such evidence is only suggestive and is always subject to doubt; it leaves open the possibility that the similarities, no matter how close they are, may be mere coincidence, the two peoples' having hit independently on a natural and obvious way of doing things.

The raw materials of which the objects were made, on the other hand, may offer an opportunity for a more decisive inquiry. If a material used by a community does not occur locally in the raw state, one must conclude it was imported, and the possibility exists that it was obtained in trade with another population. One can then start on the task

OBSIDIAN BOWL made during the fourth millennium B.C. is seen from above, its spout jutting out at the right. The translucent bowl, which is nearly eight inches in diameter, comes from the Mesopotamian site of Tepe Gawra *(see illustration on page 88)*. Trace-element analysis shows that the obsidian comes from Acigöl, 400 miles to the west in Turkey.

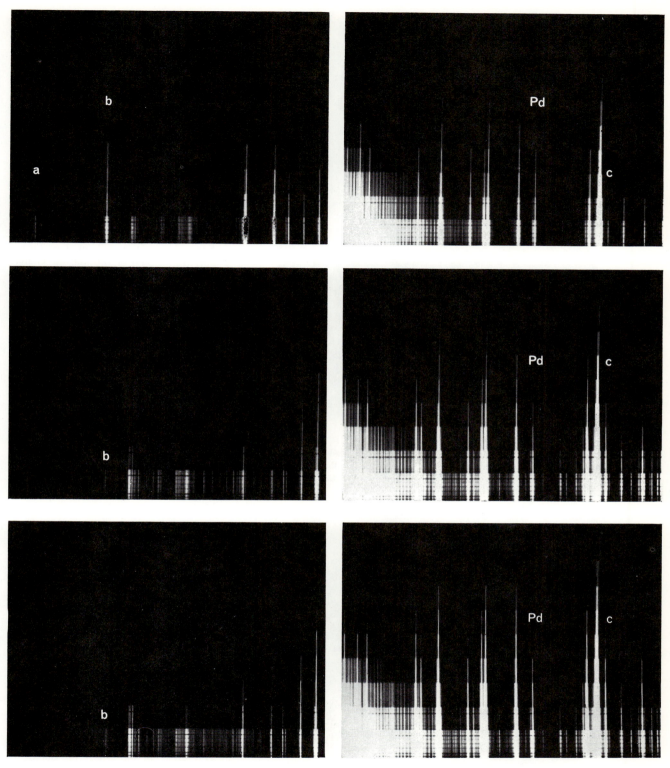

SPECTROGRAMS of three obsidian samples, reproduced here in part, show that differing proportions of trace elements make possible the identification of obsidian from different volcanic deposits. At top are two parts of the spectrogram of raw volcanic glass from Melos in the Aegean Sea. Matching parts of a spectrogram of a piece from an obsidian blade unearthed at Ali Kosh in Iran are at center. Matching parts of a spectrogram of volcanic glass from Nemrut Dag, near Lake Van in Armenia, are at bottom. In the top specimen the spectral lines of strontium ("*a*" *at left, 4,607.4 angstrom units*) and barium ("*b*" *at left, 4,554 angstroms*) are relatively long, indicating proportions of some 200 parts per million and 700 parts per million respectively. The same lines are almost invisible in the center and bottom specimens. The spectral line of zirconium ("*c*" *at right, 3,438 angstroms*) is relatively short in the top specimen, indicating a concentration of about 50 parts per million. In the other two specimens the long zirconium lines indicate a concentration of about 700 parts per million. Palladium (*spectral lines labeled "Pd" to the left of "c"*) is not a normal trace element in obsidian; the element is added to provide a standard for calibration. The trace-element differences show that the Ali Kosh artifact (*center*) could not have been made of obsidian from Melos but instead is chemically similar to the obsidian found at Nemrut Dag.

OBSIDIAN FROM MELOS, in the form of a core from which blades have been flaked, shows the characteristic glistening surface of this volcanic glass. Obsidian was probably traded in the form of glass lumps or cores that the final purchaser turned into tools himself.

SCULPTURED SEASHELL, carved from a variety of obsidian with distinctive white spots, was found in a Minoan site on Crete. Sir Arthur Evans, the pioneer student of Cretan prehistory, thought the obsidian had come from Lipari, off Sicily, where similarly spotted volcanic glass is common. Analysis now proves that it came from nearby Giali in the Aegean.

of tracing the material to its source.

It occurred to us that obsidian might be an ideal material for a tracer investigation of this kind. Obsidian is a hard, brittle volcanic glass that can be chipped like flint and fashioned into a sharp tool. It is known to have been used for knives and scrapers by prehistoric men as early as 30,000 years ago. Obsidian tools have been found in nearly every early village site in the Near East and the Mediterranean region. Yet for most of these sites it was an indubitably foreign material; it can be obtained only in certain areas of recent volcanic activity, which in that part of the world means the region around Italy, some islands in the Aegean Sea and certain areas in modern Turkey and Iran. Some of the ancient villages where obsidian tools were used were many hundreds of miles from the nearest natural source of the material.

How could one identify the particular source from which the obsidian was obtained in each case? Clearly our first task was to determine whether or not obsidian samples showed distinguishable differences that could be connected with their source. We considered several possible criteria. Physical appearance obviously would not be a reliable guide, because obsidian samples from a single volcanic deposit may vary greatly in visible characteristics such as color. Microscopic examination was not helpful: the obsidian tools were generally made of material that is uniform in structure, without crystalline inclusions. Chemical analysis of the main components was also of no avail, because all samples of obsidian are substantially alike from this point of view. We decided finally on a chemical test based on the presence of trace elements. Perhaps the obsidian samples would show distinct differences in their trace-element content that could be identified with the deposits from which they came.

In order to explore this possibility we began by analyzing samples of obsidian collected from various well-known volcanic sources in the Mediterranean area: Lipari, a volcanic island north of Sicily, two areas in Sardinia, the islands of Pantelleria and Palmarola and the island of Melos in the Aegean Sea.

For chemical analysis of the samples we used a convenient spectrographic method that archaeologists have long employed on metal objects. Every element emits characteristic wavelengths of light when it is heated to incandescence; a familiar example is the yellow light of burning sodium. By passing the light

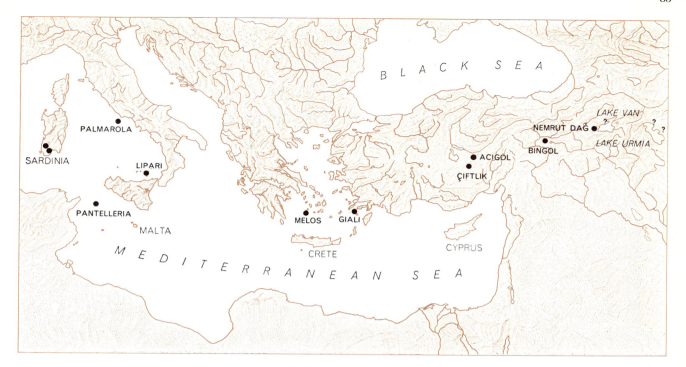

SOURCES OF OBSIDIAN in the Mediterranean and the Near East during Neolithic times included volcanic areas in Sardinia and on Palmarola, Lipari and Pantelleria in the central Mediterranean, the islands of Melos and Giali in the Aegean Sea, two central Anatolian sites, Acigöl and Çiftlik, and several places in ancient Armenia, including Bingöl in eastern Turkey and Nemrut Dağ near Lake Van.

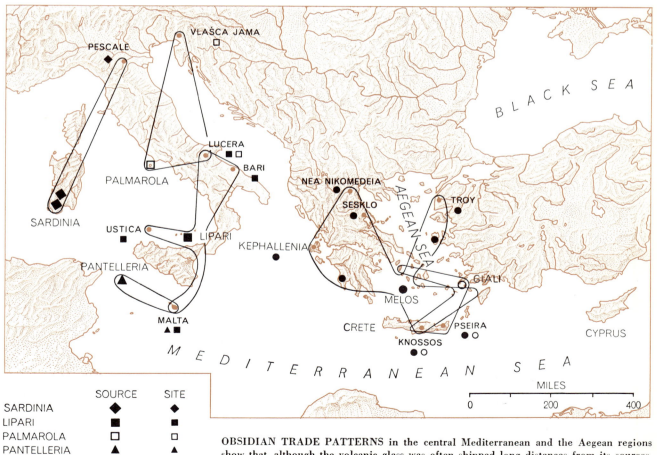

	SOURCE	SITE
SARDINIA	◆	◆
LIPARI	■	■
PALMAROLA	□	□
PANTELLERIA	▲	▲
MELOS	●	●
GIALI	○	○

OBSIDIAN TRADE PATTERNS in the central Mediterranean and the Aegean regions show that, although the volcanic glass was often shipped long distances from its sources, trade apparently did not take place between the two regions. Within each region, however, obsidian from two sources is often found at one site. Not all the sites indicated are named.

from a mixture of elements through a prism or diffraction grating that spreads out the wavelengths in a spectrum, one can separate the emissions of the various elements and detect trace elements that are present even in the amount of only a few parts per million. The beauty of the method for studying archaeological specimens is that accurate measurements can be obtained from very small amounts of material. Sixty milligrams taken from a sample is sufficient. Ground to a fine powder, mixed with an equal amount of carbon and ignited in a carbon arc, this material yields a spectrographic picture that gives a measure of the quantity of each trace element in the sample; the quantity is indicated by the intensity (photographically the height) of the element's spectral lines.

We obtained readings for 16 elements in our samples of obsidian. Among the trace elements found to be present, the two that showed the greatest quantitative variation over the range of samples were barium and zirconium. We therefore tried using the relative concentrations of these two elements as a test for identification of the source [see illustration on this page]. To our immense satisfaction these quantities were found to indicate the geographical source quite well. Samples from various flows and outcrops at Lipari, for instance, all showed much the same proportion of barium to zirconium; those from Melos had characteristic contents of these elements different from those at Lipari. The Pantelleria and Sardinia samples likewise could be distinguished on the same basis. The Palmarola samples turned out to be similar to the Lipari ones on the barium-zirconium graph, but we found we could distinguish them from the Lipari type by their content of another trace element, cesium.

Having established these markers for identifying the obsidian sources, we were in a position to determine the raw-material origins of obsidian tools found at the sites of ancient settlements. The little island of Malta, south of Sicily, offered objects for a clear-cut test. The remains of a remarkable prehistoric society of 5,000 years ago, marked by colossal stone temples, have been unearthed on this island. The finds include small obsidian tools. There are, however, no natural obsidian deposits on the island. Where, then, did the material come from? Some archaeologists had suggested that it might have been brought there by Minoan traders from the island of Melos, 600 miles to the east. Our trace-element analysis of the Malta tools disclosed that this conjecture was incorrect: the obsidian was of the types found on Lipari and on Pantelleria, a tiny island 150 miles northwest of Malta.

The findings revealed two important facts about the ancient Maltese settlement. They showed that the island people in that early Neolithic period were already accomplished seafarers, traveling frequently to Sicily, Lipari and Pantelleria. On the other hand, the obsidian evidence also indicated that the Maltese people had little or no contact with the contemporary Minoan settlements of the Aegean area. Their stone temples may well have been their own invention.

Our tests resolved another question involving the Minoan culture. Sir Arthur Evans, the illustrious archaeologist who excavated the palace at Knossos on Crete more than half a century ago, found a number of finely carved objects there that were made of a variety of obsidian marked by prominent white spots. He concluded that this material came from

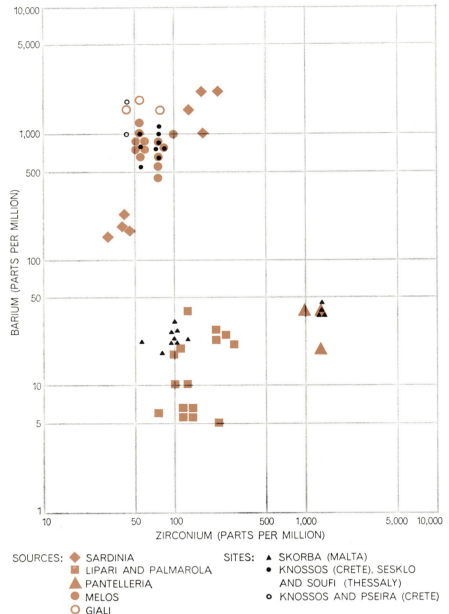

SOURCES: ◆ SARDINIA
■ LIPARI AND PALMAROLA
▲ PANTELLERIA
● MELOS
○ GIALI

SITES: ▲ SKORBA (MALTA)
● KNOSSOS (CRETE), SESKLO AND SOUFI (THESSALY)
○ KNOSSOS AND PSEIRA (CRETE)

TWO TRACE ELEMENTS, barium and zirconium, provide the principal means of identifying the sources of obsidian artifacts from central Mediterranean and Aegean sites. Obsidian from both Sardinian sources is richer in barium than obsidian from Pantelleria, Lipari and Palmarola, whereas Pantellerian obsidian is the richest of all in zirconium. Other trace elements, not plotted here, allow additional distinctions to be drawn. Although their barium and zirconium contents are similar, the high calcium content of Gialian obsidian distinguishes it from Melian, whereas Palmarolan obsidian is much richer in cesium than Liparian.

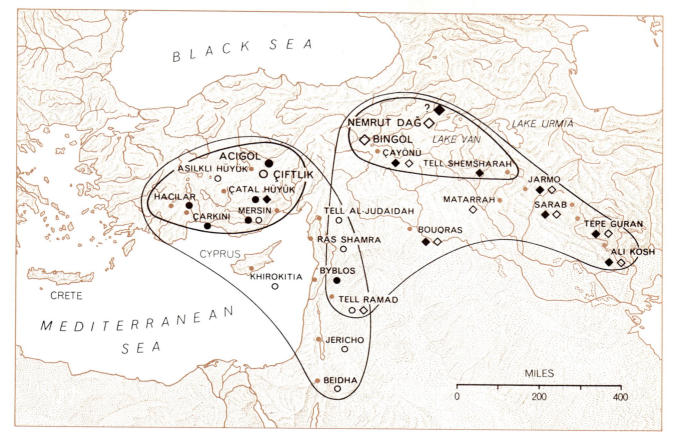

NEOLITHIC NEAR EAST was another scene of active obsidian trade. Cypriot, Anatolian and Levant villages obtained obsidian mainly from two sources in Anatolia: Acigöl and Çiftlik. Mesopotamian villages, in turn, depended on sources in Armenia. The locations of two, Nemrut Dağ and Bingöl, are known. A third variety of obsidian, found at many Mesopotamian sites, is also probably Armenian but its source is not yet known. A heavy line surrounds a nuclear zone within each trade area. These are designated "supply zones" by the authors: more than 80 percent of the chipped-stone tools at supply-zone sites are obsidian.

Lipari, some of whose obsidian also has white spots. On trace-element examination, however, it now turns out that the white-spotted obsidian at Knossos came not from Lipari but from the small island of Giali some distance north of Rhodes. The Knossos remains also include tools made of unspotted obsidian. Analysis shows that this material came from Melos, which is to be expected, since Melos is the nearest obsidian source to Crete. In general, the obsidian evidence establishes the early Aegean islanders as skilled sailors and traders, disseminating the material not only among the islands but also to settlements in Greece and Turkey.

The obsidian tracer work, begun only six years ago, has given rise to investigations at various institutions in Britain, the U.S. and elsewhere, and studies are going forward on material from early settlements in Europe, in the Middle East, in Mexico, California and the Great Lakes region of the New World, in New Zealand and in Africa, where early man

made hand axes of obsidian as long as 100,000 years ago. Our own group at the University of Cambridge, having verified the validity of the method by the Mediterranean tests, has proceeded to apply it to an investigation of the origins of trade among the earliest settlements of man in the Near East, that is to say, in Mesopotamia and in Turkey, Palestine and Egypt.

The first problem in the study of this region was to locate the natural sources of obsidian. A number of sources (all volcanic, of course) have now been identified in mountainous areas of Turkey and northern Iran [see top illustration on page 83] and in Ethiopia to the south. All the available geological evidence indicates that the entire region between these places, including Egypt, is devoid of natural deposits of obsidian. This means that every prehistoric village in the "fertile crescent," where farming began, had to import its obsidian.

Samples from all the natural deposits and from the obsidian artifacts found

in the village sites were analyzed. They were found to be definable in eight different groups, or types, according to their barium-zirconium content, and in some groups the presence of another trace element (like that of cesium in the Palmarola obsidian) served additionally to distinguish the particular source of the material. Some of the obsidian artifacts could not be matched to any known natural source. This necessarily called for searches for the missing sources. The composition of the natural obsidian samples suggested a certain geographical pattern of distribution, and this clue led to the discovery of at least one missing source. A few sources have not yet been located precisely, but the basic pattern of sources and destinations is now clear enough to provide a good picture of the movement and trade routes of obsidian in the period when the first steps toward civilization (variously called the "agricultural revolution" or the "neolithic revolution") were taking place.

By about 9000 B.C. groups of people

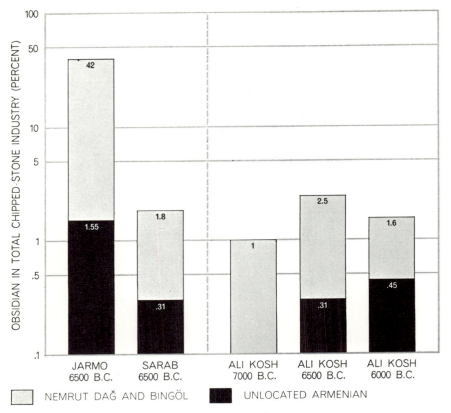

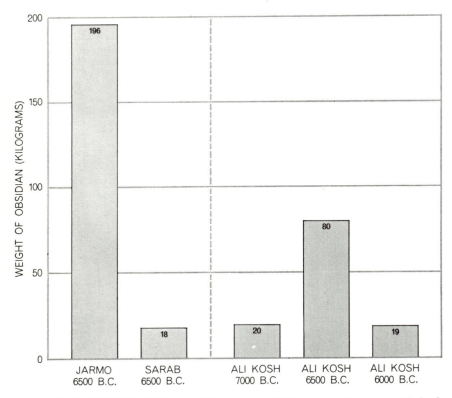

INFLUENCE OF GEOGRAPHY on trade in tool materials is apparent from the total obsidian and its proportion to other stone tools at three Zagros villages that imported Armenian obsidian during the seventh to sixth millenniums B.C. Jarmo, although outside the Armenian supply zone (*see illustration on preceding page*), was nonetheless well supplied with obsidian in terms both of percentage (*top graph*) and of estimated total weight of the material (*bottom graph*). The reduction in both percentage and weight at two more distant towns, Sarab and Ali Kosh (*plotted for three periods*), is drastic. Both distance and the difficult terrain apparently contributed to the scantiness of trade in the case of Sarab, a hill town.

in the Near East had begun to practice an incipient agriculture: selectively hunting and perhaps herding sheep and goats and harvesting wild prototypes of wheat and barley. They were not yet using obsidian to any appreciable extent. By the time the first farming villages were founded, probably a little after 8000 B.C., obsidian had come into rather general use. Naturally the extent of adoption of the material varied with distance from the sources of supply, and this is clearly traceable in the obsidian objects found at the sites of the ancient villages.

Within 150 to 200 miles of the obsidian deposits in Turkey and Armenia most of the chipped-stone tools found in the early prehistoric village sites are of obsidian: 80 percent, as against only 20 percent of flint. From that zone the proportion of obsidian falls off nearly exponentially with distance. This is clearly illustrated by the distribution of obsidian from a natural source in the volcanic area around Çiftlik, near the present town of Niğde in Turkey. At Mersin, the site of an early village on the Mediterranean coast not far from Çiftlik, obsidian was the most common chipped-tool material. From there its use diminished rapidly down the Levant coast, until at Jericho, 500 miles from the source, it is found only in very small quantities, most of the chipped tools there being made of flint. A few pieces of Çiftlik obsidian have been found, however, even at a Neolithic settlement on Cyprus, which indicates at least a trading contact across the water. Some of the obsidian from Turkish sources was distributed over distances of more than 600 miles in the early Neolithic period.

The early villages near the sources in Turkey developed a rich art and craftsmanship in obsidian. Particularly impressive are the objects found at Çatal Hüyük, a 6000 B.C. village that was so large it can be called a town. Among its obsidian products were beautifully made daggers and arrowheads and carefully polished mirrors, as sophisticated as any of those made 7,000 years later in Aztec Mexico.

Jarmo, one of the earliest-known villages in the fertile crescent, was favored by proximity to several obsidian sources. At least two of these sources furnished considerable amounts of the material, estimated to total 450 pounds or more, to Jarmo in very early times. From this it appears that well before 6000 B.C. Jarmo must have been conducting a thriving trade across the mountains that brought it into contact with the communities to the north in Armenia. There were then no wheeled vehicles (they were not invented until 3,000 years later) and not even pack animals. Hence all the traded goods, including obsidian, must have been transported on foot, or perhaps part of the way in boats down the Tigris River.

Tracing the varieties of obsidian from their sources to the villages where they turn up in manufactured objects, we can reconstruct the trade routes of

that early time in man's economic and social history. The routes, crossing mountains, deserts and water, connect the early settlements with a network of communications that must have influenced their development profoundly. No doubt goods besides obsidian were traded over these routes; indeed, it seems likely that there was a trade in perishable commodities that was much greater in size and economic significance than that in obsidian. Clearly, however, the most impor-

tant traffic must have been in ideas. The network of contacts arising from the trade in goods must have been a major factor in the rapid development of the economic and cultural revolution that within a few thousand years transformed mankind from a hunting animal to a builder of civilization.

Obsidian now furnishes us with a tool for retracing the communications at the beginning of the revolution, more than 3,000 years before the invention of writ-

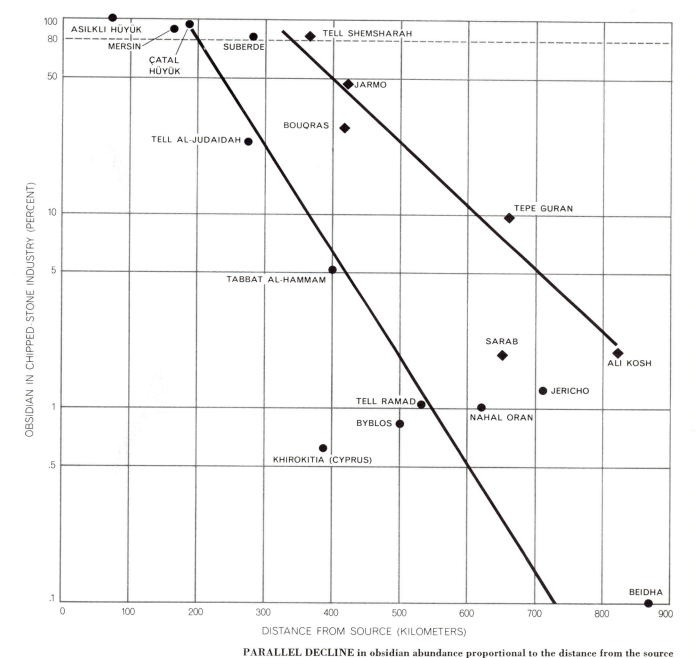

PARALLEL DECLINE in obsidian abundance proportional to the distance from the source is evident in both Near East trade areas during the period from 6500 to 5500 B.C. Not all the sites named here are included in the map on the next page. The boundary between a supply zone and the wider hinterland that the authors call a "contact zone" appears to lie about 300 kilometers from each area's obsidian sources. Poor supply of obsidian at the Cyprus site in spite of its nearness to sources in Turkey is a second example of the influence of geographical factors other than distance. The necessary ocean voyage apparently inhibited trade.

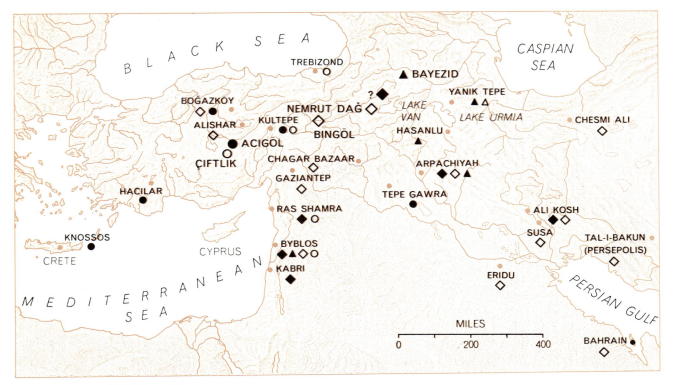

		SOURCE	SITE
ARMENIAN OBSIDIAN	1G	◆	◆
	3A	▲	▲
	4C	◇	◇
ANATOLIAN OBSIDIAN	1E·F	●	●
	2B	○	○

POST-NEOLITHIC TRADE, its directions often traceable by means of luxury items made from obsidian, was cosmopolitan in its extent. Two new sources of supply in the Lake Urmia area of Armenia were developed and Armenian obsidian was traded as far west as the Levant and as far south as Bahrain on the Persian Gulf. Obsidian from Turkey was carried westward to Crete and was transported for the first time across the desert to Mesopotamia. Ethiopian obsidian holds the Near East travel record; a slab of this material, bearing a 16th-century B.C. Egyptian inscription, has been discovered at Boğazköy, a Hittite site in Turkey.

ing. In addition to revealing the pattern and range of contacts among the prehistoric settlements, it gives us a rough picture of trade statistics (through the amounts of material involved) that indicates the strength of the communication links between particular communities. Furthermore, the development of communications over the millenniums after the villages were first established can be traced in the record of the obsidian trade.

As time went on and transportation, aided by the domestication of the ass, improved, the trade in obsidian expanded, both in the number of sources mined and in the distances of distribution. Trade routes developed across the Syrian desert in both directions, and more obsidian began to appear on the Levant coast. Obsidian from Armenia was exported to villages as far distant as Bahrain on the Persian Gulf and the Teheran area near the Caspian Sea. The use of obsidian for tools declined with the coming of the metal ages after 4000 B.C., but it continued to be prized for ornamental objects such as bowls, statuettes and even small articles of household furniture, such as tables. By that time the

Egyptians, apparently obtaining the material from Ethiopia, also had begun to use obsidian for this purpose. A remnant of a little toilette table of obsidian made in Egypt and bearing a hieroglyphic inscription of Pharaoh Chian, of the 16th century B.C., has been found at Bogazköy, the capital of the ancient Hittite kingdom in Turkey. It may have been a gift sent by the Pharaoh to the Hittite king.

By then obsidian itself was no longer an important material of commerce. Nonetheless, the great trade routes that had developed between the cities of the Near East may well have followed the same paths that had first been blazed by the obsidian trade thousands of years earlier.

The analysis of the early obsidian objects now throws new light on the revolution, some 10,000 years ago, that led to man's emergence from the hunter's way of life. There has been a tendency to think of this beginning as an isolated, small-scale phenomenon—of a little tribal group of people settling down somewhere and developing an agricultural system all by itself. In recent years an intensive search has been pursued for

the "birthplace" of this event: Did the first village spring up in the Levant or in the Zagros Mountains on the rim of the fertile crescent or in Turkey? That question now becomes less interesting or significant than it was thought to be. The farming way of life, it appears, originated not at some single location but over whole regions where the peoples of various settlements exchanged ideas and the material means of sustenance.

Throughout the 2,000 years or more during which agriculture was first developing in the Near East the communities dispersed through the region were in more or less continual communication with one another, primarily trading goods but also inevitably sharing their discoveries of agricultural techniques and skills. There is every reason to believe the region functioned essentially as a unit in moving along the road of technological advance. The early villages show considerable diversity in the customs and beliefs that make up what is called a society's "culture," but there can be little doubt that their mutual contact greatly influenced not only their material progress but also their social development and world view.

10

ANCIENT JERICHO

KATHLEEN M. KENYON
April 1954

And it came to pass at the seventh time, when the priests blew with the trumpets, Joshua said unto the people, Shout; for the Lord hath given you the city . . . and the people shouted with a great shout [and] the wall fell down flat. . . . And they utterly destroyed all that was in the city . . . with the edge of the sword. . . . And they burnt the city with fire, and all that was therein.

Jericho fell to Joshua and the Israelites sometime between 1400 and 1250 B.C. It had had a long, long history before that. Modern archaeologists are greatly interested in the site of this ancient city, for in addition to the romantic attraction of the Biblical story,

the site has other claims to importance. There is reason to believe that Jericho may be the oldest town in the world, and we are finding there a wealth of material evidences of man's first steps toward civilization some 7,000 years ago.

The site of ancient Jericho today is a great mound—a heap entombing dead towns. It contains a series of cities, each built on the ruins of those that went before. The Arabian name for a mound formed of the accumulated remains of human occupation is *tell*. The Jericho tell has a great deal to say indeed; its lowest levels go back to Neolithic times —the late stone-age period when man first took the revolutionary step from a nomadic life of hunting to the settled life of agriculture and community build-

ing. From that step has sprung all human progress: the beginning of architecture, arts, crafts and manufacture, community organization, religion, laws, the invention of writing and ultimately civilization.

Although archaeologists have long been convinced that the Near East is the region where man first made the transition from a wandering to a settled life, the early stages of this transition have been shrouded in the mists of time. There are plenty of human artifacts from the Early Bronze Age in the Near East, but very few from the Neolithic period that preceded it. When, during the latter part of the 19th century and the early years of the 20th, archaeological expeditions began to explore the site of

EARLY NEOLITHIC houses of Jericho had curved walls such as those at left center in this excavation. Running from upper left to lower right are the stones of a Neolithic city wall, probably the oldest in the world. At the left is the base of a later structure.

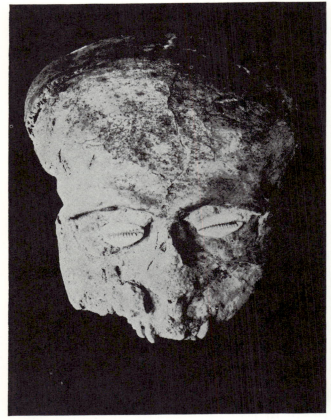

NEOLITHIC PORTRAIT HEADS were made by covering skulls with plaster. The head at the top is shown as it was found. The one at lower left has eyes of cowrie shells. The one at lower right has bands of paint across the top and eyes with vertical slits.

ancient Jericho, there was no suspicion that a prehistoric period lay beneath their spades. Their object was primarily to investigate the story of the capture of Jericho by Joshua's people, to date that event and thereby to throw light on the date of the first Israelite settlement in Palestine.

Between 1930 and 1936 the archaeologist John Garstang, of Liverpool University, carried out a series of deeper and more thorough excavations at Jericho. Far down in the mound, beneath the debris of Early Bronze Age cities, he found some flints and building remains which showed that men had occupied the site in the Neolithic age. His discoveries aroused in some archaeologists a keen desire to investigate the deep Jericho levels further.

The Second World War delayed this investigation. During the 20-year period between the two world wars Palestine in general had been the scene of much archaeological activity, principally by British and U. S. expeditions. Palestine is an area with a remarkably small written history, apart from the Bible. Very few ancient written records of the country have survived, and its history has had to be built up piece by piece from the results of excavations. These have yielded a consecutive history of Palestine from very early times, which has been set down in books such as *The Archaeology of Palestine and the Bible*, by William F. Albright of The Johns Hopkins University.

After the long interruption of World War II and the postwar political troubles in Palestine, archaeologists were keen to resume digging as soon as it became feasible. The British School of Archaeology in Jerusalem sent me to Jordan in 1951 to investigate the possibilities. I found that the Jordan Department of Antiquities was ready to welcome archaeologists and that the American School of Oriental Research in Jerusalem, with which our school had collaborated closely in the past, also wished to undertake excavations again. We had no difficulty in choosing a site: Jericho offered an ideal opportunity. So in January, 1952, a joint Anglo-American expedition of some 20 workers, with myself as director and A. Douglas Tushingham of the American School as assistant director, camped at the Jericho tell and went to work.

The ancient mound is a mile from the modern town of Jericho on the left bank of the River Jordan. It lies in a flat plain 840 feet below sea level. What

LATER NEOLITHIC houses had straight walls. Both walls and floors were covered with polished plaster. However, the people who lived in the houses had not invented pottery.

MIDDLE BRONZE AGE defenses are marked by the two farther men. The nearest man stands atop a later Bronze Age wall. In the foreground is a still later Iron Age structure.

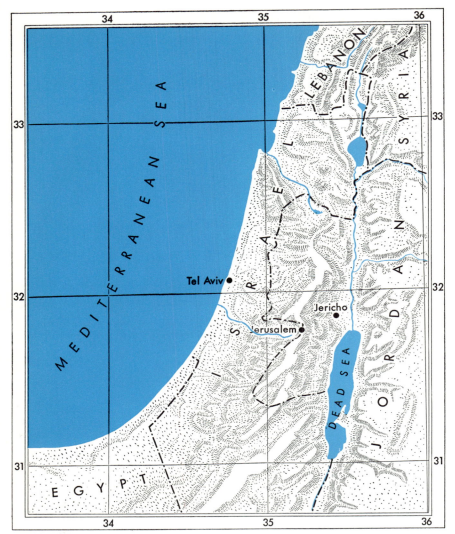

JERICHO IS LOCATED in Jordan near the Dead Sea. It is in the midst of a desert, but has been made habitable for 7,000 years by the copious waters of Elisha's Fountain.

notebook and labels the finds. Drawings are made, so that we have a permanent record of the structures excavated.

The process of excavation is a process of dissection. The archaeologist breaks down the history of the site by peeling off the layers one by one; he traces the history backward from the top down. At Jericho we have found that the surviving deposits go down in some places to depths of about 70 feet. Excavations are still in progress, and only in a very few places have we reached the earliest layers, but we have enough to tell something of a consecutive story of the site.

Garstang had discovered the Neolithic levels at the northwest end of the tell. The depth of deposit is so great there that he sounded the lowest levels only with a relatively narrow shaft. The present expedition is continuing the clearance of the levels he sounded. One of our first surprises was the discovery of Neolithic artifacts at a place on the west side of the tell some distance from where Garstang had found his. The Stone Age remains here were only about four feet below the surface, presumably because later levels in this place have been eroded or quarried away. What was remarkable about this discovery was that it showed that even in Neolithic times the settlement already covered a considerable area and had grown beyond the dimensions of a mere village.

In this area on the west side of the tell excavation has reached bedrock in some places. Just above the rock we have found rude huts which may be the Jericho settlers' earliest experiments in architecture. They are mud-brick structures with curved walls, and they look like a translation of the round tents and temporary structures of nomadic hunters into a more permanent material. This phase appears to have been short. The next stage (represented by a type of house discovered by Garstang at the north end) was a very big advance. These houses were rectangular, with solidly built walls, wide doorways and rooms grouped around courtyards. Most striking of all is the fact that the walls and floors were finished with highly burnished coats of fine plaster, giving a most sophisticated appearance. These houses belonged to a firmly established community, and moreover a well-organized one, for at this stage the settlement apparently was surrounded by a massive town wall.

These Stone Age people still had no pottery—a fact which underlines how close we are here to the beginnings of

has made it habitable through all these thousands of years is a never-failing supply of fresh water gushing from Elisha's Fountain. We began systematically to uncover the ancient Jerichos, layer by layer. Modern archaeological research is built upon foundations laid by the great 19th-century archaeologist Sir Flinders Petrie, a pioneer far ahead of his time. The dating of ancient cultures must depend, when inscriptions are lacking, upon the evolution of artifacts, especially pottery. Petrie showed that each stage of human history in the East had a distinctive pottery, and that one could establish a pottery sequence, some stages of which could be linked with inscriptions of known date in Egypt or Mesopotamia. On the foundations created by Petrie this sequence has now been built up, period by period, so that it is now possible for an archaeologist to date finds with considerable accuracy

as far back as the beginning of the Early Bronze Age, about 3000 B.C.

The basic method of stratigraphy, as Petrie enunciated it in 1890, is to establish a fixed reference point and record the level of each find (in number of feet) above that point. This technique has its limitations, because an archaeological layer may slope instead of being horizontal or may have been cut into by later occupants. Since Petrie's time the method has been considerably refined. Each layer of soil is now traced through and treated as an entity; the finds discovered in that structure (e.g., a floor level) are then dated by it.

Obviously such work requires close supervision by experts, for the workmen doing the digging cannot be expected to identify or understand the significance of the layers. Each small gang works under the direct supervision of a field assistant, who records the layers in a

settled life, for pots and pans, a primary necessity, are one of the first technical inventions of settled man. No doubt the reason men settled here lies in the natural advantages of the site. The copious stream that emerges from the rock beside the settlement made the soil of the Jordan Valley, with its tropical climate, exceedingly fertile; the modern Jericho is still a brilliant green oasis in this arid land. The inhabitants of Jericho could be assured of success in their first experiments in agriculture, and the settlement could become truly permanent.

The progress of those early settlers was not in material things alone. In the Neolithic levels we unearthed a room which in all probability was a small shrine. At one end of the room we found a niche with a rough stone pedestal, and nearby lay a carefully worked bit of volcanic stone which must have been a cult object and probably stood on the pedestal. Figurines of animals modeled in clay suggest that the religion of these early agriculturists was a fertility cult.

Our expedition's most remarkable find so far is a group of seven portrait heads. On actual human skulls the artist had modeled features in plaster. The heads have an astonishingly lifelike appearance. There can be little doubt that they are portraits, probably of venerated ancestors. Thus we are looking at the faces of individuals who died 7,000 years or more ago. These portraits are among the earliest examples of human art.

We do not yet know the exact date of this early settlement, but we guess it to be about 5000 B.C., and hope soon to have our guess tested by radiocarbon analysis of the charcoal from its layers. Its life was certainly a long one, for its successive layers of houses make a mound many feet high. Above this pre-pottery Neolithic stage we find the ruins of a second Neolithic stage in which pottery appears. This stage again lasted a considerable time, and added further height to the mound. By the time Jericho approaches the dawn of the historic period, after 3000 B.C., its walls crown a mound already some 60 feet high.

In the Early Bronze Age, a period of great urban development in Palestine, Jericho became an important walled city. It guarded a gateway through which nomads from the desert to the east were continually trying to force their way into the more fertile lands of Palestine. The Jericho city walls were breached and rebuilt no fewer than 17 times; time and again they were damaged or destroyed by enemies or by natural agencies such as earthquakes. About 2100 B.C. they

MIDDLE BRONZE AGE TOMB was occupied by a skeleton and remarkably well-preserved grave goods. The skeleton is shown at the top. In the middle is a basket containing toilet articles. At the bottom is a dish containing the remains of a large slab of meat.

were totally destroyed by the nomadic Amorites who overran much of Palestine. The city was burned to the ground.

There followed some 200 years of cultural sterility. The newcomers were not town dwellers. Their houses and equipment were simple and primitive. But about 1900 B.C. well-built houses and city walls again begin to appear at Jericho. They were built by a new people, probably from the north, who brought with them the advanced culture of the Middle Bronze Age. Under them Jericho grew to the greatest size it has ever attained. Its walls were rebuilt on a new system with the base defended by a sloping ramp, presumably against the approach of chariots.

Our best evidence for the culture of these people comes from a number of tombs which we have been fortunate enough to find intact. The hot climate of the Jordan Valley has preserved their contents—wood, textiles, basketwork, even food. Everywhere else in Palestine such objects have perished; hence the Jericho remains are the first material evidences of the culture of Palestine in the period around the 17th century B.C.

Each tomb is rich in provisions of food, drink and household equipment that were left with the dead for the afterlife. The furniture was simple: wooden tables, stools and beds, all made with considerable skill. Wooden or pottery bowls held the food, and great four-handled jars, each provided with a small dipper, contained the drink. There were rush mats, toilet accessories in wooden boxes or in alabaster flasks, many wooden combs and other small objects in baskets. We have even recovered fragments of clothing, which when they are analyzed should tell us how they were woven and of what materials.

The Middle Bronze Age came to an end with another sack of the city, probably at the hands of the Egyptians about 1560 B.C. There, unfortunately, most of the archaeological history of Jericho comes to an end. Garstang found a few remnants of structures going down to about 1350 B.C. But over most of the rest of the mound erosion and human depredations have removed all traces of the Jericho after the 16th century B.C. No sign of the walls attacked by Joshua has been found. Nevertheless, though we have been disappointed in our search for the city of the Biblical story, this disappointment has been more than compensated by the uncovering of its remarkable earlier history. It is hoped that our further excavations will continue to be as richly rewarded.

11

AN EARLY NEOLITHIC VILLAGE IN GREECE

ROBERT J. RODDEN
April 1965

The Macedonian plain of northern Greece is covered today with orchards and fields of cotton and sugar beets. The aspect of the plain was quite different 8,000 years ago: its central portion was flooded either by an arm of the Aegean Sea or by a shallow lake. Along the shore lived farmer-herdsmen who raised wheat, barley and lentils, tended sheep and goats and may also have herded cattle and pigs. These facts are known because one of the many low-lying mounds on the Macedonian plain has recently been excavated. Called Nea Nikomedeia after a nearby modern village, the mound marks the site of the oldest dated Neolithic community yet found in Europe.

Perhaps even more important than the antiquity of the site is the fact that the patterns of living it reveals, although they are basically similar to the patterns of village life in early Neolithic sites as far east as Iraq and Iran, have their own exclusively European characteristics. The evidence for the existence of a thriving village in northern Greece near the end of the seventh millennium B.C. makes it necessary to reconsider the accepted view that the agricultural revolution of the Neolithic period was relatively late in reaching Europe from its area of origin in the Middle East. In southeastern Europe, at least, the transition from hunting, fishing and food-gathering in scattered bands to farming, herding and permanent village life must have taken place far earlier than has generally been thought.

I first made an archaeological reconnaissance of the Macedonian plain with a fellow graduate student, David Clarke, during the fall of 1960. We were seeking evidence that might clarify the relation between what were then

the earliest-known farming communities in Europe—most of which are represented by sites in the Danube valley and in eastern Yugoslavia and central Bulgaria—and those early communities in central Greece whose existence had become known to archaeologists as long ago as the 1900's. Lying between the two regions, the Macedonian plain was an obvious place to look for the remains of communities that might have had connections with the first agriculturists to the north and south.

The Nea Nikomedeia mound had come to the attention of Photios Petsas of the Greek Archaeological Service in 1958, when local road builders bulldozed away three-quarters of an acre of it to use as highway fill. Petsas put a stop to this and, when we consulted him in 1960, directed us to the site. On the bulldozed surface, level with the surrounding plain, we found fragments of pottery and other artifacts that closely resembled the finds from the lowest excavated levels at Neolithic sites in central Greece.

A six-week campaign of exploratory excavation was mounted during the summer of 1961 under the direction of Grahame Clark of the University of Cambridge and myself. The work was done under the auspices of the British School of Archaeology in Athens and in cooperation with the Greek Archaeological Service; the necessary funds were provided by the Crowther-Benyon Fund of the University of Cambridge (which had sponsored my 1960 reconnaissance), the British Academy and the Wenner-Gren Foundation for Anthropological Research. Excavation quickly demonstrated that there was a rich layer of early Neolithic material at Nea Nikomedeia; pottery and other artifacts from this layer showed affini-

ties with material from the earliest pottery-using Neolithic settlements in central Greece and, as we had hoped, with artifacts from the first well-established farming communities to the north.

Impressions of cereal grains, preserved on pottery surfaces, and more than 400 fragments of animal bones demonstrated that the first settlers at Nea Nikomedeia practiced an economy of mixed farming and herding. The 1961 excavations also established the fact that the first houses at the site were rectangular structures with mud walls supported by a framework of wooden poles. Samples of organic material from the site were sent for analysis to the Radiocarbon Dating Laboratory at the University of Cambridge; the analysis yielded a figure of 6220 B.C. ± 150 years. This is the earliest date as yet assigned to Neolithic material from Europe.

It was not until the summer of 1963 that a full-scale excavation could be organized at Nea Nikomedeia. In that year much of the early Neolithic occupation level was uncovered as part of a joint Harvard-Cambridge field project sponsored by the National Science Foundation. As before, the work was done under the auspices of the British School of Archaeology in Athens. It was known from the 1961 excavations that the deposit to be explored was a very shallow one—only a little more than two feet thick at its deepest. This layer was composed partly of accumulated occupation debris but mainly of collapsed and disintegrated mud walls from the site's ancient buildings. Shallow plowing in modern times had disturbed the top four or five inches of the deposit, with the result that only 18 inches or so of undisturbed early Neolithic material remained. The digging began in

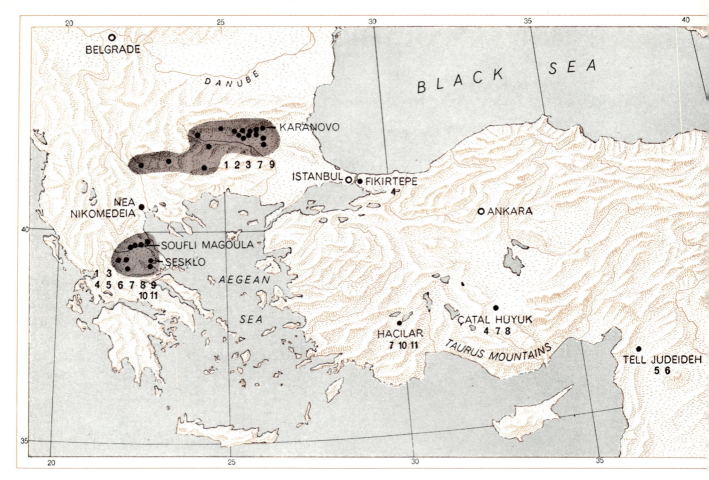

CULTURAL SIMILARITIES between Nea Nikomedeia and other early sites in Europe, Asia Minor and the Middle East are indicated by the numbers at each place name. Among the European sites, Karanovo in central Bulgaria is representative of the many Neolithic villages in that northern region; Soufli Magoula and Sesklo in central Greece similarly typify the early sites to the

early June; when it ended in October, this thin layer had been excavated over an area of about half an acre.

Archaeological techniques of the kind normally used in excavating stone or brick buildings could not be applied here. The clay that forms the subsoil at Nea Nikomedeia is the same material the early settlers used to make the walls of their houses; consequently this clay also made up the bulk of the layer being excavated. Any details of ancient structures preserved in the deposit—such as the foundations of walls or the holes that contained timber uprights—would appear only as faint discolorations in the clay. To detect these discolorations and define their outlines clearly it was necessary to apply the painstaking technique of scraping. As the term indicates, scraping involves the removal of wide areas of soil a fraction of an inch at a time. The entire section of the mound to be excavated was laid out in a grid of 12-foot squares; as digging progressed, several adjacent squares would be scraped simultaneously and the pattern of the discolorations noted. All the walls and postholes found at Nea Nikomedeia, as well as the storage and rubbish pits associated with them, were uncovered in this way [see bottom illustration on page 101].

The whole of the mound was not opened during the 1963 season, and some house outlines that continued into the unexcavated portions of the site are not completely revealed. What has been exposed, however, makes it evident that the settlement consisted of individual buildings situated two to five yards apart on a slight knoll at the edge of what was then a marshy lake or inlet. There were two periods of early Neolithic building at Nea Nikomedeia. They are separated in places by a deposit of what appears to be the beginning of a humus soil, so that the second building period evidently represents a reoccupation of the site after a period of abandonment. In any case, the earlier settlement was the smaller of the two, and it was surrounded by a pair of concentric walls on the landward side of the knoll. At the time of the second building period the settlement expanded up to the limit of these walls, which were then replaced by a deep ditch. The ditch shows evidence of having been filled with water; perhaps it served as a moat.

Seven major structures of the earlier building period were uncovered in 1963; six of them are most likely dwellings. Carbonized remains of wood indicate that the frames of the houses were made of oak. The mud walls of the buildings were constructed in the following manner: Sapling uprights were set in place three to four feet apart and the space between them was filled in with bundles of reeds standing on end. The reeds were then plastered on the inside surface with mud mixed with chaff and on the outside with white clay. Many of the footings both for the walls and for the roof supports were

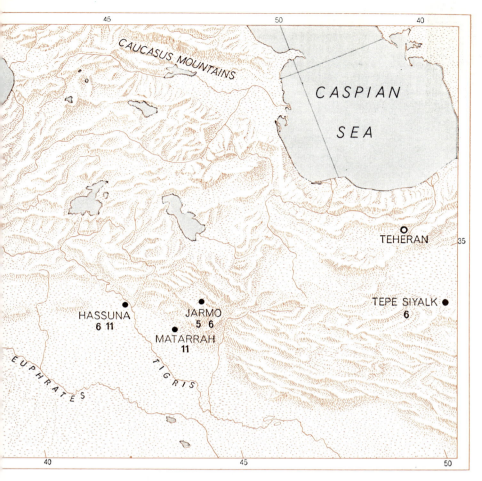

PARALLELS TO NEA NIKOMEDEIA

ARCHITECTURE

1 SQUARE HOUSE PLAN

2 WOOD FRAME AND MUD WALL

3 OPEN SETTLEMENT PLAN

SUBSISTENCE

4 CATTLE?

5 PIGS?

ADORNMENT

6 STUDS AND NAILS

7 CLAY STAMPS

8 BELT-FASTENER

POTTERY DECORATION

9 WHITE-PAINTED AND FINGER-IMPRESSED

10 RED-ON-CREAM PAINTING

11 MODELED FACE

south. These two areas, the nearest to Nea Nikomedeia, possess the largest number of traits in common with it. Nea Nikomedeia thus exhibits a distinct European character, although it has traits in common with sites as distant as Tepe Siyalk. This suggests that southeastern Europe was not peripheral to the region within which the Neolithic revolution began but was an integral part of it.

made a yard or so deep, evidently to ensure that the buildings would not be affected by frost heave or by the wetness of the waterfront subsoil. Because the mud-plastered walls would have been subject to damage by rain, it is assumed that the houses of Nea Nikomedeia had peaked and thatched roofs with overhanging eaves that would carry off rainwater [see illustration on page 99].

Although the six house plans are different, they have several features in common. The basic unit was evidently a square about 25 feet to a side. Two one-room houses show exactly these dimensions. A third building, consisting of a large main room and a narrow room along one side, was 25 feet wide; its full length could not be determined. The same plan—a large main room with a narrow room attached—is also found in the best-preserved dwelling uncovered at Nea Nikomedeia. At one end of the narrow room in this house stood a raised platform of plaster into which

were sunk a hearth basin and a storage bin; on the opposite side of the house was a fenced-off porch area.

A considerably larger structure, some 40 feet square and divided into three parts by parallel rows of heavy timbers, is also attributable to the first building period at Nea Nikomedeia. It was uncovered in the part of the excavation closest to the center of the mound. Five figurines of women were found within the bounds of its walls. Both its size and its contents suggest that the building served some ritual purpose.

Although much analytical work still remains to be done, preliminary findings by the botanists and zoologists who are working with the expedition provide a good outline of the economy of this early Neolithic community. The fact that the farmers of the first settlement grew wheat, barley and lentils is indicated by carbonized material; the particular varieties of these plants have not yet been identified. A study of the

animal bones recovered in 1961, together with a preliminary analysis of some 25,000 additional specimens recovered in 1963, suggest that sheep and goats played the primary role in animal husbandry. The bones of pigs and cattle were also present, but in far fewer numbers. In addition to tending their flocks the people of Nea Nikomedeia engaged in hunting, fowling and fishing. Deer, hare and wild pig were among the game animals; the presence of fish bones and the shells of both saltwater cockles and freshwater mussels shows that the early settlers also exploited the resources of their coastal environment.

Assuming that the carbon-14 date for Nea Nikomedeia is correct, evidence for the presence of even limited numbers of domesticated cattle and pigs at the site is a matter of considerable importance in the record of animal domestication. For one thing, this would be the earliest dated occurrence of domesticated cattle yet known anywhere in the world. If taken together with the possible evidence of cattle domestication at Fikirtepe in northwestern Turkey and at Çatal Hüyük in southeastern Turkey, this finding would argue for an original center for the domestication of cattle in Asia Minor and southeastern Europe. As for pigs, so early an occurrence of

pig bones in Greece suggests that there may have been an independent European center for the domestication of these animals, unconnected with the center implied for the Middle East by the animal-bone findings at such early village sites as Jarmo in Iraq.

It remains possible, although not probable, that the bones of both cattle and pigs found at Nea Nikomedeia represent hunters' prey rather than herdsmen's produce. The remains of both species recovered in 1961 do not all indicate the age of the animal. Of

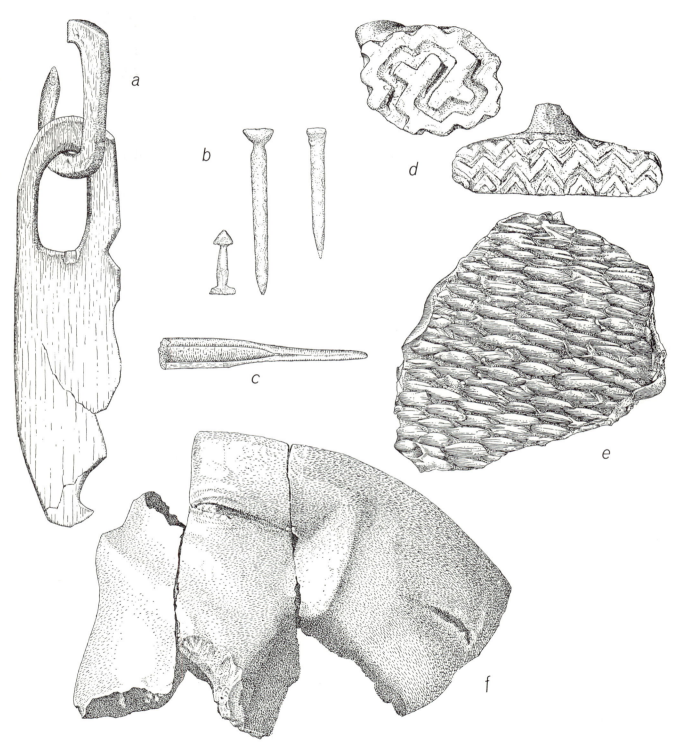

EARLY NEOLITHIC SKILLS in working with four varieties of raw material are demonstrated in this illustration. The hook-and-eye belt-fastener (a) and the awl (c) are made of bone. The two marble nails and the serpentine stud (b) show a capacity for fine lapidary work. Examples of the potter's art include geometric stamps (d), probably for body-painting, and a human face modeled below the rim of a pot (f). The bit of twined matting (e) was accidentally preserved in clay. All objects are shown natural size.

the bones that do indicate age, however, more than half belonged to immature animals; only under exceptional circumstances would such a high proportion of young animals be killed as a result of hunting. Nonetheless, the final word on cattle- and pig-domestication at this early Neolithic site must be postponed until the analysis of the vastly larger sample of bones uncovered in 1963 has been completed.

Regardless of the ultimate verdict on this point, it is evident that the economy of Nea Nikomedeia rested on a fourfold base, with wheat and barley as the major cereal crops, and sheep and goats as sources of meat and presumably of hides and milk. There is no reason to doubt that the first inspiration for the cultivation of these cereals and the husbanding of these animals came to Europe from the Middle East, although as yet the earliest links connecting the two regions have not been discovered. The essentials of the economy at Nea Nikomedeia, then, were foreign in origin; what about the other elements of village life? In reflecting on the settlement's tools, pottery, articles of personal adornment and ritual objects, one seeks similarities to material from other sites in Europe and abroad. In this way what was unique at Nea Nikomedeia can be distinguished from what was derived from—or perhaps contributed to—other areas.

The tool kit of the first settlers included both the classic artifacts of polished stone—axes, adzes and chisels—that originally gave the Neolithic, or New Stone, age its name, and a variety of chipped blades of flint and chert from which the farmers made scrapers, arrowheads and the cutting edges of rude sickles. The bow and arrow and the sling were among the hunters' weapons; hundreds of clay slingstones have been unearthed. The settlers also made bone needles (possibly including net-making needles), awls and fishhooks. Such a list, with a few exceptions or additions, would be typical of any other nearly contemporary community in southeastern Europe, Asia Minor or the Middle East. Nonetheless, there are consistent local traditions; as an example, the chipped stone artifacts from Nea Nikomedeia resemble those from sites in central Greece, eastern Yugoslavia and central Bulgaria and differ from those found in southern Greece, Asia Minor and the Middle East.

The earliest pottery at the site shows great technical competence in manufac-

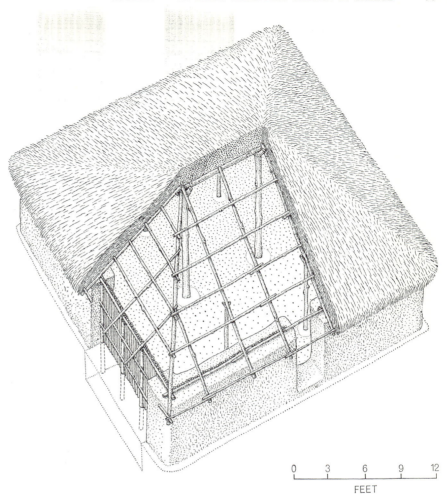

EARLY NEOLITHIC DWELLING consisted of timber uprights inside thick walls of clay plastered onto a frame of saplings and reeds. The foundations for the wall and the footings for the uprights were dug some three feet deep. The peaked pole-and-thatch roof, supported by crotched uprights, is hypothetical, but similar roofs are still built in Greece.

ture, in the range of vessel shapes and in decoration. The settlers made open bowls, large narrow-mouthed storage jars, small ladles, miniature vessels and peculiar shoe-shaped pots that may have been put into a bed of coals to heat their contents. Many of the smaller bowls were provided with lugs, which are perforated vertically or horizontally, so that they could be suspended by cords. Almost all the pots have thin walls and bases that are ring-shaped or disk-shaped. The potters decorated some of their wares by painting and some with finger impressions on the outside surface.

The earliest-known phases of Neolithic settlement in central Bulgaria and eastern Yugoslavia are characterized by pottery that bears finger-impressed decorations or designs in white paint; examples of both can be found at Nea Nikomedeia, but neither is common. That they are found at all, however,

lends weight to the conclusion that connecting links of some kind existed between these early Macedonian farmers and those to the north. The pottery evidence indicates even closer ties between Nea Nikomedeia and the earliest pottery-using settlements in central Greece. Both there and at Nea Nikomedeia wares decorated with block designs, triangles and patterns of wavy lines—all painted in red on a cream-colored background—are commonplace.

These pottery motifs provide an example of the ways in which Nea Nikomedeia may have contributed culturally to areas outside Europe. The tradition of painting pottery with red designs on a cream-colored background appears several hundred years later in southern Asia Minor with the beginnings of the Hacilar culture [see "Hacilar: A Neolithic Village Site," by James Mellaart; SCIENTIFIC AMERICAN, August, 1961]. By the same token, some of the

FIGURINE OF A WOMAN, seven inches high, is one of five similar clay sculptures unearthed inside the largest early building at Nea Nikomedeia. The presence of so many figurines, which are presumably fertility symbols, suggests that building was used ritually.

pots of Nea Nikomedeia are decorated with human faces made by pinching up a "nose" and adding ovals of clay as "eyes." Similarly decorated pots have been found in post-Neolithic levels at Hacilar and also at the earlier sites of Hassuna and Matarrah in Iraq. In the absence of well-defined intermediate steps, it must remain a matter of conjecture whether or not the presence of pots with human faces at these widely separated sites represents the diffusion of an idea or an independent invention.

Both European and Asiatic characteristics can be found among the articles of personal adornment at Nea Nikomedeia. A bone belt-fastener with a hook-and-eye clasp was uncovered during the 1963 season; a number of such fasteners have been found in the early Neolithic levels at Çatal Hüyük. A bone hook from Soufli Magoula, an early Neolithic site in central Greece, may be another European example of the same kind of object. Clay stamps, each exhibiting a different geometric pattern, are relatively common at Nea Nikomedeia; similar stamps are known from central Greece and elsewhere in southeastern and central Europe. Some of the stamps found at Nea Nikomedeia, however, have designs similar to those on stamps from Çatal Hüyük.

Some Neolithic sites in the Middle East—Tell Judeideh in Syria, Jarmo and Hassuna in Iraq and Tepe Siyalk in Iran—contain curious stone objects that look somewhat like primitive nails. The excavations at Nea Nikomedeia have yielded a great number of these objects, neatly wrought out of white marble, and a lesser number of tiny studs made of green serpentine. It is probable that the nails were headdress decorations and that the studs were earplugs. Such carefully shaped and polished articles of marble and serpentine represent a high level of technical achievement.

Of particular interest is the fact that the settlers made clay figurines of men and women; these stylized sculptures reflect a high level of artistic sensibility. The more sophisticated figurines were made in sections and then pegged together before they hardened; the component parts are the head, the torso (including the arms) and two separate legs. The head usually consists of a slightly flattened cylinder from which a prominent pointed nose is pinched up; as with the faces on the pots, the eyes are often represented by applied lumps of clay. Figurines of women outnumber those of men; in the commonest type of

MACEDONIAN PLAIN in northern Greece is level agricultural land today; 8,000 years ago its central portion was underwater and its coastline was marked by farming communities such as the one found at Nea Nikomedeia, the oldest Neolithic site in Europe.

SCRAPED HALF-ACRE at the Nea Nikomedeia mound shows the pale discolorations that outline the walls of vanished buildings. Several narrow ridges, composed of unexcavated earth, outline the grid of squares into which the site was divided before digging. Near a zigzag in this grid at the right side of the illustration appears the outline of a square structure that was subdivided into one wide and one narrow room; the disturbed outdoor area opposite the narrow room may have been a porch. Just above this house in the photograph, partly obscured by two grid ridges, is the outline of an undivided house like the one illustrated on page 99.

female figurine the thighs are modeled to an exaggerated roundness. The breasts are mere knobs, supported by the hands [see illustration on page 100].

Other clay figurines include rather less elegant models of sheep and goats. It is puzzling that these economically important animals are rendered with such relative crudity whereas three effigies of frogs found at Nea Nikomedeia were beautifully carved in green and blue serpentine and then polished. The site's marshy locale makes it reasonable to suppose that its inhabitants were well acquainted with these amphibians, but what significance the frog may have possessed that inspired the execution of its portrait in stone is unknown.

It is commonly assumed that early societies engaged in the newly discovered art of food production soon developed beliefs about the supernatural in which human, animal and plant fertility were emphasized. The exaggerated forms of the figurines of women uncovered at Nea Nikomedeia, together with the fact that five of them were found together within the confines of the site's largest structure, seem to indicate that fertility beliefs played a part in the life of this particular Neolithic community. The excavations have provided a further insight into the community's spiritual views: There was evidently little or no regard for the dead. Burial pits were located outside the house walls and sometimes in the debris of buildings that had fallen into disuse; the inhabitants appear to have taken little trouble to prepare the graves. In some instances one gains the impression that the dead were crammed into a barely adequate depression. No personal adornment, food offerings or grave goods have been found with the skeletons. In one enigmatic instance, however, a skeleton was found with a large pebble thrust between its jaws.

In summary, the characteristics of early Neolithic village life as it was practiced by the farmers of Nea Nikomedeia show basic parallels with life in similar Neolithic villages in Asia Minor and the Middle East. The most telling of these parallels are the very roots of the Neolithic revolution itself: the cultivation of wheat and barley and the domestication of sheep and goats. This village in the Macedonian marshes, however, was no mere foothold established in Europe by pioneers from the Middle East. Village plans, house plans and building methods comparable to those used at Nea Nikomedeia are known from two nearby regions. The first of these regions includes the early Neolithic sites of Karanovo and Azmak in central Bulgaria; parts of plans of

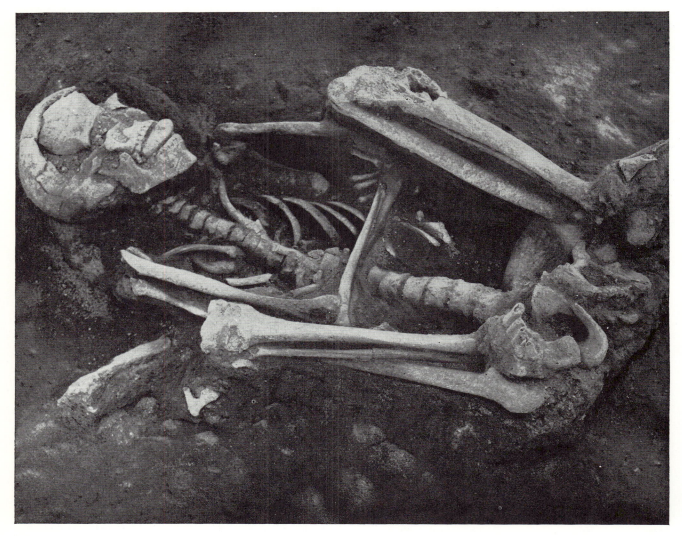

SKELETON OF ADULT, who had been buried in a contracted position, had a large, flat pebble inserted between the jaws for some unknown purpose. The burials at Nea Nikomedeia do not include funeral offerings, and the graves are cramped and shallow.

similar houses have also been exposed at several of the early sites in central Greece. It seems probable, therefore, that a Neolithic pattern of life characterized by a well-established architectural tradition adapted to the European environment and locally available materials stands behind the finds both at Nea Nikomedeia and at the sites of these other early settlements in southeastern Europe.

The precise origins of this architectural tradition remain unknown, but it is one that contrasts strongly with the custom of building houses one against another around the nucleus of a courtyard, which dominates village construction in Asia Minor and the Middle East during the late seventh millennium and early sixth millennium B.C. In the last analysis, such evidence may mean that southeastern Europe will have to be considered a part of that zone—heretofore generally deemed to lie exclusively in Asia Minor and the Middle East—in which were made the primary discoveries that led to the development of Old World civilization.

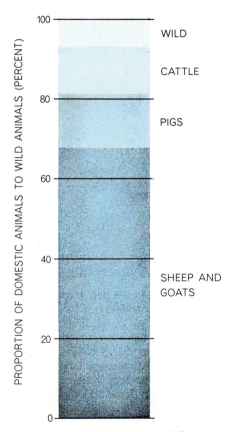

PARTIAL ANALYSIS of animal bones at Nea Nikomedeia shows the preponderance of sheep and goats. If cattle and pigs were domestic rather than wild animals, hunting provided less than 10 percent of the animal produce consumed by the villagers.

KNUCKLEBONES from the feet of four animals of the species that supplied most of Suberde's meat vary in size. They come from an ox (*top left*), a red deer (*top right*), a sheep or goat (*bottom left*) and a pig (*bottom right*). Each is a load-bearing bone, the astragalus. The size variations reflect the weight of the animals. Oxen weighed about 2,000 pounds, sheep only some 150 pounds.

METAPODIAL BONES of the same animals vary in size and also in number. Seen here is the end and part of the shaft of the single metapodial bone in the foot of a red deer (*top left*), an ox (*top right*) and a sheep (*bottom right*). Pigs have four per foot; two of them are visible here. They come from a modern boar killed at Suberde; only fragments of Neolithic pig metapodials were found.

12

A HUNTERS' VILLAGE IN NEOLITHIC TURKEY

DEXTER PERKINS, JR., AND PATRICIA DALY

November 1968

Until quite recently most prehistorians believed that the first villages, which date back to early Neolithic times, arose in response to the settled way of life made possible by man's discovery of agriculture and animal husbandry. Within the past few years, however, a number of Neolithic villages have been excavated whose inhabitants clearly depended for their livelihood on collecting wild plants or killing wild game. This is one reason why there is currently much interest in Neolithic sites in western Asia, where the oldest known remains of villages have been found. The excavator seeks to know, among other things, whether the villagers were hunters and/or gatherers or farmers and/or herdsmen.

One aspect of this general question can be approached by means of a comparatively new technique: faunal analysis, or the analysis of the animal bones unearthed at an archaeological site. Faunal analysis can demonstrate whether the occupants of the site were hunters or herdsmen, and it can provide more detailed information on their way of life. For example, if the villagers were hunters, it can indicate what hunting techniques they used.

We have recently completed the faunal analysis of an early village site in southwestern Turkey. Some 300,000 pieces of bone, the largest number yet recovered from any site in western Asia, were unearthed there in 1964 and 1965 by archaeologists from New York University working under the direction of Jacques Bordaz and the auspices of the National Science Foundation. The site, a small community of the early Neolithic period, was first located by Ralph S. Solecki of Columbia University. It occupies the top of a hill some 3,000 feet above sea level in the region where the Konya plain borders the Taurus Mountains near the modern village of Suberde [*see map on next page*]. Until recently the hill was almost entirely surrounded by the waters of a lake, and at the time the Neolithic settlement was inhabited, in the middle of the seventh millennium B.C., the lake intermittently covered a large part of the adjacent plain. Today there are still wild boars in a marshy area to the southwest of the site, and wild goats roam the nearby foothills of the Taurus. Once the region also abounded with herds of wild sheep, but they were hunted to extinction less than a century ago.

The digging of test trenches at Suberde in 1964 revealed levels of prehistoric occupation in an area half an acre in extent at the northern edge of the hill. The work of two seasons removed more than 230 cubic yards of material from the area. Below a disturbed surface layer the uppermost of two Neolithic levels was represented by a two-foot thickness of red-brown loam. In addition to tools, ornaments and bones, the upper level contained poorly preserved remains of houses with plastered floors and mud-brick walls. Underlying the red-brown loam was a second level, in places as much as six feet thick. In its light brown loam were hearths, deposits of ash and charcoal, a few unplastered floors, walls and benches, and some circular basins that had been scooped in the earth, lined with clay and then baked hard on the spot. Charcoal samples from the second level yielded carbon-14 dates that average around 6500 B.C. for the early occupation of Suberde.

By the end of the second season the excavators had collected about a ton and a half of animal bones. Our first step in dealing with this enormous accumulation was to cull out all the scraps of bone that were unidentifiable. The preliminary sorting took place at the site and reduced the collection from 3,000 pounds to 650 and from 300,000 specimens to 25,000. Although fewer than 10 percent of the potential specimens had survived the sorting, there were still plenty of bone fragments to work with.

We next sorted the bones according to the species of animal they represented. In many cases, however, it was not possible to tell what species was represented by a bone. Sheep and goat vertebrae, for example, look much alike. Worse still, the vertebrae of roe deer and fallow deer and even some pig vertebrae look enough like sheep and goat vertebrae to be confusing. Nonetheless, vertebrae are unmistakably vertebrae and are therefore not culled out when the unidentifiable scrap in a collection is eliminated. The same is true of rib bones: although they are easily identifiable as ribs, the species they represent is rarely certain. We put such bones aside and worked only with the specimens that could be identified by species.

By the time we had identified a total of 20 species, we had discarded as useless for identification nearly half of our 25,000 specimens, reducing the study collection to about 14,000 pieces of bone. The large majority of them—more than 9,000 specimens—were the bones of sheep (the Anatolian mouflon, *Ovis orientalis anatolica*) or goats (the Asian bezoar, *Capra hircus aegagrus*). Sheep and goats are lumped together in the statistics because, except for skulls, horns and a few other bones, their remains are not easily distinguished. Of the more than 9,000 specimens only 700—fewer than 10 percent of the sample—were identifiable as to species. The proportion was 85 percent sheep to 15 percent goats.

Considering Suberde's waterside location, it is curious that neither fish, shell-

SITE OF SUBERDE is located in southwestern Turkey, some 3,000 feet above sea level on the Konya plain. Two other Neolithic sites, Can Hasan and Çatal Hüyük, are its neighbors.

fish nor waterfowl seem to have played any significant role in the diet of the Neolithic villagers. Among our specimens were only a very small number of fishbones, freshwater-clam shells and bird bones (which seem to belong to a species of pelican). Better represented than any of these aquatic animals was the land tortoise, a slow-moving prey of the kind commonly collected by women and children in primitive societies even today.

The inventory of mammals other than sheep and goats at Suberde is extensive. The domestic dog was present, and the countryside supported such wildlife as jackal, fox, bear, wildcat, marten, badger, hedgehog, hare, roe deer and fallow deer. The bones of three additional mammals were found in sufficient abundance to indicate that they had shared the role of meat animals with the sheep and goats. These were the pig (*Sus scrofa*), represented by more than 1,400 bones; the red deer (*Cervus elaphus*), represented by some 340 bones, and a now extinct ox (*Bos primigenius*), represented by nearly 300 bones.

Having determined that five animal species furnished most of Suberde's meat, our next task was to find out if the relative importance of the species in each of the site's various strata indicated any change over the centuries either in the villagers' dietary preferences, in the availability of particular animals, or both. Bordaz was able to distinguish a number of stratigraphic subdivisions within the two main levels at the site, but he found that the evidence for cul-

tural change from stratum to stratum was slight. The major innovations in the upper strata were the use of polished stone in addition to the previously favored tool material, chipped obsidian, and the plastering of floors. The tools found at Suberde changed somewhat in style with the passage of time but not greatly in function. With such a record of cultural continuity, we did not expect to find much change in the villagers' diet.

The preponderance of sheep and goat bones indicates that these animals were the most important ones at Suberde. What about the other animals? The relative frequency of their bones in each stratum should provide at least part of the answer. One way to determine this relative frequency is simply to let the total number of all identifiable bone specimens represent 100 percent and then to conclude that the percentage of bones belonging to each species reflects its abundance among the animals killed. There are, however, several questionable assumptions inherent in this approach. It assumes that the survival of specimens has the same pattern for all species, and that the relative number of identifiable specimens is the same for each species. It further assumes that each of the animals was butchered in the same way.

A second approach is to determine the minimum number of individuals of each species present (based on a count of some particular bone or bones) and then to express these minimum numbers as percentages. This method largely avoids the pitfalls of the first, but it has its own drawbacks. The bone one selects as representative of a single animal may in fact prove to be so rare in a particular stratum that accidents of preservation (for example the lucky survival of two bones rather than one) could seriously distort the percentages.

The method we used avoids both difficulties. We first eliminated from our calculations the bones of the five meat animals that, for one reason or another, had not survived in approximately equal numbers among all the species. This reduced the collection from some 11,000 specimens to about 3,800. At the same time we allowed for the fact that different animals have a different number of bones in their skeleton. In the Suberde collection the bones that survived equally well among all the species were certain of the foot bones. Pigs, however, have more than twice as many foot bones than the other meat animals at the site

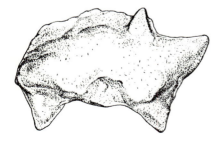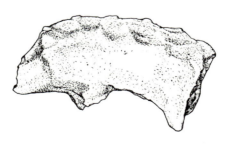

CLAY FIGURINES of pigs are among the few examples of art unearthed at Suberde. Pork was a consistently popular foodstuff throughout the site's occupation and boars' tusks were used as ornaments. Why the pig was represented in sculpture, however, remains unknown.

do: a pig's four extremities consist of 52 bones, whereas the extremities of the other animals consist of 24. A stratum that contains 100 sheep foot bones and 100 pig foot bones does not indicate, therefore, that sheep and pigs were present in a one-to-one ratio. The ratio is closer to two sheep for every pig. An ex-ample is provided by the number of identifiable pig bones in the lowest stratum of the site, designated by Bordaz as Level III–IV. They made up nearly 14 percent of all bones in the level. Moreover, the minimum proportion of pigs indicated by the pig foot bones in that level was 15 percent of all the animals. When we eliminated the bias due to the pig's characteristic skeleton, however, we found that the pig accounted for less than 7 percent of the population [*see bottom illustration on next two pages*].

Determining the relative frequency of each species in each level did not by itself indicate its economic impor-

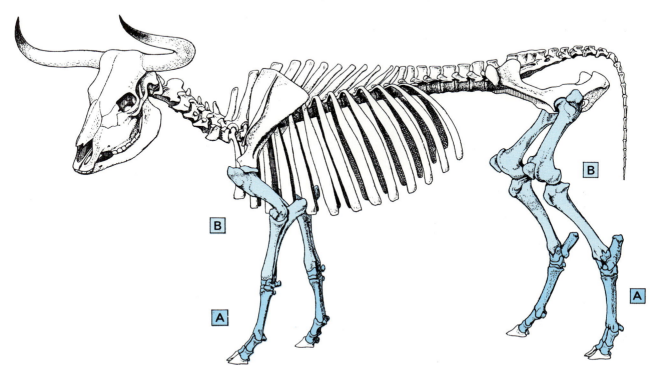

ANCESTRAL OX *Bos primigenius* became an increasingly important source of meat at Suberde over the centuries. The skeleton is shown divided into the *A* and *B* components. The *A* skeleton comprises bones of the feet, the *B* skeleton those of the legs. Many more ox foot bones than leg bones were unearthed at Suberde. This puzzle led to the authors' discovery of the "schlepp effect."

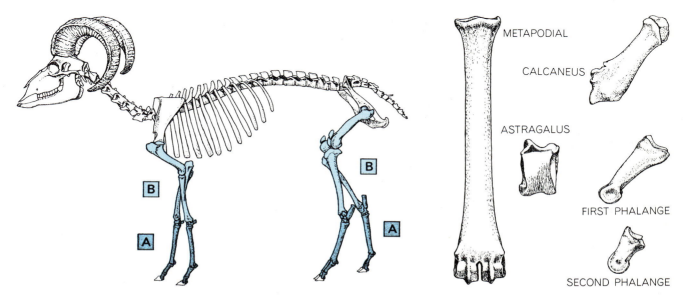

METAPODIAL

CALCANEUS

ASTRAGALUS

FIRST PHALANGE

SECOND PHALANGE

ANATOLIAN MOUFLON, a sheep of the species *Ovis orientalis*, together with lesser numbers of goats, was the primary meat animal at Suberde. The remains of sheep and goat *A* skeletons were found to be in proportion to the remains of their *B* skeletons, demonstrating that schlepp factors were inoperative in the inhabitants' treatment of smaller mammals.

BONES OF THE FEET were used by the authors to calculate how many of each meat animal had been present at Suberde because most foot bones were usually well preserved.

DIGGERS AT SUBERDE had to cut away a disturbed surface layer before reaching the underlying Neolithic remains on a hill bordering a dry lake (*background*). The countryside is ideal pasture for sheep; wild goats still roam the Taurus foothills beyond.

tance in terms of meat. An additional calculation was required. Sheep and goats are much the same size, but an ox yields more meat than a deer and much more meat than a sheep. Because the pig has short legs with more meat on the shank than there is on the legs of other animals, a pig yields about 20 percent more edible meat per pound of live weight. To estimate the proportion of meat in the Suberde diet supplied by each of the five species we assumed that sheep and goats yielded about 77 pounds of edible protein each (half the live weight), that a red deer yielded about 220 pounds and an ox about 1,000 pounds (also half the live weight). Pigs provided the same amount of edible meat as red deer because 70 percent of their live weight is edible meat. We were now in a position to calculate if the composition of the Suberde meat supply had altered over the centuries.

The excavators at Suberde had of course catalogued the animal bones according to the strata in which they were found. It was our assumption at first that, regardless of which level contained which bones, the collection as a whole would probably form a homogeneous sample. When we tested the collections from different levels for homogeneity, however, we found the statistical probability that the whole collection was

homogeneous was less than .02 percent. Working further with bones from various stratigraphic subdivisions, we found that the oldest ones (from the lowest stratum, where a particularly large quantity of animal remains extended down to bedrock) showed a better than 90 percent probability of homogeneity. The same was true of the bones from the higher strata in the older deposit, called the III levels by the excavators, and of the bones from the lower strata in the younger deposit above, known as the II levels. The bones from all the III and II

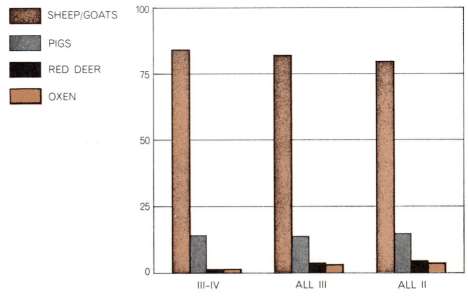

SPECIES (PERCENT OF ALL BONES)

SHEEP/GOATS
PIGS
RED DEER
OXEN

RELATIVE IMPORTANCE of the five meat animals during three time intervals at Suberde is not reflected accurately by a simple count of the number of bones of each species

levels, when taken together, also showed a better than 90 percent probability of being homogeneous. Because the site's few cultural innovations appear only in the II levels, however, we have continued to deal with the animal remains from each of these deposits as separate entities.

Applying our calculated yields of meat per species to the estimated number of animals in the earliest levels and the later ones, we found a significant difference in proportions. The amount of pork in the Suberde diet remained about the same—14 percent of all meat—from Level III–IV at the bottom up through the II levels at the top. In contrast, the amount of sheep and goat meat showed a sharp decline: from nearly 70 percent in Level III–IV to barely 50 percent in the II levels. As sheep and goats declined in dietary importance, oxen and red deer increased. Deer meat, however, seems to have been a relatively marginal item: the supply in the II levels was twice that in Level III–IV but still represented less than 7 percent of all meat. The supply of ox meat showed a notable rise: from about the same percentage as pork in Level III–IV it grew to an average of 30 percent of all meat in the III and II levels.

Do the animal bones at Suberde represent domesticated flocks or hunters' prey? There is no known instance of red deer being domesticated, but Suberde is not far from another Turkish Neolithic site, Çatal Hüyük, where domesticated cattle were known during roughly the same period. Moreover, domesticated sheep and goats were kept at the valley settlement of Zawi Chemi Shanidar in neighboring Iraq nearly 3,000 years before Suberde came into existence.

Evidence for domestication can be of several kinds. The plainest is the presence of an animal in a region outside its natural range; the pig in the New World is a recent example. In instances of this kind the suggestion is strong that the animal left its ancestral habitat under the guidance and control of man. A second kind of evidence is a change in the form of the animal, either because of the crowding that is a significant functional aspect of domestication or because of man's selective preservation of variant forms that would not survive in the wild. A third kind is a sudden rise in the proportion of one particular species for which no natural cause is apparent; the animal has obviously become a more reliable food source, possibly as a result of human control. A similar kind of evidence is the discovery that the remains of certain species all fall within certain age classes; the finding suggests either a seasonal pattern of hunting or selective culling of a domesticated herd, for example to cut down the number of animals that must be fed through the winter.

At Suberde no evidence of the first kind was available; the site is located well within the former natural range of all five of the meat animals, and two of them survive in the area today. As for any change in the form of the animals, we encountered some negative indications but only one doubtful piece of positive evidence. The evidence for and against domestication at Suberde is best described species by species.

To begin with the most numerous group, out of the more than 9,000 specimens of sheep and goat bone we found one skull fragment that seemed to be from a hornless sheep. Although the loss of horns is a change characteristic of domesticated ewes, one skull fragment is not an adequate basis for stating that the sheep at Suberde had been domesticated. Hornless females are known among some wild populations of the Asiatic mouflon, the species of sheep at Suberde. Moreover, instead of increasing in numbers and importance as time passed (an indication of possible human control) Suberde's sheep and goats declined. In order to determine if the last remaining kind of evidence—the evidence of age classes—was positive or negative, we compared the proportion of juvenile sheep to mature sheep in the Suberde sample with the proportion among the domesticated sheep in an Iron Age settlement in Europe (as reported by E. S. Higgs of the University of Cambridge) and the proportion in a population of living wild sheep (as reported by Adolph Murie of the U.S. National Park Service). The proportion in the Suberde

RELATIVE FREQUENCY OF SPECIES (PERCENT)

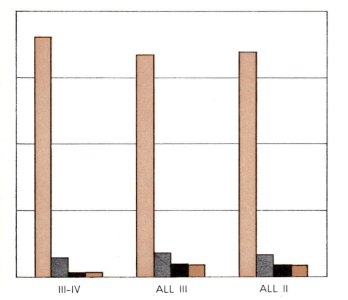

MEAT SUPPLY PER SPECIES (PERCENT)

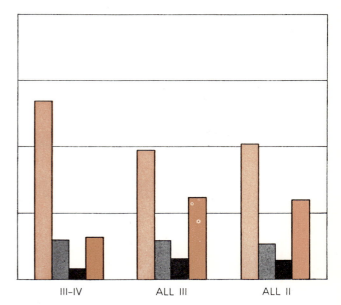

(left). The schlepp factors remain undetected and the pig, which has twice as many foot bones as the other animals, is disproportionately represented. Once the relative number of each species is known (center) one can show the percentage of meat that each provided (right).

sample was almost identical with the one found by Murie in wild sheep [*see upper illustration below*].

Subdividing our sample even further by age, we found that no sheep specimens represented animals younger than three months or older than three years, although the sample was in general evenly distributed between these two extremes. According to Murie, the old animals and the very young animals are precisely the ones that are taken by wild predators. We were therefore brought to two conclusions. First, the sheep and goats at Suberde had been wild. Second, the randomness of the sample with respect to age suggests that the Suberde villagers were not solitary hunters but rather were engaged in cooperative drives, slaughtering whole flocks at a time.

The status of the pigs at Suberde was also uncertain. They had neither declined nor increased in importance as time passed, and thus their numbers provided no evidence for or against possible domestication. Unfortunately reliable age-class information is not available for the pig. Age is commonly determined by the fusion of the ends of the long bones to the bones' main shaft. There is no information on the rate of fusion in wild pigs, and the information on domesticated pigs merely suggests that the process is too delayed to allow accurate identification of young age classes. One piece of negative evidence, however, was at our disposal. Ancient domestication might be defined as a combination of malnutrition and overcrowding. In pigs a change that soon results is a foreshortening of the jaw and face, with a consequent crowding of late-erupting tooth buds and a reduction in the length of the molar crowns. We compared the crown length of the Suberde pigs' upper third molars with the crown length of domesticated pigs from the site of Jarmo in Iraq and with the crown length of modern wild pigs. We found that the Jarmo crown length was substantially reduced but that the Suberde and wild-pig crown lengths were almost identical [*see lower illustration at left*]. We concluded that the Suberde pigs had not been domesticated.

This brought us to the oxen. Unlike the sheep and goats (whose numbers had declined) and the pigs (whose numbers had remained the same), the oxen had increased in number as time passed. Could the increase be taken as evidence for domestication? Two anomalies apparent in the bone collection argued against such a conclusion. The first is that none of the cattle specimens is from an immature animal. The same is true of the red deer specimens, which is attributable to the structure of deer herds: females and young comprise one herd and the males another. If hunters selectively stalk only the herd of males, which are notably easier prey than the alert and timid females, they will kill no juvenile deer. Perhaps the herds of ancient oxen had a similar composition. Since they are now extinct, we shall never know the answer. The total absence of juvenile cattle bones at Suberde, however, is only part of the evidence suggesting that the villagers hunted wild oxen.

Quite early in our analysis we noticed

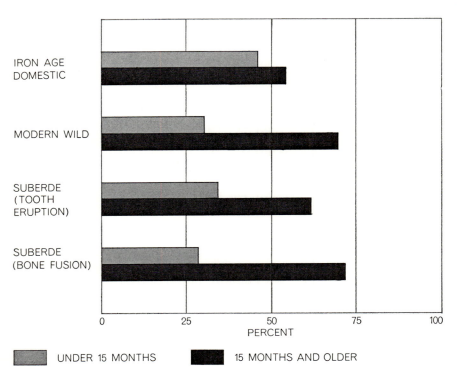

SUBERDE SHEEP were evidently wild rather than domesticated. Whether estimated on the basis of tooth eruption or on the basis of bone fusion, the age of most Suberde sheep was over 15 months. The proportion of mature to immature animals was close to that among living wild sheep and was quite unlike that among the domesticated sheep of the Iron Age.

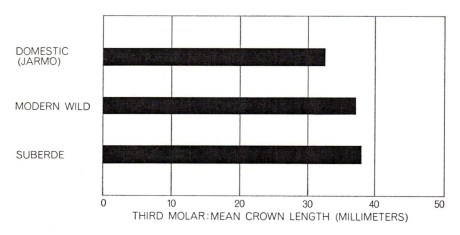

SUBERDE PIGS were also evidently wild. The crown length of the rearmost molar teeth is soon reduced in domesticated pigs because the animals' jaws grow shorter; an example is the mean crown length of the third molar teeth in domesticated pigs from Jarmo, an Iraqi site of the seventh millennium B.C. The Suberde pigs' teeth are nearer to modern wild pigs' teeth in size. Kent V. Flannery of the University of Michigan measured Jarmo and modern teeth.

that the leg bones of oxen were curiously scarce. When we compared the number of what we characterized as "A skeleton," or foot, bones with the number of "B skeleton," or leg, bones, for example, we discovered that the proportion was quite different for oxen from what it was for sheep and goats. The foot bones of sheep and goats comprised about 55 percent of the combined total; the leg bones made up the remaining 45 percent. With the oxen 83 percent of the bones were foot bones and only 17 percent were leg bones [*see lower illustration below*]. This distribution puzzled us until we remembered the various

ways the bison hunters of the American Great Plains had dealt with their prey and realized that the villagers of Suberde must have faced a quite similar problem.

If the cattle at Suberde had been domesticated, we reasoned, they would have been slaughtered conveniently near home. How, then, could one explain the absence of the leg bones? Some bones are more likely to disappear after burial than others, for various reasons. Some decay rapidly, the way hooves do. Rodents may dig into the soil and carry away small bones, and larger carnivores such as wolves and jackals may do the same. The leg bones of oxen, however,

are not more susceptible to decay than ox foot bones, and they are more difficult to carry away. Moreover, the foothills near Suberde are typical sheep terrain, but the nearest cattle country is a few miles away. The missing leg bones indicate that the cattle were not slaughtered near the village. At the same time the nature of the countryside makes it improbable that wild cattle would have been encountered near the village.

Archaeologists working at Paleo-Indian sites in the New World have shown that, if only a few parts of a bison skeleton are found, the site is probably a more or less permanent camp to which the hunters brought back meat from animals they had killed and butchered elsewhere. If, on the contrary, most of the bisons' bones are present, the site is probably a "kill" site to which the successful hunters summoned their families. Suberde was a permanent settlement, and most cattle long bones were missing from its faunal inventory. We concluded that the oxen were indeed wild and had been killed away from home.

When a Suberde hunting party killed a wild ox, they apparently butchered it on the spot and used the animal's own hide as a container for carrying the meat home. They evidently stripped the forequarters and hindquarters of meat and threw the leg bones away. They apparently left the feet attached to the hide, perhaps because the feet made convenient handles for dragging the meat-filled hide. Perhaps they also valued the feet: this part of the animal contains useful sinews and has been called "the hunter's sewing kit." We have named the disparity between the number of cattle foot bones and leg bones that resulted from this treatment of the prey the "schlepp effect," after the German verb meaning "to drag." It combines a factor related to the size of the game animal with one related to the distance between kill site and home settlement. Sheep and goats, for example, were small enough, and were killed close enough to Suberde, to be immune from the schlepp effect. The wild oxen were not.

One further consideration supports our conclusion: the proportion of ox leg bones to ox foot bones at Can Hasan, a nearby Neolithic site where cattle were domesticated. The proportion is 38 percent leg bones to 62 percent foot bones, sharply different from the Suberde proportion [*see upper illustration at left*].

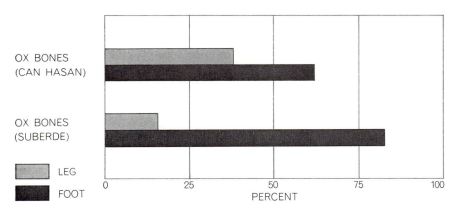

SUBERDE OXEN were also evidently wild. At Can Hasan, where cattle were domesticated, the proportion of bones from ox *B* skeletons and *A* skeletons was roughly three to two. The proportion at Suberde was closer to six to one. The authors attribute the discrepancy to the schlepp effect: the Can Hasan oxen, being domesticated, could be slaughtered close to home without leaving any bones. The Suberde oxen, in contrast, must have been butchered far from home, leaving some bones behind. Such a system suits hunters, not herdsmen.

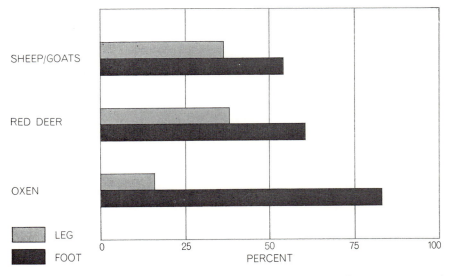

VARIABILITY of the schlepp factors at Suberde is evident in the different proportion of sheep and goat, red deer and ox *A*-skeleton and *B*-skeleton bones found at the site. The small animals, lighter loads, were apparently brought home unbutchered; they were probably killed fairly near home. The contrast between the proportions for ox and for deer, the latter identical with the proportion for Can Hasan oxen, may reflect the greater ease in dealing with a 400-pound animal rather than a 2,000-pound one when both are killed far afield.

All in all, what have the bones at Suberde told us about the lives of its Neolithic inhabitants? Suberde was a settled community of the kind that has been thought to have arisen only after men had mastered the growing of crops and the herding of animals. Analysis of the plant remains at the site has not yet been completed. Regardless of the presence or absence of domesticated plants at Suberde, however, one point is clear. The villagers fed largely on meat and were not herdsmen but hunters.

Second, in its early years Suberde depended on cooperative hunting tactics to secure nearly 70 percent of its meat supply. Sweeping through the adjacent foothills, the village hunters slaughtered entire flocks of sheep and goats at a time, perhaps driving them by setting fires. The methods used to rouse boars from the marshy thickets of the region are not apparent from the faunal remains. Among the artifacts at Suberde, however, are ornaments made from boar tusks, and the scant representational art at the site includes pottery figurines of pigs [see *bottom illustration on page 106*]. Although pork played only a limited role in the Suberde diet, the wild pig was evidently much on the villagers' minds. As for the red deer, the lack of immature deer remains make it probable that only the male herds were stalked. Because a solitary hunter would scarcely find it easy to schlepp more than 200 pounds of butchered meat and hide back to the village, group hunting again seems more likely. In the case of the wild oxen, the 1,000-pound burden of each animal's meat and hide—as well as the heavy work of butchering the animals—means that the pursuit of cattle by the inhabitants of Suberde was almost certainly a group activity.

Finally, the earlier inhabitants of Suberde depended more heavily on sheep and goat meat, or possibly found sheep and goat easier prey than their successors did. Pending a report on the plant remains at the site, we can say only that there is no obvious evidence for a change in climate that might account for the change in hunting pattern. Because the change appears in all the III layers and the site's few cultural innovations do not appear until the II layers, it seems doubtful that a cultural shift was the cause. We are left guessing. Were the local foothills overhunted, so that the villagers had to go farther afield to find other wild herds? Whatever the explanation, the analysis has shown that a change did occur and has measured its extent. Faunal analysis is capable of providing similar information about the lives of prehistoric peoples at other sites throughout the world.

13

AN EARLY FARMING VILLAGE IN TURKEY

HALET ÇAMBEL AND ROBERT J. BRAIDWOOD

March 1970

When and where did men first turn to farming and animal husbandry as a way of life? This question has increasingly come to occupy the attention of archaeologists in recent years. The first direct attempt to discover just when in human prehistory farming villages appeared was made in the Near East a little more than 20 years ago when a party from the Oriental Institute of the University of Chicago began digging at Jarmo in the foothills of the Zagros Mountains in northeastern Iraq. Today scores of such investigations are in progress in several parts of the Old World and the New World. In the Near East alone the area of interest has grown until it stretches from Turkestan and the Indus valley on the east to the Aegean and the Balkans on the west. This article concerns one Near Eastern investigation that has opened up a new area and has by chance brought to light the earliest evidence of man's use of metal.

Field results in the years since Jarmo allow a few broad generalizations about the dawn of cultivation and animal husbandry. We now know that somewhat earlier than 7500 B.C. people in some parts of the Near East had reached a level of cultural development marked by the production, as opposed to the mere collection, of plant and animal foodstuffs and by a pattern of residence in farming villages. It is not clear, however, when this level of development became characteristic of the region as a whole. Nor do we yet have a good understanding of conditions in the period immediately preceding. The reason is largely that few sites of this earlier period have yet been excavated, and that during the earliest phases of their manipulation the wild plants and animals would not yet possess features indicat-

ing that they were on the way to domestication. Moreover, even the most painstaking excavation may fail to turn up materials that constitute *primary* evidence for domestication, that is, the physical remains of the plants and animals in question. Fragments of plant material and bone—the objects that could tell us exactly which of a number of possible organisms were then in the process of domestication—are often completely missing from village sites.

What should be said of villages that yield plant and animal material that we cannot positively identify as being the remains of domesticated forms? Until recently we tended to believe that if such sites had every appearance of being permanently settled, and if their inventory of artifacts included flint "sickle" blades, querns (milling stones), storage pits and similar features, then they probably represented the next-earliest level of cultural development; we called it the level of incipient cultivation and animal husbandry. Over the years, however, it has become increasingly probable that early village-like communities of a somewhat different kind may also have existed in the Near East. At these sites the food supply tends at first to include plant and animal forms that were not subsequently domesticated. In other words, even though such items as flint sickles,

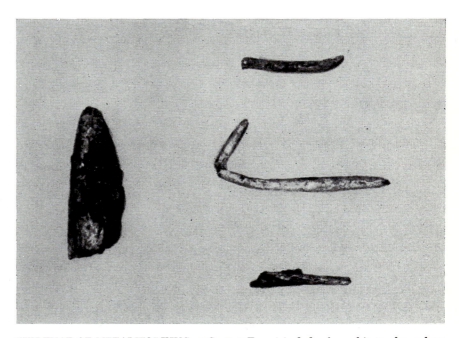

EVIDENCE OF METALWORKING at Çayönü Tepesi includes four objects, shown here twice actual size. At left is the point of a reamer, formed from a lump of native copper by hammering. Beside it are two copper pin fragments and a whole pin that has been bent. The pinpoints have been formed by abrasion. A source of native copper lies quite near the site.

querns and the like appear in their inventories, and the architectural traces of their settlement suggest some degree of permanence, it looks as if we are dealing here with villagers living on a level of intensive collection of wild foods alone. Our older notion that villages had to mean farmers has gone by the board.

A prime example of such a non-food-producing community is the village-like site of Mallaha, in northern Israel. The excavator of Mallaha, Jean Perrot of the French Archaeological Mission in Israel, was the first to suggest that when other sites of a similar nature were unearthed, they too might lack any evidence of food production. Mallaha was inhabited about 9000 B.C. The village site of Mureybet, on the middle reaches of the Euphrates in Syria, is somewhat later, say about 8250 B.C. Mureybet, which was excavated by Maurits N. van Loon for the Oriental Institute in 1964 and 1965, also shows no trace of food production. An even later example is the "hunters' village" of Suberde in Turkey, excavated by Jacques Bordaz of the University of Montreal in 1964 and 1965 [see the article "A Hunters' Village in Neolithic Turkey," by Dexter Perkins, Jr., and Patricia Daly, beginning on page 105]. As late as 6500 B.C. the people of Suberde fed themselves mainly by killing large numbers of wild sheep and wild cattle.

In very rough outline the available evidence now suggests that both the level of incipient cultivation and animal domestication and the level of intensified food-collecting were reached in the Near East about 9000 B.C. In contrast to the moderately intensive food-collecting characteristic of the preceding level of development (the level of the late Upper Paleolithic period), what allowed this second kind of community to flourish was collecting of a most intensive kind. We believe such communities can be regarded as being incipiently food-producing, in the sense that their inhabitants were doubtless already manipulating both plants and animals to some extent. It seems to us that in much of the Near East this interval of incipient food production was just before or at the same time as what in Europe is called the Mesolithic period: a phase of cultural readaption, still on a food-collecting level, to the sequence of postglacial forested environments that formed in Europe about 11,000 years ago. (Food production proper did not reach most of Europe until sometime after 5000 B.C.)

The inventory of artifacts known as the Natufian assemblage, after the valley in Palestine where it was first discovered, provides examples, found both in caves and in village-like sites, of communities without food production. The artifacts uncovered at Mallaha, for instance, fit the Natufian classification. A different but contemporary inventory,

found east of the Euphrates and Tigris rivers, is named the Karim Shahirian assemblage, after Karim Shahir, a site on the flanks of the Zagros Mountains. The artifacts from Zawi Chemi, another early site in Iraq, are of this second kind, and Zawi Chemi appears to have the earliest evidence for domesticated sheep (about 9000 B.C.). A somewhat later site in neighboring Iran—Ganj Dareh, near Kermanshah—contains an assemblage that, although it is similar, is somewhat more developed than the basic Karim Shahirian. It is not yet clear, however, either along the Mediterranean littoral or in the regions east of the Euphrates, through how many successive phases the incipient food producer—hunters' village level may have passed before the next developmental step took place.

The early phase of that next step— the level of effective village-farming communities—is now known from sites throughout the Near East. Representative early-phase villages have been unearthed in most of the region's grassy uplands, in some middle reaches of its major river valleys, along the Mediterranean and even beyond the Near East in Cyprus, Crete and Greece. Originally one of us (Braidwood) believed the most ancient evidence of this early phase

● SITES WITH ESTABLISHED FOOD PRODUCTION.

○ SITES WITH SEVERAL PERIODS OF OCCUPATION. SOME FOOD-PRODUCING.

◆ SITES WITH EVIDENCE OF "INCIPIENT" FOOD PRODUCTION.

◇ SITES WITH INSUFFICIENT EVIDENCE OR NO EVIDENCE OF FOOD PRODUCTION.

☐ SITES KNOWN FROM BRIEF TESTS OR SURFACE COLLECTIONS; NO EVIDENCE OF FOOD PRODUCTION.

SOUTHWESTERN ASIA, from beyond the Caspian (right) to the Mediterranean shore (left), contains many of mankind's earliest farming settlements, most of them in or near the hilly regions flanking the Fertile Crescent of Mesopotamia. The region also contains a number of village-like sites whose inhabitants were only incipient food producers or won a living by means of intensified hunting and gathering (see key above).

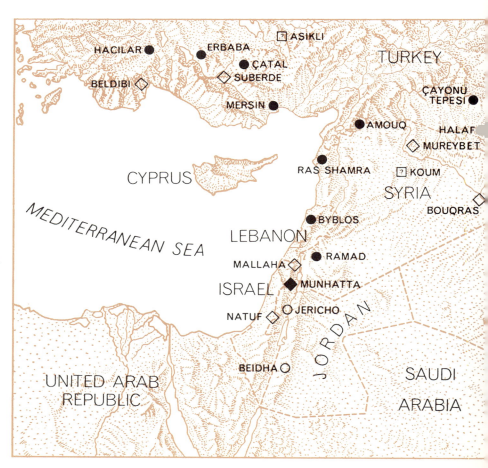

would be found only within a geographically restricted area, which was defined as the hilly flanks of the Fertile Crescent [*see illustration below*]. Moreover, even within this area the expectation was that the evidence would be confined to the zone naturally occupied today by certain wild but potentially domesticable plants and animals. One consequence of this view was that for a time the search for early sites was restricted to the "hilly flank" area, with the result that a large proportion of the early village sites now known are either in that area or immediately adjacent to it.

Recently it has become apparent that in past millenniums the natural range of the potentially domesticable forms of what may be called the "wheat-barley/sheep-goat-cattle-pig complex" extended well beyond the hilly flanks of the Fertile Crescent. For example, while extending earlier investigations by the Oriental Institute in Iran, Herbert E. Wright, Jr., of the University of Minnesota and Willem van Zeist of the University of Groningen have collected samples from the beds of lakes and ponds for analysis of their pollen content. Wright and van Zeist find that since about 17,000 years ago the vegetation and climate along the flanks of the Zagros Mountains have

changed much more than had been supposed. At the same time test excavations by an Oriental Institute group at Koum, in the dry steppe country west of the Euphrates in Syria, have added another site to the growing list of early non-food-producing settlements. Koum, like Mureybet, lies well south of the hilly-flanks zone, just as Suberde in Asia Minor lies well north of it. We have yet to learn precisely how wide the natural range of the domesticable plants and animals constituting this Near Eastern complex was in early times. The question will be answered only with the continued help of our colleagues in the natural sciences.

In the 1950's there was a substantial increase of archaeological activity in the Near East, but not until the 1960's did it become possible to investigate one untouched area that formed a virtual keystone in the arch. This was the southern slopes and the piedmont of the Taurus Mountains in southeastern Turkey, an area that includes the entire northern watershed in the upper reaches of the Tigris and the Euphrates. We reasoned that, however extensive the ancient range of domesticable plants and animals may have been, the upper basin of the Tigris and the Euphrates must have been

somewhere near the center of the zone.

Much of this unexplored territory lay within three Turkish border provinces (Urfa, Diyarbakir and Siirt), which for reasons of national security are normally out-of-bounds to foreign visitors. It seemed to us that if the area was to be reconnoitered, a joint Turkish-American venture was in order. In late 1962 the Oriental Institute joined forces with the department of prehistory of Istanbul University to establish a joint Prehistoric Project, and the authors of this article were made its codirectors. The project received the support of the National Science Foundation and the Wenner-Gren Foundation for Anthropological Research.

We proposed that a surface survey of the three provinces be made in the fall of 1963 and that exploratory digging be undertaken in the spring of 1964. We presently received the necessary approvals, which in this border region meant not only the cooperation of the Directorate of Antiquities of the Turkish Republic but also the active support of the Prime Minister, of many high civil and military authorities and of the governors of the three provinces and their staffs.

Thanks to the interest of all concerned, we were able to begin our sur-

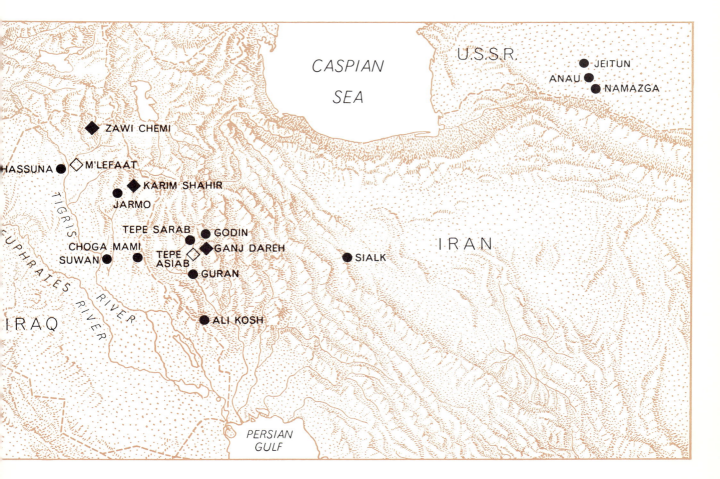

face survey in the province of Siirt early in October of 1963. We moved on to Diyarbakir in mid-November and ended the season with a five-day survey in Urfa in mid-December. Since the three provinces cover a total of more than 46,000 square kilometers, the reconnaissance could scarcely be an intensive one. The most detailed work was done in two valley regions: the plains of Kurtalan in Siirt and the Ergani plain in Diyarbakir. We found a total of 134 archaeological sites, plotted their location and roughly classified the materials we could collect on the surface at the main sites.

Our survey showed that this part of Turkey had been continuously occupied by men at least from the time (between 100,000 and 200,000 years ago) when stone tools of the Acheulean type were commonplace. So far as our particular interests were concerned, sites that looked as though they might be the remains of early farming villages were located in both the Kurtalan and the Ergani valleys. Still other sites in these val-

leys evidently represented more fully evolved village-farming communities. Some of the sites belonged to the developed village-farming phase termed Halafian (after Tell Halaf in northern Syria).

So far as settlements that might have belonged to the initial level of incipient food production are concerned, the most we can say at the moment is that our survey turned up no artifacts that, even in general terms, could be called representative of either the Natufian or the Karim Shahirian assemblages. Although it is probable that an unrelated third cultural tradition at the general level of incipient food production existed in this part of Turkey, we have yet to identify its traces.

In late April of 1964 we returned to the area of our survey prepared to undertake a number of test excavations. Bruce Howe of Harvard University, who had joined the project with the support of the American Schools of Oriental Re-

search, tackled two small open sites in the area northwest of the provincial capital of Urfa. Named Biris Mezarligi and Söğüt Tarlasi, the sites contained numerous specialized stone tools produced from blades of flint. The inventory seems to represent some end phase of the Paleolithic period in the region. The sites did not yield samples adequate for carbon-14 dating, so that the age of this blade industry is a matter of conjecture; our guess is that the tools were made around 10000 B.C. or perhaps a little later. At Söğüt Tarlasi, but not at Biris Mezarligi, the blade-tool horizon was overlain by material of a time somewhat before 3000 B.C., contemporary with the Uruk phase of Sumerian culture in neighboring Mesopotamia.

While Howe worked in Urfa, the majority of the workers on the project moved on to Diyarbakir in order to investigate a promising mound some five kilometers southwest of the town of Ergani. Known as Çayönü Tepesi, the mound is about 200 meters in diameter;

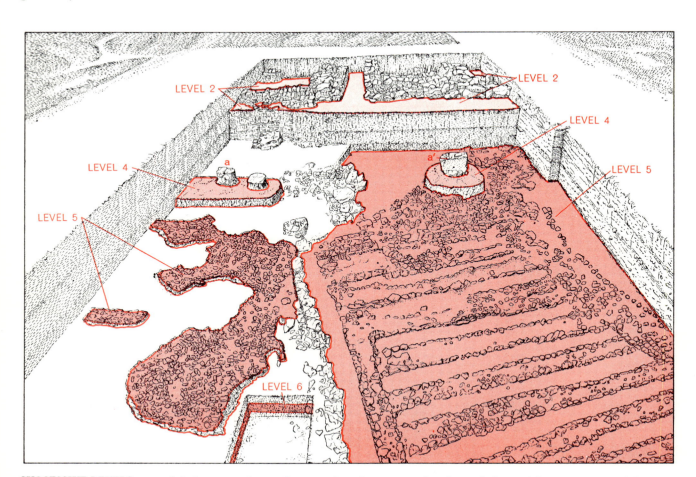

SUCCESSIVE LEVELS exposed during excavation on the crest of the mound are shown in a drawing based on composite photographs. At the rear of the dig, only a little below the mound surface, are the stone foundations of mud-brick structures that had been built at Level 2. In the middle distance (*a, a'*), still surrounded by unremoved earth, are the bases of the two stone monoliths found at Level 4. Sections of the cobble pavement found at Level 5 are in the foreground at left. In the foreground at right is the grill-like stone foundation of the elaborate structure exposed at Level 5. The two-by-two-meter pit, foreground, descends beyond Level 6.

it stands on the north bank of a minor tributary of the Tigris. At some time in the past part of the mound's south side was washed away. At the foot of the talus slope on the river side we found fragments of crude and easily crumbled pottery that had been made by hand, rather than with the potter's wheel. Some additional potsherds were present on the northeast slope of the mound and in the top 10 or 15 centimeters of soil in our test excavations (about the depth to which the soil had been disturbed by modern plowing). Below that our 1964 excavations revealed no pottery. The presence in these lower levels of figurines made of clay shows that clay was known and used in the early days of Çayönü Tepesi. Like the people of Jarmo and some other early village-farming communities, however, the inhabitants of Çayönü Tepesi evidently got along without the clay bowls, jars and other containers that are commonplace in the villages of later farmers.

We worked at Çayönü Tepesi for two seasons—in 1964 and again in 1968—and we expect to work there again this year. Our main evidence concerning the early occupation of the site comes from a 10-by-15-meter area we excavated on the crest of the mound and a five-by-eight-meter trench we cut into the mound on the river side; both excavations were undertaken during the 1964 season [see illustrations on page 118]. Those who explore village sites in southwestern Asia come to expect that each new excavation will exhibit an exuberant characteristic that is distinctively its own. Çayönü Tepesi was no exception: its special characteristic is its architecture. Among the buildings we uncovered, several must have been quite imposing. The trench we cut back from the river revealed part of what could have been a building interior or perhaps an open court. The area was floored with a broad pavement of smooth flagstones, around which the stone bases of thick walls rose to a height of a meter or more. Spaced along the main axis of the paved area were the broken bases of a pair of large stone slabs that had once stood upright. From one of the stone walls buttresses projected at the points nearest the broken slabs. Another partly intact slab marked the area's short axis. Unfortunately erosion had eaten away the southern portions of this elaborate structure, so that its full plan is beyond recovery.

At the crest of the mound we dug down to a depth of more than three meters, encountering traces of at least six

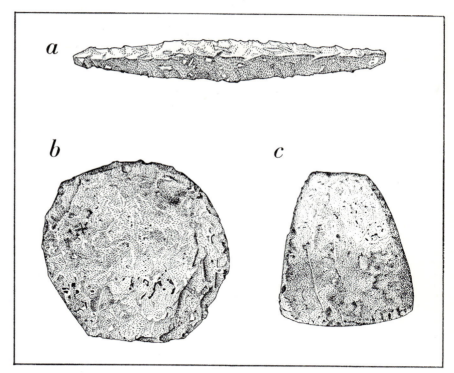

THREE STONE IMPLEMENTS from Çayönü Tepesi are a flint projectile point (a), found during the 1968 season, a scraper of flint (b) and a polished stone celt, the bit of a compound cutting tool (c), unearthed in 1964. The artifacts are shown at their actual size.

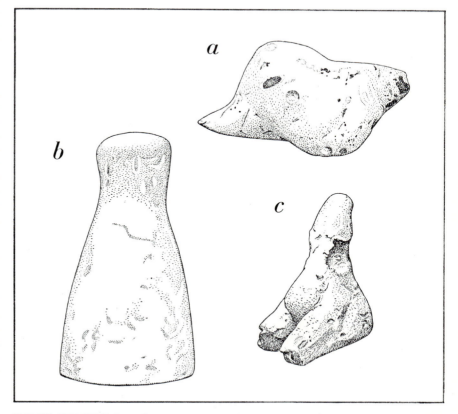

THREE ODDITIES from the site are a snail shell (a), a polished stone object (b) and a crude clay figurine (c). The shell, imported from the Mediterranean, has been smoothed and drilled with holes, presumably for decorative inserts. The stone, about three inches high, is one of 22 found in a cache during the 1968 season; their function is unknown. The figure seems to represent a pregnant woman; it may be a portrayal of the familiar "fertility deity."

AIR VIEW of Çayönü Tepesi, on the bank of a tributary of the Tigris River in southwestern Turkey, shows the work done by the authors in 1964. Near the river (*right*) digging uncovered stone walls and a floor of flagstones. On the crest of the village mound (*left*) six successive levels of occupation have been exposed; the next-to-lowest level contained objects made from copper.

GROUND VIEW of Çayönü Tepesi, from a rise on the south side of the river, shows a stretch of the broad Ergani plain beyond the site. On the northern horizon are the first ranges of the Taurus Mountains, here distinctively marked by light-colored bands of rock.

successive levels of occupation. At the fourth level the bases of two more upright slabs rose from a broad pavement of fist-sized limestone cobbles; the broken upper portion of one slab lay beside its base. The fifth level, also paved with cobbles, contained the stone foundations of still another substantial structure. What we could perceive of the foundation plan showed a curious grill-like pattern [see illustration on page 116]. Our work in 1968 exposed another of these grill-like foundations. A similar foundation, although it is smaller and built of sun-dried mud walling rather than stone, was unearthed at Jarmo. We are still puzzled as to the function of such foundations.

The purpose of the upright slabs at Çayönü Tepesi is equally puzzling. We are of two minds about whether they could have been supports for roof beams. Our first notion was that the slabs might have been ceremonial stones set up within unroofed courts, but the actual function of the structures containing them is not yet clear. We are much impressed by the substantial proportions of the buildings and by the relative sophistication of their construction, but we are still loath to press any suggestion that they served a public or a sacred purpose.

In addition to its impressive architecture, Çayönü Tepesi yielded tools chipped from flint and obsidian or fashioned from stone by grinding, ornaments made of polished stone, the clay figurines mentioned above and one shell ornament. The last object indicates contact, direct or indirect, with the Mediterranean coast. If one adds to this inventory evidence what seems to be a primitive form of wheat and the remains of domesticated dogs, pigs, sheep and probably goats, one gains some sense of the quality of life here and in similar communities across southwestern Asia as the arts of farming and animal husbandry became established during the eighth millennium B.C. If that were all Çayönü Tepesi had to tell us, it would be enough. A combination of geological propinquity and archaeological good fortune, however, has made the site even more significant. We have found here what is so far the earliest evidence of man's intentional use of metal.

Turkey is rich in minerals; one of its major mining centers today—a deposit of native copper, copper ores and related minerals such as malachite—is less than 20 kilometers from Çayönü Tepesi. In our excavation at the crest of the mound we noticed, from just below the surface downward, dozens of fragments of a bright green substance that we took to be malachite. Below the fourth occupation level we began to find actual artifacts made of malachite: drilled beads, a carefully smoothed but undrilled ellipsoid and a small tablet. Next we found part of a tool—one end of a reamer with a square cross section—that had been hammered into shape out of a lump of native copper. Finally we uncovered three tiny objects of copper that are perhaps analogous to the ordinary modern straight pin. In two of these pins, which do not appear to be complete, the metal had been abraded to form a point at one end; the third pin was pointed at both ends and was sharply bent [see illustration on page 113].

Metallurgy, of course, involves the hot-working of metals, including such arts as smelting, alloying, casting and forging. We are making no assertion that any kind of metallurgy, however primitive, existed at Çayönü Tepesi; there is not even any unanimity of opinion among the experts about whether the reamer, the only article that had certainly been hammered, was worked cold or hot. The fact remains that sometime just before 7000 B.C. the people of Çayönü Tepesi not only were acquainted with metal but also were shaping artifacts out of native copper by abrading and hammering.

What we suggest is that the Çayönü Tepesi copper reveals the moment in man's material progress when he may first have begun to sense the properties of metal as metal, rather than as some peculiar kind of stone. Looking back from the full daylight of our own age of metals, these first faint streaks of dawn are exciting to behold.

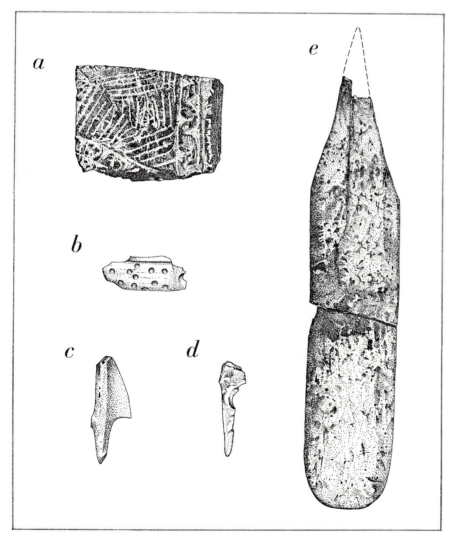

CRAFTSMANSHIP at Çayönü Tepesi included the decoration of stone bowls with incisions (a) and bone objects with drilled patterns (b). Drills flaked from flint (c, d) were used to work the bone. Bone awls (e) were probably used to produce wooden and leather items.

14

A NEOLITHIC CITY IN TURKEY

JAMES MELLAART
April 1964

Excavations on the Anatolian plateau of Turkey a few years ago provided an answer to an archaeological question of long standing about Neolithic culture. The Neolithic is the stage of civilization at which men began to cultivate crops and to domesticate animals and as a result of these activities to dwell in permanent settlements; in the Near East this stage occurred roughly between 7000 B.C. and 5000 B.C. The question was how Neolithic culture had moved from the Near East into Europe. The answer was that the movement was overland, by way of the Anatolian plateau. Such a route had long seemed to archaeologists a logical supposition, but until Neolithic communities were excavated on the plateau there had been no direct evidence to support the supposition [see "Hacilar: A Neolithic Village Site," by James Mellaart, SCIEN-TIFIC AMERICAN, August, 1961].

In answering one question, however, these excavations raised another: What were the origins of the culture of which Hacilar was representative? The Late Neolithic culture found at Hacilar had arrived there fully developed. The long gap between its arrival, probably about 6000 B.C., and the desertion of a pre-pottery village on the same site some 500 years earlier needed investigation. The gap appeared to correspond to the Early Neolithic period. If an Early Neolithic site could be excavated on the plateau, it might indicate the origin of the Hacilar culture and provide a longer culture sequence.

We had such a site in mind. I had found it about 30 miles southeast of the modern city of Konya in 1958: an ancient mound (*hüyük* in Turkish) bearing the name Çatal. The mound, covered with weeds and thistles, stood in the middle of a great plain. Lying on what

was once the bank of a river (now canalized into other channels to prevent flooding) that flows from the Taurus Mountains onto the plain, it rose gently from the fields to a height of 50 feet.

Çatal Hüyük seemed to be the most promising of some 200 sites we had visited on the Konya plain. A preliminary investigation indicated, to our delight, that the site belonged substantially, if not wholly, to the Early Neolithic period. Small fragments of pottery and broken obsidian arrowheads showed an unmistakable resemblance to those found in the deepest Neolithic levels at Mersin on the southern coast of Turkey, and at Çatal Hüyük they were on top of the mound. Moreover, the pottery looked more primitive than anything we had found at Hacilar.

So it was that Çatal Hüyük's 8,000 years of slumber came to an end on May 17, 1961, when our party began excavations. Ten days later the first Neolithic paintings ever found on man-made walls were exposed, and it was clear that Çatal Hüyük was no ordinary site. Succeeding excavations in 1962 and 1963 have confirmed this impression. With its story only partly revealed by the excavations to date, Çatal Hüyük has already added to the archaeological evidence that the development of towns and cities (as distinct from villages) goes farther back in antiquity than had been thought. Çatal Hüyük deserves the name of city: it was a community with an extensive economic development, specialized crafts, a rich religious life, a surprising attainment in art and an impressive social organization.

For the opportunity to explore this story we are indebted to several organizations. Our excavations have been supported by the Wenner-Gren Foundation for Anthropological Research, the Bol-

lingen Foundation, the British Academy, the University of London, the University of Edinburgh, the Royal Ontario Museum, the Australian Institute of Archaeology, the University of Canterbury in New Zealand and the late Francis Neilson. The Shell Oil Company and British Petroleum Aegean Limited provided technical help. Numerous other institutions have contributed in such ways as sending experts to the site or making analyses of material found at the site.

Çatal Hüyük covers 32 acres and so is easily the largest known Neolithic site, although how much of the site was occupied at any given period cannot be said with certainty. Apparently the settlement grew up from the riverbank, and the substantial part of the mound that spreads back from the river therefore dates from later phases of settlement. Our excavations, covering about one acre, have so far been concentrated on the southwest side of the mound, in a quarter that appears to have been sacred and residential. Because we have found nothing but finished goods in this area, we assume that the bazaar quarter with the workshops lies elsewhere in the mound.

With different quarters for different activities, a clear specialization in crafts and a social stratification that is obvious in both the size of the houses and the quality of burial gifts, this settlement was not a village of farmers, however rich. It was far more than that. In fact, its remains are as urban as those of any site from the succeeding Bronze Age yet excavated in Turkey.

We have found at Çatal Hüyük 12 superimposed building levels, which we have numbered from 0 to VI-A and VI-B to X according to their apparent

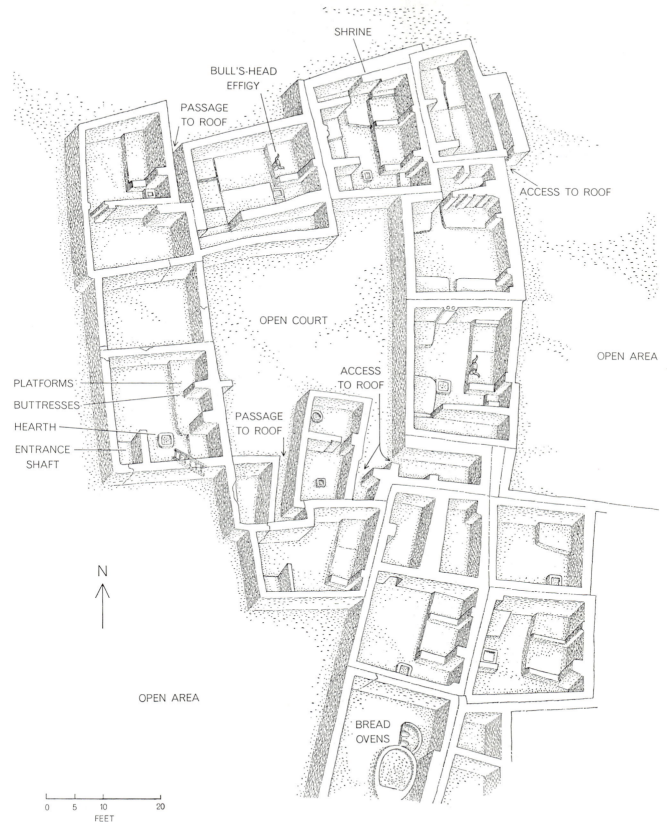

SHRINE

BULL'S-HEAD
EFFIGY

PASSAGE
TO ROOF

ACCESS TO ROOF

OPEN COURT

OPEN AREA

PLATFORMS

BUTTRESSES

HEARTH

ENTRANCE
SHAFT

ACCESS
TO ROOF

PASSAGE
TO ROOF

ACCESS
TO ROOF

N

OPEN AREA

BREAD
OVENS

0   5   10   20
FEET

COMMUNITY ARRANGEMENTS of 8,000 years ago in a Neo-lithic city are depicted on the basis of recent excavations. This is a reconstruction of an area in the fifth of 12 building layers so far found at the Çatal Hüyük site on the Anatolian plateau of Turkey.

Access to the buildings was solely from the roof, so that the exterior walls presented a solid blank face, which served effectively as a defense against both attackers and floods. Çatal Hüyük showed a surprising evolution of civilization for so early a community.

chronology from latest to earliest [*see illustration on page 125*]. All these levels belong to a single culture that was uninterrupted in development and shows no signs of destruction attributable to outside forces. The entire sequence so far discovered appears to cover the seventh millennium B.C., although radiocarbon dating of Çatal Hüyük materials now in progress at the University of Pennsylvania may provide a more precise time scale. The core of the mound, however, remains to be sounded, and a full 10 meters of deposit there may take the origins of Çatal Hüyük back to the end of the last continental glaciation.

Houses at Çatal Hüyük were built of shaped mud brick of standard sizes. Because the nearest stone was several

miles away and would have been difficult to bring to the site, the foundations of the houses also consist of mud brick, laid in several courses. By these foundations it is possible to recognize buildings even if their floors are gone, as is the case in Level 0. The houses were rectangular, usually with a small storeroom attached [*see illustration on preceding page*]. Apparently these dwellings were one-story structures, perhaps with a wooden veranda.

The houses show a remarkable consistency of plan inside. Along the east wall there were two raised platforms with a higher bench at the southern end. This arrangement constituted a "divan," used for sitting, working and sleeping. The smaller corner platform evidently belonged to the male owner and the

larger central platform to the women and children. This hierarchic convention appears from Level X to Level II and probably existed in Levels I and 0, of which little remains. There are numerous variations on this arrangement of built-in furniture, including situations in which platforms appear along the north or west wall. The hearth was invariably at the south end of the room, sometimes accompanied by an oven and less often by a kiln. There was a reason for this location of the fires: it had to do with the manner in which the houses were entered.

The entrance was, as in some American Indian villages, a hole in the roof, over which there was surely some sort of canopy-like shelter. The roof opening was always on the south side of the

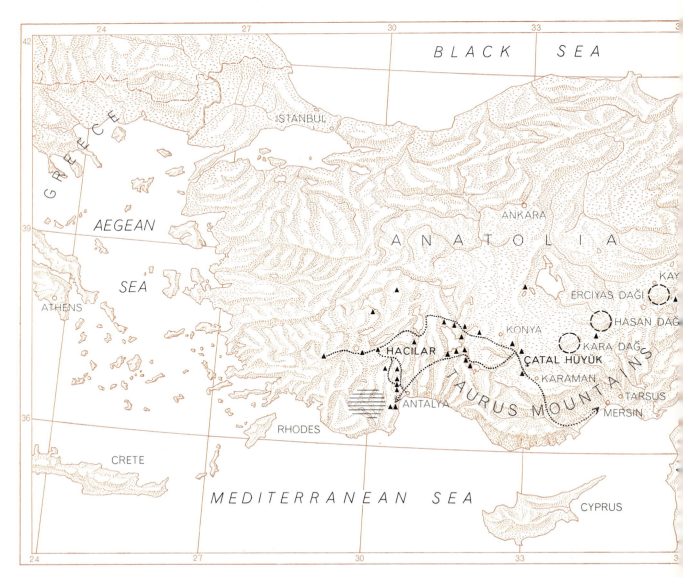

AREA OF NEAR EAST in which the culture represented by Çatal Hüyük was located is shown. Triangular symbols show Neolithic sites; circled areas indicate sources of obsidian; hatched areas, sources of flint. Çatal Hüyük was chosen for extensive archaeological work after excavations at Hacilar revealed a Late Neolithic culture that had arrived fully developed from some other place. Çatal

dwelling; thus it served both as a smoke hole and as an entrance. All access from the outside to the roof was by a movable ladder. From the roof into the dwelling the usual access was by a fixed ladder, although some buildings had another entrance through a well-plastered ventilation shaft that apparently had a movable ladder. Communication between dwellings was accomplished over the rooftops. There is little evidence of lanes and passages, and the courtyards that exist (often merely a ruined house) appear to have been used only for rubbish disposal and excreta.

The system of roof entrances meant that the outside of the settlement presented a solid blank wall. This was a check against enemies and also against

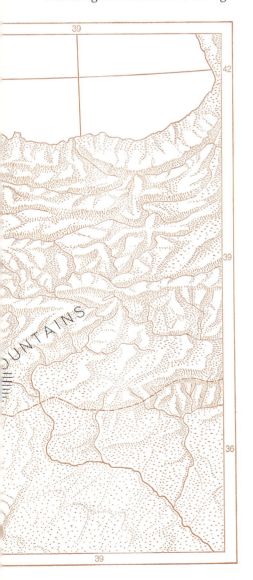

Hüyük apparently represents a culture that was a forerunner of Hacilar's and eventually may be traced back farther than 7000 B.C.

floods. It was evidently a successful defense system, as is indicated by the absence of any signs of massacre. About all any attackers could do—armed as they were with nothing more than bow and arrow, slings and stone tools—was to raid the cattle kept in corrals on the edge of the settlement or to set fire to the roofs. The defenders, in contrast, had the advantage of height and probably of superior numbers. In any case, because of the successful defense the only form of destruction suffered by Çatal Hüyük was fire. Most of the buildings in levels from VI to II were destroyed by fire; but with numerous hearths and ovens and the high winds of the region a disastrous fire about once a century is no more than could be expected.

As a result of these fires the carbonized remains of cereal grains and other foods are plentiful at Çatal Hüyük. There are also many animal bones. The food remains and the bones tell a great deal about the domestic economy of the settlement; the studies being made of them by the paleoethnobiologist Hans Helbaek of the National Museum of Denmark and the zoologist Dexter Perkins, Jr., of Harvard University will probably yield important additional information.

On the basis of what is now known Helbaek has described the grain finds as "the largest, richest and best preserved of all early cereal deposits so far recovered," providing "some of the most significant genetical and cultural" data yet obtained about early civilization. The grains, unlike the finds in other early Near Eastern settlements of cultivated plants little removed from their wild ancestors, include such hybrids and mutants as naked six-row barley and hexaploid free-threshing wheat, which were introduced into Europe from Anatolia in the sixth millennium B.C. The use made of the grains is indicated by the grain bins found in every house and the many mortars for dehusking and querns for grinding. In addition to cereals, peas and lentils the community grew bitter vetch and, some other crops; the residents also collected nuts, fruits and berries.

The zoological remains are no less interesting: they show the presence of domesticated sheep even below Level X and cows as early as Level VII. Goats and dogs also appear to have been domesticated, but there is no indication that pigs were. Their absence may be due to religious considerations. Although the domesticated animals provided the community with wool, milk, meat and

skins, the people had by no means abandoned hunting. Wild cattle and red deer were extensively hunted, as were wild asses, wild sheep, boars and leopards.

With such an abundant diet it is not surprising to find from the skeletons that the inhabitants were generally healthy. Bone disease was rare, teeth were good and this dolichocephalic (long-headed) people were fairly tall: the males ranged from about five feet six inches to five feet 10 and the females from five feet to five feet eight. Still, as is to be expected of such an ancient era, few individuals reached middle age.

The burials were inside the houses, beneath the platforms. Most of the skeletons we have found are those of women and children; presumably many of the males died away from home on hunting or fighting forays. The dead were buried in a contracted position, usually lying on their left side with feet toward the wall. Isolated burials were rare; some buildings contain several generations of a family, with 30 or more burials. It appears to have been the practice before final burial to strip the bodies of flesh by a preliminary interment, or by exposure to vultures, insects or microorganisms on an outdoor platform, sheltered by gabled structures built of reeds and mats. Thereafter the bones, still more or less held in position by the ligaments, were wrapped in cloth and given final burial, often being laid out on mats of cloth, skin or fur.

The burials provide information about the dress, weapons and jewelry of the Çatal Hüyük people. Male dress consisted of a loincloth or a leopard skin, fastened by a belt with a bone hook and eye; the men appear also to have worn cloaks fastened with antler toggles in the winter. The women wore sleeveless bodices and jerkins of leopard skin, with fringed skirts or string skirts—the ends of the string being encased in copper tubes for weighting. The women used bone pins for fastening garments.

Weapons buried with the men included polished stone maceheads, obsidian arrowheads and javelin heads and sometimes an obsidian spearhead. Frequently there was a fine flint dagger with a chalk or bone handle and a leather sheath.

Jewelry was mainly for the women and children. They wore the necklaces, armlets, bracelets and anklets we found made of beads and pendants in a great variety of stone, shell, chalk, clay, mother-of-pearl and (as early as Level IX) copper and lead. Cosmetics were

SITE OF NEOLITHIC CITY is this mound on the Anatolian plateau of Turkey. The Turkish word for mound is *hüyük*, and this one, which rises 50 feet above the plain, has the modern name of Çatal. After the inhabitants left about 6000 B.C. it lay deserted for 8,000 years; when excavations were started in 1961, it was heavily overgrown. In this photograph the view is from west of the site.

GENERAL VIEW OF EXCAVATIONS at Çatal Hüyük shows work in progress in Level VI, which is near the middle of the 12 levels of construction explored to date. The author chose Çatal Hüyük as the most promising of more than 200 sites he visited on the Anatolian plateau in a search for a representative Early Neolithic community. The site proved to have been a major settlement.

widely used, judging from the number of related articles we found, such as palettes and grinders for their preparation, baskets or the shells of fresh-water mussels for their containers and delicate bone pins for their application. The cosmetics probably consisted of red ocher, blue azurite, green malachite and perhaps galena. The women, once arrayed, used mirrors of highly polished obsidian to see the effect.

Several times we found food remains with the dead: berries, peas, lentils, eggs or a joint of meat put next to the deceased in baskets or in wooden bowls and boxes, which are carved with great delicacy. These wooden vessels are a characteristic of the Çatal Hüyük culture, and even when pottery began to appear in quantity around 6500 B.C., baskets and wooden bowls continued in use and had a strong influence on the pottery. The ovals and boat shapes, the lozenges and rectangles that appear in the pottery, not only from Level VI-A upward at Çatal Hüyük but also in the following Late Neolithic of Hacilar, have their origins in the wood-carving tradition of early Çatal Hüyük. In the same way numerous pottery vessels have features such as handles that derive from the earlier basketry.

The first production of pottery at Çatal Hüyük is found in Levels X and IX, but evidently this soft ware could not compete with traditional wood and woven products. It was not until the end of Level VI-A, when technical improvements had led to the production of an excellent hard baked ware, that pottery came into general use. The pottery was handmade and highly burnished. At first it was all dark brown or black; cooking pots were left that way but other objects were soon turned out in red, buff or mottled tones. In the upper levels of the mound animal heads start to appear on oval cups, and an over-all red slip, or coating, is in use, but painting on pottery was apparently never achieved. This pottery develops without a break into that of Late Neolithic Hacilar.

Another area in which Çatal Hüyük shows a people of remarkable technical competence and sophistication is textiles. We found some carbonized textiles in burials as far down as Level VI. They appear to have been wool, and at least three different types of weaving can be distinguished. These are the earliest textiles yet known; Helbaek has written of them that "we shall be hard put to it to find evidence of more perfect work anywhere within the following thousand years."

It is singular that with all these products of human workmanship we have found so few traces of the workmen. None of the 200 houses and shrines excavated so far has shown any evidence that any art or craft other than food preparation was carried on within. We have much fine woolen cloth but only one or two spindle whorls or loom weights, and these are from fill rather than from floor deposits. We have thousands of finely worked obsidian tools but only two small boxes of chips, thousands of bone tools but no piles of waste or splinters. Somewhere in the mound there must be the workshops of the weavers and basketmakers; the matmakers; the carpenters and joiners; the men who made the polished stone tools (axes and adzes, polishers and grinders, chisels, maceheads and palettes); the bead makers who drilled in stone beads holes that no modern steel needle can penetrate and who carved pendants and used stone inlays; the makers of shell beads from dentalium, cowrie and fossil oyster; the flint and obsidian knappers who produced the pressure-flaked daggers, spearheads, lance heads, arrowheads, knives, sickle blades, scrapers and

borers; the merchants of skin, leather and fur; the workers in bone who made the awls, punches, knives, scrapers, ladles, spoons, bowls, scoops, spatulas, bodkins, belt hooks, antler toggles, pins and cosmetic sticks; the carvers of wooden bowls and boxes; the mirror makers; the bowmakers; the men who hammered native copper into sheets and worked it into beads, pendants, rings and other trinkets; the builders; the merchants and traders who obtained all the raw material; and finally the artists—the carvers of statuettes, the modelers and the painters.

The unusual wealth of the city of Çatal Hüyük, as manifested by this great variety of sophisticated workmanship, is a phenomenon as yet without parallel in the Neolithic period. At the base of course lay the new efficiency of food production, transplanted from its probable origin in the hills to the fertile alluvial plain. Although that may account for the unprecedented size of the city, something else is needed to explain the community's almost explosive development in arts and crafts.

The key undoubtedly lies in the community's dependence on the import of

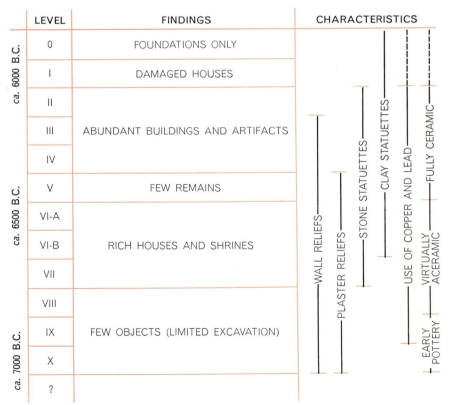

LEVEL		FINDINGS	CHARACTERISTICS
ca. 6000 B.C.	0	FOUNDATIONS ONLY	
	I	DAMAGED HOUSES	
	II	ABUNDANT BUILDINGS AND ARTIFACTS	
	III		
	IV		
ca. 6500 B.C.	V	FEW REMAINS	
	VI-A		
	VI-B	RICH HOUSES AND SHRINES	
	VII		
	VIII		
ca. 7000 B.C.	IX	FEW OBJECTS (LIMITED EXCAVATION)	
	X		
	?		

CHRONOLOGY OF HABITATION at Çatal Hüyük is indicated in this chart. Each level above VI-B apparently was built because of fire damage to the preceding level; the site appears to have been deserted after a fire in Level 0. Levels may yet be found below X.

EXCAVATED SHRINE is in Level VI. Three plaster heads of bulls appear atop one another on the west wall, with a half-meter scale below them; on the north wall is a ram's head made of plaster. At bottom right is the remaining part of a small pillar.

RECONSTRUCTED SHRINE is the same as that shown above. The drawing represents the author's conception, based on excavations of several shrines at Çatal Hüyük, of how the room might have looked in Neolithic times. The stylized heads of animals and women's breasts probably were fertility symbols. Many of the city's shrines also had wall paintings of remarkable sophistication.

raw materials (other than clay, timber and food) from near and far. One cannot possibly be wrong in suggesting that it was a well-organized trade that produced the city's wealth. Moreover, it appears likely that the trade in obsidian was at the heart of this extensive commerce. This black volcanic glass, which first appeared in the preceding Mesolithic period, became the most widespread trading commodity during the Neolithic period in the Near East. It has been found in the "proto-Neolithic" and prepottery Neolithic periods at Jericho; it occurs as far south as Beidha near Petra; it reached Cyprus in the sixth millennium. The origin of this obsidian, which was the best material of the time for cutting tools, was almost certainly central Anatolia, and it is extremely likely that the city of Çatal Hüyük controlled this source and organized the trade. The then active volcanoes of Hasan Dağ, Karaca Dağ, Mekke Dağ and others lie on the edge of the Konya plain. The nearest is some 50 miles east of Çatal Hüyük, and all are visible on a clear day. These sources of obsidian were well within the limits of the culture area of which Çatal Hüyük was the undisputed center.

This hegemony was not only economic but also religious and therefore political; in the ancient world no authority could exist without religious sanction. About the political system of Çatal Hüyük one can do little more than guess because there are no writings from the community. It seems likely, however, that at such an early stage of civilization only the priests could have been the bearers of authority.

Of the religious system one can say more because of the shrines and religious art we have found at Çatal Hüyük. In my view they constitute the community's most important archaeological contribution. I would maintain, perhaps wrongly, that the Neolithic religion of Çatal Hüyük (and of Hacilar) was created by women. In contrast to nearly all other earlier and later "fertility cults" of the Near East, it significantly lacks the element of sexual vulgarity and eroticism that is almost automatically associated with fertility and probably is the male's contribution. If the Çatal Hüyük religion is a creation of women, one has the rare opportunity of exploring Neolithic woman's mind by studying the symbolism she used in her effort to comprehend and influence the mysteries of life and death.

Of these symbols there is an abundance. In addition to schematic clay fig-

NEOLITHIC ARTIFACTS found at Level VI of Çatal Hüyük and dating from about 6500 B.C. include bone necklace, bone pin, stone beads, limestone bracelet and obsidian mirror.

WALL PAINTING found in Level VI shows children's hands. Çatal Hüyük yielded the earliest known paintings on man-made walls. Most of the painting had a religious purpose.

CLAY SEALS, most about the size of a postage stamp, apparently were used for identification. No house had more than one, and all the designs differed. These were in Levels II–IV.

STATUE OF GODDESS, done in clay and about eight inches high, shows her giving birth. Many representations of the goddess were found at Çatal Hüyük; this was in Level II.

urines of people and more naturalistic animal figures, there is a unique collection of fine statuettes. Those from the upper layers are modeled in clay; those in the lower layers are carved from stone. Beyond these, which together with burial rites are usually the archaeologist's only sources of information about religion, Çatal Hüyük has produced no fewer than 40 shrines and sanctuaries. They are at every level, but the nine in Level VI-A, the 12 in Level VI-B and the eight in Level VII are particularly rich in information. Wall decorations occur in most: painted scenes with numerous human figures in Levels III and IV; modeled and sometimes painted reliefs in Levels VI-A through X.

The shrines, although frequently large and well appointed, do not differ in plan from the houses, but they are much more lavishly decorated [*see illustration on page 126*]. Even if they were not continuously lived in, they served as burial places, presumably for their priestesses and the priestesses' families. It is only in the shrines that we have found reliefs and symbolism connected with life and death. From these it is possible to reconstruct in some degree the Neolithic pantheon.

The supreme deity was the Great Goddess. Often represented beside her are a daughter and a young son. A bearded god, who is always shown on a bull, was perhaps the Great Goddess' husband. No other deities appear. This group, therefore, probably constitutes the "holy family." Statues and reliefs represent the female deities either as two goddesses or as twins. The idea behind the duplication is evidently that of age and fertility, the whole aim of the religion being to ensure the continuity of life in every aspect: wildlife for the hunter, domesticated life for the civilized communities and finally the life of Neolithic man himself.

It is doubtful that Neolithic thought regarded these as four distinct deities. More likely the representations show aspects of the goddess as mother or as daughter and virgin, with the god as consort or son. The role of the male deity is more pronounced at Çatal Hüyük than it is at Hacilar, perhaps because in Çatal Hüyük hunting and the domestication of wild animals still held major importance, but in general the male plays a subsidiary role.

Scenes dealing with life are generally found on the west wall of the shrines. A typical scene shows the goddess giving birth to a bull or ram. Scenes dealing with death are found on the east wall: in three shrines the east-wall paintings show vultures attacking headless human corpses. Usually, however, the subject of death is expressed in more subtle ways. Representations of women's breasts, for example, which are of course symbolic of life, contained such items as the skulls of vultures, the lower jaws of wild boars and the heads of foxes and weasels—all scavengers and devourers of corpses.

The symbolism of west and east walls, or right and left, is matched by black and red: the red associated with life, the black with death. Panels of red hands are common, and several burial sites show remains of a coating of red ocher, which was evidently intended to be a substitute for blood and so a means of restoring life, at least symbolically. A great black bull covered the vulture paintings; both were symbolic of death. Contrasted with these was another painting of an enormous red bull surrounded by minute jubilant people.

There are some strange figures in the shrines. A stern-looking representation of the goddess was found with a headless bird, probably a vulture. Numerous figures roughly carved out of stalactites suggest a link with the dark world of caves, man's first refuge and sanctuary. An odd painting seems to represent a honeycomb with eggs or chrysalises on boughs and with bees or butterflies, which perhaps symbolize the souls of the dead. It is framed by alternate red and black hands along the top and gray and pink hands along the base. An earlier painting shows alternate red and black lines, resembling a net, similarly framed by hands. Net patterns decorate several other religious scenes, together

with symbols of horns, crosses and hands. Crosses, perhaps a simplified form of a four-petaled flower, were painted on a statuette of the goddess as well as on numerous walls; probably they are to be interpreted as fertility symbols. Rosettes and the double ax (or butterfly) are in the same category.

In several shrines and houses schematized heads of bulls in the form of a pillar serve as a cult symbol for protection. We have found curious benches with one, two, three or seven pairs of the bone cores of horns stuck in the sides. These defy explanation. Perhaps they figured in the burial rites, conceivably serving as a bier while the grave was dug.

Of the rites performed in the shrines little can be said. It is apparent, however, from the absence of blood pits and animal bones that there was no sacrificing of animals in the shrines. There were offerings of other kinds. In a shrine in Level II we found grain that had been burned on the plastered ceremonial altar and then covered by a new coat of plaster; this suggests the first offering after the harvest. In the earlier buildings, particularly in Level VI, there are offerings of all sorts: pots that doubtless contained food and drink; groups of hunting weapons, maces, axes and ceremonial flint daggers; tools; bags of obsidian; beads and many other objects, all unused or in pristine condition.

The wall paintings were mostly created for religious occasions and were covered with white plaster after they had outlived their usefulness. The paint was made of minerals mixed with fat; the painter worked with a brush on a white, cream or pale pink surface. The

range of colors is extensive. Red in all shades, including pink, mauve and orange, is predominant. The other colors are white, lemon yellow, purple, black and (very infrequently) blue. We have yet to find green. In a class apart from the religious paintings are several paintings of textile patterns, which attest the importance attached to weaving. Many of them show kilims, or woven carpets, making carpet weaving an art that can now be traced back to Neolithic times.

Many seasons of work remain at Çatal Hüyük. It is therefore premature to speak definitively about the origins of this remarkable civilization. It can be said, however, that the discovery of the art of Çatal Hüyük has demonstrated that the Upper Paleolithic tradition of naturalistic painting, which died in western Europe with the end of the ice age, not only survived but flourished in Anatolia. The implication is that at least part of the population of Çatal Hüyük was of Upper Paleolithic stock.

These people may not have been the first to learn the arts of cereal cultivation and animal husbandry, but they improved on the techniques to such an extent that they were able to produce the surplus of food that permits the beginning of leisure and specialization. By the seventh millennium they had created the first Mediterranean civilization, of which Çatal Hüyük is such an impressive representative. In time the offshoots of that civilization reached the Aegean shore, and by the sixth millennium Anatolian colonists were laying the foundations for the ultimate development of civilization in Europe.

III

BRONZE AGE CITIES AND CIVILIZATIONS

III

BRONZE AGE CITIES AND CIVILIZATIONS

INTRODUCTION

The readings in this section detail several of the major Bronze Age civilizations in the Old World: Sumerian, Harappan, Persian Gulf, Proto-Elamite, and Egyptian. The readings hardly exhaust the earliest civilizations that arose in the Old World. The Shang civilization of ancient China (1500 B.C.), the Minoan and Mycenaean civilizations of the Aegean and mainland Greece (1500 B.C.), the Zimbabwe of Africa (A.D. 1000), are but a few that are conspicuous by their absence.

Archaeologists have long been searching for a meaningful and inclusive definition for "civilization" and "city," which to many archaeologists are synonymous. The search has been an elusive one. In the early nineteenth century the stage of civilization was restricted to the Egyptian, Assyrian, Greek, and Roman peoples of antiquity who were reported on in the Bible. It has only been within the past hundred years that this list has been more than tripled. By archaeological excavations, the Sumerians, after 4,000 years of being "lost," were rediscovered, as the civilizations of the Minoans, Mycenaeans, Harappan, and Shang have also been since then. In fact, two of the papers included here reveal civilizations that we have only begun to appreciate within the past decade, the Persian Gulf and Proto-Elamite (see the articles by Glob and Bibby and by Lamberg-Karlovsky (in this section).

In 1877, Ernest de Sarzac, a French consul at Basra, Iraq, began digging at a large mound called Telloh; during the next quarter-century he exposed, after 4,000 years of silence, the Sumerians. In 1870 Heinrich Schliemann had begun digging at Hissarlik, a mound in western Turkey, and fulfilled his life-long dream: the discovery and excavation of Homeric Troy. Between his four archaeological campaigns at Troy, he excavated at Mycenae and Tiryns, and revealed to the world the civilization of the Mycenaeans, a civilization of Greek-speaking peoples that existed a thousand years before classical Greek culture. A few months before his unexpected death in 1890, Schliemann had requested from the government officials on Crete permission to undertake excavations on that island. His death prevented this undertaking. The first excavations on Crete were undertaken in 1899 by Arthur Evans, who after nine weeks of digging at Knossos uncovered a vast building, the palace of Minos, an ancient Cretan king. The next year he announced the existence of an early civilization on that island: the Minoan, after the palace that he had uncovered the year before. As recently as 1924, Sir John Marshall announced in the *Illustrated London News* that excavations at Moheno-daro and Harappa had revealed a prehistoric civilization that had been lost to our records of the past for millennia. Today we recognize the Harappan civilization as having the largest geographical distribution of all the Old World civilizations. In Asia the last civilization to be announced was discovered in 1928, when an expedition sponsored by the Academica Sinica and the Smithsonian Institution began to dig at Anyang and revealed the Bronze Age culture of China, identified as the Shang Dynasty of Chinese historians. As the readings in this section attest, archaeologists have spent much effort in the past few decades in excavating the remains of these civilizations and in attempting to understand their natures and the processes that began their formation and their eventual decline.

Let us return to the vexing problem of "what is civilization?" The Oxford English Dictionary defines it as "the active process of . . . being civilized," which of course begs the question, for what is "civilized"? The word civilization is by no means an old word or concept. Boswell reported that in 1772 he urged Johnson to insert the word "civilization" in his dictionary, but the doctor declined; he preferred the older word "civility," which in being derived from the Greek *civitas* reflects the world of the city dweller. V. G. Childe (who defined the Neolithic Revolution, as we saw in Part II) listed the elements that he believed were involved in man's transition from Neolithic communities to urban centers. In his books *Man Makes Himself* and *What Happened in History*, he provided a list of material inventions that he believed were responsible for transforming man into an urban dweller: writing, use of animals for traction, wheeled carts, the plough, metallurgy, standard units of weight and volume, sailing boats, surplus production, specialization of craftsmen, irrigation technology, and mathematics. Such a list is of very little help in defining a civilization, and it adds absolutely nothing to our understanding of how and why these inventions came about in the first place. We have already noted that at Neolithic Çayönü, *ca.* 7000 B.C. (see Çambel and Braidwood, page 113) there was metallurgy; sailing was already evident in Europe by 5000 B.C., as was irrigation at Neolithic Beidha; and specialized craftsmen may be posited for the artists of the Paleolithic. It is quite clear that neither a single criterion nor a list of criteria will succeed in defining civilization. Yet, if any single invention stands out as creating a dramatic change in social organization, I think it must be writing.

An attempt to define "civilization" made at a symposium held in 1958 at the Oriental Institute of the University of Chicago was perhaps more successful than others. (The proceedings of the symposium were published in 1960 in a book entitled *City Invincible*.) At that symposium, the anthropologist Clyde Kluckhohn argued that there were three essential criteria for civilization: (1) towns containing 5,000 or more people, (2) writing, and (3) monumental ceremonial centers. The Assyriologist C. Gelb stated, "I have reached the conclusion that writing is of such importance that civilization cannot exist without it, and, conversely, that writing cannot exist except in a civilization." With this I would agree, were it not for the Inca and Maya of the New World: civilizations that lacked full writing and yet cannot be denied the status of civilization, however one chooses to define the concept. Robert M. Adams (see his "Origin of Cities," page 137), an archaeologist and anthropologist, perhaps came closest to a working definition. He argued for the definition of civilization as a society with functionally interrelated sets of social institutions, which he listed as:

1. Class stratification, each stratum marked by a highly different degree of ownership or control of the main productive resources.
2. Political and religious hierarchies complementing each other in the administration of territorially organized states.
3. Complex division of labor, with full-time craftsmen, servants, soldiers, and officials existing alongside the great mass of primary, peasant producers.

Professor Adams' criteria concentrated thus on sociological phenomena that, when found working together, constitute a civilization.

Because the rapid advance of archaeological research is continually changing our understanding of man's past, five of the papers in this section merit additional comment: those dealing with the civilizations of the Sumerians, the Proto-Elamites, the Egyptians, the Harappans, and the Persian Gulf. All appear to have begun in the first half of the third millennium B.C. It can be fairly asked whether civilization was "invented" only once by a single people in a given geographical area, from where it was diffused to other areas, or whether we can support the independent invention of civilization by all five of the above cultures. Until recently it was argued that the Sumerians created writing and the first civilization, which, once established, was diffused throughout the Near East to distant India and Europe. However, today we know that the very different writing system of the Proto-Elamites is at least contemporary with, if not earlier than, the Sumerian (see the article by the Lamberg-Karlovskys). We have also recognized that explaining the rise of the different civilizations throughout the Old World as resulting from diffusion of the Sumerian "invention" is far too simplistic. Today a more complex model becomes necessary to understand the almost-simultaneous rise of civilization in different geographical areas with different cultures that evidence little if any cultural contact between them. We have come to realize that the "nuclear area" concept for the Neolithic is a fallacy; it would appear to be likewise a fallacy for the urban revolution.

A more complex model that has been recently advanced begins to provide a fuller understanding. This model sees the Sumerians of southern Mesopotamia, together with the Persian Gulf, Proto-Elamite, Egyptian, and Early Harappan civilizations as distinctive spheres of cultural interaction that were already separate polities by 3500 B.C.; these areas were already coordinating their distinctive specialized functions, manufacturing their own resources, establishing their own distinctive administrative centers, and maintaining a pattern of cultural and economic exchange among themselves. There is an increasing body of information, coming from sites like Tepe Yahyā (see the article by the Lamberg-Karlovskys) and even more distant Namazga Tepe in Soviet Turkmenistan, to support the contention that by 3500 B.C. all the distinctive cultures throughout western Asia were in contact with each other and that all shared distinctive sets of the interrelated phenomena that Adams used to define civilization. It must also be appreciated that this is some 500 years earlier than the date at which the Sumerians could be credited with the diffusion of civilization. This model supports none of the principal geographical areas (e.g., Mesopotamia) as "nuclear," none as peripheral (e.g., the Indus). Thus, Mesopotamia cannot be supported as the nuclear area generating the development toward civilization in all peripheral areas. Rather, it was the economic dialogue among *all* these areas that apparently stimulated the political and social development in each. Mesopotamia depended on outside resources that it entirely lacked and greatly demanded, e.g., timber, ores, stone, and such luxury items as lapis lazuli. The process (i.e., large-scale interregional trade) that led toward urban development cannot be wholly accounted for by the diffusion and adoption of the Mesopotamian Sumerian urban "stage."

Although we have expanded our geographical horizons and come to understand better the processes that gave rise to civilizations, we are still far from understanding the processes that brought about their demise. George Dales (see his article in this section) argues that a cataclysmic flood brought about the end of the city of Mohenjo-daro, surely one of the major cities of the Harappan civilization. The destruction of Mohenjo-daro by a natural phenomenon does not, however, explain the demise of the entire civilization, a civilization that spread over tens of thousands of square miles. Archaeologists have expended the vast majority of their energy so far in attempting to explain the origins of civilizations. It remains for those of the future to expend an equal effort in understanding the processes that led to the "deaths" of these civilizations.

ROYAL GRAVE OFFERINGS from later tombs at Ur indicate the concentration of wealth that accompanied the emergence of a kingly class. Dated at about 2500 B.C., the objects include large gold earrings (*top*); a headdress with gold leaves; beads of gold, lapis and carnelian; gold rings; a gold leaf; a hairpin of gold and lapis; an ornament with a gold pendant; an adz head of electrum.

15

THE ORIGIN OF CITIES

ROBERT M. ADAMS
September 1960

The rise of cities, the second great "revolution" in human culture, was pre-eminently a social process, an expression more of changes in man's interaction with his fellows than in his interaction with his environment. For this reason it marks not only a turning but also a branching point in the history of the human species.

Earlier steps are closely identified with an increasing breadth or intensity in the exploitation of the environment. Their distinguishing features are new tools and techniques and the discovery of new and more dependable resources for subsistence. Even in so advanced an achievement as the invention of agriculture, much of the variation from region to region was simply a reflection of local differences in subsistence potential.

In contrast the urban revolution was

MAP OF NIPPUR on a clay tablet dates from about 1500 B.C. Two lines at far left trace the course of Euphrates River; adjacent lines show one wall of the city. Square structures at far right are temples; the two vertical lines at right center represent a canal.

EARLY GRAVE OFFERINGS from Mesopotamian tombs of about 3900 B.C. consist mainly of painted pottery such as two vessels at left. Vessels of diorite (*center and right center*) and alabaster (*far right*), found in tombs of about 3500 B.C. and later, reflect growth of trade with other regions and increasing specialization of crafts. These vessels and objects on opposite page are in the University Museum of the University of Pennsylvania.

a decisive cultural and social change that was less directly linked to changes in the exploitation of the environment. To be sure, it rested ultimately on food surpluses obtained by agricultural producers above their own requirements and somehow made available to city dwellers engaged in other activities. But its essential element was a whole series of new institutions and the vastly greater size and complexity of the social unit, rather than basic innovations in subsistence. In short, the different forms that early urban societies assumed are essentially the products of differently interacting political and economic—human—forces. And the interpretive skills required to understand them are correspondingly rooted more in the social sciences and humanities than in the natural sciences.

Even the term urban needs qualification. Many of the qualities we think of as civilized have been attained by societies that failed to organize cities. At least some Egyptologists believe that civilization advanced for almost 2,000 years under the Pharaohs before true cities appeared in Egypt. The period was marked by the development of monumental public works, a formal state superstructure, written records and the beginnings of exact science. In the New World, too, scholars are still searching the jungles around Maya temple centers in Guatemala and Yucatán for recognizably urban agglomerations of dwellings. For all its temple architecture and high art, and the intellectual achievement represented by its hieroglyphic writing and accurate long-count calendar, classic Maya civilization apparently was not based on the city.

These facts do not detract from the fundamental importance of the urban revolution, but underline its complex character. Every high civilization other than possibly the Mayan did ultimately

produce cities. And in most civilizations urbanization began early.

There is little doubt that this was the case for the oldest civilization and the earliest cities: those of ancient Mesopotamia. The story of their development, which we will sketch here, is still a very tentative one. In large part the uncertainties are due to the state of the archeological record, which is as yet both scanty and unrepresentative. The archeologist's preoccupation with early temple-furnishings and architecture, for example, has probably exaggerated their importance, and has certainly given us little information about contemporary secular life in neighboring precincts of the same towns.

Eventually written records help overcome these deficiencies. However, 500 or more years elapsed between the onset of the first trends toward urbanism and the earliest known examples of cuneiform script. And then for the succeeding 700 or 800 years the available texts are laconic, few in number and poorly understood. To a degree, they can be supplemented by cautious inferences drawn from later documents. But the earliest chapters rest primarily on archeological data.

Let us pick up the narrative where Robert J. Braidwood left it in the article on page 71, with the emergence of a fully agricultural people, many of them grouped together in villages of perhaps 200 to 500 individuals. Until almost the end of our own story, dating finds little corroboration in written records. Moreover, few dates based on the decay of radioactive carbon are yet available in Mesopotamia for this crucial period. But by 5500 B.C., or even earlier, it appears that the village-farming community had fully matured in southwestern Asia. As a way of life it then stabilized internally for 1,500 years or more, although it con-

tinued to spread downward from the hills and piedmont where it had first crystallized in the great river valleys.

Then came a sharp increase in tempo. In the next 1,000 years some of the small agricultural communities on the alluvial plain between the Tigris and Euphrates rivers not only increased greatly in size, but changed decisively in structure. They culminated in the Sumerian city-state with tens of thousands of inhabitants, elaborate religious, political and military establishments, stratified social classes, advanced technology and widely extended trading contacts [see the article "The Sumerians," by Samuel Noah Kramer, beginning on page 145]. The river-valley agriculture on which the early Mesopotamian cities were established differed considerably from that of the uplands where domestication had begun. Wheat and barley remained the staple crops, but they were supplemented by dates. The date palm yielded not only prodigious and dependable supplies of fruit but also wood. Marshes and estuaries teemed with fish, and their reeds provided another building material. There was almost no stone, however; before the establishment of trade with surrounding areas, hard-fired clay served for such necessary agricultural tools as sickles.

The domestic animals—sheep, goats, donkeys, cattle and pigs by the time of the first textual evidence—may have differed little from those known earlier in the foothills and northern plains. But they were harder to keep, particularly the cattle and the donkeys which were needed as draft animals for plowing. During the hot summers all vegetation withered except for narrow strips along the watercourses. Fodder had to be cultivated and distributed, and pastureland was at a premium. These problems of management may help explain why the herds rapidly became a responsibility of people associated with the temples. And control of the herds in turn may have provided the stimulus that led temple officials frequently to assume broader control over the economy and agriculture.

Most important, agriculture in the alluvium depended on irrigation, which had not been necessary in the uplands. For a long time the farmers made do with small-scale systems, involving breaches in the natural embankments of the streams and uncontrolled local flooding. The beginnings of large-scale canal networks seem clearly later than the advent of fully established cities.

In short, the immediately pre-urban society of southern Mesopotamia consisted of small communities scattered along natural watercourses. Flocks had to forage widely, but cultivation was confined to narrow enclaves of irrigated plots along swamp margins and stream banks. In general the swamps and rivers provided an important part of the raw materials and diet.

Where in this pattern were the inducements, perhaps even preconditions, for urbanization that explain the precocity of the Mesopotamian achievement? First, there was the productivity of irrigation agriculture. In spite of chronic water-shortage during the earlier part of the growing season and periodic floods around the time of the harvest, in spite of a debilitating summer climate and the ever present danger of salinity in flooded or over-irrigated fields, farming yielded a clear and dependable surplus of food.

Second, the very practice of irrigation must have helped induce the growth of cities. It is sometimes maintained that the inducement lay in a need for centralized control over the building and maintaining of elaborate irrigation systems, but this does not seem to have been the case. As we have seen, such systems came after the cities themselves. However, by engendering inequalities in access to productive land, irrigation contributed to the formation of a stratified society. And by furnishing a reason for border disputes between neighboring communities, it surely promoted a warlike atmosphere that drew people together in offensive and defensive concentrations.

Finally, the complexity of subsistence pursuits on the flood plains may have indirectly aided the movement toward cities. Institutions were needed to medi-

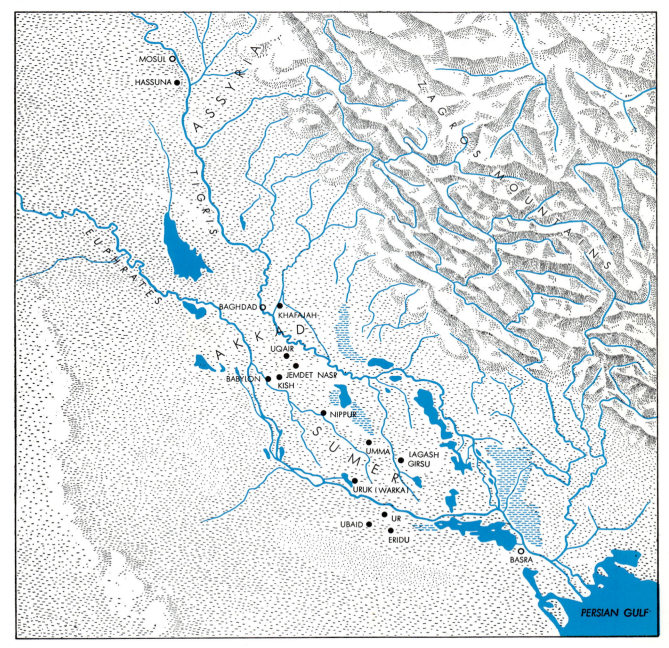

ANCIENT CITIES of Mesopotamia (*black dots*) were located mainly along Tigris and Euphrates rivers and their tributaries. In ancient times these rivers followed different courses from those shown on this modern map. Modern cities are shown as open dots.

CITY OF ERBIL in northern Iraq is built on the site of ancient city of Arbela. This aerial view suggests the character and appearance of Mesopotamian cities of thousands of years ago, with streets and houses closely packed around central public buildings.

ate between herdsman and cultivator; between fisherman and sailor; between plowmaker and plowman. Whether through a system of rationing, palace largesse or a market that would be recognizable to us, the city provided a logical and necessary setting for storage, exchange and redistribution. Not surprisingly, one of the recurrent themes in early myths is a rather didactic demonstration that the welfare of the city goddess is founded upon the harmonious interdependence of the shepherd and the farmer.

In any case the gathering forces for urbanization first become evident around 4000 B.C. Which of them furnished the initial impetus is impossible to say, if indeed any single factor was responsible. We do not even know as yet whether the onset of the process was signaled by a growth in the size of settlements. And of course mere increase in size would not necessarily imply technological or economic advance beyond the level of the village-farming community. In our own time we have seen primitive agricultural peoples, such as the Yoruba of western Nigeria, who maintained sizable cities that were in fact little more than overgrown village-farming settlements. They were largely self-sustaining because most of the productive inhabitants were full-time farmers.

The evidence suggests that at the beginning the same was true of Mesopotamian urbanization: immediate economic change was not its central characteristic. As we shall see shortly, the first clear-cut trend to appear in the archeological record is the rise of temples. Conceivably new patterns of thought and social organization crystallizing within the temples served as the primary force in bringing people together and setting the process in motion.

Whatever the initial stimulus to growth and reorganization, the process itself clearly involved the interaction of many different factors. Certainly the institutions of the city evolved in different directions and at different rates, rather than as a smoothly emerging totality. Considering the present fragmentary state of knowledge, it is more reasonable here to follow some of these trends individually rather than to speculate from the shreds (or, rather, sherds!) and patches of data about how the complete organizational pattern developed.

Four archeological periods can be distinguished in the tentative chronology of the rise of the Mesopotamian city-state. The earliest is the Ubaid, named for the first site where remains of this period were uncovered [*see map on page 139*]. At little more than a guess, it may have lasted for a century or two past 4000 B.C., giving way to the relatively brief Warka period. Following this the first written records appeared during the Protoliterate period, which spanned the remainder of the fourth millennium. The final part of our story is the Early Dynastic period, which saw the full flowering of independent city-states between about 3000 and 2500 B.C.

Of all the currents that run through the whole interval, we know most about religious institutions. Small shrines existed in the early villages of the northern plains and were included in the cultural inventory of the earliest known agriculturalists in the alluvium. Before the end of the Ubaid period the free-standing shrine had lost its original fluidity of plan and adopted architectural features that afterward permanently characterized Mesopotamian temples. The development continued into the Early Dynastic period, when we see a complex of workshops and storehouses surrounding a greatly enlarged but rigidly traditional arrangement of cult chambers. No known contemporary structures were remotely comparable in size or complexity to these establishments until almost the end of the Protoliterate period.

At some point specialized priests appeared, probably the first persons released from direct subsistence labor. Their ritual activities are depicted in Protoliterate seals and stone carvings. If not immediately, then quite early, the priests also assumed the role of economic administrators, as attested by ration or wage lists found in temple premises among the earliest known examples of writing. The priestly hierarchies continued to supervise a multitude of economic as well as ritual activities into (and beyond) the Early Dynastic period, although by then more explicitly political forms of organization had perhaps become dominant. For a long time, however, temples seem to have been the

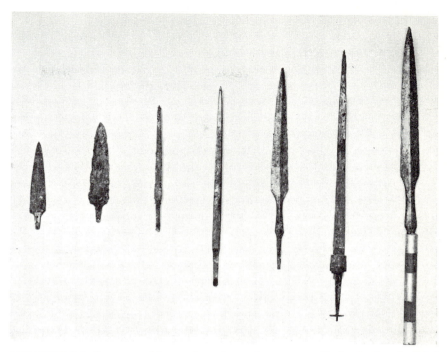

SPEARHEADS of copper and bronze from the royal cemetery at Ur date back to the third millenium B.C. The workmanship of these weapons matches that of the jewelry on page 138.

largest and most complex institutions that existed in the communities growing up around them.

The beginnings of dynastic political regimes are much harder to trace. Monumental palaces, rivaling the temples in size, appear in the Early Dynastic period, but not earlier. The term for "king" has not yet been found in Protoliterate texts. Even so-called royal tombs apparently began only in the Early Dynastic period.

Lacking contemporary historical or archeological evidence, we must seek the origins of dynastic institutions primarily in later written versions of traditional myths. Thorkild Jacobsen of the University of Chicago has argued persuasively that Sumerian myths describing the world of the gods reflect political institutions as they existed in human society just prior to the rise of dynastic authority. If so, they show that political authority in the Protoliterate period rested in an assembly of the adult male members of the community. Convoked only to meet sporadic external threat, the assembly's task was merely to select a short-term war leader.

Eventually, as the myths themselves suggest, successful war leaders were retained even in times of peace. Herein lies the apparent origin of kingship. At times springing up outside the priestly corporations, at times coming from them,

ROYAL WAR-CHARIOT carved on limestone plaque from city of Ur reflects increasing concern of Mesopotamian cities about methods of warfare in middle of third millennium B.C.

RELIGIONS of ancient Mesopotamia were dominated by the idea that man was fashioned to serve the gods. Here a worshipper followed by figure with pail brings a goat as an offering to goddess seated at right. A divine attendant kneels before her. This impression and the one below were made from stone cylinder-seals of Akkadian period (about 2400 B.C.).

new leaders emerged who were preoccupied with, and committed to, both defensive and offensive warfare against neighboring city-states.

The traditional concerns of the temples were not immediately affected by the new political leadership. Palace officials acquired great landed estates of their own, but the palace itself was occupied chiefly with such novel activities as raising and supplying its army, maintaining a large retinue of servants and entertainers and constructing a defensive wall around the city.

These undertakings took a heavy toll of the resources of the young city-states, perhaps too heavy to exact by the old "democratic" processes. Hence it is not surprising that as permanent, hereditary royal authority became established, the position of the assembly declined. In the famous epic of Gilgamesh, an Early Dynastic king of Uruk, the story opens with the protests of the citizenry over their forced labor on the city walls. Another episode shows Gilgamesh manipulating the assembly, obviously no longer

depending on its approval for his power. Rooted in war, the institution of kingship intensified a pattern of predatory expansionism and shifting military rivalries. The early Mesopotamian king could trace his origin to the need for military leadership. But the increasingly militaristic flavor of the Early Dynastic period also can be traced at least in part to the interests and activities of kings and their retinues as they proceeded to consolidate their power.

As society shifted its central focus from temple to palace it also separated into classes. Archeologically, the process can best be followed through the increasing differentiation in grave offerings in successively later cemeteries. Graves of the Ubaid period, at the time when monumental temples were first appearing, hold little more than a variable number of pottery vessels. Those in the cemetery at Ur, dating from the latter part of the Early Dynastic period, show a great disparity in the wealth they contain. A small proportion, the royal tombs

(not all of whose principal occupants may have belonged to royal families), are richly furnished with beautifully wrought weapons, ornaments and utensils of gold and lapis lazuli. A larger number contain a few copper vessels or an occasional bead of precious metal, but the majority have only pottery vessels or even nothing at all. Both texts and archeological evidence indicate that copper and bronze agricultural tools were beyond the reach of the ordinary peasant until after the Early Dynastic period, while graves of the well-to-do show "conspicuous consumption" of copper in the form of superfluous stands for pottery vessels even from the beginning of the period.

Early Dynastic texts likewise record social and economic stratification. Records from the main archive of the Baba Temple in Girsu, for example, show substantial differences in the allotments from that temple's lands to its parishioners. Other texts describe the sale of houseplots or fields, often to form great estates held by palace officials and worked by communities of dependent clients who may originally have owned the land. Still others record the sale of slaves, and the rations allotted to slaves producing textiles under the supervision of temple officials. As a group, however, slaves constituted only a small minority of the population until long after the Early Dynastic period.

Turning to the development of technology, we find a major creative burst in early Protoliterate times, involving very rapid stylistic and technical advance in the manufacture of seals, statuary and ornate vessels of carved stone, cast copper or precious metals. But the number of craft specialists apparently was very small, and the bulk of their products seems to have been intended only for cult purposes. In contrast the Early Dynastic period saw a great increase in production of nonagricultural commodities, and almost certainly a corresponding increase in the proportion of the population that was freed from the tasks of primary subsistence to pursue their craft on a full-time basis. Both stylistically and technologically, however, this expansion was rooted in the accomplishments of the previous period and produced few innovations of its own.

Production was largely stimulated by three new classes of demand. First, the burgeoning military establishment of the palace required armaments, including not only metal weapons and armor but also more elaborate equipment such as chariots. Second, a considerable vol-

GILGAMESH, early Mesopotamian king and hero of legend, may be figure attacking water buffalo (*right center*). Figure stabbing lion may be his companion, the bull-man Enkidu.

ume of luxury goods was commissioned for the palace retinue. And third, a moderate private demand for these goods seems to have developed also. The mass production of pottery, the prevalence of such articles as cylinder seals and metal utensils, the existence of a few vendors' stalls and the hoards of objects in some of the more substantial houses all imply at least a small middle class. Most of these commodities, it is clear, were fabricated in the major Mesopotamian towns from raw materials brought from considerable distance. Copper, for example, came from Oman and the Anatolian plateau, more than 1,000 miles from the Sumerian cities. The need for imports stimulated the manufacture of such articles as textiles, which could be offered in exchange, and also motivated the expansion of territorial control by conquest.

Some authorities have considered that technological advance, which they usually equate with the development of metallurgy, was a major stimulant or even a precondition of urban growth. Yet, in southern Mesopotamia at least, the major quantitative expansion of metallurgy, and of specialized crafts in general, came only after dynastic city-states were well advanced. While the spread of technology probably contributed further to the development of militarism and social stratification, it was less a cause than a consequence of city growth. The same situation is found in New World civilizations. Particularly in aboriginal Middle America the technological level remained very nearly static before and after the urban period.

Finally we come to the general forms of the developing cities, perhaps the most obscure aspect of the whole process of urbanization. Unhappily even Early Dynastic accounts do not oblige us with extensive descriptions of the towns where they were written, nor even with useful estimates of population. Contemporary maps also are unknown; if they were made, they still elude us. References to towns in the myths and epics are at best vague and allegorical. Ultimately archeological studies can supply most of these deficiencies, but at present we have little to go on.

The farming villages of the pre-urban era covered at most a few acres. Whether the villages scattered over the alluvial plain in Ubaid times were much different from the earlier ones in the north is unclear; certainly most were no larger, but the superficial appearance of

one largely unexcavated site indicates that they may have been more densely built up and more formally laid out along a regular grid of streets or lanes. By the end of the Ubaid period the temples had begun to expand; a continuation of this trend is about all that the remains of Warka and early Protoliterate periods can tell us thus far. Substantial growth seems to have begun toward the end of the Protoliterate period and to have continued through several centuries of the Early Dynastic. During this time the first battlemented ring-walls were built around at least the larger towns.

A few Early Dynastic sites have been excavated sufficiently to give a fairly full picture of their general layout. Radiating out from the massive public buildings of these cities, toward the outer gates, were streets, unpaved and dusty, but straight and wide enough for the passage of solid-wheeled carts or chariots. Along the streets lay the residences of the well-to-do citizenry, usually arranged around spacious courts and sometimes provided with latrines draining into sewage conduits below the streets. The houses of the city's poorer inhabitants were located behind or between the large multiroomed dwellings. They were approached by tortuous, narrow alleys, were more haphazard in plan, were less well built and very much smaller. Mercantile activities were probably concentrated along the quays of the adjoining river or at the city gates. The marketplace or bazaar devoted to private commerce had not yet appeared.

Around every important urban center rose the massive fortifications that guarded the city against nomadic raids and the usually more formidable campaigns of neighboring rulers. Outside the walls clustered sheepfolds and irrigated tracts, interspersed with subsidiary villages and ultimately disappearing into the desert. And in the desert dwelt only the nomad, an object of mixed fear and scorn to the sophisticated court poet. By the latter part of the Early Dynastic period several of the important capitals of lower Mesopotamia included more than 250 acres within their fortifications. The city of Uruk extended over 1,100 acres and contained possibly 50,000 people.

For these later cities there are written records from which the make-up of the population can be estimated. The overwhelming majority of the able-bodied adults still were engaged in primary agricultural production on their own holdings, on allotments of land received

from the temples or as dependent retainers on large estates. But many who were engaged in subsistence agriculture also had other roles. One temple archive, for example, records that 90 herdsmen, 80 soldier-laborers, 100 fishermen, 125 sailors, pilots and oarsmen, 25 scribes, 20 or 25 craftsmen (carpenters, smiths, potters, leather-workers, stonecutters, and mat- or basket-weavers) and probably 250 to 300 slaves were numbered among its parish of around 1,200 persons. In addition to providing for its own subsistence and engaging in a variety of specialized pursuits, most of this group was expected to serve in the army in time of crisis.

Earlier figures can only be guessed at from such data as the size of temple establishments and the quantity of craft-produced articles. Toward the end of the Protoliterate period probably less than a fifth of the labor force was substantially occupied with economic activities outside of subsistence pursuits; in Ubaid times a likely figure is 5 per cent.

It is not easy to say at what stage in the whole progression the word "city" becomes applicable. By any standard Uruk and its contemporaries were cities. Yet they still lacked some of the urban characteristics of later eras. In particular, the development of municipal politics, of a self-conscious corporate body with at least partially autonomous, secular institutions for its own administration, was not consummated until classical times.

Many of the currents we have traced must have flowed repeatedly in urban civilizations. But not necessarily all of them. The growth of the Mesopotamian city was closely related to the rising tempo of warfare. For their own protection people must have tended to congregate under powerful rulers and behind strong fortifications; moreover, they may have been consciously and forcibly drawn together by the elite in the towns in order to centralize political and economic controls. On the other hand, both in aboriginal Central America and in the Indus Valley (in what is now Pakistan) great population centers grew up without comprehensive systems of fortification, and with relatively little emphasis on weapons or on warlike motifs in art.

There is not one origin of cities, but as many as there are independent cultural traditions with an urban way of life. Southern Mesopotamia merely provides the earliest example of a process that, with refinements introduced by the industrial revolution and the rise of national states, is still going on today.

144

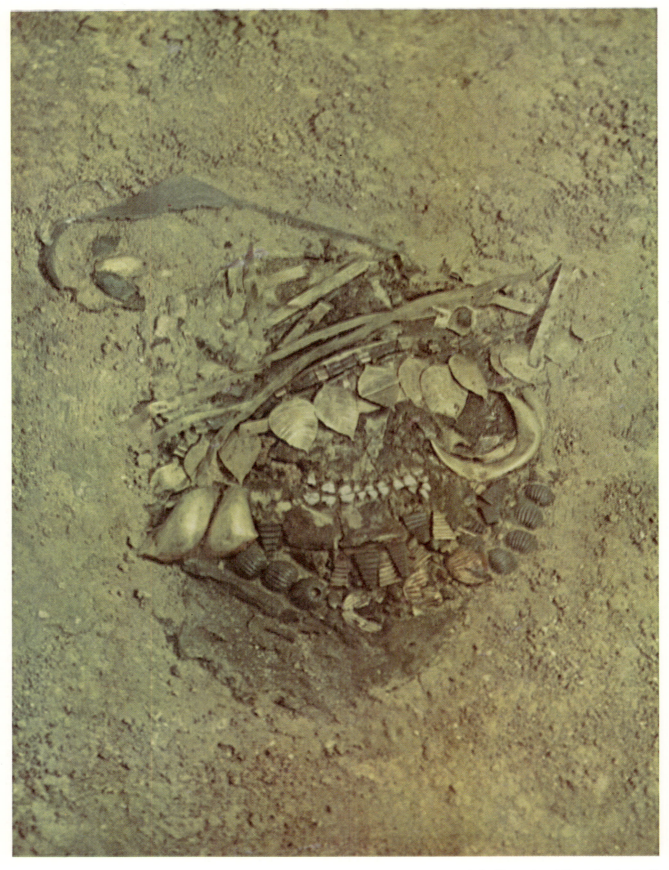

PARTLY EXCAVATED BURIAL of a lady-in-waiting to a Sumerian royal family of 2500 B.C. was moved intact from Ur to the University Museum of the University of Pennsylvania. Amid the rich ornaments of gold may be seen the teeth of their wearer.

16

THE SUMERIANS

SAMUEL NOAH KRAMER
October 1957

The Tigris-Euphrates plain is a hot, arid land. Six thousand years ago it was a wind-swept barren. It had no minerals, almost no stone, no trees, practically no building material of any kind. It has been described as a land with "the hand of God against it." Yet it was in this desolate region that man built what was probably the first high civilization. Here were born the inventions of writing, farming technology, architecture, the first codes of law, the first cities. Perhaps the very poverty of the land provided the stimulus that mothered these inventions. But the main credit must go to the people who created them—a most remarkable people called the Sumerians.

These Sumerians, as now revealed by long archaeological research, were a surprisingly modern folk. In many ways they were like the pioneers who built the U. S.—practical, ambitious, enterprising, jealous of their personal rights, technologically inventive. Having no stone or timber, they built with marsh reeds and river mud, invented the brick mold and erected cities of baked clay. They canalled the waters of the Tigris and Euphrates rivers into the arid fields and turned Sumer into a veritable Garden of Eden. To manage their irrigation systems they originated regional government, thus emerging from the petty social order of the family and village to the city-state. They created a written language and committed it to permanent clay tablets. They traded their grain surpluses to distant peoples for metals and other materials they lacked. By the third millennium B.C. the culture and civilization of Sumer, a country about the size of the state of Massachusetts, had spread its influence over the whole Middle East, from India to the Mediterranean. And there is hardly an area of our culture

today—in mathematics or philosophy, literature or architecture, finance or education, law or politics, religion or folklore—that does not owe some of its origins to the Sumerians.

One might suppose that the story of the Sumerians and their accomplishments would be one of the most celebrated in history. But the astonishing fact is that until about a century ago the modern world had no idea that Sumer or its people had ever existed. For more than 2,000 years they had simply vanished from the human record. Babylonia and ancient Egypt were known to every history student, but the earlier Sumerians were buried and forgotten. Now, thanks to a century of archaeological labor and to the Sumerians' own cuneiform tablets, we have come to know them intimately—as well as or better than any other people of the early history of mankind. The story of how the lost Sumerian civilization was discovered is itself a remarkable chapter. This article will review briefly how the history of the Sumerians was resurrected and what we have learned about them.

The Cuneiform Tablets

Modern archaeologists began to dig in Mesopotamia for its ancient civilizations around a century ago. They were looking for the cities of the Assyrians and Babylonians, who of course were well known from Biblical and Greek literature. As the world knows, the diggers soon came upon incredibly rich finds. At the sites of Nineveh and other ancient Assyrian cities they unearthed many clay tablets inscribed with the wedge-shaped writing called cuneiform. This script was taken to be the invention of the Assyrians. Since the Assyrians were apparently a Semitic people, the language was as-

sumed to be Semitic. But few clues were available for decipherment of the strange cuneiform script.

Then came a development which was to be as important a key to discovery in Mesopotamia as the famous Rosetta Stone in Egypt. In western Persia, notably on the Rock of Behistun, European scholars found some cuneiform inscriptions in three languages. They identified one of the languages as Old Persian, another as Elamite, and the third as the language of the Assyrian tablets. The way was now open to decipher the cuneiform writing—first the Old Persian, then the Assyrian, of which it was apparently a translation.

When scholars finally deciphered the "Assyrian" script, they discovered that the cuneiform writing could not have been originated by the Assyrian Semites. Its symbols, which were not alphabetic but syllabic and ideographic, apparently were derived from non-Semitic rather than Semitic words. And many of the cuneiform tablets turned out to be written in a language without any Semitic characteristics whatever. The archaeologists had to conclude, therefore, that the Assyrians had taken over the cuneiform script from a people who had lived in the region before them.

Who were this people? Jules Oppert, a leading 19th-century investigator of ancient Mesopotamia, found a clue to their name in certain inscriptions which referred to the "King of Sumer and Akkad." He concluded that Akkad was the northern part of the country (indeed, the Assyrians and Babylonians are now called Akkadians), and that Sumer was the southern part, inhabited by the people who spoke the non-Semitic language and had invented cuneiform writing.

So it was that the Sumerians were rediscovered after 2,000 years of oblivion. Oppert resurrected their name in 1869. In the following decades French, American, Anglo-American and German expeditions uncovered the buried Sumerian cities—Lagash, Nippur, Shuruppak, Kish, Ur (Ur of the Chaldees in the Bible), Erech, Asmar and so on. The excavation of ancient Sumer has proceeded almost continuously for three quarters of a century; even during World War II the Iraqi went on digging at a few sites. These historic explorations have recovered hundreds of thousands of Sumerian tablets, great temples, monuments, tombs, sculptures, paintings, tools, irrigation systems and remnants of almost every aspect of the Sumerian culture. As a result we have a fairly complete picture of what life in Sumer was like 5,000 years ago. We know something about how the Sumerians looked (from their statues); we know a good deal about their houses and palaces, their tools and weapons, their art and musical instruments, their jewels and ornaments, their skills and crafts, their industry and commerce, their *belles lettres* and government, their schools and temples, their loves and hates, their kings and history.

The Peoples of Sumer

Let us run quickly over the history. The area where the Sumerians lived is lower Mesopotamia, from Baghdad down to the Persian Gulf [*see the map at the right*]. It is reasonably certain that the Sumerians themselves were not the first settlers in this region. Just as the Indian names Mississippi, Massachusetts, etc., show that North America was inhabited before the English-speaking settlers came, so we know that the Sumerians were preceded in Mesopotamia by another people because the ancient names of the Tigris and Euphrates rivers (*Idigna* and *Buranun*), and even the names of the Sumerian cities (Nippur, Ur, Kish, etc.), are not Sumerian words. The city names must be derived from villages inhabited by the earlier people.

The same kind of clue—words that turn up in the Sumerian writing but are plainly not Sumerian in origin—tells us something about those first settlers in Sumer. As Benno Landsberger of the University of Chicago, one of the keenest minds in cuneiform research, has shown, among these pre-Sumerian words are those for farmer, herdsman, fisherman, plow, metal smith, carpenter, weaver, potter, mason and perhaps even

merchant. It follows that the predecessors of the Sumerians must already have developed a fairly advanced civilization. This is confirmed by excavations of their stone implements and pottery.

The dates of Sumer's early history have always been surrounded with uncertainty, and they have not been satisfactorily settled by tests with the new method of radiocarbon dating. According to the best present estimates, the first settlers occupied the area some time before 4000 B.C.; new geological evidence indicates that the lower Tigris-Euphrates Valley, once covered by the Persian Gulf, became an inhabitable land well before that date. Be that as it may, it seems that the people called Sumerians did not arrive in the region until nearly 3000 B.C. Just where they came from is in doubt, but there is some reason to believe that their original home had been in the neighborhood of a city called Aratta, which may have been near the Caspian Sea: Sumerian epic poets sang glowingly of Aratta, and its people were said to speak the Sumerian language.

Wherever the Sumerians came from, they brought a creative spirit and an extraordinary surge of progress to the land of Sumer. Uniting with the people who already inhabited it, they developed a rich and powerful civilization. Not long after they arrived, a king called Etana became the ruler of all Sumer: he is described in Sumerian literature as "the man who stabilized all the lands," and he may therefore be the first empire builder in human history. Sumer reached its fullest flowering around 2500 B.C., when its people had developed the cuneiform symbols and thereby originated their finest gift to civilization—the gift of written communication and history. Their own history came to an end some 800 years later: about 1720 B.C. In that year Hammurabi of Babylon won control of the country, and Sumer disappeared in a Babylonian kingdom.

Life in Sumer

The Sumerians' writings and disinterred cities, as I have said, make it possible to reconstruct their life in great detail. Their civilization rested on agriculture and fishing. Among their inventions were the wagon wheel, the plow and the sailboat, but their science and engineering went far beyond these elementary tools. For irrigation the Sumerians built intricate systems of canals, dikes, weirs and reservoirs. They developed measuring and surveying instru-

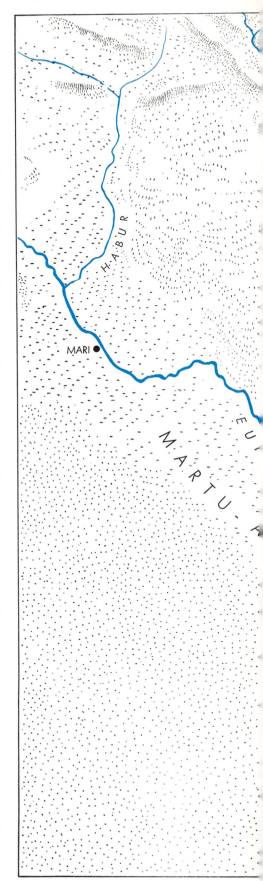

SUMER and its neighbors are located on this map of the area between modern

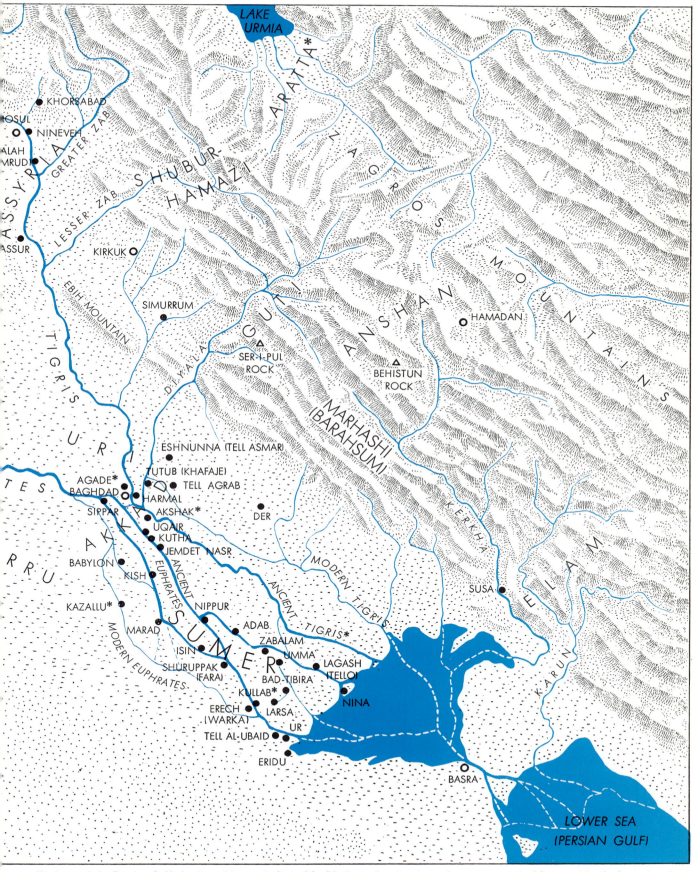

LAKE URMIA

ASSYRIA
KHORSABAD
MOSUL
NINEVEH
ALAH
NIMRUD
ASSUR

SHUBUR-HAMAZI

ARATTA *

ZAGROS

ANSHAN

GREATER ZAB
LESSER ZAB

KIRKUK

EBIH MOUNTAIN
TIGRIS

SIMURRUM

GUTI

DIYALA
SER-I-PUL ROCK

MOUNTAINS

HAMADAN

BEHISTUN ROCK

MARHASHI (BARAHSUM)

URI

ESHNUNNA (TELL ASMAR)
TUTUB (KHAFAJE)
AGADE *
BAGHDAD
SIPPAR
HARMAL
AKSHAK *
UQAIR
KUTHA
JEMDET NASR
BABYLON
KISH
KAZALLU *
EUPHRATES
MARAD
NIPPUR
ISIN
MODERN EUPHRATES
SHURUPPAK (FARA)
KULLAB *
ERECH (WARKA)
TELL AL-UBAID
ERIDU

TELL AGRAB
AKKAD

DER

ANCIENT EUPHRATES
MODERN TIGRIS
ANCIENT TIGRIS *

ADAB
ZABALAM
UMMA
LAGASH (TELLO)
BAD-TIBIRA
NINA
LARSA
UR

SUMER

KERKHA

SUSA

ELAM

KARUN

BASRA

LOWER SEA (PERSIAN GULF)

Turkey and the Persian Gulf. Ancient cities are indicated by black dots; modern cities, by open dots. Cities and areas whose exact location is not known are marked by asterisks. In Sumerian times a large fresh-water lake lay beyond the head of the Persian Gulf.

SUMERIAN TABLETS are inscribed with cuneiform signs. At upper left is the medical tablet of which a section is shown on the cover (about 2000 B.C.). At upper right is a fragment of the epic poem "Enmerkar and the Lord of Aratta" (about 1800 B.C.). At lower left is part of the law code of Hammurabi (about 1700 B.C.). At lower right is a textile inventory (about 1950 B.C.).

ments, and a sexagesimal number system (*i.e.*, based on the number 60) with a place notation device not unlike our decimal system. Their farming was highly sophisticated: among their tablets is a veritable farmer's almanac of instructions in agriculture.

In the crafts, the Sumerians' inventions included the potter's wheel, metal casting (of copper and bronze), riveting, soldering, engraving, cloth fulling, bleaching and dyeing. They manufactured paints, leather, cosmetics, perfumes and drugs. Prescriptions recorded on some of their tablets show that the Sumerian physician had command of a large assortment of *materia medica*, prepared from plants, animals and inorganic sources.

Although the Sumerians' economy was primarily agricultural, their life was centered mainly in the cities. Here lived many of the farmers, herdsmen and fishermen, as well as merchants, craftsmen, architects, doctors, scribes, soldiers and priests. Artisans and traveling merchants sold their products in the central town market, and were paid in kind or in money—usually silver coin in the form of a disk or ring. The dozen or so cities in Sumer probably ranged from 10,000 to 50,000 in population. Each was enclosed by a wall and surrounded with suburban villages and hamlets.

The dominant feature of every Sumerian city was a massive temple mounted on a high terrace. It usually had the form of a ziggurat, Sumer's most distinctive contribution to religious architecture. This is a pyramidal tower with a series of ascending terraces winding around the outside. To break the unattractive blankness of the temple's mud-brick walls, the Sumerian architects introduced buttresses and recesses, and they also beautified the building with columns decorated in colored mosaics. Inside the temple were rooms for the priests and a central shrine with a niche for the statue of the god. Each city in Sumer had a different tutelary god, and the Sumerians considered the city the god's property. Thus the city of Nippur, for example, belonged to Enlil, the god of the air. Nippur became Sumer's chief religious and cultural center, and Enlil was elevated to the highest rank as father of all the gods.

Originally the cities were governed by the citizens themselves, presided over by a governor of their selection. On all important decisions the citizens met in an assembly divided into two chambers —the "elders" and the "men." But for military reasons they gradually relin-

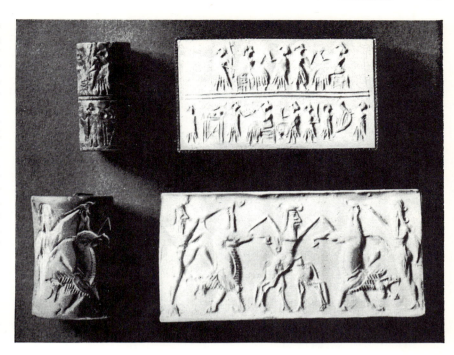

TWO SUMERIAN CYLINDER SEALS are shown at left. Impressions were made with the seals by rolling them over wet clay. At right are two impressions made by this method.

quished this democratic system. Each city acquired a ruler—at first elected, later hereditary—who organized its defense against the other cities and against foreign invaders. In the course of time the king rivaled the city's religious leaders in wealth and influence. The rulers of Sumer's dozen or so city-states also contended with one another for control of the whole country, and the history of Sumer is largely a record of bitter conflicts among its cities, which eventually led to its downfall.

The life of the individual citizen in a Sumerian city was remarkably free and prosperous. The poorest citizen managed to own a farm and cattle or a house and garden. To be sure, slavery was permitted, and a man could sell his children or his entire family to pay off his debts. But even slaves had certain legal rights: they could engage in business, borrow money and buy their freedom. (The average price for an adult slave was 10 shekels— less than the price of an ass.) The great majority of Sumerians were free citizens, going about their business and the pursuit of happiness with a minimum of restrictions. This did not, however, apply to children, who were under the absolute authority of their parents, could be disinherited or sold into slavery, and had to marry mates chosen by the parents. But in the normal course of events Sumerian families cherished their children and were knit closely together by love

and mutual obligations. Women had many legal rights, including the right to hold property and engage in business. A man could divorce his wife on comparatively slender grounds, or, if they had no children, he was allowed to take a second wife.

Most Sumerian families lived in a one-story, mud-brick house consisting of several rooms grouped around an open court. The well-to-do had two-story houses of about a dozen rooms, plastered and whitewashed inside and out; these houses boasted servants' rooms and sometimes even a private chapel. Often the house had a mausoleum in the basement where the family buried its dead. The Sumerians believed that the souls of the dead traveled to a nether world where existence continued more or less as on earth. They therefore buried pots, tools, weapons and jewels with the dead. When a king died, the palace sometimes buried with him some of his courtiers and servants and even his chariot and animals.

Sumerian men were often clean-shaven, but many of them wore a long beard and had long hair parted in the middle. In early times their usual dress was a flounced skirt and felt cloak; later these were replaced by a long shirt and a big fringed shawl draped over the left shoulder, leaving the right arm bare. The common dress for women was a long shawl covering the body from head to foot, except for the right shoulder. Women usually braided their hair into a heavy pigtail and wound it around the head, but on important occasions they wore elaborate headdresses consisting of ribbons, beads and pendants.

Music apparently occupied a large place in the life of the Sumerians—at home, in school and in the temple. Beautifully constructed harps and lyres were found in the royal tombs at Ur. Research has also turned up references to drums, tambourines, reed and metal pipes, and hymns written on tablets. Some of the important personages in the palaces and temples of the Sumerian cities were musicians.

The Sumerians cannot be said to have produced any great art, but they did show considerable skill in carving and sculpture. Perhaps their most original contribution to the graphic arts was the cylinder seal—a stone cylinder with a carved design which was impressed in clay by rolling the cylinder over it. These designs, or seals, appear on clay tablets, jar covers and so on. They depict scenes such as a king on the battlefield, a shepherd defending his flock from wild beasts, heraldic arrangements of animals. Eventually the Sumerians settled on one favorite seal design which became almost their trademark—a scene showing a worshipper being presented to a god by his personal good angel.

Religion

The Sumerians lived by a simple, fatalistic theology. They believed that the universe and their personal lives were ruled by living gods, invisible to mortal

EARLIEST PICTOGRAPHS (3000 B.C.)	DENOTATION OF PICTOGRAPHS	PICTOGRAPHS IN ROTATED POSITION	CUNEIFORM SIGNS CA. 1900 B.C.	BASIC LOGOGRAPHIC VALUES		ADDITIONAL LOGOGRAPHIC VALUES		SYLLABARY (PHONETIC VALUES)
				READING	MEANING	READING	MEANING	
	HEAD AND BODY OF A MAN			LÚ	MAN			
	HEAD WITH MOUTH INDICATED			KA	MOUTH	KIRI₃ ZÚ GÙ DUG₄ INIM	NOSE TEETH VOICE TO SPEAK WORD	KA ZÚ
	BOWL OF FOOD			NINDA	FOOD, BREAD	NÍG GAR	THING TO PLACE	
	MOUTH + FOOD			KÚ	TO EAT	ŠAGAR	HUNGER	
	STREAM OF WATER			A	WATER	DURU₅	MOIST	A
	MOUTH + WATER			NAG	TO DRINK	EMMEN	THIRST	
	FISH			KUA	FISH			KU₆ HA
	BIRD			MUŠEN	BIRD			HU PAG
	HEAD OF AN ASS			ANŠE	ASS			
	EAR OF BARLEY			ŠE	BARLEY			ŠE

EVOLUTION OF SUMERIAN WRITING is outlined in the chart at left. The earliest pictographs were inscribed vertically on tablets. Around 2800 B.C. the direction of this writing was changed from vertical to horizontal, with a corresponding rotation of the pictographs. The pictographs were now reduced to collections of linear strokes made by a stylus which had a triangular point. Some of these cuneiform signs are logographic, i.e., each sign represents a spoken word. Some of the signs represent more than one word;

eyes. The chief gods were those of water, earth, air and heaven, named respectively Enki, Ki, Enlil and An. From a primeval sea were created the earth, the atmosphere, the gods and sky, the sun, moon, planets and stars, and finally life. There were gods in charge of the sun, moon and planets, of winds and storms, of rivers and mountains, of cities and states, of farms and irrigation ditches, of the pickax, brick mold and plow. The major gods established a set of unchangeable laws which must be obeyed willy-nilly by everything and everybody.

Thus the Sumerians were untroubled by any question of free will. Man existed to please and serve the gods, and his life followed their divine orders. Because the great gods were far away in the distant sky and had more important matters to attend to, each person appealed to a particular personal god, a "good angel," through whom he sought salvation. Not that the people neglected regular public devotions to the gods. In the Sumerian temples a court of professionals, including priests, priestesses, musicians and eunuchs, offered daily libations and sac-

rifices of animal and vegetable There were also periodic feasts and ce brations, of which the most important was a royal ceremony ushering in each new year.

This ceremony is traceable to the cycle of nature in Mesopotamia. Every summer, in the hot, parched months, all vegetation died and animal life languished. In the autumn the land began to revive and bloom again. The Sumerian theology explained these events by supposing that the god of vegetation retired to the nether world in the summer and returned to the earth around the time of the new year; his sexual reunion with his wife Inanna, the goddess of love and procreation, then restored fertility to the land. To celebrate this revival and ensure fecundity, the Sumerians each year staged a marriage ceremony between their king, as the risen god, and a priestess representing the goddess Inanna. The marriage was made an occasion of prolonged festival, ritual, music and rejoicing.

The Sumerians considered themselves to be a chosen people, in more intimate contact with the gods than was the rest of mankind. Nevertheless they had a moving vision of all mankind living in peace and security, united by a universal faith and perhaps even by a universal language. Curiously, they projected this vision into the past, into a long-gone golden age, rather than into the future. As a Sumerian poet put it:

Once upon a time there was no snake,
*   there was no scorpion,*
There was no hyena, there was no lion,
There was no wild dog, no wolf
There was no fear, no terror,
Man had no rival.

Once upon a time . . .
The whole universe, the people in unison,
To Enlil in one tongue gave praise.

To students of the ancient religions of the Near East, much of the Sumerian cosmology and theology is easily recognizable. The order of the universe's creation, the Job-like resignation of sinful and mortal man to the will of the gods, the mystic tale of the dying god and his triumphant resurrection, the Aphrodite-like goddess Inanna, the ideals of "humaneness"—these and many other features of the Sumerian creed survive without much change in the later religions of the ancient world. Indeed, the very name of the Sumerian dying god, Dumuzi, endures as Biblical Tammuz, whose descent to the nether regions was still

CUNEIFORM SIGNS	TRANSLITERATION	TRANSLATION
	AMA-AR-GI₄	FREEDOM
	ARHUŠ	COMPASSION
	DINGIR	GOD, GODDESS
	DUB-SAR	SCRIBE
	É-DUB-BA	SCHOOL, ACADEMY
	HÉ-GÁL	PLENTY, PROSPERITY
	ME	DIVINE LAWS
	NAM-LÚ-LU₇	HUMANITY, HUMANENESS
	NAM-LUGAL	KINGSHIP
	NAM-TAR	FATE, DESTINY
	NÍG-GA	PROPERTY
	NÍG-GE-NA	TRUTH
	NÍG-SI-SÁ	JUSTICE
	SAG-GÍG	BLACK-HEADED ONES, THE SUMERIAN PEOPLE
	UKKIN	ASSEMBLY

some are syllabic, *i.e.*, they also represent syllables. The accents and subscript numbers on the modern transliteration of the cuneiform signs are used by modern scholars to distinguish between signs having the same pronunciation but different meanings. In the chart at right are 15 cuneiform words, their transliteration and their English translation.

STATUETTES show the appearance of the Sumerians. The four statuettes at left, made about 2500 B.C., were found at Tutub (modern Khafaje). The statuette at right, made about 1850 B.C., was found at Ur. It represents Princess Enannatumma, high priestess

mourned by the women of Jerusalem in the days of the prophet Ezekiel. It is not too much to say that, with the decipherment of the Sumerian tablets, we can now trace many of the roots of man's major religious creeds back to Sumer.

Cuneiform

But the Sumerians' chief contribution to civilization was their invention of writing. Their cuneiform script is the earliest known system of writing in man's history. The cuneiform system served as the main tool of written communication throughout western Asia for some 2,000 years—long after the Sumerians themselves had disappeared. Without it, mankind's cultural progress would certainly have been much delayed.

The Sumerian script began as a set of pictographic signs devised by temple administrators and priests to keep track of the temple's resources and activities. They inscribed the signs in clay with a reed stylus, and this accounts for the curious wedge-shaped characters. In the course of the centuries Sumerian scholars developed the signs into purely phonetic symbols representing words or syllables.

More than 90 per cent of the tablets that have been excavated in Sumer are economic, legal and administrative documents, not unlike the commercial and governmental records of our own day. But some 5,000 of the finds are literary works: myths and epic tales, hymns and lamentations, proverbs, fables, essays. They qualify as man's oldest known literature—nearly 1,000 years older than the *Iliad* and the Hebrew Bible. In addition the tablets include a number of Sumerian "textbooks," listing the names of trees, birds, insects, miner-

als, cities, countries and so forth. There are even commemorative narratives which constitute mankind's first writing of history.

From the Sumerians' invention of writing grew the first formal system of education—another milestone in human intellectual progress. They set up "professional" schools to train scribes, secretaries and administrators; in time these vocational schools became also centers of culture where scholars, scientists and poets devoted their lives to learning and teaching.

The head of the school was called "the school father"; the pupils, "school sons." Among the faculty members were "the man in charge of drawing," "the man in charge of Sumerian," "the man in charge of the whip." There was no sparing of the rod. The curriculum consisted in copying and memorizing the lists of

of the moon-god Nanna and sister of Lipit-Ishtar, king of Isin. Enannatumma presided at some of the most important reconstruction of Ur after it had been destroyed by the Elamites.

record was Lugalannemundu of the city of Adab; he is reported to have ruled 90 years and to have controlled an empire extending far beyond Sumer. But his empire also fell apart, and a king of Kish named Mesilim became the dominant figure in Sumer. Later rule over the country was won by the city of Lagash. The last ruler of the Lagash dynasty, a king named Urukagina, has the distinction of being the first recorded social reformer. He suppressed the city's harsh bureaucracy, reduced taxes, and brought relief to widows, orphans and the poor. One of King Urukagina's inscriptions contains the word "freedom"—the first appearance of this word in man's history. But within less than 10 years a king of the neighboring city of Umma overthrew Urukagina and put the city of Lagash to the torch.

The Fall of Sumer

The cities' incessant struggle for power exhausted Sumer. A Semitic people from the west, under the famous warrior Sargon the Great, marched into the country and established a new dynasty. Sargon founded a capital called Agade (from which came the name Akkadian) and made it the richest and most powerful city in the Middle Eastern world. He conquered almost all of western Asia and perhaps also parts of Egypt and Ethiopia. Sargon's sons held on to the empire, but his grandson, Naramsin, brought Sumer to disaster. For reasons unknown, he destroyed the holy city of Nippur, and soon afterward he was defeated by semibarbaric invaders from the mountains of Iran who overran Sumer and completely wiped out the city of Agade.

It took the Sumerians several generations to recover. But their civilization did come to life again, under a governor of Lagash named Gudea, whose face is the best known to us of all the Sumerians because a score of statues of him have been found in the ancient temples of Lagash. Gudea re-established contacts and trade with the rest of the known world and put Sumer on the path to prosperity. After Gudea, however, the rivalry among its cities broke out again and became Sumer's final undoing. The city of Ur, under a king named Ur-Nammu, defeated Lagash; Ur-Nammu founded a new rule called the Third Dynasty of Ur. It was to be Sumer's last dynasty.

Ur-Nammu was a strong and benevolent ruler. According to inscriptions that have recently come to light, he removed "chiselers" and grafters and established

words and names on the textbook tablets, in studying and composing poetic narratives, hymns and essays and in mastering mathematical tables and problems, including tables of square and cube roots.

Teachers in ancient Sumer seem to have been treated not unlike their counterparts in the U. S. today: their salaries were low and they were looked upon with a mixture of respect and contempt. The Sumerians were an aggressive people, prizing wealth, renown and social prestige. As their tablets suggest, they were far more concerned with accounts than with academic learning.

Their restless ambition and aggressive spirit are reflected in the bitter rivalry among their cities and kings. The history of Sumer is a story of wars in which one city after another rose to ascendancy over the country. Although there are many gaps in our information, we can

reconstruct the main outlines of that history from references in the tablets. The first recorded ruler of Sumer, as I have mentioned, was Etana, king of Kish. Probably not long afterward a king of Erech by the name of Meskiaggasher founded a dynasty which ruled the whole region from the Mediterranean to the Zagros Mountains northeast of Sumer. The city of Kish then rose to dominance again, only to be supplanted by the city of Ur, whose first king, Mesannepadda, is said to have ruled for 80 years and made Ur the capital of Sumer. After Mesannepadda's death, Sumer again came under the rule of the city of Erech, under a king named Gilgamesh who became the supreme hero of Sumerian history—a brave, adventurous figure whose deeds were celebrated throughout the ancient world of western Asia. The next great ruler who appears in the

AREA AROUND NIPPUR, one of the principal cities of Sumer *(see map on pages 146 and 147)*, is covered with barren dunes today. Six thousand years ago much of the area was similarly barren. The Sumerians and their predecessors made it fertile by irrigation.

NIPPUR WAS EXCAVATED in 1951 and 1952 by a joint expedition of the University Museum of the University of Pennsylvania and the Oriental Institute of the University of Chicago. In this photograph the houses of Nippur's scribal quarter are uncovered.

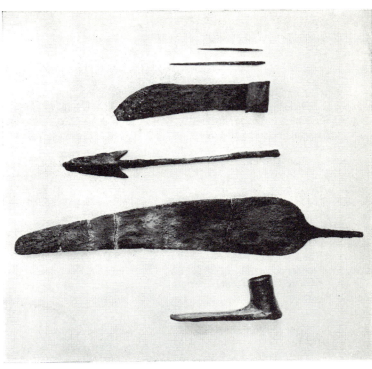

ARTIFACTS at left are Sumerian stone weights. The weight at top is one *mana* (505 grams); the weight at bottom, one *gin* (8.416 grams); the weight in middle, one *gin* 160 *shē* (15.896 grams).

At right is a group of copper and bronze tools and weapons. They are, from top to bottom, two bronze drills, a copper axhead, a copper spearhead, a copper saw blade and a bronze adzhead.

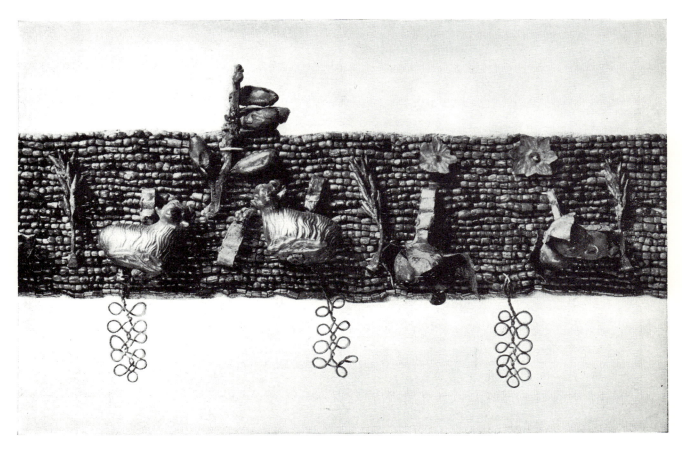

DIADEM of Queen Shub-Ad, who lived about 2500 B.C., was found in the royal cemetery of Ur. The horizontal band of the diadem is fashioned out of beads of lapis lazuli. Mounted on the band are tiny leaves, fruits, flowers and figures of rams, all made of gold.

a law code which insured honest weights and measures and took care that the poor should not "fall a prey to the wealthy." Ur-Nammu's code is especially significant for the fact that instead of the barbarous rule of "an eye for an eye and a tooth for a tooth" common among early societies it established a money fine as punishment for assaults.

In spite of Sumer's civilized kings and prosperity, time was running out for the Sumerians. Their internal rivalries and the growing pressure of surrounding peoples soon overwhelmed them. Semitic nomads from the Arabian desert to the west (the Amorites of the Bible) took over the Sumerian cities of Isin, Larsa and Babylon. Ur itself was conquered by the Elamites to the east, who carried off its last king, Ibbi-Sin. In the following two and a half centuries the Semitic rulers of Isin and Larsa, and then Larsa and Babylon, struggled for control of the country. Finally, in about the year 1720 B.C., Hammurabi defeated Rim-Sin, the last king of Larsa, and Babylon emerged as the dominant city of southern Mesopotamia. The Sumerians were submerged by the Semites and lost their identity as a people. In time their name was erased from the memory of man; the Sumerian language disappeared as a living, spoken tongue, though for centuries it continued to be the written language studied in schools.

The Sumerians firmly believed that when man died, his emasculated spirit descended to a dark, dreary nether world. The spirit and fame of this proud, vigorous people certainly suffered a remarkable eclipse after their empire fell. But what their minds created survives throughout the living corpus of present-day civilization: it appears in the form of a Biblical proverb, a statutory law, a heroic folktale, an Aesopic fable, a zodiacal sign, a Euclidean theorem, the weight of a coin, the degree of an angle. And in the cuneiform tablets which were the Sumerians' pre-eminent gift we have found the earliest intellectual record of man's strivings toward civilization.

EDITOR'S NOTE

The author wishes to thank the following individuals for their generous cooperation and help in the presentation of this article: F. G. Rainey, A. V. Kidder, Robert Dyson, Edmund I. Gordon, Jane Kohn, and the Board of Managers of the University Museum of the University of Pennsylvania.

17

THE DECLINE OF THE HARAPPANS

GEORGE F. DALES
May 1966

Four thousand years ago the world's first three civilizations were flourishing. The Sumerians of Mesopotamia and the Egyptians of the Nile valley are reasonably well known to us. The third civilization embraced an area more extensive than either Egypt or Mesopotamia, yet it is far less known. Its most impressive remains—the dead cities of Mohenjo-daro and Harappa in the Indus valley of what is now West Pakistan—were first excavated four decades ago [see "A Forgotten Empire of Antiquity," by Stuart Piggott; SCIENTIFIC AMERICAN, November, 1953]. Our knowledge of this remarkable culture of South Asia, which is called the Harappan civilization, has been limited until recently to what could be gleaned from archaeological findings at these two sites, mainly because the written records of the culture are scanty and not yet deciphered. New discoveries in both Pakistan and India, however, are now adding much to our understanding of certain events in Harappan times.

In the past few years many Harappan towns and villages have been discovered well outside the civilization's nucleus in the Indus basin, indicating that the Harappan state extended much farther than earlier investigators had realized. It is now known that Harappan authority reached westward at least to the modern border between Iran and Pakistan, that it touched the foothills of the Himalayas to the north, even extending to the headwaters of the Ganges, and that it stretched southward along the west coast of India as far as the Gulf of Cambay to the north of modern Bombay. The Harappan civilization thus controlled or dominated a triangle roughly 1,000 miles on a side [*see illustration on next page*]. A series of carbon-14 dates from Harappan sites

along the coast of India also shows that many of these southerly towns and trading posts had continued to be occupied much later than the sites in the Indus valley. This and other bits of unexplained evidence have raised doubts concerning a fundamental hypothesis about the Harappan civilization: that Harappa and Mohenjo-daro had been sacked, and the Harappan civilization liquidated or absorbed, by the Aryan invaders who presumably brought the Indo-European language and culture to prehistoric India sometime during the second millennium B.C.

With the intention of learning more about the life and death of Harappan civilization the University of Pennsylvania and the Pakistan Government Department of Archaeology agreed on a joint reopening of the Mohenjo-daro site during the winter of 1964–1965. The expedition undertook, as part of a three-year program, to determine the total depth of the site's deposits of human occupation, something earlier workers had been unable to establish because groundwater lies only 15 feet below the surface of the plain at Mohenjo-daro. Efforts were made to devise some means of excavating these flooded occupation levels and to analyze evidence at the site, in the form of abundant accumulations of water-deposited silt, that the city had more than once been exposed to major floods.

During its mature period, from a few centuries before to a few centuries after 2000 B.C., the city of Mohenjo-daro housed an estimated 40,000 inhabitants in an area about a mile square. Today its ruins consist of two parts; a western mound that contains the so-called citadel is separated by a broad gully from a much larger eastern mound that con-

tains the lower town [*see illustration on page 159*]. At the southwest corner of the lower-town mound an undisturbed area rises some 35 feet above the surrounding plain. In 1964 this area was selected for excavation in the hope of obtaining a sequence of stratified materials that could be correlated with the artifacts unearthed by earlier expeditions.

As a start it was decided to sink drill holes straddling the selected area to discover the depth of the earliest occupation levels. Core samples were collected at two-foot intervals; before the drills struck sterile soil 39 feet of core containing evidence of occupation had been raised to the surface. Thus the total depth of occupation in this part of Mohenjo-daro is 74 feet, about the equivalent of a seven-story building. Of the entire deposit, the deepest and therefore the earliest 24 feet (or almost a third) is still not available for study because of groundwater.

In the 1920's and 1930's, when the first digging was done at Mohenjo-daro, carbon-14 dating techniques were unknown and the only firm evidence of the city's antiquity came from the discovery of a few Harappan artifacts, principally stone seals, in ancient Mesopotamian sites. The Harappan seals found in reliably dated Mesopotamian strata belonged to a period extending from about 2350 B.C. to about 1800 B.C. The early investigators concluded that Mohenjo-daro and Harappan civilization in general had flourished during this same period. The carbon-14 dates now available for a number of Harappan and pre-Harappan sites tend to confirm this dating but also suggest that from 50 to 100 years might be added at each end of the period. When several new carbon samples collected from late levels at Mohenjo-daro in 1964–1965 are analyzed, they should establish the date when that city—and civilization in the southern Indus valley—met its end.

Before discussing why and how Harappan civilization declined, something should be said about its origins. No formative phase, or early stage, of Harappan culture has yet been positively identified in the archaeological record of South Asia, although current excavations in Pakistan and India are beginning to yield some clues. Numerous pre-Harappan cultures have been found in the hills and valleys of Baluchistan, to the west of the Indus valley. Pre-Harappan groups also lived in the Indus valley itself just before Harappan culture appeared there in mature form. The Baluchistan sites have strong ties with Afghanistan and the Near East,

but their relation to the origin and development of Harappan civilization is little understood. The same is true of the civilization's precursors in the Indus basin. At sites such as Amri, Kot-diji and Kalibangan materials belonging to the mature Harappan phase are found mixed with materials from late phases of the indigenous cultures. Such findings suggest that Harappan civilization arrived full-blown from some other area. At the same time earlier levels of these and other pre-Harappan Indus sites contain objects that are characteristic of Harappan civilization in its maturity. These findings argue either for an on-the-spot evolution from one culture to the other or, at the very least, for heavy borrowing from the local inhabitants by the Harappans when they first settled in the Indus valley. Perhaps the 24 feet of

waterlogged occupation layers at Mohenjo-daro, containing as they should a record of the city's earliest development, will help to illuminate this question of Harappan origins.

The problem of the decline and disappearance of Harappan civilization has been a matter of primary concern during the expedition's first two years of work. One of the discoveries made at Mohenjo-daro in the 1920's that is cited in support of the hypothesis that Aryan invaders destroyed the Harappan civilization was the presence of some 30 human skeletons in what appeared to be the upper levels of the site. The bodies had evidently been left where they fell rather than receiving burial; this seemed a dramatic archaeological confirmation of the postulated invasion and massacre. In 1964 the poorly preserved remains of five more bodies were unearthed in

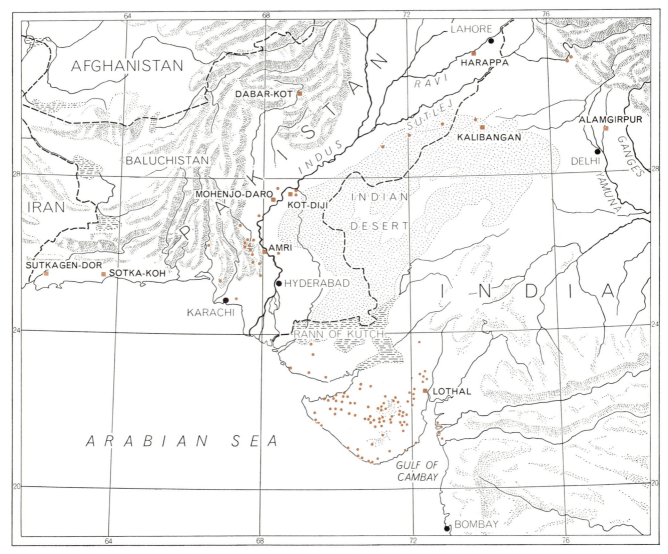

HARAPPAN CIVILIZATION at its maturity some 4,000 years ago controlled a triangular territory with sides roughly 1,000 miles long. The Indus valley was its central focus; Harappa, near modern Lahore, and Mohenjo-daro to the south were its great cities.

the upper levels of the excavation, only two to three feet below the surface of the mound. They lay in a narrow alley amid an accumulation of collapsed brick, broken pottery and ash. The period to which these dead belong is evidently late, but it has not yet been precisely determined. The fact that they had not had any normal kind of burial suggests that all five were the victims of some common disaster. Nonetheless, we are reluctant to believe that either the earlier discoveries or our own support the hypothesis of an Aryan invasion. For one thing, no one has any exact knowledge of the date when the Aryans first entered the Indus valley area; they have not yet been identified archaeologically. For another, the sole purpose served by the invasion hypothesis is to explain the demise of Harappan civilization. If evidence can be found that Mohenjo-daro declined for other reasons, the invasion hypothesis goes by the board. Such evidence, in the form of traces of catastrophic floods, is now being subjected to close scrutiny.

The presence of water-deposited silts at Mohenjo-daro had been recognized by early workers at the site as an indication that floods had played a role in the city's history, but no one suggested that the silts represented anything more significant than periodic brief overflows of the Indus River. Excavators who later worked at such sites to the south of Mohenjo-daro as Amri and Chanhu-daro found abundant evidence of flooding in these areas also. It was not until 1940, however, that anyone suggested a relation between the archaeological evidence of ancient floods and a number of topographic and geological anomalies of the Indus valley. In that year the Indian paleontologist M. R. Sahni noticed silt deposits perched many feet above the level of the Indus plain near the city of Hyderabad in what is now West Pakistan. This and other evidence suggested to him that the area's ancient floods had not been mere river overflows but events on a far larger scale. Major tectonic upheavals, Sahni proposed, might have blocked the Indus River from time to time; each such stoppage would have caused the gradual formation of a huge upstream lake that might then have persisted for decades.

Sahni's suggestion went virtually unnoticed until 1960. By that time two totally independent lines of research had led to the identical conclusion: natural disasters must have played a major

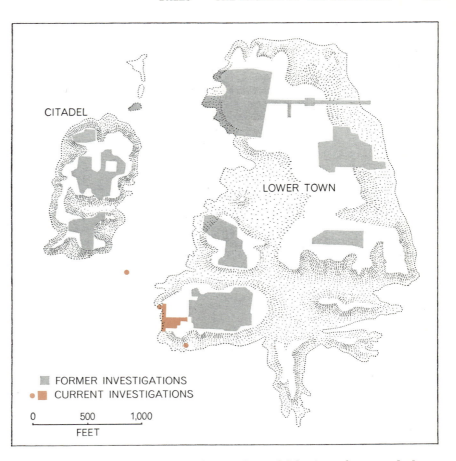

URBAN AREA of Mohenjo-daro is divided into the citadel district to the west and a larger district, called the lower town, to the east. The part of the lower town that was excavated in 1964 and the location of three test borings are shown in color. In this part of the site the culture-bearing strata are 72 feet thick; 24 feet of the accumulation is under water.

role in the decline of Harappan civilization. In that year the University Museum undertook an archaeological survey of the Arabian Sea coast of West Pakistan. The field party discovered settlements of the Harappan era that had clearly been seaports but were now located as far as 30 miles inland. These displaced ports made it evident that the coastline in this part of Pakistan had risen considerably during the past 4,000 years, with the initial rise apparently having occurred during the Harappan period. In the same year Robert L. Raikes, a hydrologist, was conducting extensive surveys in southern Baluchistan and the lower Indus valley. Raikes's keen antiquarian interests led him to investigate the possibility that ancient topographic changes in the area might well be related to the decline of Harappan civilization. The mutual desire to combine archaeological evidence with the findings of another discipline led to a joining of forces. Raikes is now working with the Mohenjo-daro expedition as engineering consultant and is

in charge of geological and hydrological investigations.

Just as Sahni had been puzzled by the silts near Hyderabad, so Raikes in 1964 sought an explanation for the thick silt deposits that are preserved in the ruins of Mohenjo-daro at points as high as 30 feet above ground level. The 1964 test borings that revealed the thickness of the underlying archaeological strata at the site showed that silt deposits also existed below the surface of the plain. When the layers above ground are added to those below, the silts sandwiched between the city's successive occupation levels span a vertical distance of 70 feet. A better explanation than occasional floods is obviously needed to account for such a multilevel accumulation.

Raikes's preliminary research not only suggests that the dam-and-lake hypothesis proposed 25 years ago by Sahni is tenable but also singles out an area near Sehwan, some 90 miles downstream from Mohenjo-daro, as the most probable area of tectonic disturbance

EXCAVATORS' HANDICAP at Mohenjo-daro is the presence of groundwater near the surface of the plain. This cut was made to un- cover the bottom of the city wall (brickwork at rear). The work was halted by flooding at a depth of only 15 feet below the plain level.

affecting the city. Both at Mohenjo-daro and at smaller sites between the city and Sehwan the silt deposits are of the kind characteristic of still-water conditions in a lake rather than the kind deposited by the fast-moving waters of a flooded river. Moreover, there is abundant geological evidence of rock faulting on a large scale near Sehwan. The faulting by itself could have raised a natural dam and turned the upstream portion of the Indus into a slow-filling lake. More probably, however, the same disturbances that caused the faulting were accompanied by massive extrusions of mud, aided by the pressure of accumulated underground gases. Such mud extrusions are not uncommon in Pakistan even today; for example, a number of mud islands abruptly appeared off the Arabian Sea coast in 1945.

Let us assume that some such barrier was thrown up near Sehwan. Thereafter the normal discharge of the Indus would not have reached the sea but instead would have accumulated in a steadily growing reservoir [*see illustration at right*]. As the rising waters encroached on the valley's villages and towns, many small settlements undoubtedly disappeared below the surface and were completely obliterated by silt. When the waters approached such a major population center as Mohenjo-daro, however, it seems logical to suppose that efforts were made to protect the city. The archaeological evidence strongly suggests that large-scale community projects were indeed undertaken at Mohenjo-daro for this purpose. As an example, massive mud-brick platforms were erected and faced with fired brick, apparently with the objective of raising the level of the city safely above the lake waters. One such embankment, partially excavated by the expedition in 1964, is some 70 feet wide and well over 25 feet high [*see top illustration on following page*].

Eventually the waters accumulating behind the natural dam would have risen until they had spilled over it and begun to cut it away. Thereafter the Indus would have resumed its normal flow to the sea and re-erosion of the silt-covered floodplain would have begun. After each immersion the inhabitants of Mohenjo-daro found it necessary to rebuild or reinforce most of the city's buildings. Although they usually rebuilt directly on top of the older foundations and walls, they eventually encountered serious problems of decay and sinking. The ruins today dramatical-

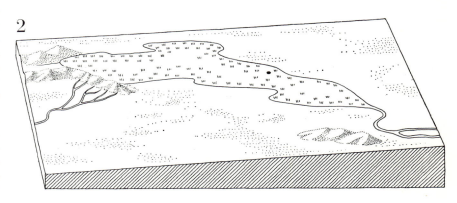

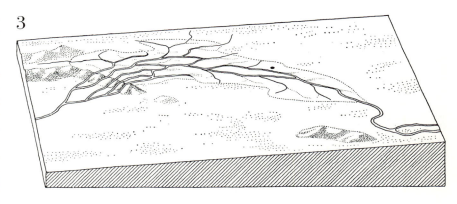

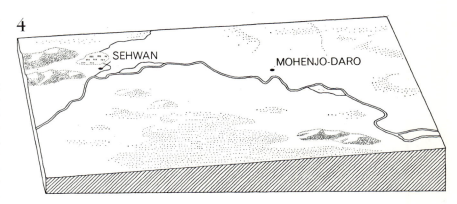

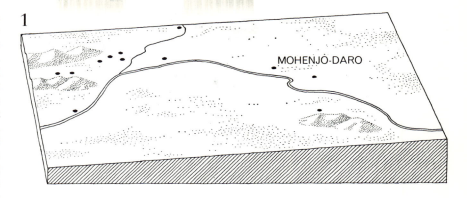

PERIODIC FLOODING of Mohenjo-daro and other Harappan settlements in the Indus River valley was apparently caused by geologic disturbances in the vicinity of modern Sehwan. In *1* the Indus follows an unhindered course to the sea (*south is at left, north at right*). In *2* a massive mud extrusion or a rock fault dams the river and produces a shallow, marshy lake upstream, flooding Mohenjo-daro. In *3* the lake waters have topped the barrier; as it erodes, the lake empties. In *4* the cycle is complete and the valley is habitable again.

FLOOD COUNTERMEASURES taken at Mohenjo-daro included the construction of massive brick embankments to keep the level of the city above water. A pit (*center*) was dug down through 25 feet of unfired brick in one such embankment without reaching bottom.

FLOOD DAMAGE at Mohenjo-daro is evidenced by slumping brick masonry (*center*), which presumably reflects erosion of the city's unfired brick foundations during their prolonged immersion in lake water. The Harappans simply leveled masonry and built on top of it.

ly illustrate the problems they faced [*see bottom illustration on opposite page*].

Both the multiple layers of silt at Mohenjo-daro and the evidence of multilevel reconstruction suggest that the city was flooded in this prolonged and damaging fashion no less than five times and perhaps more. At present it is impossible to estimate just how long each cycle of lake intrusion and withdrawal may have lasted, but it seems doubtful that the duration of any one cycle would have exceeded 100 years.

Could such a series of natural catastrophes, rather than the Aryan invasion, have brought about the collapse of Harappan civilization? The city of Harappa itself and lesser sites in the Indus valley to the north of Mohenjo-daro do not seem to have ever suffered significant flooding. Instead they give the appearance of having been abruptly abandoned, after which they stood empty for centuries. Such a pattern is certainly compatible with the invasion hypothesis. It is also compatible with a situation in which the Harappan state's weakened heartland to the south was unable to send help to the inhabitants of the northern frontier when they were threatened. The people who presented the threat could quite well have been hill raiders rather than Aryan invaders. An archaeological fact must also be taken into account in any effort to reconstruct the Harappan demise: The northern Indus sites show no evidence of a decline in material prosperity before their abandonment but quite the opposite is true of Mohenjo-daro and other southern sites. What does this contrast signify?

The mature phase of Harappan civilization at Mohenjo-daro appears to have degenerated into a well-defined late phase that in turn fades into a squatter phase. Both the materials and style of later artifacts and the quality of later architecture demonstrate a gradual process of degeneration. The traditional Harappan painted pottery of the mature phase, with its intricate black-on-red designs, is replaced in the late phase by plain unpainted ware. In contrast to the typical seals of the mature phase, carved out of soapstone and superbly engraved with animal figures in negative relief, the late-phase seals are not made of soapstone and bear only a few simple geometric designs. The deftly executed and spirited animal figurines of the mature phase are replaced by much cruder effigies. Even the buildings erected during the squatter phase reflect the same

degeneration: they are jerry-built and often made of broken or secondhand bricks. These examples of diminishing prosperity in the south, or at least of a debasement in the Harappan civilization's standard of values, suggest an associated breakdown in the efficiency of state administration. Perhaps not only Harappan prosperity but also the Harappan spirit was being mired in an unrelenting sequence of invading water and engulfing silt.

What was the final fate of the Harappans? Findings at more than 80 Harappan sites recently identified in the Gujarat area of India provide a partial answer. A majority of the Indian sites belong to the late phase of Harappan civilization, but the culture had also been present in force in this area during its mature phase. The seaport at Lothal, for example, contains the largest structure of fired brick erected anywhere in the Harappan realm; it is identified by its excavator as a docking basin, ingeniously designed so that the ships within it remained afloat even at low tide.

With the onset of the late phase of Harappan civilization the Gujarat sites present a sad picture of gradual

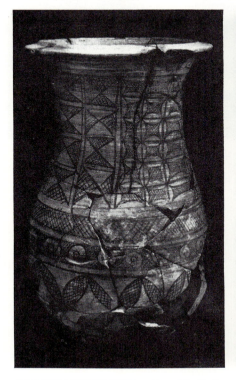

HARAPPAN DECLINE is reflected in the lowered standards of workmanship characteristic of the late Harappan phase. A skillfully carved stone stamp seal of the mature Harappan phase (*top left*) is contrasted with a simple geometric one (*top right*), typical of the late phase at Mohenjo-daro. A similar contrast is seen between a polychrome painted pot of the mature phase (*bottom left*) and an unpainted pot from late-phase levels (*bottom right*).

HARAPPAN ARTISTRY is exemplified by this miniature terra-cotta mask, one and a half inches wide, found at Mohenjo-daro in 1964. Typical of mature Harappan workmanship, the mask has a boldly outlined human face topped by the ears and horns of some animal.

degeneration. Sophisticated Harappan traits are watered down by a mingling with impoverished local cultures until what was once distinctively Harappan is diluted to the point of nonexistence. No urban centers rise along the Gulf of Cambay, no more soapstone seals are carved, no more clay figurines are modeled. Trade with the civilized centers of the Near East, once the *raison d'être* for these Indian coastal ports, comes to a stop. The Harappan script, with its 400 or so still undeciphered symbols, disappears.

These findings are compatible with a hypothesis that envisions the disastrous sequence of floods at Mohenjo-daro and elsewhere in the southern Indus valley as the stimulus that drove the Harappans from the heartland of the far-flung state to take refuge in the Gujarat area. Suddenly crowded with refugees and deprived of support from the once prosperous realm that had fostered them, the Harappan trading towns on the southern frontier could have done little else than gradually merge with the countryside they had formerly dominated. On the basis of present evidence it seems probable that the Harappans, to borrow a figure of speech from T. S. Eliot, met their end not with an Aryan bang but with an Indus expatriate's whimper.

18

A FORGOTTEN CIVILIZATION OF THE PERSIAN GULF

P. V. GLOB AND T. G. BIBBY

October 1960

Bahrain Island, halfway down the Persian Gulf from the delta of the Tigris and Euphrates rivers, has been known to archeologists and grave robbers as an island of the dead. The yellow sand of the island is covered with uncounted large grave mounds—an estimated 100,000 of them. They rise in such weird profusion that they give the impression of some natural cataclysm, as though a boiling, bubbling wasteland had suddenly solidified at the dawn of time. Yet all is the work of man: each of the mounds covers a stone chamber (often two chambers one above the other), and each contains a human burial.

The wonder of the grave mounds became a mystery when several archeological expeditions came to the island after the turn of the century and found

GRAVE MOUNDS in this photograph are some of the estimated 100,000 that lie on Bahrain Island. Each of the mounds covers one or two stone chambers. The chambers contain human burials and objects of gold, copper and ivory that are more than 3,000 years old.

LARGE MOUND in this photograph is about 35 feet high. Most of the large mounds lie at the edge of the desert. Their size probably explains why they were robbed centuries ago.

of smaller settlements and an extensive temple-complex, all dating to the period of the grave mounds and representing a hitherto unknown civilization. From this auspicious beginning, the work has continued on an expanding scale for the past seven years. While excavations have yielded an increasingly complete revelation of the center in Bahrain, reconnaissance has extended the outer marches of this civilization ever farther to the north and east along the curving coastline of Arabia. In the 1960 season the expedition consisted of 27 Scandinavian archeologists and was operating over a front of 600 miles, from Kuwait at the head of the Persian Gulf to Abu Dhabi and Buraimi in the east. Bahrain has proved to be the legendary Dilmun referred to in the cuneiform texts of Sumer, the bridge between that primary seat of the urban revolution and the civilization of the Indus Valley in what is now Pakistan.

That we were the vanguard of one of the largest archeological expeditions ever to operate in the Middle East was not to be guessed when we landed at Moharraq airport on the northern island of the Bahrain archipelago and negotiated for the ancient station wagon that was to take us on our reconnaissance of the main island. Bahrain itself is a small island about twice the size of Manhattan. It is widest in the north, where most of the grave mounds lie, and tapers in the south to a sandy spit pointing to the head of the deep bay that lies between the peninsula of Qatar and the Arabian mainland, clearly visible on the western horizon. Along the north and northwestern coastal strip of Bahrain lie extensive plantations of date palms, interspersed with fields of alfalfa that provide fodder for humped Indian cattle, for goats and donkeys. The rest of Bahrain consists of open, windswept desert, plains of gravel and eroded limestone buttes, with the 440-foot Jebel Dukhan —the Mountain of Smoke—rising in the center. Of the 150,000 Arabic-speaking inhabitants of the archipelago, a third live in the capital city of Manama on the northeastern coast, a close-packed town of narrow streets, slender minarets and tall, windowless, whitewashed merchants' palaces. Another third live on the northern island of Moharraq, and the remainder in the villages strung out along the coasts. Here, in houses of interwoven palm fronds, the villagers live a life that can have changed little

no trace of towns or cities. Inevitably the expeditions tended to concentrate on the excavation of the larger mounds. These proved to have been already visited by robbers in remote antiquity. But the gold, copper and ivory objects that still remained here and there in the massive tomb-chambers bore witness to the wealth they once contained, and indicated that the graves were at least as old as the Bronze Age—earlier than 1000 B.C. The fact that no settlements were discovered gave rise to the theory that Bahrain was solely a burial island, a cemetery for peoples dwelling on the mainland of Arabia.

This theory had an essential weakness: The island has a plentiful water supply and a soil that is productive where it is watered, while nearby Arabia is sandy and waterless. Accordingly in 1953 the Prehistoric Museum of Aarhus in Denmark dispatched a small expedition, comprising the two authors of this article, to Bahrain. Our objective was to reconnoiter the island as a whole and to resolve the mystery of the grave mounds by locating, if we could, the settlements of their builders.

This limited objective was achieved in the course of the first season's work. We discovered one large city, a number

over the centuries, working in the date and vegetable gardens, tending the fish traps that line the tidal channels around the coast and in the summer months sailing to the oyster banks to dive for pearls.

Pearling, however, is a dying occupation. A new source of wealth has come to Bahrain, the first state in the Persian Gulf in which oil was discovered. Now in increasing numbers the new generation is leaving its fish traps and gardens to work in the machine shops and offices of the oil company and at the huge refinery that dominates the east coast. In the center of the island, north of Jebel Dukhan, in a town of pastel-colored bungalows and green gardens, live the American and European oilmen and their families, in an area that 30 years ago was desert.

It was in this desert that the first traces of prehistoric settlements were discovered. These settlements, however, dated back to a time long before the burial mounds. Where the wind had exposed the ancient surface of the desert lay hundreds of chipped flakes of flint. They marked the chipping floors and settlements of men of the Stone Age, and they followed closely an ancient coastline now lying some two miles inland. A small number of finely chipped barbed

and tanged arrowheads and toothed flint sickle-blades belonging to the first agriculturalists of the Neolithic period turned up among these artifacts, but the vast majority were the points and scrapers of the hunters of the Middle Paleolithic. These evidenced clear relationship with the early Stone Age cultures of northwestern India. The work in this realm of Middle East archeology has since been advanced with the finding on the Qatar peninsula of a succession of artifacts that lead back to the hand axes of 100,000 years ago. But these works of primitive, perhaps pre-*sapiens*, culture were scarcely clues to the mystery of the grave mounds.

The first month's wandering over the island also resulted, however, in the discovery of a large number of settlement sites: sand-covered ruins with scraps of pottery of many different types. Clearly it was necessary to determine whether the grave mounds contained the same types of pottery. We accordingly excavated two grave mounds and explored the slab-roofed burial chambers within. These are of a shape unknown outside Bahrain, with two alcoves at the western end giving the chamber a T-shaped plan. While both proved to have

been robbed, they produced, in addition to copper spearheads and a drinking cup formed of an ostrich eggshell, a small quantity of distinctive red pottery.

With this encouragement we began to dig at a site where a large number of squared stone blocks, lying on the surface, argued an important building below the ground. A small underground well-chamber was found, with a flight of steps leading down to the wellhead, formed of a single square block pierced by a hole. Two decapitated statues of seated rams, which originally had stood at the head of the stairs, showed that this site was pre-Islamic. Further work was stopped, however, by water from underground and by the discovery in the meantime of a site of much greater importance.

This was a large mound near the village of Barbar on the northwestern coast. There a large block of hewn stone, projecting above the surface, tempted investigation. A trial trench laid bare a stone-flagged court surrounded by the lowest courses of a wall of cut limestone. In the center of this court the trench exposed part of a double circle of curved blocks. A widening of the trench showed these to be a plinth that must have borne statues or cult objects. To the east of the plinth two stone slabs stood upright,

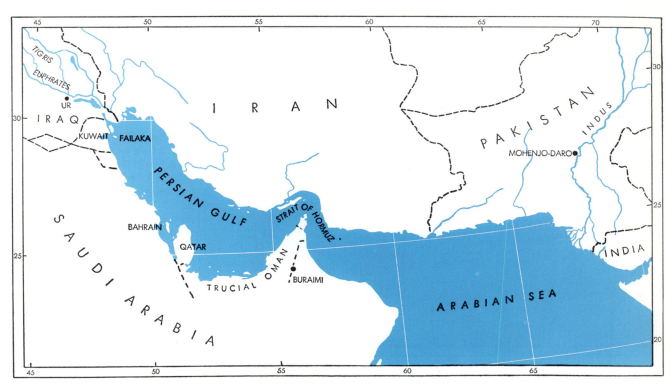

ANCIENT SITES are located on this modern map of the Middle East. Bahrain Island lies halfway down the Persian Gulf from the joint mouth of the Tigris and Euphrates rivers. Cuneiform texts describe the island as being some two days' sail from Mesopotamia.

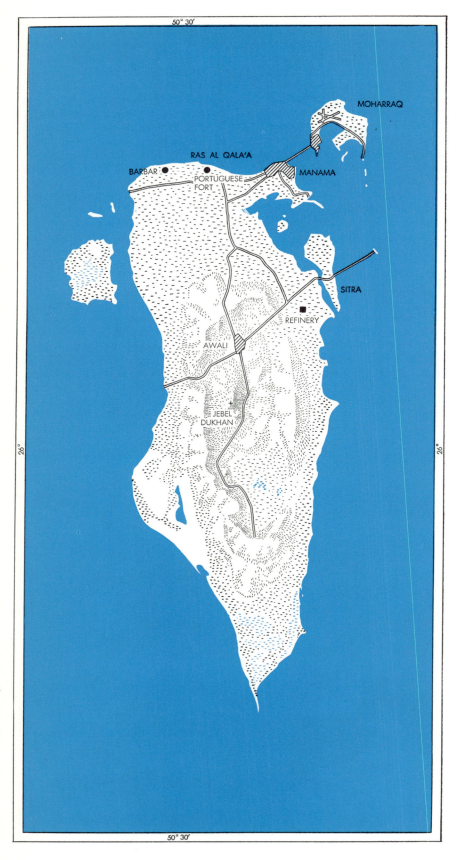

BAHRAIN ISLAND is about twice the size of Manhattan. Most of the grave mounds lie in the northern part of the island. The cross at center marks the 440-foot Jebel Dukhan (Mountain of Smoke). Shaded areas are modern towns; double lines represent modern roads.

with a recess in the upper edge to take a seat top, and before them was a square libation altar with a hollowed top, served by a stone-lined drain passing through the walls. To the north a square pit in the flags of the courtyard proved to contain a wealth of objects: lapis-lazuli beads and pendants, alabaster jars and objects of copper, including a figure of a naked and shaven priest in an attitude of prayer. We had uncovered the holy of holies of a temple. The statuette evidenced unmistakable Sumerian affinities —secure evidence for an early date. Moreover, several of the lapis-lazuli pendants were of a type found in the cities of the Indus Valley.

Now, after seven seasons of work on the temple of Barbar, the central area has been completely cleared. The square temple has been shown to stand upon a terrace supported by walls of finely cut and fitted limestone. A ramp leads down to the east to an oval enclosure full of charcoal from extensive and repeated burnings and containing stone foundations, perhaps blocks on which animals were sacrificed. To the west a flight of steps leads down from the terrace to a small tank or bathing pool. The temple is thus reminiscent in its layout of the temples of Early Dynastic Sumer, but, with its bathing pool, it also recalls the ritual baths of the Indus Valley cities. We have found the structure to be only the final stage of three successive building phases, each representing additions to the terrace and to the temple above it.

A wealth of small objects has been discovered within the complex—axes and spears of copper, a magnificent bull's head that calls to mind those that adorned the harps in the Early Dynastic royal graves at Ur of the Chaldees and eight circular soapstone seals. These seals are of a type well known to archeologists and much discussed. Among the thousands of cylindrical seals found in Mesopotamia there are a mere 17 of these round seals. They were not native to Mesopotamia, and appeared to date to the period between 2300 and 2000 B.C. Several bore inscriptions in the unknown language of the Indus Valley civilization. Moreover, three examples of the same type of seal had actually been found in the prehistoric Indus Valley city of Mohenjo-Daro. But they were obviously not native to the Indus Valley, where large square seals, found by the hundreds, had been shown to be the native type. It was now apparent to us that the round seals were native to Bahrain. The temples at Barbar could thus be placed in the third millennium B.C.; they belonged to a people who traded with both Mesopotamia and India and had a culture distinct from both.

The temples of Barbar have also yielded a large quantity of pottery. It is of a distinctive type—round-bellied jars of a red ware, decorated with horizontal ridges and often bearing a short spout. Further excavation of several more grave mounds with the distinctive T-shaped chambers has produced jars of precisely the same type. The link between the grave mounds and the temple-complex at Barbar is thus established beyond doubt.

Still another large site, discovered during the first season, has revealed the same Barbar pottery, and has at the same time greatly extended our knowledge of this forgotten civilization. Some miles to the east of Barbar, at a bend in the coast known as Ras al-Qala'a, a huge low mound is crowned by the ruins of a fort built by the Portuguese during their 100-year domination of the Gulf in the 16th century. The excavations of the first year showed this mound to be composed of the debris and ruins of a large city. The work of the subsequent years has laid bare a large area (though small in relation to the 200,000 square yards covered by the mound), and has shown that here lie seven cities, one buried below the other. The city second from the bottom has yielded the red-ridged pottery and round stamp-seals characteristic of the Barbar period. In the same levels are ruins of stone houses and a rectangular layout of streets, all surrounded by a massive wall of hewn stone, 14 feet thick. The city that lies below the Barbar city also yields round stamp-seals. But these are more primitive, with designs resembling more closely those of the Indus Valley cities than those found in Mesopotamia. The pottery, too, is related, but bears ridges pressed into a chainlike pattern.

The five successive cities that overlie the two third-millennium cities give a broad panorama of the history of Bahrain almost up to our own day. After the great days of the third millennium there comes a clean break in the style of pottery and other artifacts. It would seem that a different people now occupies the island. In many ways they are poorer and less artistic, and they seem to have deserted part of the city. And yet it is to their time that the most magnificent phase in the construction of a colossal building apparently belongs. This building was discovered at Ras al-Qala'a during the closing weeks of the first campaign. Built of squared stones a yard in length and more, it still stands

CLOSE-UP OF A MOUND shows the ruins of the circular stone walls that ring it. The stone-lined entrance shaft at top center leads to two T-shaped burial chambers within.

BURIAL CHAMBERS within the mounds are roofed with slabs of stone and sealed with large rocks. Although robbed, chambers contained spearheads, shell cups and pottery.

to a monumental height of 16 feet, with imposing doorways and sheer walls. Begun perhaps at the close of the Barbar period, it was completed and occupied by the new invaders. Some time in the second millennium this third city was destroyed and left desolate.

After a lapse of years a new people with new fashions of pottery and implements reoccupied the site. The ruins of the immense building were now cleaned out, repaired and partially rebuilt of inferior materials, apparently as a temple to a snake goddess. In the huge entrance hall two mighty square pillars had originally borne a roof. But in this period the hall was roofless; one pillar had disappeared, and of the other only the bottom block, a yard square and two feet high, still stood like an altar. In front of this block we found 14 offerings in pottery bowls deposited in shallow holes in the floor. In seven of the bowls lay the skeletons of snakes, some up to five feet in length. With the skeletons in

some cases were beads, while one of the offerings consisted entirely of a necklace of 26 beads of agate, amethyst, glass and porcelain, held by a silver clasp. Clearly these gifts of snakes and jewelry were either the offerings of women or were offerings to a female deity (or, most probably, both). They call to mind the snake goddess of fertility worshiped in the second and first millennia over a wide area, from India to Scandinavia, and best known from the Cretan statuettes of goddesses holding snakes.

Early in the first millennium the building was again abandoned, though it was for some time used as a burial vault. Its rooms now lay entirely below ground. Adults were buried in clay coffins, bathtub-shaped and painted with bitumen inside and out, while babies were buried curled up in large bowls. Most of these graves had been robbed, but in one lay a fine bronze wine-service, consisting of pitcher, bowl, strainer and ladle, together with an agate seal that securely dates the grave to about 700 B.C.

Outside the abandoned building the city extended its area, and its surface rose with the accumulation of rubbish and the demolition and rebuilding of houses. In these late levels we suddenly find sherds of black-painted pottery, the products of Athens in the fourth century B.C. Terra-cotta figures and a Greek name scratched on a potsherd show that not only Greek trade goods but also Greek art and speakers of Greek traveled the Persian Gulf before the time of Alexander the Great.

With the beginning of the Christian era and the fall of the successors of Alexander, the city of Ras al-Qala'a appears to have been once more deserted for some centuries. The two uppermost building levels of the city are Islamic, dated very neatly by Chinese pottery of the Sung and Ming dynasties to the 10th and the 16th centuries A.D. respectively. The last city is therefore contemporary with the 16th-century Portuguese fort that crowns the mound and within which the Danish archeological expe-

EXCAVATIONS AT BARBAR uncovered a stone-lined pool (*center*) similar to the ritual baths of the ancient cities of the Indus Valley. In the background is the terrace of a temple. The layout of the temple resembles that of Sumerian temples of the Early Dynas-

dition has pitched its camp these last five years.

It now seems clear that Bahrain was a center of urban life for at least 3,000 years before the Christian era. In the centuries around 2000 B.C. it was a place of considerable wealth and power. Its unique civilization was in close cultural contact with the Sumerians of Mesopotamia 150 miles up the Persian Gulf to the north and with the cities of the Indus Valley, 1,000 miles across land and sea to the east.

References to such a center of civilization turn up again and again in the extensive literature dug up in the cities of Mesopotamia over the past century. Commercial documents describe trading voyages down the Persian Gulf from the cities of Ur, Larsa, Lagash and Nippur. The historical accounts of the campaigns of the kings of Sumer, Babylon and Assyria tell of tribute and submission received from the countries of the "lower sea." Three lands down the Gulf are named with particular frequency: the

kingdoms of Dilmun, Makan and Meluhha. They are always named in that order, presumably the order of their distance from Mesopotamia.

Henry Rawlinson, the British colonial official and scholar who deciphered cuneiform more than a century ago, was also the first to suggest that Bahrain might be the site of Dilmun. He based his theory on the discovery on Bahrain of a cuneiform inscription naming the god Inzak, who is cited in the god lists of Mesopotamia as the chief god of Dilmun. With the discovery of the rich cities and temples of Bahrain this theory may now be regarded as confirmed. Dilmun is described in the cuneiform records of Mesopotamia as an island with abundant fresh water lying some two days' sail, with a following wind, from Mesopotamia. Ships are frequently recorded as sailing to Dilmun with cargoes of silver and woolen goods to be exchanged there for the products of Makan (copper and diorite) and those of

Meluhha (gold, ivory and precious woods). This would suggest that Meluhha was none other than the Indus Valley civilization, and that Makan must be sought between Bahrain and India. Dilmun is also named as supplying products of its own: dates and pearls. Clearly, however, Dilmun's main importance was as a clearing house for goods from farther east, the abode of merchants and shippers engaged in widespread commerce. This view agrees closely with the new archeological evidence.

But Dilmun was more than this. The Sumerian poems and epics of gods and heroes tell of another Dilmun, a land that before the creation of man was the abode of the gods, the home of immortality, a paradise of gardens and fresh water in which neither sickness nor old age was known. It was to Dilmun that Zius-udra, the sole survivor of the Deluge, retired when the waters subsided and he had been granted immortality. And it was to Dilmun that the greatest hero of ancient Sumer, Gilgamesh, came

tic Period. Another view of this temple appears on next page.   EXCAVATIONS AT RAS AL-QALA'A unearthed the ancient water closet in center foreground. Dating back to first millennium B.C., water closet was complete with tank and running water.

in his vain quest for immortality. But of that golden age of Dilmun no traces have yet been found in the record.

In order to follow the ancient trade routes to the east and to the west the Danish archeologists have extended their research far beyond Bahrain to cover 600 miles off the coast of Arabia from Kuwait to the Trucial Oman on the Strait of Hormuz, the eastern entrance to the Gulf. Near Kuwait three seasons' work on the little island of Failaka, a

three-hour sail from the coast, has uncovered two adjacent sites of unusual importance. One is an outpost of the Dilmun culture, a small but very rich settlement, producing the typical ridged red pottery so well known from the Barbar temples of Bahrain, as well as fragments of soapstone bowls carved with figures of animals and men, amulets bearing cuneiform inscriptions, and almost 200 round seals identical with those of the Barbar period of Bahrain. The

other site, a fort, was built almost 2,000 years later by veterans of the army of Alexander the Great on their return from India. In and near it have been found Rhodian wine jars and molds for casting statuettes of Greek goddesses and even of the divine Alexander himself. And the campaign just completed has laid bare a pillared temple of Greek style. Standing before it is a slab that bears a long Greek inscription giving the instructions issued by the Greek king for

WALL OF TERRACE of the latest of the ancient temples at Barbar (*bottom*) masked the wall of the earlier terrace and its stone staircase (*top*). Three pierced stone blocks at extreme upper left were possibly tethering poles for animals awaiting sacrifice.

the foundation of this colony so far from the Greek homeland.

But perhaps the greatest perspectives are opened by the work that has now been going on for two years in the Trucial Oman. There, on a little island off the coast, and again at the oasis of Buraimi, three days' camel journey into the interior, groups of grave mounds have been found. The graves are of a completely new and imposing type, with perpendicular circular walls built with stones cut to fit the curve and standing to above the height of a man. Squeezing through tiny "porthole" entrances, one finds within cross walls supporting arched roofs. Unlike the single burials of the Bahrain mounds, these burial chambers each contains up to 50 skeletons, lying in disorder as they were successively pushed aside to make room for more bodies. Among them lie thousands of beads and a wealth of finely made painted pottery. This pottery resembles the pottery found in the Dilmun levels of Bahrain closely enough to determine that the burial vaults are of the same date as the Dilmun civilization. But it resembles even more closely the pottery of the Kulli culture of India, which is believed to have preceded the Indus Valley civilization. In this new culture, with its unique burial practices, we may be touching the fringe of the next great civilization toward the east, the kingdom of Makan.

GREEK TEMPLE at Kuwait, 250 miles north of Bahrain, was built at the order of Alexander the Great. A stone slab found in front of the temple contains a long inscription in Greek giving the instructions issued by Alexander for the founding of a Greek colony.

19

AN EARLY CITY IN IRAN

C. C. AND MARTHA LAMBERG-KARLOVSKY
June 1971

The kingdom of Elam and its somewhat better-known neighbor, Sumer, were the two earliest urban states to arise in the Mesopotamian area during the fourth millennium B.C. Archaeological findings now show that the Elamite realm also included territory at least 500 miles to the east. For more than 10 centuries, starting about 3400 B.C., the hill country of southeastern Iran some 60 miles from the Arabian Sea was the site of a second center of Elamite urban culture.

Today all that is left of the city that stood halfway between the Euphrates and the Indus is a great mound of earth located some 4,500 feet above sea level in the Soghun Valley, 150 miles south of the city of Kerman in the province of the same name. Known locally as Tepe Yahyā, the mound is 60 feet high and 600 feet in diameter. Its record of occupation begins with a 6,500-year-old Neolithic village and ends with a citadel of the Sassanian dynasty that ruled Persia early in the Christian Era. Intermediate levels in the mound testify to the connections between this eastern Elamite city and the traditional centers of the kingdom in the west.

Such a long archaeological sequence has much value for the study of man's cultural development from farmer to city dweller, but three unexpected elements make Tepe Yahyā a site of even greater significance. First, writing tablets made of clay, recovered from one of the lower levels in the mound, have been shown by carbon-14 analysis of associated organic material to date back to 3560 B.C. (±110 years). The tablets are inscribed with writing of the kind known as proto-Elamite. Proto-Elamite inscriptions and early Sumerian ones are the earliest known Mesopotamian writings, which are the oldest known anywhere. The Tepe Yahyā tablets are unique in

that they are the first of their kind that can be assigned an absolute date. It comes as a surprise to find these examples of writing—as early as the earliest known—in a place that is so far away from Mesopotamia.

The second surprise is evidence that Elamite trade with neighboring Sumer in an unusual commodity—steatite, the easily worked rock also known as soapstone—formed a major part of the commerce at Tepe Yahyā. Unlike Sumer, which was surrounded by the featureless floodplains of lower Mesopotamia, Elam was a hill kingdom rich in natural resources. Elamite trade supplied the Sumerians with silver, copper, tin and lead, with precious gems and horses, and with commoner materials such as timber, obsidian, alabaster, diorite and soapstone. To find that the soapstone trade reached as far east as Tepe Yahyā adds a new dimension to our knowledge of fourth-millennium commerce.

Third, the discovery of Tepe Yahyā has greatly enlarged the known extent of ancient Elam, which was hazily perceived at best. Susa, the most famous Elamite city, lies not far from such famous Sumerian centers as Ur and Eridu. As for other Elamite cities named in inscriptions (Awan, for example, or Madaktu), their location remains a mystery. To discover a prosperous Elamite city as far east of Mesopotamia as Tepe Yahyā is both a surprise and something of a revelation. It suggests how urban civilization, which arose in lower Mesopotamia, made its way east to the valley of the Indus (in what is now West Pakistan).

The British explorer-archaeologist Sir Aurel Stein was the first to recognize that southeastern Iran is a region with important prehistoric remains. Two sites that Stein probed briefly in the 1930's—Tal-i-Iblis near Kerman and Bampur in Per-

sian Baluchistan—have recently been excavated, the first by Joseph R. Caldwell of the University of Georgia and the second by Beatrice de Cardi of the Council for British Archaeology. Although it is the largest mound in southeastern Iran, Tepe Yahyā remained unknown until the summer of 1967, when our reconnaissance group from the Peabody Museum at Harvard University discovered it during an archaeological survey of the region.

We have now completed three seasons of excavation at Tepe Yahyā in coopera-

LARGE EARTH MOUND, over a third of a mile in circumference, was raised to a

tion with the Iran Archaeological Service and have established a sequence of six principal occupation periods. The site was inhabited almost continuously from the middle of the fifth millennium B.C. until about A.D. 400. Following the end of the Elamite period at Tepe Yahyā, about 2200 B.C., there is a 1,000-year gap in the record that is still unexplained but finds parallels at major sites elsewhere in Iran. Tepe Yahyā remained uninhabited until 1000 B.C., when the site was resettled by people of an Iron Age culture.

Our main work at Tepe Yahyā began in the summer of 1968 with the digging of a series of excavations, each 30 feet square, from the top of the mound to the bottom [see illustration below]. Small test trenches were then made within the series of level squares. During our second and third season the excavations were extended by means of further horizontal exposures on the top of the mound and to the west of the main explorations. In addition we opened a stepped trench 12 feet wide on the opposite face of the mound as a check on the sequences we had already exposed.

The earliest remains of human occupation at Tepe Yahyā, which rest on virgin soil in a number of places, consist of five superimposed levels of mud-brick construction. We have assigned them to a single cultural interval—Period VI—that is shown by carbon-14 analysis to lie in the middle of the fifth millennium B.C. The structures of Period VI seem to be a series of square storage areas that measure about five feet on a side. Most of them have no doorways; they were probably entered through a hole in the roof. The walls are built either of sun-dried mud bricks that were formed by hand or of hand-daubed mud [see top illustration on page 179]. Fragments of reed matting and timber found on the floors of the rooms are traces of fallen roofs.

The tools of Period VI include implements made of bone and flint. Many of the flints are very small; they include little blades that were set in a bone handle to make a sickle. The most common kind of pottery is a coarse, hand-shaped ware; the clay was "tempered" by the addition of chaff. The pots are made in the form of bowls and large storage jars and are decorated with a red wash or painted with red meanders. Toward the end of Period VI a few pieces of finer pottery appear: a buff ware with a smooth, slip-finished surface and a red ware with decorations painted in black.

Human burials, all of infants, were found under the floor in a few of the structures. The limbs of the bodies had been tightly gathered to the trunk before burial, and accompanying the bodies are unbroken coarse-ware bowls. In one room a small human figurine was found face down on the floor, resting on a collection of flint and bone tools. The sculpture is 11 inches long and was carved out of dark green soapstone [see illustration on next page]. The carving clearly delineates a female figure. Its elongated form and the presence of a hole at the top of the head, however, suggest a dual symbol that combines male and female characteristics.

The Neolithic culture of Period VI evidently included the practice of agriculture and animal husbandry. Identifiable animal bones include those of wild gazelles and of cattle, sheep and goats. Camel bones are also present, but it is not clear whether or not they indicate that the animal had been domesticated at this early date. The domesticated plants include a variety of cereal grains. In the Tepe Yahyā area today raising crops involves irrigation; whether or not this was the case in Neolithic times is also unclear. At any rate the Neolithic occupation of the mound continued until about 3800 B.C.

The transition from Period VI to the Early Bronze Age culture that followed

height of 60 feet over a 5,000-year period as new settlements were built on the rubble of earlier ones. Located in southeastern Iran and known locally as Tepe Yahyā, the site was first occupied by a Neolithic community in the middle of the fifth millennium B.C.

NEOLITHIC FIGURINE was found in one of the storerooms in the earliest structure at Tepe Yahyā, associated with tools made of flint and bone. The sculpture was apparently intended to be a dual representation: a female figure imposed on a stylized phallic shape.

occurred without any break in continuity. The structures of Period V contain coarse-ware pottery of the earlier type. The finer, painted pottery becomes commoner and includes some new varieties. One of these, with a surface finish of red slip, has a decorative geometric pattern of repeated chevrons painted in black. We have named this distinctive black-on-red pottery Yahyā ware, and we call the material culture of Period V the Yahyā culture.

The commonest examples of Yahyā ware are beakers. These frequently have a potter's mark on the base, and we have so far identified nine individual marks. Evidence that outside contact and trade formed part of the fabric of Early Bronze Age life at Tepe Yahyā comes from the discovery at Tal-i-Iblis, a site nearly 100 miles closer to Kerman, of almost identical painted pottery bearing similar potter's marks. There is other evidence of regional contacts. Yahyā ware shows a general similarity to the painted pottery at sites elsewhere in southeastern Iran, and a black-on-buff ware at Tepe Yahyā closely resembles pottery from sites well to the west, such as Bakun. Moreover, the Period V levels at Tepe Yahyā abound in imported materials. There are tools made of obsidian, beads made of ivory, carnelian and turquoise, and various objects made of alabaster, marble and mother-of-pearl. One particularly handsome figure is a stylized representation of a ram, seven inches long, carved out of alabaster [*see top illustration on page 182*]. No local sources are known for any of these materials.

Although the architecture of Period V demonstrates a continuity with the preceding Neolithic period, the individual structures are larger than before. Several of them measure eight by 11½ feet in area and are clearly residential in character. Some rooms include a hearth and chimney. In the early levels the walls are still built of hand-formed mud bricks. Bricks formed in molds appear in the middle of Period V, which carbon-14 analyses show to have been around 3660 B.C. (±140 years).

The bronze implements of Period V, like much of the earliest bronze in the world, were produced not by alloying but by utilizing copper ores that contained "impurities." This was the case in early Sumer, where the ore, imported from Oman on the Arabian peninsula, contained a high natural percentage of nickel. Early bronzesmiths elsewhere smelted copper ores that were naturally rich in arsenic. Chisels, awls, pins and spatulas at Tepe Yahyā are made of such an arsenical bronze.

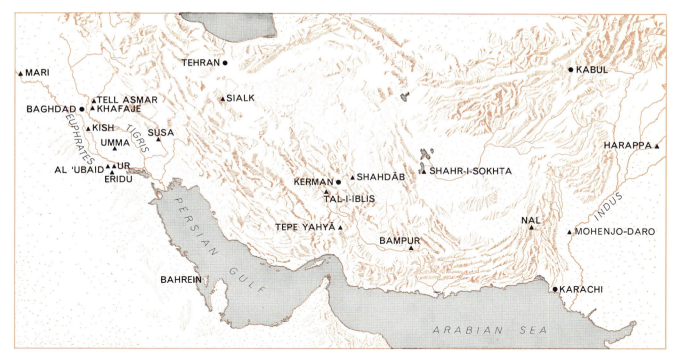

FIRST CITIES arose in the kingdom of Sumer in lower Mesopotamia (*left*). The earliest known forms of writing appeared in Sumer and in nearby Elam at cities such as Susa and Sialk. The discovery of proto-Elamite writing at Tepe Yahyā (*center*), which is 500 miles to the east, suggests that trade between the region and the early cities of Mesopotamia led to the rise of cities in this part of ancient Persia in the fourth millennium B.C. and to the later development of the urban Harappan civilization in the Indus region.

Six artifacts from the site have been analyzed by R. F. Tylecote and H. McKerrell of the University of Newcastle upon Tyne. They found that the bronze had been produced by smelting, which shows that the metalworkers of Period V were able to obtain the high temperatures needed to smelt copper ores into molten metal. The final shapes were not made by casting, however, but by hot and cold forging, a more primitive technique. One of the articles, a chisel, proved to contain 3.7 percent arsenic, which leads us to believe that the metalworkers consciously selected for smelting ores with a high arsenic content. This finding is further testimony in support of trade at Tepe Yahyā; none of the copper deposits native to the region could have been used to make arsenical bronze.

With the beginning of Period IV, around 3500 B.C., the appearance of writing at Tepe Yahyā allows the city to be identified as a proto-Elamite settlement. Much of the pottery representative of the first two phases of this period, IV-C and IV-B, is typical of the preceding Yahyā culture in both shape and decoration. Although there is plentiful evidence of external contact, the transition to Period IV at Tepe Yahyā, like the one that preceded it, occurred without any break in continuity. There is no need at Tepe Yahyā to conjure up that hackneyed instrument of cultural change: a new people arriving with luggage labeled "Proto-Elamite."

Architecture, however, was considerably transformed. The site ceased to be a residential area and became an administrative one. A large structure we have unearthed at the IV-C level of the mound is carefully oriented so that its walls run north-south and east-west. The walls consist of three courses of mold-formed brick in a new size. The earlier mold-formed bricks had been six by six by 12 inches; the new ones were 9½ by 9½ by 4¾ inches—a third wider and less than half as thick. So far we have identified five of an undetermined number of rooms within the large structure, although we have fully cleared only part of one room. Both the structure and the partially excavated room continue toward the center of the mound; the size of each remains to be determined.

The part of the room that has been cleared measures about 10 by 20 feet. Its contents strongly suggest a commercial function. Among the objects in the room are bowls with beveled rims made of a coarse ware. The vessels have counterparts at numerous sites in Mesopotamia. They are believed to have served as standard measures. Three large storage jars, which proved to be empty, were also found in the room; near them were some 24 "sealings": jar stoppers made of clay and marked with a seal impression. The seals used to mark the sealings were cylindrical; the designs resemble those on cylinder seals found at Susa, the Elamite capital in the Mesopotamian area. The finding creates the possibility that goods from Susa were reaching Tepe Yahyā early in Period IV.

Lying on the floor of the room were 84 blank clay tablets and six others that bore inscriptions. The tablets are all the same shape; they are made of unbaked dark brown clay, are convex in profile and measure 1⅛ by two inches. The six inscribed tablets bear a total of 17 lines of proto-Elamite writing. The inscriptions were impressed in the soft clay with a stylus; they read from right to left along the main axis of the tablet and from top to bottom. When an inscription continues from one side of a tablet to the other, the writer rotated the tablet on its main axis so that the bottom line of the obverse inscription and the top line of the reverse inscription lie opposite each other.

The Tepe Yahyā inscriptions are being deciphered now. Preliminary examination indicates that they are records or receipts dealing with goods. The fact that inscribed and otherwise identical blank tablets were found in the same room is strong evidence that the writing was done on the spot. Therefore the goods they describe must have been either entering or leaving the administrative area.

Until the discovery at Tepe Yahyā the only other proto-Elamite tablets known were from Susa or from Sialk in northwestern Iran. Susa yielded nearly 1,500 such tablets, Sialk only 19. Proto-Elamite writing has been found recently at Shahdāb, a site north of Kerman that is being excavated by the Iran Archaeological Service. The writing there is not on tablets but consists of brief inscriptions, with a maximum of seven signs, incised on pottery.

A second change in architectural style is evident in the single IV-B structure examined so far. It is a building, nine by 24 feet in area, that is oriented without reference to north-south and east-west. It is built of bricks of a still newer size and shape. They are oblong rather than square, and are either 14 or 17 inches long; the other two dimensions remained the same. The structure is subdivided into two main rooms and a few smaller rooms that contain large storage bins built of unbaked clay. Its walls are only one brick thick, and their inside surfaces are covered with plaster.

Storage vessels in one of the main

rooms still held several pounds of grain. The grain was charred, which together with the fact that the matting on the floor and the bricks in the wall were burned indicates that the building was destroyed by fire. Amid the debris on the floors were cylinder seals and, for the first time at Tepe Yahyā, stamp seals as well.

Some bronze tools of the IV-B period have also been discovered. Needles and chisels, unearthed in association with soapstone artifacts, were probably used to work the soapstone. A bronze dagger some seven inches long was found by Tylecote and McKerrell to have been made by forging smelted metal, as were the bronze tools of Period V. Analysis showed that the dagger, unlike the earlier artifacts of arsenical bronze, was an alloy comprising 3 percent tin. Tin is not found in this part of Iran, which means that either the dagger itself, the tin contained in it or an ingot of tin-alloyed bronze must have been imported to Tepe Yahyā.

The proof that writing was known at Tepe Yahyā as early as it was known anywhere is a discovery of major importance to prehistory. Perhaps next in

importance, however, is the abundant evidence suggesting a unique economic role for the city beginning late in the fourth millennium B.C. The IV-B phase at Tepe Yahyā is known from carbon-14 analyses to have extended from near the end of the fourth millennium through the first two centuries of the third millennium. During that time the city was a major supplier of soapstone artifacts.

Objects made of soapstone, ranging from simple beads to ornate bowls and all very much alike in appearance, are found in Bronze Age sites as far apart as Mohenjo-Daro, the famous center of Harappan culture on the Indus, and Mari on the upper Euphrates 1,500 miles away. Mesopotamia, however, was a region poor in natural resources, soapstone included. The Harappans of the Indus also seem to have lacked local supplies of several desired materials. How were the exotic substances to be obtained? Sumerian and Akkadian texts locate the sources of certain luxury imports in terms of place-names that are without meaning today: Dilmun, Maluhha and Magan.

Investigations by Danish workers on the island of Bahrein in the Persian Gulf have essentially confirmed the belief that the island is ancient Dilmun. There is also a degree of agreement that the area or place known as Maluhha lay somewhere in the valley of the Indus. Even before we began our work at Tepe Yahyā it had been suggested that the area known as Magan was somewhere in southeastern Iran. Our excavations have considerably strengthened this hypothesis. A fragmentary Sumerian text reads: "May the land Magan [bring] you mighty copper, the strength of . . . diorite, 'u-' stone, 'shumash' stone." Could either of the untranslated names of stones stand for soapstone? Were Tepe Yahyā and its hinterland a center of the trade? Let us examine the evidence from the site.

TWO CYLINDER SEALS from the level at Tepe Yahyā overlying the first proto-Elamite settlement appear at left in these photographs next to the impressions they produce. The seal designs, which show pairs of human figures with supernatural attributes, are generally similar to the designs on seals of Mesopotamian origin but appear to be of local workmanship.

More soapstone has been found at Tepe Yahyā than at any other single site in the Middle East. The total is more than 1,000 fragments, unfinished pieces and intact objects; the majority of them belong to Period IV-B. Among the intact pieces are beads, buttons, cylinder seals, figurines and bowls. Unworked blocks of soapstone, vessels that are partially hollowed out and unfinished seals and beads are proof that Tepe Yahyā was a manufacturing site and not merely a transshipment point.

Some of the soapstone bowls are plain, but others are elaborately decorated with carvings. The decorations include geometric and curvilinear designs, animals and human figures. Among the decora-

EARLIEST STRUCTURE at Tepe Yahyā is a storage area consisting of small units measuring five feet on a side. Few of the units have doorways; apparently they were entered through a hole in the roof. The walls were built either of sun-dried mud bricks, formed by hand rather than in molds, or simply of hand-daubed mud. White circle (*left*) shows where female figurine was found.

TWO ELAMITE BUILDINGS at Tepe Yahyā left the traces seen in this photograph. The walls of the earlier building (*left*) were built sometime around 3500 B.C. of mold-formed mud bricks 9½ inches on a side. The walls run from north to south and from east to west. The walls of the later structure (*right*) are not oriented in these directions. It was built sometime after 3000 B.C. of oblong mold-formed mud bricks of two lengths. Both structures seem to have been administrative rather than residential. The earlier one contained storage pots and measuring bowls. Near one angle of its walls a pile of 84 unused writing tablets is visible.

tions are examples of every major motif represented on the numerous soapstone bowls unearthed at Bronze Age sites in Mesopotamia and the Indus valley. Moreover, motifs found on pottery unearthed at sites such as Bampur, to the east of Tepe Yahyā, and Umm-an-Nai on the Persian Gulf are repeated on soapstone bowls from IV-B levels.

During our 1970 season we located what was probably one of the sources of Tepe Yahyā soapstone. An outcrop of the rock in the Ashin Mountains some 20 miles from the mound shows evidence of strip-mining in the past. This is unlikely to have been the only source. Soapstone deposits are often associated with deposits of asbestos and chromite. There is a chromite mine only 10 miles from Tepe Yahyā, and we have noted veins of asbestos in stones unearthed during our excavation of the mound. Reconnaissance in the mountains to the north might locate additional soapstone exposures.

Taking into consideration the large quantities of soapstone found at the site, the evidence that many of the soapstone

articles were manufactured locally, the availability of raw material nearby and the presence in both Mesopotamia and Harappan territory of soapstone bowls that repeat motifs found at Tepe Yahyā, it is hard to avoid the conclusion that the city was a major producer of soapstone and a center of trade in the material. Before turning to the broader significance of such commercial activity in this geographically remote area, we shall briefly describe the remaining occupation periods at Tepe Yahyā.

At present there is little to report concerning the final phase of Period IV, which drew to a close about 2200 B.C. It is then that the break occurs in the continuity at Tepe Yahyā. The Iron Age reoccupation of the site, which lasted roughly from 1000 to 500 B.C., comprises Period III. It is evidenced by a series of living floors and by pottery that shows strong parallels to wares and shapes produced during the same period in northwestern Iran. We have not yet uncovered a major structure belonging to Period III; both the nature of the culture and Tepe Yahyā's relations with

its Iron Age neighbors remain unclarified.

Period II at Tepe Yahyā, which consists of more than 200 years of Achaemenian occupation, was a time of large-scale construction. The building material remained mud brick, but we have yet to uncover a complete structure. The appearance of the two large rooms excavated thus far suggests, however, that the site had once more become at least partly residential.

A subsequent 600 years or so of Parthian and Sassanian occupation, representing Period I, is the final period of urban civilization at Tepe Yahyā. We have uncovered suggestions of large-scale architecture, including courtyards and part of a massive mud-brick platform made by laying four courses of brick one on the other. By Sassanian times (early in the third century) the accumulated debris of thousands of years had raised the mound to an imposing height; the structure that has been partly exposed probably was a citadel standing on the summit.

Most of the Sassanian pottery consists

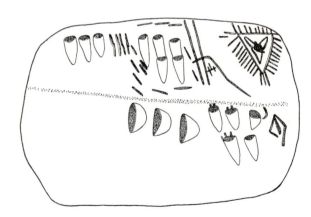

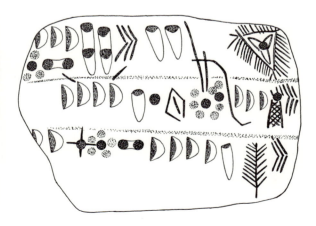

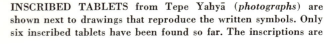

INSCRIBED TABLETS from Tepe Yahyā (*photographs*) are shown next to drawings that reproduce the written symbols. Only six inscribed tablets have been found so far. The inscriptions are in proto-Elamite, written from right to left across the length of the tablet by pressing the blunt or sharp end of a stylus into the soft clay. Similar written tablets have been unearthed at Susa and Sialk.

of coarse, thick-walled storage jars. An abundance of beads and several small glass and pottery bottles, perhaps containers for perfume, suggest a degree of prosperity during Period I. The presence of iron and bronze swords, axes and arrowheads adds a military flavor. A single work of art, a small clay figurine, represents a warrior with a distinctive headdress [*see bottom illustration on next page*]. Thereafter, from sometime in the fifth century on, Tepe Yahyā was occupied only by occasional squatters or transient nomads. The few scattered surface finds are of early Islamic age; none of the visitors lingered or built anything of substance.

What role did Elamite Tepe Yahyā play in the transmission of the urban tradition from west to east? The city's position suggests that Elamite culture, which is now revealed as being far more widespread than was realized previously, was instrumental in the contact between the first urban civilization in Mesopotamia and the civilization that subsequently arose in the Indus valley. It appears that the Elamites of eastern Persia may have accomplished much more than that. To assess this possibility it is necessary to examine the evidence for direct contact, as distinct from trade through middlemen, between Mesopotamia and the Indus valley.

A small number of artifacts that are possibly or certainly of Harappan origin have been found at sites in Mesopotamia. Because much of the archaeological work there was done as long as a century ago, it is not surprising that both the age and the original location of many of these artifacts can only be roughly estimated. Nonetheless, Mesopotamia has yielded six stamp seals, one cylinder seal and a single clay sealing, all of the Harappan type, that are evidence of some kind of contact between the two civilizations. Certain seals are engraved with Harappan writing. On others the writing is combined with animal figures that are indisputably Harappan in style: a "unicorn," an elephant, a rhinoceros. Evidence of contact, yes. But was the contact direct or indirect?

The single Indus sealing found in Mesopotamia was discovered by the French archaeologist G. Contenau at Umma in southern Iraq during the 1920's. It suggests the arrival there of freight from Harappan territory that had been identified with the sender's personal mark before shipment. The seven seals, however, are evidence of a more equivocal kind. Mesopotamian contact with the Indus evidently did not resemble the later trade

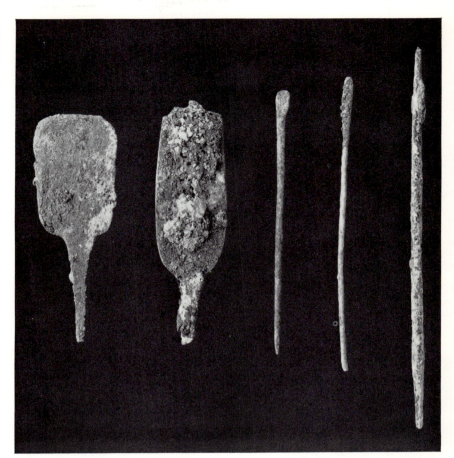

BRONZE OBJECTS contemporaneous with peak of work and trade in soapstone at Tepe Yahyā include two chisels (*left*) and three needle-like forms; the longest object measures 6½ inches. The bronze was not produced by alloying but by utilizing copper that naturally included significant amounts of arsenic. The enriched ores were obtained through trade.

SOAPSTONE BOWLS, many of them elaborately decorated, were among the numerous objects made at Tepe Yahyā and traded eastward and westward during the first half of the third millennium B.C. Fragments of bowls with decorations like the ones on these bowl fragments from Tepe Yahyā have been found from Mesopotamia to the Indus valley.

FIGURINE OF A RAM carved out of alabaster is one of the numerous articles made from imported materials that are found at Tepe Yahyā at the time of its first urban settlement about 3800 B.C. Evidences of trade between the city and outlying areas include, in addition to alabaster, mother-of-pearl from the Persian Gulf, marble, turquoise and carnelian.

FIGURINE OF A WARRIOR modeled in clay is from the final period of occupation at Tepe Yahyā, when a Sassanian military outpost stood on the top of the mound from sometime in the third century B.C. to about A.D. 400. Thereafter only nomads visited the dead city.

between Mesopotamia and, say, the Hittite realm to the west. In that instance Assyrian trading colonies were housed within special quarters of such Hittite strongholds as Kültepe and Hattusha [see the article "An Assyrian Trading Outpost," by Tahsin Özgüç, beginning on page 243]. There is simply no good evidence that Mesopotamians ever visited the Indus to set up residence and trade or that Harappans did the reverse.

What, then, were the seals of Harappan traders doing in Mesopotamia? What was the function of the three unearthed at Ur, the two at Kish and the two at Tell Asmar? So far there is no persuasive answer to these questions. It is tempting to look on these seals not as credentials but as souvenirs of indirect trade contact; all of them are handsome objects. At the same time another equally puzzling question presents itself. Some objects of Indus origin have been found in Mesopotamia. Why has nothing of any kind from Mesopotamia been found at any Indus site?

Evidence of direct trade contact between the two civilizations thus remains almost entirely absent. Other kinds of trade, however, are equally well known. One of the oldest and most widespread is simple exchange, which can interpose any number of witting or unwitting intermediaries between two principals. Exchange is notable for presenting the archaeologist with difficulties of interpretation; intangibles such as style and function are likely to travel along with the goods.

A system of exchange that involves a single intermediary seems to provide the theoretical model that best approximates the situation at Tepe Yahyā. Such a system is known as "central place" trade; we suggest that Tepe Yahyā was just such a central place in southeastern Persia during Elamite times.

A central place can lie outside the sphere of influence of either principal and at the same time produce goods or control natural resources desired by both. In addition to (or even instead of) exporting its own products, a central place can transship goods produced by either principal. Bahrein—ancient Dilmun—provides a good example of a central place whose prosperity was based on the transshipment of goods bound for Mesopotamia. Whether or not transshipment was important at Tepe Yahyā, the city's basic central-place role in Elamite times was clearly that of a producer manufacturing and exporting articles made of soapstone.

The names of the Mesopotamian sites that contain soapstone bowls identical in shape and decorative motif with those we unearthed at Tepe Yahyā read like an archaeologist's checklist: Adab, Mari, Tell Asmar, Tell Aqrab, Khafaje, Nippur, Telloh, Kish, Al ʻUbaid and Ur. Bowls of Tepe Yahyā style have also been found at Mohenjo-Daro on the Indus and at Kulli-Damb in Pakistani Baluchistan. In addition to bevel-rim bowls of the Uruk type at Tepe Yahyā as evidence of contact with the west, the mound has yielded Nal ware, a kind of Indus painted pottery that predates the rise of Harappan civilization, as evidence of contact with the east.

Tepe Yahyā was not, however, the only central place in eastern Persia. It seems rather to have been one of several that comprised a local loose Elamite federation astride the middle ground between the two civilizations. Shahr-i-Sokhta, a site 250 miles northeast of Tepe Yahyā, appears to have been another central place, exporting local alabaster and transshipping lapis lazuli from Afghanistan. The links between Tepe Yahyā and other possible central places in the region such as Tal-i-Iblis, Shahdāb and Bampur—mainly demonstrated by similarities in pottery—have already been mentioned.

How did this remote Elamite domain, which in the case of Tepe Yahyā predates the appearance of Harappan civilization by at least three centuries, influence developments in the Indus valley? In spite of exciting new evidence that trade networks existed as long ago as the early Neolithic, a strong tendency exists to view trade exclusively as an ex post facto by-product of urbanism. Trade, however, has certainly also been one of the major stimuli leading to urban civilization. This, it seems to us, was exactly the situation in ancient Kerman and Persian Baluchistan.

We suggest that trade between resource-poor Mesopotamia and the population of this distant part of Persia provided the economic base necessary for the urban development of centers such as Tepe Yahyā during the fourth millennium B.C. It can further be suggested that, once an urban Elamite domain was established there, its trade with the region farther to the east provided much of the stimulus that culminated during the third millennium B.C. with the rise of Harappan civilization. Sir Mortimer Wheeler has declared that "the idea of civilization" crossed from Mesopotamia to the Indus. It seems to us that the Elamite central places midway between the two river basins deserve the credit for the crossing.

20

THE TOMBS OF THE FIRST PHARAOHS

WALTER B. EMERY
July 1957

When the famous British archaeologist Flinders Petrie published his *History of Egypt* in 1894, he devoted only 10 pages of it to the period before 2680 B.C. Yet by that time there had already been three dynasties of Egyptian kings. Egyptologists had learned much about the succeeding 27 dynasties by archaeological excavation, but their knowledge of the first pharaohs was based only on the lists of kings compiled by later Egyptians and on the writings of Greek and Roman historians. Indeed, some authorities believed that these kings were figures of myth and legend rather than men who really lived. But at the turn of the century the pick of the excavator revealed many monuments of the First Dynasty, and the shadowy figures of the first pharaohs stepped forth onto the stage of history to tell their story of the rise of civilization in the valley of the Nile.

The most important of these discoveries was made in 1895 at Abydos, a site on the Nile 300 miles south of Cairo. Here the French Egyptologist Emile-Clément Amélineau discovered a group of graves consisting of great pits lined with brick. In 1899 Petrie began to work at Abydos, and in two years of brilliant research he established its tombs as monuments of the kings of the First and Second Dynasties. He was also able to identify the royal owner of each tomb and to establish the order of his succession. Originally each brick-lined pit was roofed with timber and surmounted with a superstructure. In all cases this part of the building has disappeared, and no indication of its precise form exists. We do know, however, that because the tombs are so close to one another the superstructures cannot have covered an area

much larger than the pits themselves. Each tomb was surrounded by numerous graves which contained the bodies of slaves sacrificed to continue their service to the king in the afterworld.

Petrie believed that the kings of the First Dynasty were actually buried at Abydos, and until recently there was no reason to doubt this conclusion. Later excavations strongly suggest, however, that the kings were buried not at Abydos but at Sakkara, far down the Nile [*see map on page 186*]. Sakkara, the vast cemetery of ancient Memphis, is best known as the site of a great stepped pyramid of the Third Dynasty. At its north end are the remains of tombs which had long been recognized as perhaps even older than this pyramid. But it was not until 1912 that any really serious research was undertaken at North Sakkara. The late J. E. Quibell, then Chief Inspector of the Egyptian Department of Antiquities, excavated for two seasons and proved the existence of First Dynasty tombs far better preserved than those at Abydos.

The site was still not considered especially promising because it had been systematically ravaged by tomb-robbers for more than 5,000 years, and so after the interruption of Quibell's work by World War I the site lay untouched until 1930. Then his successor, the late C. M. Firth, resumed the excavations. Firth cleared several more First Dynasty tombs, the most notable of which was known as 3035. The paneled exterior and burial pit of this great structure were excavated, but its interior was left untouched. This was because it was believed that the interior of the superstructures of such monuments was a solid network of brick walls filled with rubble. The excavation of Tomb 3035

was not very productive, for the burial chamber had been plundered and replundered in ancient times. Nonetheless Firth was able to establish that the tomb had been built during the reign of Udimu, fifth king of the First Dynasty. Firth

EXCAVATED TOMBS of the pharaohs of the First Dynasty are on the right side of

died suddenly in 1932, and once again the exploration of North Sakkara was interrupted.

In 1935, when the Director General of the Department of Antiquities instructed me to reclear the tombs, I also turned my attention to Tomb 3035. In order to determine certain details of its construction I cut rather ruthlessly into the big brick superstructure and found that it was not just a solid mass of brickwork and rubble but was divided up into a series of 45 storerooms, many of which had escaped the attention of the ancient tomb-robbers. In these storerooms we found a great collection of funerary equipment—food, tools, weapons, games and drinking vessels—lying where they had been placed 5,000 years before. Inscriptions on the clay seals of jars led us to believe that the tomb belonged to a great noble named Hemaka, vizier of the pharaoh Udimu. This was the greatest single discovery of First Dynasty material that had been made up

to that time. Its importance was at once appreciated by the Egyptian Government and I was given permission to explore the whole area systematically.

Digging continued from 1935 until the beginning of World War II; one great tomb after another was cleared, each showing that civilization during the period of the First Dynasty was far more advanced than we had supposed. Tombs contemporaneous with the kings Hor-Aha, Zer, Udimu, Enezib and Ka-a were discovered—all much larger and more elaborate in design than their counterparts at Abydos. We knew that these kings originated at This near Abydos, but that they conquered the lower Nile Valley and established their capital at Memphis. Thus it seemed possible and even probable that the tombs at Sakkara were their actual burial places, and that the structures at Abydos were empty monuments. Only further excavation could confirm this theory, but at the outbreak of the war the work was shut down. With the exception of

a short season in 1946, nothing further was done at North Sakkara until 1952. In that year an arrangement was made whereby the Egypt Exploration Society reopened the excavations on behalf of the Department of Antiquities. The clearance is still in progress.

In 1952 we discovered a tomb which probably belonged to Uadji, the third pharaoh of the First Dynasty; in the following year we excavated another which we ascribed to Ka-a, the last king of the dynasty. A third large tomb was cleared in 1955, and although its ownership could not be established it supplies conclusive evidence that all the burials almost certainly belonged to the kings, queens and princes of the First Dynasty.

These big tombs of the First Dynasty have the same fundamental design: a large pit cut in the ground, within which were built the burial chamber and subsidiary rooms [see drawings on pages 188 and 189]. Here were stored the owner's most precious possessions. This

this photograph of the area around North Sakkara, 15 miles from Cairo. In the distance at the far left are three pyramids of the Fifth Dynasty. Beyond them are the three famous pyramids built by the Fourth Dynasty kings Khufu (Cheops), Khafra and Menkaura.

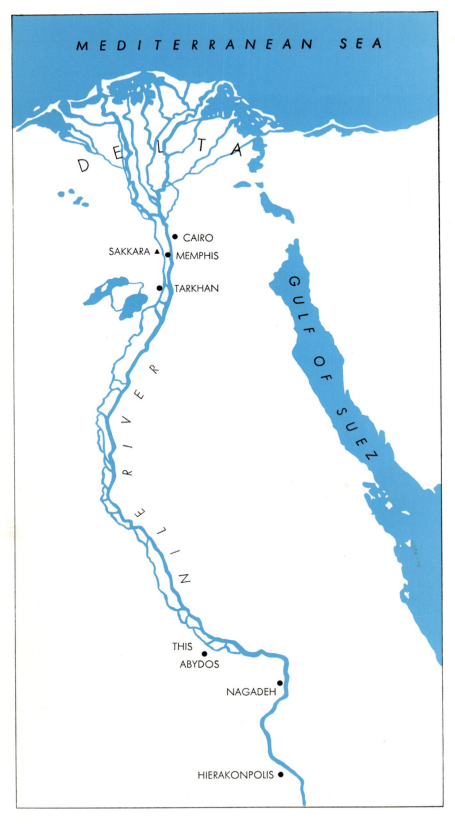

SITES mentioned in this article are located on a map of the Nile Valley. The pharaohs of the First Dynasty originated at This but later established their capital at Memphis. It was once thought that they were buried at Abydos, but it now appears that their graves· are at Sakkara. Tarkhan, Nagadeh and Hierakonpolis are other sites of the First Dynasty.

substructure was covered by a large rectangular superstructure of brick, enclosing chambers in which were stored reserve supplies for the use of the deceased in afterlife. This was only the general scheme of the funerary edifice; refinements and developments occurred in rapid succession throughout the 250-odd years of the dynasty. The developments were confined principally to the substructure; the superstructure increased in size but remained largely unchanged. These great buildings, made only of unbaked brick, were undoubtedly dummy copies of the actual palaces of the kings. Although they now stand only five feet above their foundations, there is evidence that they originally rose to a height of not less than 30 feet. The elaborate recess-paneling of their exteriors was gaily painted with geometrical designs simulating the colored matting which adorned the interior walls of buildings at that time.

Although the burial chambers were ravaged and, in many cases, set afire by plunderers, we can reconstruct them with considerable certainty. The deceased lay slightly bent on his right side within a great wooden sarcophagus measuring about 10 by six feet. Outside the sarcophagus were furniture, games for the amusement of the deceased, and his last meal, served in vessels of alabaster, diorite, schist and pottery. These meals were of an elaborate character, consisting of soup, ribs of beef, pigeon, quail, fish, fruit, bread and cake. We found such a meal remarkably preserved in a tomb of the early Second Dynasty, and from fragments found with burials of the First Dynasty we have every reason to suppose that the same rich repast was left during the earlier period. Other rooms in the substructure were devoted to the storage of wine and food, furniture, clothing, games, tools and weapons of flint and copper. Similar objects were stored in the chambers of the superstructure: hundreds of great wine jars, furniture inlaid with ivory, toilet implements, agricultural equipment—all the appurtenances of a well-organized and highly developed civilization.

The principal evolution in the design of the substructure was the introduction of a stairway entrance which enabled the architect to build the whole funerary edifice before the burial. Before this innovation had been introduced the superstructure was built after the burial—obviously an unsatisfactory arrangement. At the end of the First Dynasty a small funerary temple was built at the north side of the tomb; both tomb and temple

SUPERSTRUCTURE of a First Dynasty tomb is exposed by excavation. The recessed walls of the superstructure originally stood at least 30 feet high and were painted with geometrical designs. This is probably the tomb of Queen Meryt-Nit of the First Dynasty.

CLAY MODEL of an ancient Egyptian estate is excavated beside the tomb of Hor-Aha, the first king of the First Dynasty. Such models may have been small-scale copies of the royal estates, presumably to be re-created for the use of their owners in the afterlife.

were enclosed by walls with an entrance to the east. In this final evolution of the First Dynasty tomb we have the prototype of the pyramid complex of later dynasties.

We still have much to learn about the earliest First Dynasty tombs, which are perhaps the oldest examples of monumental architecture in the world. They are not entirely what they seem. In the course of our excavations we have often been puzzled to discover stairways and passages which lead nowhere. For a time we were inclined to dismiss these mysterious features as the result of alterations in the architect's plans. Now we know that the tombs were built in two distinct stages. First they were raised to serve some unknown purpose; then, after this purpose was fulfilled, they were altered so that they could serve

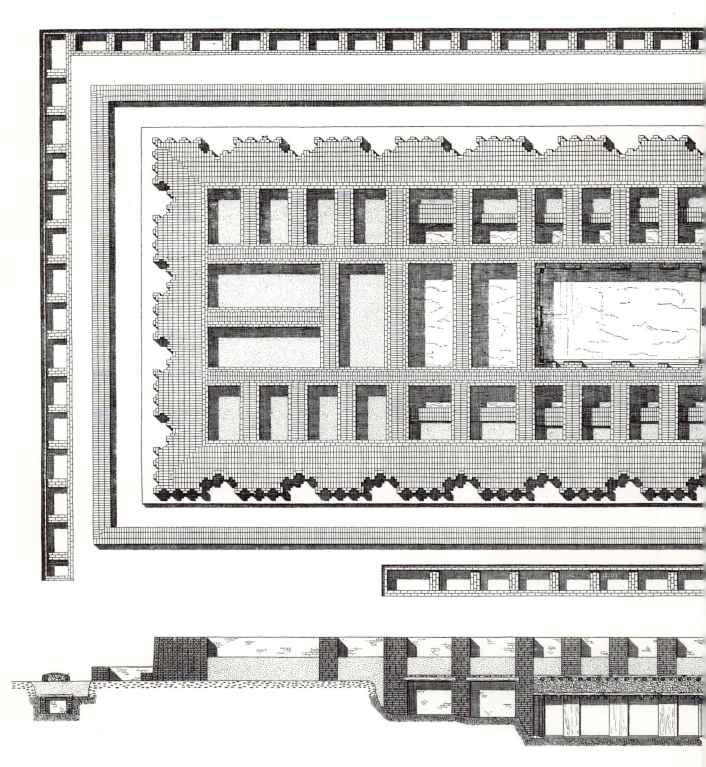

TOMB IS RECONSTRUCTED in plan and elevation by these drawings. This is Tomb 3504 at Sakkara. It is dated to the reign of Uadji, third king of the First Dynasty. The tomb is roughly 200 feet long and 100 feet wide. In the center is the burial chamber. Around

their final function as a house of the dead. We are still entirely ignorant as to the purpose of the original structure, and we can only hope that further excavation will give us the answer to this fascinating question.

The complete funerary installation consisted not only of the tomb, but also of surrounding graves of retainers sacrificed to accompany the king in death as in life. These small graves are of great interest, for we often find objects buried with the dead retainer which indicate his occupation: paint pots with the art-ist, model ships with the shipmaster, varieties of pottery with the potter, and so on. Around the tombs we frequently find the remains of gardens with rows of trees and plants. Near one tomb is a clay model of an estate with houses, granaries and fields. It is tempting to see in this model an exact copy of the royal estate, to be re-created in the next world for the service of its dead owner. Beside the tomb of Udimu are the remains of a wooden ship to carry the pharaoh with the celestial gods in their voyage across the heavens. This vessel, which was 50 feet long, was built 400 years before the recently discovered ship of Cheops.

There are still other sites of the First Dynasty awaiting excavation. It is thus a little early to come to any conclusion regarding the origin of civilization in the Nile Valley. Enough has been disclosed, however, to show that a highly developed culture existed in Egypt by 3000 B.C. In assessing this culture we must remember that we do so on evidence which has survived 5,000 years of destruction by nature and man. But even in their ruined state the magnificent monuments of Sakkara, Abydos and other sites show that they were built by a people with an advanced knowledge of architecture and a mastery of construction in both brick and stone. The scattered contents of their tombs show that they had a well-developed written language, a knowledge of the preparation of papyrus and a great talent for the manufacture of stone vessels, to which they brought a beauty of design that is not excelled today. They also made an almost unlimited range of stone and copper tools, from saws to the finest needles. Their decorative objects of wood, ivory and gold are masterly, and their manufacture of leather, textiles and rope was of a high standard. Above all they had great artistic ability: the motifs of painting and sculpture that were characteristic of Egypt for 3,000 years had already appeared.

This advanced civilization appears suddenly in the early years of the third millennium B.C.; it seems to have little or no background in the Nile Valley. Yet the Valley had been inhabited for a long period before the First Dynasty. Excavation has indicated that during this period burial customs developed little; the passage of time is marked only by changes in the design of pottery and other objects. The people of the period had an advanced neolithic culture which certainly made a contribution to the later Egyptian civilization. In my opinion, however, their culture does not pro-

it are many rooms for the storage of food and other goods. The long rows of small chambers on three sides of the tomb are the graves of retainers sacrificed to accompany the king.

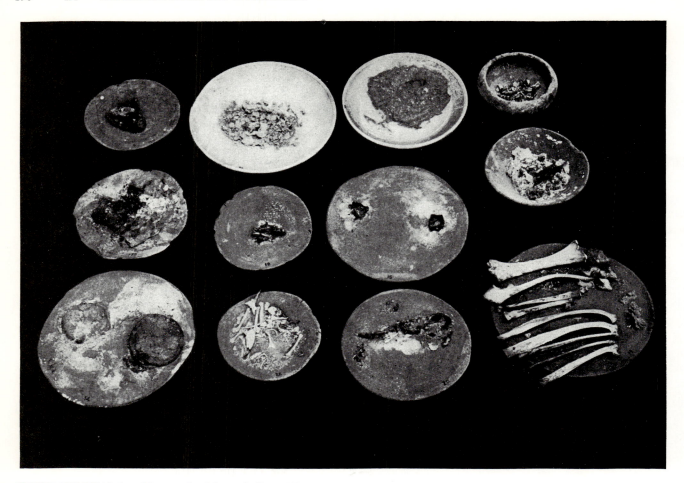

FUNERARY MEAL found in a tomb of the early Second Dynasty is in a remarkable state of preservation, considering that it was set out some 5,000 years ago. Fragments found in tombs of the First Dynasty indicate that similar meals were buried with its pharaohs.

vide a complete foundation for the Egypt of the pharaohs. It is of course possible that the architecture of the First Dynasty was the product of a superior people inhabiting the delta of the Nile, where constant flooding and agriculture has destroyed all remains of the period before the pharaohs. Since there is no evidence for or against this theory, it must remain speculative. In any case I feel it is unlikely that such a civilization could develop independently in the marshlands of the delta and suddenly impose itself on the upper Nile Valley. It is significant that during the First Dynasty only the nobles and officials were buried in monumental tombs. The mass of the people were buried in graves consisting of shallow

pits with no superstructure beyond a circular mound of earth. The body lay in a huddled position on its left side; except for the objects in it such a grave had little to distinguish it from those of the period before the First Dynasty. By the end of the Second Dynasty we find the mass of the people had adopted the burial customs of their betters: the design of their tombs was the same in almost every detail except size. All this plainly suggests the existence of a superior culture which gradually imposed its burial customs on the conquered indigenes.

If we accept the theory that the civilization of the pharaohs was brought to the Nile Valley by a new people, we must ask: Who were they and where

did they come from? The British historian Reginald Engelbach suggested a horde invasion, and there is evidence to suggest something of the sort. We must not overlook, however, the possibility of gradual infiltration over a long period. The monumental architecture of the First Dynasty has been compared to that of the Jemdet Nasr period in Mesopotamia, and I think the similarity is beyond dispute. But there are also great differences, so a direct connection between the Euphrates and the Nile at that time is still a matter of doubt. Thus the problem of how the civilization of the pharaohs originated remains unsolved. It is to be hoped that the further work of the Egypt Exploration Society will contribute to its solution.

IV

RECENT PERSPECTIVES AND PROBLEMS

IV

PERSPECTIVES AND PROBLEMS

INTRODUCTION

The first four articles in this section need further comment because of archaeological developments since their publication that make them incomplete but not obsolete. The next two articles detail, from opposite ends of the European continent, specific European prehistoric cultures. The villages of prehistoric Swiss lake dwellers (see the article by Müller-Beck) were among the first major prehistoric sites to be excavated in Europe, well over a hundred years ago, and many of the great tombs of the Scythians (see the article by Artamonov) were excavated under the sponsorship of the Russian czars. These two papers report the most recent results in the excavation of sites once occupied by Swiss lake dwellers and Scythians. It is to the problems presented by the first four papers that we now turn.

The article by Edward Deevey on radiocarbon dating was written at a time when most archaeologists believed that this technique would provide a clear and incontestably absolute chronology, and it was hailed as a revolution in archaeological control of chronology. It is twenty years since Professor Deevey's article was written, and the archaeologists' faith in radiocarbon dating has become a bit less than enthusiastic. (For a completely up-to-date evaluation and discussion of radiocarbon data, see J. U. Olson, 1969). The shortcomings and abuses of carbon-14 dating are becoming proverbial in the archaeological literature. Although radiocarbon dates (or determinations, as the skeptics prefer to call them) are beginning to offer a relatively coherent pattern of absolute chronology, there are increasing concerns, on the part of both archaeologists and physicists, about the nature, care, and feeding of radiocarbon samples (Stuckenrath, 1965). It has become clear that the assumption made by W. F. Libby and his collaborators, who developed the technique, that the carbon-14 content in the atmosphere has always been constant, cannot be upheld (Bucha and Neustupny, 1968). The half-life of carbon-14 reported here by Deevey has been changed to a newer and presumably more accurate one: that is, from 5,568 to $5,730 \mp 40$ years. Such a change makes radiocarbon dates based on the 5,568-year half-life actually earlier than they were reported to be.

As if archaeologists were not already confounded by the challenge and changes in the radiocarbon system, physicists are now proposing major readjustments that they say will bring radiocarbon dates more into line with historical reality (Michael and Ralph, 1971). Correction factors have been determined from inconsistencies between radiocarbon dates and tree-ring dates, and control measurements, using dendrochronologically dated wood from giant sequoias and bristlecone pines, have established several variations in the carbon-14 level. For the B.C. period, the correction factors that should be applied to the standard radiocarbon dates grow progressively larger as one goes back in time, from plus 50 years at 300 B.C. to plus 650 years at 2700 B.C. For example, a published radiocarbon date of 1950 B.C.

would have 400 years added to it, and be thus corrected to a more nearly correct date of 2350 B.C. The radiocarbon cycle, like all natural phenomena, deviates from the ideal; but until more sophisticated techniques of dating prehistoric materials are discovered, it remains the best timepiece for the prehistoric past. In spite of its real and alleged imperfections, it remains a vital tool for the construction of the archaeologists' absolute chronology and the establishment of cultural sequences.

The revolutionary impact of calibrating the radiocarbon dates, and finding they are actually earlier than was first reported, is dealt with in the article by Colin Renfrew. Previously, archaeologists argued that the primary stimulus for the development and elaboration of the prehistory of Europe resulted from the diffusion of technological achievements (i.e., metallurgy, writing, etc.) from the Near East into Europe. With the new calibrated dates, diffusion becomes an impossible explanation for in certain developments (e.g., metallurgy) because, as Professor Renfrew argues, the new dates assign primacy for the invention to Europe. Thus, if the new radiocarbon calibrations are correct, then the Tartaria tablets, reported on in the article by M. S. F. Hood, are 500 years older than the earliest evidence of Near Eastern writing. It is, however, still debatable whether the Tartaria tablets were found in their correct archaeological context (the Vinca-Tordos Culture, *ca.* 4000 B.C.) and whether the radiocarbon dates have correctly dated the context of the tablets. It is equally debatable whether the Tartaria tablets are related in script to the Near Eastern Uruk tablets: although this is the most commonly held opinion, Professor Hood argues that they may belong to the later Aegean script of Eteo-Cretan. The argument, pending additional evidence, remains unresolved. One thing is clear: the calibrations of radiocarbon dates, e.g., the adding of 650 years to a reported date of 2700 B.C., has introduced the Second Radiocarbon Revolution. It is far too early to agree with positive conviction with Renfrew that such a basic change in European prehistory, which pushes back the dates of prehistoric European cultures several centuries, can be tolerated in the totality of our archaeological understanding. One can wholly agree with him that archaeologists have all too long accepted the alternative hypothesis about European prehistory: *Ex Oriente Lux.*

The last article that needs some comment because of recent work on its subject is the one on Stonehenge. A series of articles in *Nature* in 1963 and 1964 by Gerald Hawkins advanced the idea that Stonehenge was built for a singular purpose: the monumental stone structure was an astronomical observatory. The idea that Stonehenge was oriented in relation to the sun is at least a hundred years old, but Professor Hawkins, an astronomer, suggested far more than this. His computer-assisted research on the stone alignments at Stonehenge seemed to show that the entire megalithic monument was built to predict important events in the heavens—solar and lunar eclipses, summer and winter solstices, and even more. His articles were followed by a book, *Stonehenge Decoded* (1965), whose publication created a world-wide stir. The argument between Hawkins and his detractors can be followed in the pages of *Antiquity* from 1965 through 1967. Ms. Jacquetta Hawkes, whose article included here was written in 1953, would have none of Hawkins "scientism." She wrote a scathing rebuttal to his argument which was published in *Antiquity* as "God and the Machine." Since then current opinion has settled perhaps more in favor of Hawkins' view. Surely, Stonehenge appears to have been built to serve some astronomical function. Perhaps the most striking support of Hawkins' ideas came from a Scottish mathematician, Alexander Thom, who had, for years before Hawkins advanced his theory, been studying the alignments and measurements of the many megalithic structures that dot the landscape of England. He concluded, independently and most convincingly, that these stone structures of 2500 B.C. (and earlier) were carefully constructed in standardized measurements and were all aligned to serve as astronomical observatories. Their function seems undeniable.

The article by Tahsin Özgüç, which concludes the selected readings, is a reminder to the archaeologist of how selective is the evidence with which he deals. The Assyrian Empire has long been regarded as one of the most expansive and military of Near Eastern civilizations. In the city of ancient Kanesh, Professor Özgüç has had the good fortune to isolate a commercial colony, a foreign Assyrian outpost in the heartland of an indigenous Anatolian culture. The excavations here have thrown a great deal of new light on the commercial activities of the Assyrians in foreign lands. But how has the archaeologist actually detected the presence of this Assyrian colony? From the conventional way of isolating Assyrian materials associated with materials of a different culture? No! The only way we are informed of the Assyrian presence is by their own writings. Clay tablets have been found at Kanesh that report the presence of Assyrians in that city and their commercial role there. It would appear that, while living at Kanesh, the Assyrians adopted foreign ways, living in houses, using pottery, metals, and so on, which cannot be distinguished from those of the local population. This is a reminder of how fragile and dependent the archaeological record is on certain categories of information, and of the great distinction between archaeology with textual guidance and archaeology in the absence of the written record.

There appears to be no end to the surprises in store for the archaeologist in his ever-increasing appreciation of the accomplishments of prehistoric man. The "savage brute" in the form of Paleolithic man is today far less savage than he was to our grandfathers, for today we can follow him recording the seasons in a symbolic system (writing?). Still, we have come but a short distance in fully appreciating man's prehistoric past. The articles printed here offer only glimpses into the richness and complexity of that past, a past that, in our increasingly technological world, becomes the harder, but the more important, to comprehend.

REFERENCES

Bucha, V., and E. Neustupny. 1968. Changing the Earth's Magnetic Field and Radiocarbon Dating. *Nature*, July 15.

Michael, H. N., and E. K. Ralph. 1971. *Dating Techniques for the Archaeologist*. MIT Press.

Olsson, I. U., ed. 1969. *Radiocarbon Variations and Absolute Chronology*. Twelfth Nobel Symposium, Uppsala University. John Wiley.

Stuckenrath, R., Jr. 1965. On the Care and Feeding of Radiocarbon Dates. *Archaeology*, vol. 18, no. 4, pp. 277 *et seq.*

21

RADIOCARBON DATING

EDWARD S. DEEVEY, JR.
February 1952

NO BRANCH of learning is tame to its enthusiasts—not even grammar, as Browning reminded us. Some sciences, of course, have a more urgent appeal than others. The lure of nuclear physics, at least since 1945, is a force that feeds itself; like Cleopatra, physics "makes hungry where most she satisfies." The identification of fossil pollen grains in ancient lake beds is not commonly held fascinating to the same degree, nor would the study of Aztec calendric manuscripts get many votes as the most bewitching of occupations. Yet each has its allure. The most delightful fact about radiocarbon dating, a new research field that has captivated scientists of all descriptions, is that it combines the fascination of the immediate and the bizarre, of physics and history. While it was conceived in nuclear physics, much of its verve is contributed by such eccentrics as the students of fossil elephants and of the architecture of ancient Peru. Radiocarbon dating has brought science and the humanities together in the laboratory for the first time.

The credit for starting this union belongs to Willard F. Libby, of the University of Chicago's Institute for Nuclear Studies. His postwar discovery that radioactive carbon 14 in nature could be used for dating the past has already given birth to radiocarbon laboratories at the Universities of Chicago, Columbia, Michigan and Yale, and others are being constructed at the Universities of Cambridge, Copenhagen and Pennsylvania, by the U. S. Geological Survey and by the government of New Zealand. Compact assemblies for dating objects by radiocarbon analysis may soon be as easy to buy as dentists' chairs.

Why all the excitement? Is this new dating method as good as it looks? The Chicago laboratory has now published some 300 radiocarbon dates, and on the basis of cross-checks on these dates one can say that in general the method has fulfilled its original promise. In detail, however, there are puzzles, contradictions and weaknesses. It will be a long time before radiocarbon dating is as straightforward as an electric dishwasher.

The basis of the method is magnificently simple. Carbon 14 is continuously produced in the upper atmosphere by the action of cosmic rays, which set free neutrons that transmute nitrogen in the air into the radioactive carbon. Incorporated in carbon dioxide, the radiocarbon moves through the atmosphere and is absorbed by plants. Animals in turn build radiocarbon into their tissues by eating the plants. As long as they are alive, plants and animals go on ingesting radiocarbon. When an organism dies, and ceases to take in fresh carbon, its built-in clock begins to run down. The disintegrations of its carbon-14 atoms tick away the seconds and the years: in 5,568 years (on the average) only half of its original store of radiocarbon atoms is left, and in another 5,568 years only half of those, or one quarter of the original number.

Long before that time, of course, most plants and animals have decayed into dust. But when the remains of an organism are fortuitously preserved, as a fossil or a house beam or a bit of charcoal, the age of the remains can be calculated. The amount of radiocarbon the organism possessed when it was alive is known, and so is the rate of its radioactive disintegration. It is easy to compute the relic's age from the amount of radioactivity it still retains.

The radiocarbon time-scale, to be sure, covers only the last few thousand years. The initial quantity of radiocar-

CARBON 14 METHOD requires that materials to be dated be sent to a specially equipped laboratory.

SAMPLE IS SPLIT from a block of wood being dated in Geochronometric Laboratory of Yale University.

SAMPLE IS PLACED in a heating tube at the beginning of the process of converting it into carbon dioxide.

bon, at the organism's death, is exceedingly small—about one atom of carbon 14 to a trillion atoms of ordinary carbon. Three half-lives (16,700 years) later only one eighth of that amount remains, and its detection is hardly possible. Hence radiocarbon cannot be used as a long-term clock like uranium, which decays to lead with a half-life of 4.5 billion years: it merely adds a second-hand to the cosmic clock.

AS SOON as Libby and his collaborators conceived the idea of using radiocarbon for dating, they began to check the accuracy of their clock on old objects of known age. Heartwood from a giant sequoia tree, laid down nearly 3,000 years ago, gave a satisfactory check; this was especially gratifying because it showed that wood already formed in a tree is not contaminated with carbon from younger wood as the tree grows. From Egyptologists (of whom some of the best in the world live or have lived in Chicago) Libby obtained specimens of mummy cases and house beams, whose dates are among the best-established in all archaeology. Radiocarbon analysis gave accurate measurements of the age of these objects also.

All this was splendid as far as it went, but the oldest of these specimens was only about 4,600 years old. Back of that date the supply of organic matter of accurately known age ran out, and not even one half-life of carbon 14 had yet been reached. Could radiocarbon dating be used with confidence on objects older than 5,000 years? What if the cosmic shower had varied in intensity in the past? Furthermore, the radiocarbon method was based on the assumption that the movement of carbon 14 from the upper to the lower atmosphere and its thorough mixing was a rapid process compared with the carbon's radioactive decay. What if this assumption was wrong? This could easily be the case, for

great ice sheets stood over the Northern continents 20,000 years ago, and the world's weather must have been notably different from today.

There was only one way to check the reliability of radiocarbon dating over a longer span, and that was to test it on the materials of geology and prehistoric archaeology. The age of such material is not "known" in the same sense as that of mummy cases or trees, but some of the geologic dates have a high probability of being correct. The results of this checking process, as far as it has gone, are exceedingly interesting.

GEOLOGIC chronology depends on the study of stratified deposits that represent elapsed time. One way to date the deposits is to examine their content of fossilized pollen from plants. The pollen proportions in one of these layers show what types of plants predominated when the deposit was laid down, and this in turn indicates the climate at that time and place. A predominance of spruce pollen, for instance, means that the climate was cold; if oak was dominant, the weather was warmer. The method involves stabbing with coring devices into the beds of old lakes or peat bogs, where pollen fell and was buried in successive layers of mud as time and stratification went on, and then counting the percentages of pollen in the successive strata. The chronology that is built up from the changing pollen percentages is a sequence of climatic changes—cold, cool and warmer, moister and drier.

This makes it possible to date, in terms of relative age, events which at first sight seem remote from bogs, or even from climate. The pollen remains can fix the time of a rise in sea level that covered fresh-water deposits with marine material. If the archaeologist is lucky enough to find human remains stratified in bog or salt-marsh peat, he can date the ancient culture directly;

more indirectly, he may be able to date it by the stratigraphic relation between a village site or shell heap and a former sea level, or by its debris of animal bones, the time of whose prevalence in the region is known from the level at which remains of the same animals lie in bogs.

Useful as it is, the pollen chronology has limitations. It is helpful only during the time when pollen sequences were continuously forming. Mostly this means the time since the last ice age, for lakes and bogs are transitory features, and those in which we find the pollen sequences were formed in the youthful landscape left behind by the glaciers as they retreated northward. In the light of that movement we can see what an odd sort of chronology this is: it begins at different times in different latitudes, and the chronology itself shifts with the northward migration of climatic belts and of trees. The schoolboy, asked why the days are longer in summer than in winter, replied: "Because heat expands and cold contracts." So a unit of pollen time is not a constant but varies in a peculiar way with the temperature. In Connecticut spruce pollen time (when spruce prevailed) apparently means at least 8,000 years ago, but in much of Canada it marks "today." Fortunately the smearing of the time-scale is not so serious as this particular situation would imply, for the present prevalence of spruce in Canada reflects a recent return to cooler climate. Nonetheless a more typical marker such as pine pollen time, in its march northward from West Virginia to Maine, covers a spread of 3,000 years—from 9,000 to 6,000 years ago. There is, consequently, a certain fuzziness about pollen dates which suggests caution in using them to check radiocarbon dating.

BACK OF postglacial time the geologist gauges time by the advances and retreats of the glaciers. Here again

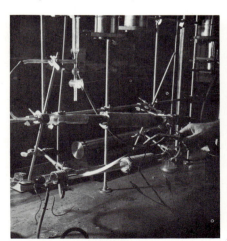

SAMPLE IS BURNED in the tube. The reaction is started by a torch and continued by an electric furnace.

CARBON DIOXIDE from the sample is dried by freezing (*center*) and stored in glass bottles (*upper right*).

GEIGER COUNTER finally measures the amount of radioactivity in the carbon prepared from the sample.

he runs into important difficulties, particularly in trying to correlate independent sequences. The succession of advances and retreats of the North American ice sheet in the Middle West is reasonably well understood. So is the similar sequence in northern Europe. But how can they be fitted together? True, both continents, and Asia as well, seem to have known four major glacial ages in the Pleistocene epoch, and the coastlines of all the continents show traces of the long, warm interglacial ages when the oceans were fuller. On the whole the evidence supports the idea that the stately alternation of glacial and interglacial climates was essentially synchronous everywhere. But for the short period of the past 20,000 years, which is only two per cent of the total estimated duration of the ice ages, one would hardly expect the climatic sequences in different places to agree in detail.

During the last glacial age the North American ice sheet was three times as large as its Scandinavian counterpart, and lay on the opposite side of an ocean and its moisture-bearing air masses. Enough can be deduced about the weather of those days to suggest that the waxing and waning of two such different glaciers should not have followed identical patterns. Yet radiocarbon dating of materials from the last ice age indicates that the ice sheets on both sides of the Atlantic did follow a similar pattern, at least in their retreat. If so surprising a result can be accepted, stratigraphers need have no further hesitation in relying on the radiocarbon method and using it to dispel the doubts and contradictions of the stratigraphic chronology. Has this happy time arrived?

It looks to most geologists as though it has, but it is really too early to say for certain. This much seems sure:

The melting of both ice sheets was intermittent. Before they dwindled away for good both paused in their retreat and readvanced in places. The readvance brought colder climate into regions that had been temperate enough for trees to grow. In Denmark a birch woodland grew up during a relatively warm spell and then was replaced by a treeless tundra. That is, the climate got as warm as that of Lappland and later became more like that of Spitsbergen; as the reindeer may have said to the musk ox, "It will get worse before it gets better." All this is told by evidence of pollen and other fossils in bogs. In Wisconsin, too, there was a mild phase when trees grew, only to be killed when the returning glacier plowed into them. Indeed, if we compress the last few chapters of the Pleistocene into parallel sequences, it is plain that Wisconsin and Denmark have more than cheese-making in common.

At each place the story has four chapters. In Wisconsin there was (1) an early glaciation; then (2) the mild, tree-growing time, named Two Creeks from a place where the waters of Lake Michigan cut back a cliff exposing the spruce forest stratum; then (3) a new ice sheet, called Mankato after a place in Minnesota where the glacier's moraines are especially well displayed, and finally (4) postglacial time. In Denmark there is an exactly parallel sequence: (1) an early glaciation; (2) the mild time of the birch woodland, named Alleröd after a Danish town; (3) a cold time when new glaciation called Fennoscandian reached southern Sweden, and (4) postglacial time.

Now radiocarbon analyses have been made of five separate specimens of wood and peat from the buried Two Creeks forest in Wisconsin, and the average age of these is computed to be 11,400 ± 700 years. The average radiocarbon age of four typical specimens of lake mud of the parallel Alleröd interlude in Europe is 10,800 ± 1,200 years. The agreement is essentially perfect, and it is especially impressive in view of the fact that three of the four Alleröd samples came from England and Ireland, where the glaciers had seceded from the Scandinavian parent body long before Alleröd time; radiocarbon dating carries chronologies across the North Sea as easily as it does across the Atlantic.

A TRAP may be concealed in these figures, because we are not sure that the Mankato ice sheet is the last glaciation that approached Wisconsin, the region to the north being an almost unexplored wilderness. It is possible there were post-Mankato cycles of readvance and retreat. So long as this suspicion remains, the skeptic of radiocarbon dating is free to doubt that the Two Creeks forest bed is in the same stratigraphic position as the Alleröd mud. But the radiocarbon age of 11,000 years for the latter agrees closely with previous geological estimates and provides a good check on the radiocarbon method.

It is conceivable that there may be a systematic error in "old" dates obtained by radiocarbon analysis, for a great number of them come out about 10,000 years. But if this is the case, it is hard to see how such an error could apply to the Two Creeks analysis, because radiocarbon determinations on at least nine samples of material known to be a little older than the Two Creeks forest came out "older than 16,000 years." The supposed error would not be systematic, in other words, but must affect the Two Creeks date independently. The skeptic may still argue that, since the Two Creeks forest was buried, the fossils might have become contaminated by younger carbon from subterranean waters. But the spruce wood and the

POLLEN ANALYSIS is a method of dating which, together with other methods, can be used to test the validity of radiocarbon dates; the principles of this method are outlined in the illustration on the opposite page. If mud is taken from the bottom of a lake (upper left), it will be found to contain the pollen of various plants. If a vertical sample is taken from several layers, however, the relative amount of pollen from each species at each level of the mud will vary (diagram at the right). From the kinds of pollen that predominate at any one level the pollen analyst can infer the vegetation, and hence the climate, when the pollen drifted down from the surface of the lake. To extend the usefulness of the method backward in time the same kind of analysis can be applied to the bed of an extinct lake (lower left).

peat were measured separately, and both gave the same age. This would not be expected if contamination had occurred. The wary geologist can still reserve judgment, but more and more evidence is relieving his doubt.

Several other events connected with the retreat of the last ice sheets in North America have been dated by radiocarbon in the neighborhood of 10,000 years ago. The connection is somewhat hazy, because what the dates actually refer to is the last stage of moist climate in the arid West. A charred bone of an extinct bison, left over from a picnic of Folsom man, gave 9,900 ± 700 years. Charcoal from hunting camps occupied by Scottsbluff Yuma people gave 10,500 ± 3,000 years, and excreta of ground sloths, in faraway Chile as well as in Nevada, also gave figures of about 10,000 years (see "The Early Americans," by Frank H. H. Roberts; SCIENTIFIC AMERICAN, February, 1951).

A number of radiocarbon dates therefore agree with each other in saying that the last ice advance occurred about 10,000 years ago, both in North America and in Europe. They also agree with the stratigraphic chronology, making due allowance for traps. Some popular articles have given the impression that this result caused consternation among geologists, who for many years had considered the Mankato glaciation to be about 25,000 years old. But that figure had already been questioned before the radiocarbon analysis. It had been based originally on estimates of the time it took the Niagara River to cut back 6½ miles to the present position of the Falls; more recently geologists had found that the river had not been biting its rocky lip throughout post-Mankato time but had been excavating an old gravel-filled valley—a more rapid process. To geologists the new idea that one might prove agreement between stages of retreat of

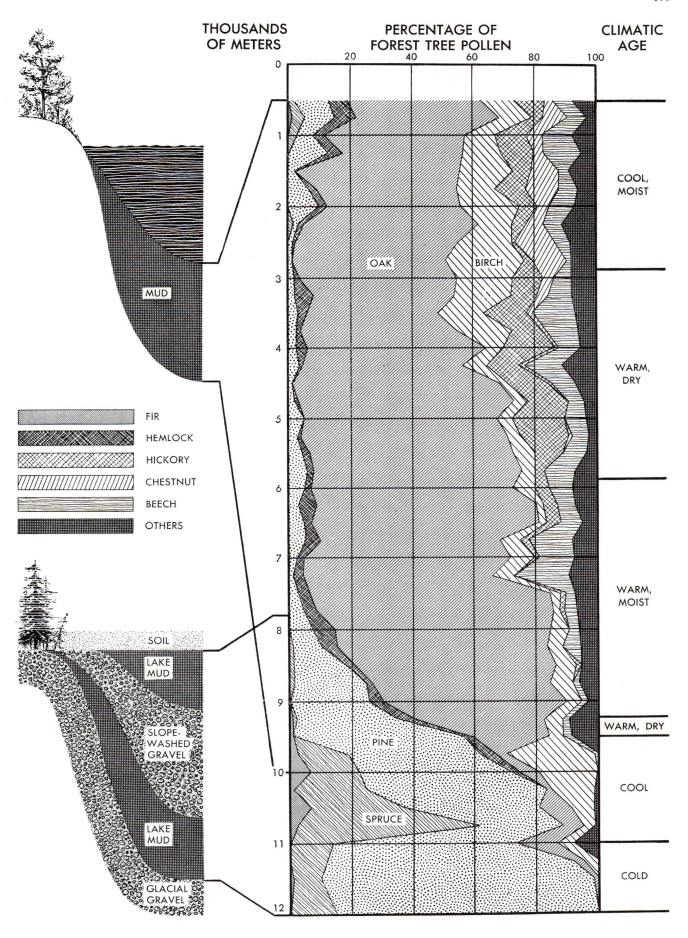

THOUSANDS OF METERS

PERCENTAGE OF FOREST TREE POLLEN

CLIMATIC AGE

two major ice sheets was far more exciting than the loss of a few thousand years' antiquity that Folsom man wasn't entitled to in the first place.

CLEARLY the stratigraphic chronology is too full of pitfalls for an isolated date to tell us very much. A figure like 15,500 ± 1,800 years (the oldest radiocarbon date so far determined) for charcoal from the famous Lascaux Cave in France, the "Versailles of prehistoric man," is not especially informative, for it cannot even be proved that the charcoal belonged to the gifted people who decorated the walls of the cave. Clusters of radiocarbon dates are more enlightening. An example is a group of more than a dozen for archaeological objects found in Peru. Six of these were on samples from the same mound. Most of the dates agreed with the stratigraphic position—but not all. Of two samples that came from the same level, one gave 3,600 ± 440, the other 4,400 ± 540 years. The younger date was from shell, the older from plant remains. At another site there was a more remarkable discrepancy: the radiocarbon dates of wooden artifacts from two graves, which must have been made at about the same time because one contained broken pots whose missing pieces were found in the other, were 900 years apart. What is the archaeologist to say of such a finding? Offhand it seems that both dates cannot be right, but the archaeologic position is not certain enough to show which is correct, or whether both are wrong. In Denmark the radiocarbon dates for objects found in old houses stratified in a peat bog were so badly out that it seems certain that the bog sediments were stirred up by the ancient Danes. In fact, one writer, worrying about the dates of some hazel nuts from this site, and perhaps trying too hard to avoid quoting Hamlet's opinion about Denmark, suggested that the inhabitants had gone in for collecting thousand-year-old hazel nuts! No doubt, like the Chinese with their elderly eggs, they enjoyed the flavor.

The fact is, then, that radiocarbon dating has not been an unalloyed blessing to geologists. What did they expect: that proof of their wildest guesses would be handed over to them, tied in pink ribbon with Mother Nature's compliments? If science were as easy as that, most of us would be doing something really difficult, like playing poker.

Dating the past by radioactive carbon, as a matter of fact, is in some respects akin to poker. In both games there are two sorts of probability—one calculable and the other not. The geologist contributes to dating the kind of inspired guesswork that is involved in deciding when to bluff and when to call; the physicist's kind of probability corresponds to the chances of filling a four-card straight That is to say, the physical measurement of the radiocarbon in a sample is subject to the laws of chance in the same way as the distribution of cards.

The reasons for this become clear when we look at the method by which a sample of material is analyzed. The carbon of the sample, both ordinary carbon 12 and radioactive carbon 14, is converted to carbon dioxide, purified and reduced to pure carbon by passing it over hot magnesium. After washing it is spread in a thin film around the inside of a Geiger counter, and carbon-14 disintegrations are counted electronically. The best counters made have a background radiation of their own, which is no lower than 2½ counts per minute even after cosmic rays and other sorts of stray radiation have been screened out. The net radioactivity of the carbon is obtained by subtracting the background from the total, but both measurements are averages, usually of 24 hours' observation for each.

Like other averages, these figures are subject to a probable error that can be estimated. The probability that the radiocarbon dates so far determined are off the true value by as much as one standard deviation is ⅓; in other words, of all the dates published by the Chicago laboratory, one in three is "wrong" by an amount exceeding the published errors—but one cannot tell which particular dates are wrong. The two discrepant dates from the Peruvian graves are not necessarily 900 years apart; they could easily differ by as little as three years.

There are at least two ways of improving the accuracy of radiocarbon dates. One is to count for longer periods; another is to enrich the carbon 14 of the sample. Both are costly and cumbersome, and neither has seemed worth while up to now. If the counting time is four times as long, four times as many physicist-hours have to be paid for by someone, but the accuracy is only doubled (on account of the rule that the standard deviation is approximately equal to the square root of the number of observations). And if one attempts to enrich the sample, new sources of error are introduced by the new instruments. There is still a third way of improving the present measurements,. and that is to improve the efficiency of the Geiger counter; this offers hope of more immediate success.

GEOLOGISTS and archaeologists can learn to live with a dating method that has only this moderately high probability. After all, a unit of radiocarbon time is constant, and does not vary with the latitude, as the pollen chronology does, and it gives absolute rather than relative dating. These are big advantages, and if it is necessary to measure all the dates several times in order to get accurate averages, historians can afford to be patient. There are other difficulties to be cleared up, however, before we are sure that nothing but chance is producing the errors. At present it is not certain that the physicist and the historian are playing with the same 52 cards.

Among these difficulties the most obvious is that the nature of the material, or the circumstances of its preservation during thousands of years, might affect the radiocarbon content of a specimen. A sample of fresh shell contains about 10 per cent more radiocarbon than fresh wood; no one knows why. Ancient shell and ancient wood or charcoal, buried in a geologic formation or an archaeologic site, may respond in different ways to the carbon dioxide in the ground water that has percolated over them since their burial. If they respond at all, we are in for trouble, and this is a problem of interest to chemists.

Aquatic plants, which of course make up most of the fossils in peat, present a different kind of theoretical difficulty: they do not restrict themselves to the carbon dioxide of the air in making their bodies, but take in bicarbonate from the water. Radiocarbon is incorporated in the bicarbonates in water as well as in the carbon dioxide in air. But some of the bicarbonate that plants get from water will have been derived from an ancient, and therefore radioactively dead, limestone rock. There is a long chain of chemical processes: from carbon dioxide in the air to carbonic acid in ground water percolating over limestone, to bicarbonate in stream or lake water, to protoplasm in an aquatic plant, to organic mud on a lake bottom. Each of these reactions is partly cyclical, and no one knows enough about the rates and quantities concerned to say what the carbon-14 content of peat should be.

The direct approach is to measure it, and let the results give guidance to the theory. Naturally, this is being done. When enough such measurements have been made, we shall not merely know more about the reliability of radiocarbon dating, which brings the physicist and the historian into the same friendly game; we shall know much more than we do about the chemical history of lakes, the atmosphere and the oceans. The main thing about radiocarbon dating, then, is not the dates themselves, exciting though they are. It is the dawning realization that a new field has come into being, one that is worthy of the best talent that natural science, social science and the humanities can collectively command.

22

CARBON 14 AND THE PREHISTORY OF EUROPE

COLIN RENFREW
October 1971

Our knowledge of European pre-history is currently being revolutionized. The immediate cause of the revolution is a recently discovered discrepancy between the actual ages of many archaeological sites and the ages that have been attributed to them on the basis of carbon-14 analysis. Some sites are as much as seven centuries older than they had been thought to be. This revelation has destroyed the intricate system of interlocking chronologies that provided the foundation for a major edifice of archaeological scholarship: the theory of cultural diffusion.

For more than a century a basic assumption of prehistorians has been that most of the major cultural advances in ancient Europe came about as the result of influences from the great early civilizations of Egypt and Mesopotamia. For example, megalithic tombs in western

Europe feature single slabs that weigh several tons. The prevailing view of their origin was that the technical skills and religious motivation needed for their construction had come from the eastern Mediterranean, first reaching Spain and Portugal and then France, Britain and Scandinavia. To take another example, it was generally supposed that the knowledge of copper metallurgy had been transmitted by Mediterranean intermediaries to the Iberian peninsula and to the Balkans from its place of origin in the Near East. The revolution in chronology shows, however, that the megalithic tombs of western Europe and the copper metallurgy of the Balkans are actually older than their supposed Mediterranean prototypes.

When the scholars of a century ago wanted to date the monuments and objects of prehistoric Europe, they had

little to help them. C. J. Thomsen, a Danish student of antiquities, had established a "three ages" frame of reference in 1836; structures and objects were roughly classified as Stone Age (at first there was no distinction between Paleolithic and Neolithic), Bronze Age or Iron Age. To assign such things an age in years was a matter of little more than guesswork.

Prehistoric finds are of course by their nature unaccompanied by written records. The only possible recourse was to work from the known to the unknown: to try to move outward toward the unlettered periphery from the historical civilizations of Egypt and Mesopotamia, where written records were available. For example, the historical chronology of Egypt, based on ancient written records, can be extended with considerable confidence back to 1900 B.C. because

MEGALITHIC MONUMENT near Essé in Brittany is typical of the massive stone structures that were raised in France as long ago as the fifth millennium B.C. Called "Fairies' Rock," it is made of 42 large slabs of schist, some weighing more than 40 tons. Because of the great effort that must have been required to raise such monuments, scholars traditionally refused to credit the barbarian cultures of prehistoric Europe with their construction and instead attributed them to influences from civilized eastern Mediterranean.

the records noted astronomical events. The Egyptian "king lists" can then be used, although with far less confidence, to build up a chronology that goes back another 11 centuries to 3000 B.C.

The need to establish a link with Egypt in order to date the prehistoric cultures of Europe went naturally with the widespread assumption that, among prehistoric sites in general, the more sophisticated ones were of Near Eastern origin anyway. In 1887, when the brothers Henri and Louis Siret published the results of their excavations in the cemeteries and settlements of "Copper Age" (late Neolithic) Spain, they reported finding stone tombs, some roofed with handsome corbeled stonework and others of massive megalithic construction. In the tombs there were sometimes human figurines carved in stone, and daggers and simple tools made of copper. That these structures and objects had evolved locally did not seem likely; an origin in the eastern Mediterranean—in Egypt or the Aegean—was claimed for all their more exotic features.

In the first years of this century this method of building up relationships and using contacts with the early civilized world to establish a relative chronology was put on a systematic basis by the Swedish archaeologist Oskar Montelius. In 1903 Montelius published an account of his "typological method," where the development of particular types of tools or weapons within a given area was reconstructed and the sequence was then compared with those of neighboring areas. Adjacent regions could thus be linked in a systematic manner, until a chain of links was built up stretching from the Atlantic across Europe to Egypt and Mesopotamia. It was still assumed that most of the innovations had come from the Near East, and that the farther from the "hearthlands" of civilization they were found, the longer it would have taken them to diffuse there.

Some diffusionist scholars went to extremes. In the 1920's Sir Grafton Smith argued the view that nearly all the innovations in the civilizations around the world could be traced back to Egypt. In this hyperdiffusionist theory the high cultures of the Far East and even the early civilizations of Central America and South America had supposedly stemmed from Egypt. Today very few continue to suppose that the essential ingredients of civilization were disseminated from Egypt to the rest of the world, perhaps in papyrus boats. There were, of course, scholars whose views lay at the other extreme, such as the German ultranationalist Gustaf Kossinna, whose chauvinist writings fell into a predictable pattern. For these men the truly great advances and fundamental discoveries always seem to have been made in the land of their birth. The *Herrenvolk* fantasies of Aryan supremacy in the Nazi era were rooted in Kossinna's theory of Nordic primacy.

Appalled by both of these extremes, the British prehistorian V. Gordon Childe tried to steer a middle course. In *The Dawn of European Civilisation*, published in 1925, Childe rejected Smith's fantasy that the ancient Egyptians were responsible for all the significant advances in prehistoric Europe. Working in the same framework as Montelius but with a detailed and sympathetic consideration of the prehistoric cultures of each region, he built up a picture in terms of what one colleague, Glyn E. Daniel, has termed "modified diffusionism."

Childe saw two main paths whereby a chronological link could be established between Europe and the Near East. First there were the Spanish "Copper Age" finds. Earlier writers had likened the megalithic tombs of Spain, particularly those with corbeled vaults, to the great tholos tombs of Mycenae, which were built around 1500 B.C. Childe saw that the Mycenaean tombs were too recent to have served as a model, and he suggested instead a link between the Spanish tombs and the round tombs of Bronze Age Crete, which had been built

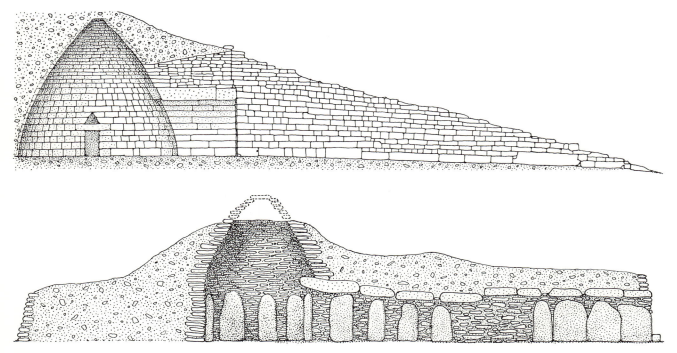

TWO SIMILAR STRUCTURES with corbeled domes are the famous "Treasury of Atreus," a Mycenaean tomb built around 1500 B.C. (*top*), and a megalithic passage grave, Île Longue in Brittany, which is probably some 6,000 years old (*bottom*). Unaware of the true age of the French passage graves, the prehistorian V. Gordon Childe nonetheless dismissed the notion that they were inspired by a civilization as recent as Mycenae. He suggested that they were probably modeled on earlier Minoan tombs built around 2500 B.C.

about 2500 B.C. As subsequent work provided more detail, it was even suggested that colonists from the Aegean had set up settlements in Spain and Portugal. With them they would have brought their knowledge of architecture, their custom of collective burial, their belief in a "mother goddess" and their skill in metallurgy. The fortifications at one or two of these early Iberian sites resemble those at the settlement of Chalandriani on the Aegean island of Syros [*see bottom illustration at right*].

It was on this basis that the earliest megalithic tombs of the Iberian peninsula were assigned an age of around 2500 B.C. The similar French and British tombs, some of which also have stone vaults, were assigned to times a little later in the third millennium.

Similar logic was used in assigning dates to the striking stone temples of Malta. Sculptured slabs in some of the island's temples are handsomely decorated with spirals. These spirals resemble decorations from Crete and Greece of the period from 1800 to 1600 B.C. The Maltese temples were therefore assumed to date from that time or a little later.

Childe's second path for chronological links between western Europe and the Near East was the Danube. Artifacts of the late Neolithic period found at Vinča in Yugoslavia were compared by him to material from the early Bronze Age "cities" at Troy. The Trojan finds can be dated to within a few centuries of 2700 B.C. It was concluded that metallurgy had arisen in the Balkans as a result of contacts with Troy. This view was strengthened by certain similarities between the clay sculptures found at Vinča and various artistic products of the early Bronze Age Aegean.

These twin foundations for the prehistoric chronology of Europe have been accepted by most archaeologists since Childe's day. The appearance of metallurgy and of other striking cultural and artistic abilities in the Balkans, and of monumental architecture on the Iberian peninsula, were explained as the result of contacts with the Aegean. Such skills make their appearance in the Aegean around 2500 B.C., a point in time that is established by finds of datable Egyptian imports in Crete and of somewhat later Cretan exports in datable contexts in Egypt. The chronology of Crete and the southern Aegean is soundly based on the chronology of Egypt and has not been affected by the current revolution.

It should be noted that, as Childe himself pointed out, these conclusions rested on two basic assumptions. First, it

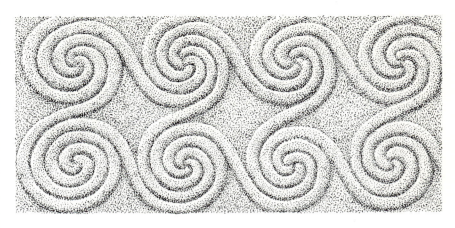

TWO SIMILAR SPIRALS are the decorations on a stele from a Mycenaean shaft grave (*top*) and decorations at temple of Tarxien in Malta (*bottom*). Mycenaean spirals were carved about 1650 B.C. Maltese ones were held on grounds of resemblance to be same age.

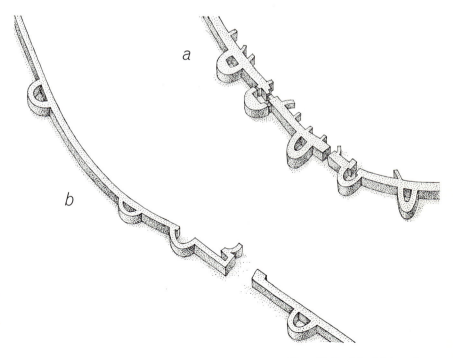

TWO SIMILAR FORTIFICATIONS are the bastioned walls at Chalandriani (*a*), a site on the Aegean island of Syros, and the walls of Los Millares (*b*), a "Copper Age" site near Málaga in Spain. The likeness was once attributed to the work of Aegean colonists in Spain.

was assumed that "parallel" developments in different regions—the appearance of metallurgy or the beginning of monumental tomb architecture—were not entirely independent innovations. Second, it was assumed that if the developments had indeed diffused from one region to another, the ancient civilizations of the Near East were the innovators and the barbarians of Europe were the beneficiaries. Childe realized that these assumptions could be questioned, but in the absence of any independent dating method the only way prehistoric Europe could be dated at all was to relate it to the dated civilizations of the Near East. In practice this meant full acceptance of the assumptions. As Childe remarked of his work, "the sole unifying theme was the irradiation of European barbarism by Oriental civilization."

The discovery of carbon-14 dating in 1949 offered, in principle at least, the possibility of establishing a sound absolute chronology without the need for the assumptions that Childe had had to make. Even without carbon-14 dating, however, some of the arguments of the modified diffusionist school were susceptible to criticism. For example, there are no megalithic tombs in the Aegean, so that some special pleading is needed to argue a Near Eastern origin for those of western Europe. Again, detailed studies in the Aegean area show that the resemblances between the pottery and fig-

urines of the Iberian peninsula and those of Greece, the supposed homeland of the "colonists," are not as close as had been supposed. Nor are the Balkan Neolithic finds really very closely related to the Aegean ones from which they were supposedly derived. There was certainly room for doubt about some of the details in the attractive and coherent picture that diffusionist theory had built up.

Although the introduction of carbon-14 dating did not disrupt the diffusionist picture or the chronology based on it, the dates did produce a few anomalies. A decade ago there were already hints that something was wrong. The carbon-14 method, originated by Willard F. Libby, ingeniously exploits the production of atoms of this heavy isotope of carbon in the upper atmosphere. The carbon-14 atoms are produced by the absorption of neutrons by atoms of nitrogen 14. The neutrons in turn are produced by the impact of cosmic ray particles on various atoms in the atmosphere. Carbon 14 is radioactive, and like all radioactive elements it decays in a regular way. Its half-life was originally estimated by Libby to be some 5,568 years.

The manufacture of the radioactive isotope by cosmic radiation and its diminution through decay sets up a balance so that the proportion of carbon 14 to carbon 12, the much more abundant nonradioactive isotope, is approximately constant. The atoms of the radioactive isotope in the atmosphere, like the atoms

of normal carbon, combine with oxygen to form carbon dioxide. This substance is taken up by plants through photosynthesis and by animals feeding on the plants, and in that way all living things come to have the two kinds of carbon in the same proportion in their tissues while they are alive. At death, however, the cycle is broken: the organisms no longer take up any fresh carbon and the proportion of the two isotopes steadily changes as the radioactive isotope decays. Assuming that the proportion of the two isotopes in the atmosphere has always been constant, one can measure how much carbon 14 is left in plant or animal remains (in charcoal, say, or bone) and, knowing the half-life of the radioactive isotope, can calculate how long the decay process has been going on and therefore how old the sample is.

This, put rather simply, is the principle of the dating method. In practice it is complicated by the very small number of carbon-14 atoms in the atmosphere and in living things compared with the number of carbon-12 atoms: approximately one per million million. The proportion is of course further reduced in dead organic material as the rare isotope decays, making accurate measurement a delicate task. Nonetheless, samples from archaeological sites began to yield coherent and consistent dates soon after 1949. In general the carbon-14 dates in Europe tallied fairly well with those built up by the "typological method"

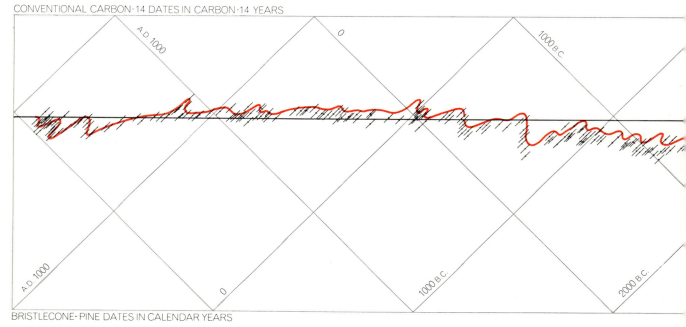

BRISTLECONE-PINE CALIBRATION worked out by Hans E. Suess of the University of California at San Diego makes it possible to correct carbon-14 dates. The dates running across the top and the lines on which they rest refer to carbon-14 dates in carbon-14 years; the dates running across the bottom and the lines on which they rest refer to bristlecone-pine dates in calendar years. The colback to about 2500 B.C. The great surprise was how early the Neolithic period, defined by the appearance of farming villages, began everywhere. Instead of yielding the expected dates of around 4000 or 4500 B.C., the earliest villages in the Near East proved to date back to as early as 8000 B.C.

These dates for the early Neolithic period were most important. Indeed, their impact on prehistoric archaeology can be regarded as the first carbon-14 revolution. The sharp increases in age did not, however, actually disrupt the diffusionist picture. Farming developments in the Near East remained in general earlier than those in Europe. The pattern did not change nor did the Near East lose its primacy; it was just that all the dates were earlier than had been expected. Everyone had always been aware that, for the period before 3000 B.C., which is when the Egyptian chronology begins, all dates were guesswork. What the first carbon-14 dates demonstrated was that the guesses had not been bold enough.

Thus the first carbon-14 revolution did not seriously challenge the relationships that had previously been established in terms of relative chronology between the different areas of Europe and the Near East. Even with respect to the crucial period after 3000 B.C., for which the Egyptian historical chronology provided a framework of absolute rather than relative dating, the new dates seemed to harmonize fairly well with the traditional ones. Just three troublesome problems hinted that all was not yet well. First, whereas many of the early carbon-14 dates for the megalithic tombs in western Europe fell around 2500 B.C., which fitted in with Childe's traditional chronology, the dates in France were somewhat earlier. In Brittany, for example, the dates of several corbeled tombs were earlier than 3000 B.C. This did not agree with the established picture of megalithic tombs diffusing from Spain to France sometime after 2500 B.C. Most scholars simply assumed that the French laboratories producing these dates were no better than they ought to be, and that the anomaly would probably disappear when more dates were available.

Second, the dates for the Balkan Neolithic were far too early. Sites related to the Vinča culture gave carbon-14 readings as early as 4000 B.C. This implied that not only copper metallurgy but also the attractive little sculptures of the Balkans were more than a millennium older than their supposed Aegean prototypes. Clearly something was wrong. Some archaeologists, led by Vladimir Milojčić, argued that the entire carbon-14 method was in error. Others felt that some special factor was making the Balkan dates too early, since the dates in other regions, with the exception of Brittany, seemed to be in harmony with the historical dates for the third millennium B.C.

Third, the dates for Egypt were too late. In retrospect this now seems highly significant. Egyptian objects historically dated to the period between 3000 and 2000 B.C. consistently yielded carbon-14 dates that placed them several centuries later. With the early inaccuracies and uncertainties of the carbon-14 method these divergences could at first be dismissed as random errors, but as more dates accumulated such an excuse was no longer possible. The archaeologists kept on using their historical dates and did not bother too much about the problems raised by the new method.

The physicists were more concerned, but they supposed, to use Libby's words, "that the Egyptian historical dates beyond 4000 years ago may be somewhat too old, perhaps five centuries too old at 5000 years ago, with decrease in error to [zero] at 4000 years ago.... It is noteworthy that the earliest astronomical fix is at 4000 years ago, that all older dates have errors and that these errors are more or less cumulative with time before 4000 years ago." For once, however, the archaeologists were right. The discrepancy was to be set at the door of the physicist rather than the Egyptologist. The consequences were dramatic.

Remote as it may seem from European archaeology, it was the venerable pine trees in the White Mountains of

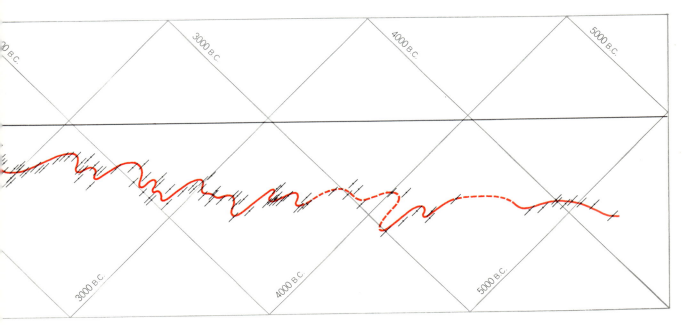

ored curve, which follows many individual measurements, shows how the carbon-14 dates go off with time. To calibrate a carbon-14 date, say 2000 B.C., one follows the line for that date until it meets the colored curve. At that point a diagonal is drawn parallel to the bristlecone-pine lines and the date is read off on the bristlecone-pine scale. The corrected date would be about 2500 B.C.

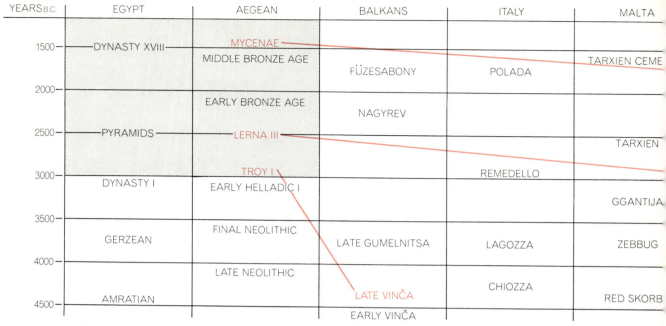

YEARS B.C.	EGYPT	AEGEAN	BALKANS	ITALY	MALTA
1500	DYNASTY XVIII	MYCENAE			TARXIEN CEME
		MIDDLE BRONZE AGE	FÜZESABONY	POLADA	
2000		EARLY BRONZE AGE	NAGYREV		
2500	PYRAMIDS	LERNA III			TARXIEN
3000	DYNASTY I	TROY I		REMEDELLO	
		EARLY HELLADIC I			GGANTIJA
3500	GERZEAN	FINAL NEOLITHIC	LATE GUMELNITSA	LAGOZZA	ZEBBUG
4000		LATE NEOLITHIC		CHIOZZA	
4500	AMRATIAN		LATE VINČA		RED SKORB
		EARLY VINČA			

REVISED CHRONOLOGY, taking the Suess calibration into account, destroys the basis for the diffusionist theory of European prehistory. Colored area at left marks the portion of Egyptian and Aegean chronology that is related to historical records. Colored

California that brought about the revolution in Old World prehistory. These trees have provided a reliable check of the carbon-14 method and have produced significant modifications. By 1960 one major assumption of the method was already coming into question. This was that the rate of production of carbon 14 in the atmosphere, and hence its proportion in all living things, had been constant over the past 40,000 years. The assumption was first really checked when Eric H. Willis, Henrik Tauber and Karl Otto Münnich analyzed samples of wood from the stump of a giant sequoia that could be dated exactly by counting its annual growth rings. Although the carbon-14 dates and the tree-ring dates agreed to within 100 years all the way back to A.D. 650, some minor but real fluctuations were observed. This suggested that there had been definite small changes in the rate of carbon-14 production in the past.

It was obviously desirable to check back to even earlier periods. Fortunately the fantastically long life of the California bristlecone pine (*Pinus aristata*) was known to the late Edmund Schulman of the Laboratory of Tree-Ring Research at the University of Arizona. Bristlecone pines as old as 4,600 years had been authenticated. Since Schulman's death the study of the trees has been energetically pursued by Charles Wesley Ferguson of the same laboratory. With ring sequences from many bristlecones, Ferguson has succeeded in building up a continuous absolute chronology

reaching back nearly 8,200 years. The compilation of such a chronology, with due provision for multiple growth rings and missing rings, is a formidable task. Ferguson and his colleagues have developed computer programs for the comparison and matching of the ring sequence of different trees. This admirably systematic work has been the indispensable foundation of the second carbon-14 revolution.

Ferguson supplied wood samples whose absolute age had been determined by ring-counting to three independent carbon-14 laboratories: one at the University of Arizona, one at the University of Pennsylvania and one at the University of California at San Diego. The carbon-14 determinations, which in general agree fairly well with one another, reveal major discrepancies between previously accepted carbon-14 dates and actual dates. At San Diego, Hans E. Suess has analyzed more than 300 such samples and has built up an impressively clear and coherent picture of these discrepancies.

The divergence between the carbon-14 and tree-ring dates is not serious after 1500 B.C. Before that time the difference becomes progressively larger and amounts to as much as 700 years by 2500 B.C. The carbon-14 dates are all too young, but Suess's analysis can be used to correct them [*see illustration on preceding two pages*].

One problem that has emerged is that, in addition to a large first-order divergence, Suess's calibration curve shows

smaller second-order fluctuations or "kinks." Sometimes the rate of carbon-14 production has fluctuated so rapidly that samples of different ages show an identical concentration of carbon 14 in spite of the fact that the older sample allowed more time for radioactive decay. This means that a given carbon-14 date can very well correspond to several different calendar dates.

The reasons for the fluctuations are not yet known with certainty, but the Czechoslovakian geophysicist V. Bucha has shown that there is a striking correlation between the divergence in dates and past changes in the strength of the earth's magnetic field. The first-order variation is probably due to the fact that as the strength of the earth's field changed it deflected more or fewer cosmic rays before they could enter the atmosphere. There are strong indications that the second-order fluctuations are correlated with the level of solar activity. Both the low-energy particles of the "solar wind" and the high-energy particles that are the solar component of the cosmic radiation may affect the cosmic ray flux in the vicinity of the earth. Climatic changes may also have influenced the concentration of carbon 14 in the atmosphere.

To the archaeologist, however, the reliability of the tree-ring calibration is more important than its physical basis. Libby's principle of simultaneity, which states that the atmospheric level of carbon 14 at a given time is uniform all

IBERIA	FRANCE	BRITISH ISLES	NORTH EUROPE
EL ARGAR		MIDDLE BRONZE AGE	BRONZE HORIZON III
	EARLY BRONZE AGE	STONEHENGE III	HORIZON II
			HORIZON I
BEAKER			
	BEAKER		
	SEINE-OISE-MARNE CULTURE	STONEHENGE I	MIDDLE NEOLITHIC (PASSAGE GRAVES)
OS MILLARES			
		NEW GRANGE	
ALMERIAN	LATE PASSAGE GRAVE	NEOLITHIC	TRICHTERBECKER "A"
RLY ALMERIAN			ERTEBØLLE
		EARLY NEOLITHIC	
	EARLY CHASSEY		

area at right indicates periods when megalithic monuments were built in the European areas named. Lines and names in color show "connections" now proved to be impossible.

over the world, has been in large measure substantiated. Tests of nuclear weapons have shown that atmospheric mixing is rapid and that irregularities in composition are smoothed out after a few years. The California calibration should therefore hold for Europe. There is no need to assume that tree growth or tree rings are similar on the two continents, only that the atmospheric level of carbon 14 is the same at a given time.

There remains the question of whether some special factor in the bristlecone pine itself might be causing the discrepancies. For example, the diffusion of recent sap across the old tree rings and its retention in them might affect the reading if the sap were not removed by laboratory cleaning procedures. Studies are now in progress to determine if this is a significant factor; present indications are that it is not. Even if it is, it would be difficult to see why the discrepancy between carbon-14 dates and calendar dates should be large only before 1500 B.C.

The general opinion, as reflected in the discussions at the Twelfth Nobel Symposium at Uppsala in 1969, is that the discrepancy is real. Suess's calibration curve is the best now available, although corrections and modifications can be expected. It is particularly satisfying that when the carbon-14 dates for Egypt are calibrated, they agree far better with the Egyptian historical calendar. Further work is now in progress at the University of California at Los Angeles and at the British Museum on

Egyptian samples specially collected for the project, so that a further check of the extent to which the calibrated carbon-14 dates and the historical chronology are in harmony will soon be available.

The revision of carbon-14 dates for prehistoric Europe has a disastrous effect on the traditional diffusionist chronology. The significant point is not so much that the European dates in the third millennium are all several centuries earlier than was supposed but that the dates for Egypt do not change. Prehistorians have always used the historical dates for Egypt because they seemed more accurate than the carbon-14 dates. They have been proved correct; the calibrated carbon-14 dates for Egypt agree far better with the historical chronology than the uncalibrated ones did. Hence the Egyptian historical calendar, and with it the conventional Egyptian chronology, remains unchanged. The same is true for the Near East in general and for Crete and the southern Aegean. The carbon-14 dates for the Aegean formerly seemed too young; they too agree better after calibration.

For the rest of Europe this is not true. Over the past decade prehistorians in Europe have increasingly been using carbon-14 dates to build up a chronology of the third millennium B.C. Except in Brittany and the Balkans, this chronology had seemed to work fairly well. The dates had still allowed the megalithic tombs of Spain to have been built around 2500 B.C. There was no direct contradiction between the diffusionist

picture and the uncalibrated carbon-14 chronology.

All that is now changed. A carbon-14 date of about 2350 B.C. for the walls and tombs at Los Millares in Spain must now be set around 2900 B.C. This makes the structures older than their supposed prototypes in the Aegean. Whereas the carbon-14 inconsistency in western Europe was formerly limited to Brittany, it now applies to the entire area. In almost every region where megalithic tombs are found the calibrated carbon-14 dates substantially predate 2500 B.C. The view of megalithic culture as an import from the Near East no longer works.

The same thing seems to be happening in Malta, although there are still too few carbon-14 dates to be certain. A date of 1930 B.C. for the period *after* the temples now becomes about 2200 B.C. Clearly the spirals in the temples cannot be the result of Aegean influence around 1800 B.C.

The Balkans are affected too. The figurines of the Vinča culture now have dates earlier than 4500 B.C.; to associate them with the Aegean of the third millennium becomes ludicrous. The revision of dates also shows that in the Balkans there was a flourishing tradition of copper metallurgy, including such useful artifacts as tools with shaft holes, before metal production was well under way in the Aegean.

Similar changes are seen all over Europe. Stonehenge was until recently considered by many to be the work of skilled craftsmen or architects who had come to Britain from Mycenaean Greece around 1500 B.C. The monument is now seen to be several centuries older, and Mycenaean influence is clearly out of the question.

All is not confusion, however. As we have seen, the chronology of Egypt, the Near East, Crete and the Aegean is not materially changed in the third millennium B.C. Although the actual dates are altered in the rest of Europe, when we compare areas dated solely by carbon 14 the relationships between them are not changed. The great hiatus comes when we compare areas that have calibrated carbon-14 dates with areas that are dated by historical means. The hiatus may be likened to a geological fault; the chronological "fault line" extends across the Mediterranean and southern Europe.

On each side of the fault line the relationships and the successions of cultures remain unaltered. The two sides have shifted, however, *en bloc* in relation to each other, as the geological stra-

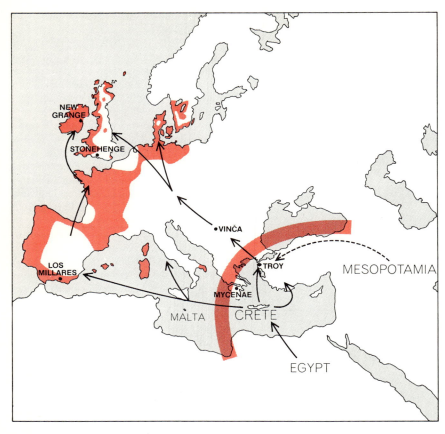

CHRONOLOGICAL "FAULT LINE" (*curved bar*) divides all Europe except the Aegean from the Near East. Arrows above the fault line are supposed chronological links now discredited. Areas of Europe that contain megalithic chamber tombs are in color at left.

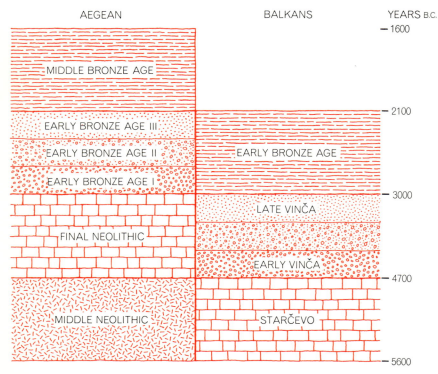

FAULT-LINE SLIPPAGE is shown schematically as it affects the chronological connection between the barbarian Balkans and the civilized Aegean. Strata with the same markings were once thought to be contemporary. Estimated Balkan dates, however, were too recent.

ta on two sides of a fault might. As a result much of what Montelius and Childe wrote about relationships and relative chronologies within continental Europe still stands. It is only the absolute chronology in calendar years and certain key links—between Spain and the Aegean and between the Balkans and the Aegean—that are ruptured. The dates for Europe as a whole have moved back in time, and the old diffusionist view of links connecting Europe and the Near East is no longer tenable.

The really important effect of tree-ring calibration is not that it changes the dates for prehistoric Europe by a few centuries. What matters is that it transforms our picture of what happened in prehistoric Europe and of how Europe developed. No longer can the essential theme of European prehistory be Childe's "irradiation of European barbarism by Oriental civilization." Indeed, the very early dates for some of the achievements of the prehistoric inhabitants of Europe make the term barbarism quite inappropriate.

Now it is clear that megalithic chamber tombs were being built in Brittany earlier than 4000 B.C., a millennium before monumental funerary architecture first appears in the eastern Mediterranean and 1,500 years before the raising of the pyramids. The origins of these European burial customs and monuments have to be sought not in the Near East but in Europe itself. The temples of Malta must likewise be viewed as remarkable, indeed unique, local creations: the oldest freestanding stone monuments in the world.

Even metallurgy may have been independently invented in the Balkans, and possibly in Spain as well. Certainly it was flourishing in the Balkans earlier than it was in Greece. The possibility remains, however, that the art of metalworking was learned from the Near East, where it was known even earlier than in the Balkans.

The central moral is inescapable. In the past we have completely undervalued the originality and the creativity of the inhabitants of prehistoric Europe. It was a mistake, as we now can see, always to seek in the Near East an explanation for the changes taking place in Europe. Diffusion has been overplayed. Of course, contact between prehistoric cultures often allowed ideas and innovations to pass between them. Furthermore, evidence might easily emerge for occasional contacts between western or southern Europe and the Near East in very early times. This, however, is not an adequate model for the explanation of culture change. Nor is there any case for turning the tables on the old diffusionists by suggesting that the early monuments and innovations in Europe inspired the pyramids of Egypt or other achievements in the Near East. That would merely be to reverse the arrows on the diffusionist map, and to miss the real lesson of the new dating.

The initial impact of the carbon-14 revolution will be to lead archaeologists to revise their dates for prehistoric Europe. This is the basic factual contribution that the tree-ring calibration has to make, although inevitably it will be some years before we can develop a definitive and reliable calibrated chronology for the entire area. The more profound impact, however, will be on the kind of explanation that prehistorians will accept in elucidating cultural change. A greater reluctance to swallow "influences" or "contacts" as sufficient explanations in themselves, without a much more detailed analysis of the actual mechanisms involved, is to be expected. This is in keeping with much current archaeological thinking. Today social and economic processes are increasingly seen as more important subjects for study than the similarities among artifacts.

When the textbooks are rewritten, as they will have to be, it is not only the European dates that will be altered. A shift in the basic nature of archaeological reasoning is necessary. Indeed, it is already taking place in Europe and in other parts of the world. This is the key change that tree-ring calibration, however uncertain some of its details remain, has helped to bring about.

ANCIENT PINE, its trunk scarred and its branches twisted, is one of the many trees of the bristlecone species (*Pinus aristata*) that grow in the White Mountains of California. An analysis of this tree's growth rings proves it to be more than 4,500 years old. Using this and other specimens, Charles Wesley Ferguson and his co-workers at the University of Arizona have built up a continuous tree-ring chronology with a span of more than 8,000 years.

23

THE TARTARIA TABLETS

M. S. F. HOOD
May 1968

The earliest known writing appears on clay tablets uncovered at Uruk, a Sumerian city that flourished in Mesopotamia during that region's early Bronze Age. The tablets are known to be a little more than 5,000 years old. Prehistorians were surprised, therefore, when what appears to be much earlier writing was found a few years ago in the ruins of a Neolithic village in the Balkans. The Neolithic find, consisting of three small clay tablets, was made at Tartaria in the Transylvanian region of Romania. On the widely accepted basis of carbon-14 dating, the Tartaria tablets could be more than 1,000 years older than the oldest Sumerian ones. This was not the only surprise at Tartaria. Some of the signs incised on the Tartaria tablets proved to be almost identical with Sumerian ones of the period around 3000 B.C. The Tartaria tablets also looked much like the written records produced in Crete around 2000 B.C., when the earliest archives uncovered at Knossos were established. The Tartaria discovery obviously raises a number of puzzling questions.

The least troublesome questions concern the distance between the Balkans on the one hand and Crete and Mesopotamia on the other. It is now established beyond doubt that in Neolithic times the Near East and other areas around the Mediterranean were crisscrossed by trade routes over which the volcanic glass obsidian, for example, was carried hundreds of miles from mine to toolmaker [see the article "Obsidian and the Origins of Trade," by J. E. Dixon, J. R. Cann and Colin Renfrew, beginning on page 80]. Other materials may have moved over these routes, and written records could easily have been among them.

The questions that arise because of the differences in age between Neolithic Tartaria, early Bronze Age Sumer and late Bronze Age Crete are much more troublesome. Are the Tartaria tablets in fact older than the earliest writing at Uruk? Could writing have first been invented in Neolithic Europe? Was this key element in civilization disseminated from Europe to the Near East, in contradistinction to the usually accepted view that the movement was in the opposite direction? Assuming that such was the case, how can one account for the arrival of writing in distant Mesopotamia perhaps 1,000 years before archives first appear in comparatively nearby Crete? These are only a few of the questions one might ask.

I hope to show that reasonably satisfactory answers can be given to most of such questions, if not all of them. First, however, the reader will need to be acquainted with the Tartaria site and its

SUMERIAN WRITING of the period around 3000 B.C. covers a clay tablet found at Jemdet Nasr in Mesopotamia. Several parallels exist between Sumerian writing and the inscriptions on tablets found at Tartaria in Romania (*see illustration on opposite page*). The Tartaria site belongs to the Neolithic period and thus the tablets have been thought to be older than the earliest Sumerian writing. The Jemdet Nasr tablet is reproduced by permission of the Keeper of the Department of Antiquities, Ashmolean Museum, University of Oxford.

contents, and with some facts about Balkan archaeology and about early writing in general. Tartaria is a town some 70 miles south of the city of Cluj; it lies on the Maros River near a part of Transylvania that was famous in classical times for its rich gold deposits. The Tartaria site is a mound some 250 yards long and 100 yards wide. It was first excavated in 1942 and 1943 but the war forced a halt; digging began again, under the direction of N. Vlassa of the Cluj Institute of History and Archaeology, only in 1961.

The main reason for excavating the Tartaria mound was that it was an undisturbed site and might provide a much-needed key to a more famous Neolithic site nearby: the mound at Tordos. This was one of the first Neolithic sites to be studied in Europe; excavations had been made there off and on since 1874. The most recent excavation had been undertaken in 1910. Soon afterward a nearby stream shifted its course and washed away most of the mound. Not all the digging had been up to modern standards, and it was hoped that a clear stratigraphic record from Tartaria would enable prehistorians to put the large number of artifacts from Tordos in their proper chronological sequence.

The culture represented at both Tordos and Tartaria is called Vinca after a major Neolithic village site in Yugoslavia, 120 miles southwest of the two mounds in Romania. The Vinca people were farmers who built simple huts with a framework of wooden posts and walls woven from thin branches and daubed with clay. When such a dwelling fell into disrepair or was destroyed, the villagers built a new hut on top of the leveled wreckage of the old one. Settlement mounds thus rose in the Balkans in the same way as did the *hüyüks* of Asia Minor and the *tepes* and *tells* of the Near East. The mound at Vinca is more than 30 feet high and has many successive building levels. The Tartaria mound is only six feet high but four periods of occupation can be distinguished.

The Vinca culture evidently lasted a long time, perhaps for 1,000 years or more. It is traditionally classified as a Neolithic culture, that is to say, a culture in which metal and its uses were unknown. In actuality two main phases of the culture can be distinguished, and throughout the later phase the Vinca farmers possessed axes and other tools made of copper, as well as axes and adzes made of polished stone and knives and arrowheads made of chipped flint and obsidian. Traces of copper have also been found in strata belonging to the

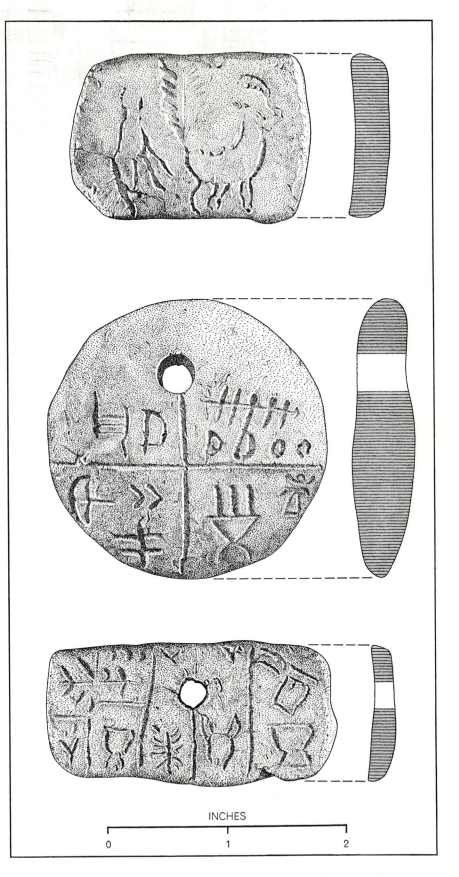

INCHES

0   1   2

THREE INSCRIBED TABLETS, found at the bottom of an ash-filled pit at Tartaria, are reproduced slightly larger than actual size. The tablets are marked on one face only. Many of the marks resemble the signs used for numerals and for syllables in Sumerian writing.

earlier phase of the Vinca culture; these traces are thought to be the remains of imported metal ornaments rather than objects made locally.

Of the upper three occupation levels at Tartaria, the lower two belong to the later phase of the Vinca culture and the uppermost to a still later period. The lowest level at the site belongs to the earlier Vinca phase. Vlassa and his co-workers discovered that a pit had been dug down below the lowest level, apparently during the time when that level was occupied. The pit was filled with ashes. In a small heap at its bottom the diggers found 26 clay figurines, two stone figurines, a seashell bracelet and the three inscribed tablets. Nearby were the disjointed and scorched bones of an adult human. The pit had evidently been used for a ritual, perhaps a sacrifice involving some form of cannibalism, and the tablets may owe their preservation to their having been baked in the same

fire that scorched the bones and filled the pit with ashes.

The Tartaria tablets are small. Two of them are rectangular; they are respectively two inches and two and a half inches across, an inch high and a quarter of an inch thick. The third tablet is a roundel, or disk; it is two and a quarter inches in diameter and is thicker than the other tablets [see illustration on preceding page]. The tablets are inscribed on only one face. The roundel and the larger of the rectangles have a hole in them through which a string may have been passed; they are also incised with signs that appear to be more than simple pictographs. The third tablet seems to be exclusively pictographic; at its right side is the figure of a goat, in the middle what may be the branch of a tree or an ear of grain, and at the left another animal, perhaps a second goat.

Most of the signs on the roundel resemble symbols the early Sumerians

incised in clay to record numerals or syllables. Their closest Sumerian counterparts are signs written during a period around 3000 B.C. This fact was noted by Vlassa at the time the tablets were discovered and was subsequently confirmed by the late Adam Falkenstein of the University of Heidelberg, the principal student of the written records of Uruk. Tablets that bear writing of this period, known as the Jemdet Nasr phase, have been unearthed both at the city of Uruk and at the lesser site of Jemdet Nasr itself. Among the more striking resemblances are the following.

To write the number 10 the Sumerians at that time held a round stick upright and pressed its end straight into the clay, making a circular mark. They represented two other numbers by pressing the end of the stick into the clay at an angle, making a semicircular mark: a small semicircle represented the number one, a large semicircle the number 60.

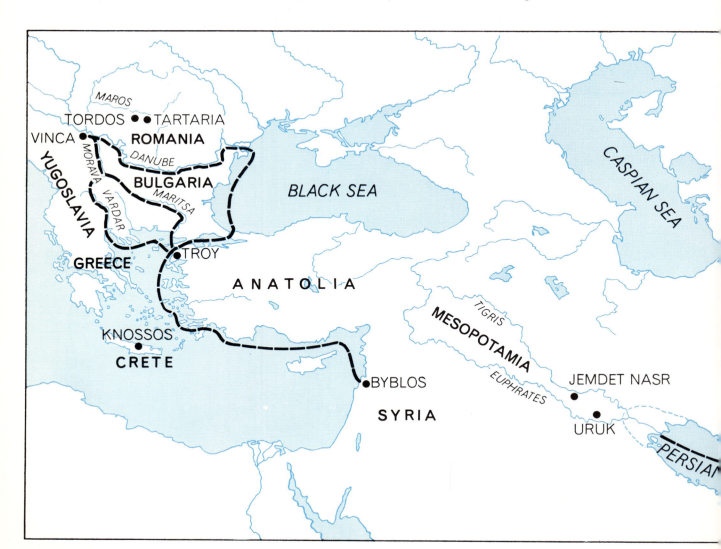

ANCIENT WORLD, from the Indus to the Danube, may have been familiar to the merchant voyagers of the Near East. In the latter half of the third millennium B.C. the Mesopotamian monarch Sargon of Akkad conquered Syria and also raided into eastern Anatolia. In

The Tartaria roundel is incised with similar circles and semicircles in two sizes, rendered in outline rather than punched into the clay.

To denote the syllables *En-Gi*, the name of a god, the Sumerians linked one sign, a long line crossed by a number of short dashes, with another, a grid with several parallel bars. A sign resembling each of the Sumerian ones appears on the Tartaria roundel, although they are incised separately rather than together. Perhaps the most striking resemblance is a candelabrum-shaped sign in the lower right quadrant of the roundel. A sign just like it is very common on the tablets from Jemdet Nasr. A number of other parallels between the Jemdet Nasr and the Tartaria signs can be noted [see *bottom illustration on page 215*].

The parallels are not limited to signs alone. For example, the Sumerians incised their tablets with horizontal and vertical lines to separate one group of signs from another. There are similar dividing lines on the Tartaria roundel and the larger rectangle. In addition, on the Sumerian tablets a single word sign or a pair of signs is regularly found within a marked-off space along with signs that represent numbers. Two of the four divisions of the Tartaria roundel contain similar combinations. Finally, the Sumerians usually wrote on rectangular tablets.

There are differences as well as parallels. Rectangular Sumerian tablets with holes in them have been found, but they are extremely rare. Moreover, although most of the Tartaria signs are comparable to Sumerian signs, and some are strikingly comparable, they are by no means always identical with them.

Some of the differences between the Tartaria tablets and early Sumerian writing are points of resemblance with respect to the early written records of Crete. The earliest known Cretan tab-

lets, including rectangles and roundels, often have string holes [see *top illustration on page 215*]. At least four signs on the Tartaria tablets resemble signs on the tablets found in the 1900's by Sir Arthur Evans in the part of the palace at Knossos that he named the Hieroglyphic Deposit. Since then similar tablets have been found in the ruins of the palace at Phaistos in southern Crete and at Mallia, east of Knossos.

There are also differences between the Tartaria tablets and those of Crete. A few of the earliest Cretan tablets, for instance, have lines that mark off groups of signs, but the practice was evidently becoming obsolete and most tablets have no lines. Every Tartaria sign that has a Cretan equivalent also has a Sumerian one, but some signs with Sumerian equivalents have no Cretan counterparts.

The Jemdet Nasr phase of Sumerian history is dated around 3000 B.C. In Crete, where the earliest evidence of writing is in the form of stone seals engraved with signs and of clay impressions made with seals, no sign-bearing seal is yet known that can be dated more than a century or so before 2000 B.C. The oldest written tablets discovered so far do not appear until later; the tablets in the Hieroglyphic Deposit at Knossos, for example, may not have been made until 1700 B.C. The early forms of Sumerian and Cretan writing may therefore have been separated in time by as much as 1,300 years. They have a minimum separation of some 900 years.

A number of carbon-14 dates from Neolithic sites in the Balkans indicate that the Vinca culture rose well before 4000 B.C. and perhaps even before 5000. This means that the Tartaria tablets could be a good deal more than 1,000 years older than their Sumerian counterparts and more than 2,000 years older than the Cretan ones. Is it possible somehow to bring these dates into line?

One way to do so is to deny that the Tartaria tablets are from the earlier phase of the Vinca culture. One might suggest that the pit where they were found had been dug down not from the lowest level of the Tartaria mound but from somewhere higher up. The pit's contents could then be given a considerably later date. But the excavation was a careful one, and Vlassa certainly got the impression that the pit had been dug down from the mound's lowest level. Vlassa's position is independently supported by the opinion of most experts that the figurines found in the pit are characteristic of the earlier phase of the

his successors' day traders visited the Indus delta (*right*). The author suggests that Syrian traders may have traveled beyond Troy to the middle Danube (*left*) in even earlier times.

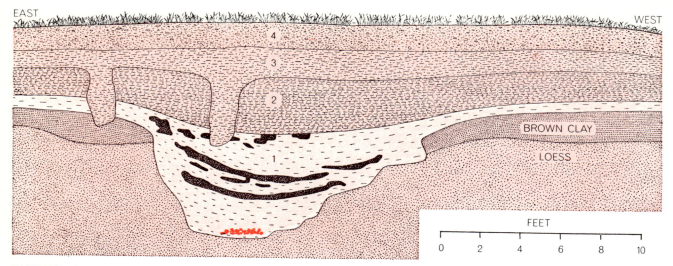

EAST   WEST

BROWN CLAY

LOESS

FEET

0   2   4   6   8   10

TARTARIA MOUND is seen in cross section. The three upper strata represent the later phase of the Vinca culture and a period thereafter. Two small pits had been dug down from the surface of the third level. The lowest stratum belongs to the earlier Vinca phase; here a large pit had been dug down into the underlying loess. It contained the tablets, human bones and other remains.

Vinca culture and not of the later phase, although this view is not held unanimously.

If we accept the Tartaria tablets as being from an authentically early period, what other ways are there to explain the puzzle? One would be to deny that the tablets had any real connection with early Sumerian writing, but the resemblances are so strong that such an argument is difficult to accept. Another way would be to challenge the validity of the carbon-14 dates obtained from Neolithic sites in the Balkans. This does not, of course, mean doubting the scientific principles of carbon-14 dating. The many carbon-14 dates for Neolithic cultures in central and eastern Europe are reasonably consistent and also in good agreement with the sequence of relative chronology suggested independently by archaeological correlations. There may nonetheless be room for thinking that the entire sequence of carbon-14 dates obtained for Neolithic Europe north of the Mediterranean is both too early and too long.

It has been suggested that carbon-14 dates may vary slightly in relation to latitude. Perhaps the variations due to latitude were greater in the Neolithic period than is now supposed. Perhaps factors of climate, or other factors that are not yet understood, have drastically influenced the carbon-14 dates for certain areas during early periods. Whatever the truth of the matter, once it is agreed that the Tartaria tablets' connection with Sumerian writing is authentic, and that they were written during the earlier phase of the Vinca culture, I find one conclusion inescapable. This is that the Vinca culture must have arisen some

1,500 years later than its carbon-14 dates suggest, that is, later than 3000 B.C.

One way to escape even this conclusion is to propose that the art of writing originated in the Balkans. But the origin of writing in Sumer can be traced with considerable precision from pictographic beginnings just before the Jemdet Nasr phase through the comparatively advanced writing of Jemdet Nasr—part ideographic and part phonetic—to the cuneiform of later Sumerian times. In contrast, the Tartaria tablets are a unique phenomenon in Balkan prehistory. They appear for an instant in time, boldly outlined against a barbaric background, and are succeeded by long ages of continuing barbarism that harbor no further suggestion of an acquaintance with writing. It seems impossible that the Balkan Neolithic was the milieu in which man first achieved literacy.

Let us assume, then, that the carbon-14 record is sufficiently wrong to allow setting the date of the Tartaria tablets at some time after 3000 B.C. It still remains to be shown how Sumerian writing of that period could have reached the wilds of eastern Europe. To consider the journey one step at a time, one can start by seeking an explanation for the similarity between Sumerian writing and the early archival writing of Crete.

Syria and Lebanon are clearly potential intermediaries between Sumer and Crete. At Byblos, Lebanon's ancient seaport, the large clay jars that were used for burials in the period that precedes the Jemdet Nasr phase in Sumer are stamped with groups of signs. The signs have been interpreted as a rudimentary form of writing at the pictographic stage,

the same stage that had then been reached by the Sumerians. If the signs stamped on the Byblos jars represent writing, it is plausible to suppose that the idea had come from Mesopotamia.

No formal writing of the kind indicated by collections of tablets is known in Syria before about 2000 B.C. Long before that, however, Syrians scratched marks on their pottery, apparently so that the owners could tell which pots were theirs. The practice is first evident in Syria at the time of the Jemdet Nasr phase in Sumer, when writing had become comparatively advanced. The Syrian owners' marks are not true writing, but they may reflect some acquaintance with the art. Certainly Syria and Mesopotamia had close relations during this period: cylinder seals of the Jemdet Nasr type, as well as the impressions made by them, are found in Syrian sites. It is conceivable that, in addition to owners' marks, Syrians at this time had a system of writing inspired by the Sumerian example and using many of the same signs.

The Jemdet Nasr phase was the last in which the Sumerians wrote on their tablets by scratching signs in the soft clay. In the Early Dynastic period that followed all tablets are written in cuneiform, a system that uses a special, wedge-shaped implement to mark the clay. If, as I suggest, a system of writing in the Jemdet Nasr style was then known in Syria, it could have continued in use there for some time after cuneiform was adopted in Mesopotamia. Such a development could have enabled Syria to transmit a system of writing with incised signs to Crete even a long time after incised writing had vanished from its original home. Such a hypothesis helps to solve one of our dating difficulties; it means that neither the early writing of Crete nor the Tartaria tablets need to be contemporaneous with the Jemdet Nasr phase in Mesopotamia.

Looking at the other end of the line for connections that would tie the Balkans to the Mediterranean, we readily find a geographic one. Only a short distance from Vinca down the Danube the main stream is joined by the north-flowing Morava River. Traveling southward along the valley of the Morava one crosses easily into the valley of the south-flowing Vardar River and can follow that route to the shores of the Aegean Sea. Exotic elements in the Vinca culture reflect this propinquity. It has even been suggested that the Vinca people, or at least some of them, came to the Danube from Macedonia and before that from Asia Minor beyond the Dardanelles. This is open to question, but in some respects the Vinca culture certainly resembles a simplified and barbarized form of Macedonian culture, which in turn is a simplified version of the early cultures of Troy in Asia Minor.

Many of the vases made by Vinca potters have shapes that are basically akin to Trojan ones. Pots with dark, polished surfaces, often decorated with incisions filled with a white paste, are common both in the first settlement at Troy and in the earlier phase of the Vinca culture. Vinca wares also show affinities with later pottery at Troy. In particular, pot lids strikingly decorated with representations of the human face are found in the lowest level and above at Vinca. They are not unlike the face-decorated pot lids found at Troy in the second settlement (Troy II) and later.

Even more compelling evidence of influences from Asia Minor in the Vinca culture is found in the numerous signs the Vinca people scratched on their pots, presumably as owners' marks. There are comparable marks—in many cases identical ones—on Trojan pots and spindle whorls dating from the period of Troy II and later. During this period similar marks appear in other parts of western Asia Minor, scratched or painted on pots. Within the area of the Vinca culture, owners' marks are particularly abundant at Tordos; the signs were usually incised on the bottom of a pot or low on the side before firing. Most Tordos pots that carry such marks have only one, but some have two or more.

Several of the marks used by both Trojan and Vinca potters are identical with signs that appear in the earliest Sumerian writing. Because the signs are

CRETAN WRITING that appears on the tablets found in the ruins at Knossos includes a few signs that resemble inscriptions on the Tartaria tablets. Other points of resemblance include tablets rectangular in shape (*top*), circular in shape (*bottom*) and with string holes.

JEMDET NASR PHASE			KNOSSOS HIEROGLYPHIC DEPOSIT		TARTARIA TABLETS		

PARALLELS are apparent between the signs used in Sumerian writing of about 3000 B.C. (*left*), those of Cretan writing 1,000 years later (*center*) and the marks incised on the Tartaria tablets (*right*). Here only the Tartaria inscriptions are shown at a common scale.

216

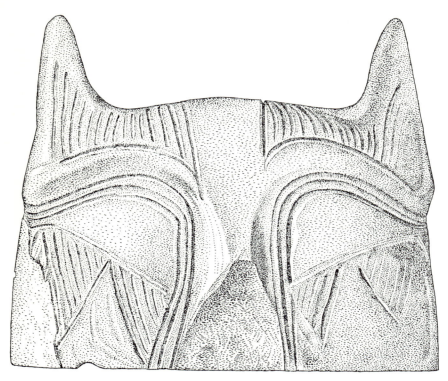

DECORATED POT LID from the lower levels of the Vinca mound, a Neolithic village site in Yugoslavia, shows a representation of a human face, a motif evidently derived from Asia.

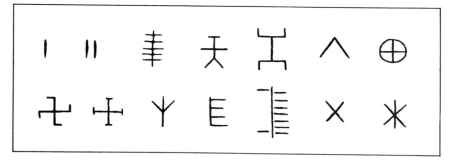

OWNERS' MARKS were placed on the sides or bottoms of pots by the potters of the Vinca culture. Pottery marked in this fashion is particularly abundant in the Tordos mound, a Neolithic site in the Transylvanian region of Romania only a few miles from Tartaria.

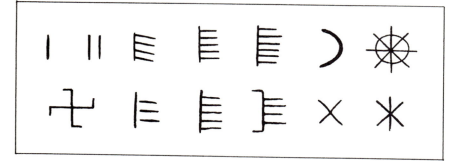

SIMILAR MARKS appear on the pottery and the spindle whorls unearthed from the second settlement and later levels at Troy, as well as elsewhere in western Asia Minor. The ones illustrated here are all from Troy II finds. Some are identical both with owners' marks of the Vinca culture and with signs that appear in early Sumerian writing. The author suggests that Trojan and Vincan marks, like the Tartaria ones, were brought from the Near East. This would mean that the Vinca culture is much younger than has generally been supposed.

simple ones, this coincidence has usually been explained away as an example of independent invention. In the light of the Tartaria discovery another interpretation suggests itself. Might not some of the signs, if not most of them, have been copied from the early writing of the Near East?

The traits that Troy and Vinca have in common imply that the Vinca culture could not have arisen much before the time of Troy II. Carbon-14 analysis of material from sites in western Asia Minor places Troy II some centuries after 2600 B.C., but the carbon-14 dates are not for Troy itself or for sites in the city's immediate neighborhood. On the basis of other criteria dates have been proposed for Troy II that range from 2600 to 2100 B.C. If one accepts a date of 2300 to 2200 B.C. for the start of Troy II, the Tartaria tablets need not have been made until as late as the turn of the second millennium B.C. Such a date would make the tablets not much older than the comparable tablets in Crete.

It is not hard to imagine how Trojan owners' marks could have reached the potters of Tordos. But how were the Trojan potters able to borrow the signs from Mesopotamia in the first place? Again Syria seems a probable intermediary. The people of Troy II evidently had many contacts with Cilicia, the southeastern coastal region of Asia Minor that borders Syria on the west. Cilician vase shapes were copied at Troy, and the "fast" potter's wheel, which was first used at Troy early in the Troy II period, may have been an import from Cilicia. The arrival of Mesopotamian influences in the Balkans by way of Syria, Cilicia and Troy is therefore far from impossible. Syrian and Cilician merchants may actually have had direct commercial contacts with the Balkans as early as the time of Troy II. When copper and bronze tools, weapons and ornaments came into general use in the Balkans, they were largely Syrian (ultimately Mesopotamian) types. The reader will recall that copper tools were present during the later phase of the Vinca culture and that traces of imported copper also appear in earlier Vinca strata.

What could have drawn Near Eastern goods, and perhaps Near Eastern traders as well, to the Balkans? It may have been mineral riches. The treasures of gold and silver unearthed from the ruins of Troy II attest to the city's wealth. Much of the Trojan jewelry is comparable in design and craftsmanship to Syrian and Mesopotamian work; some of it resembles the jewelry found in the royal tombs of Ur in Mesopotamia. Whence came the gold for these Trojan treasures? Perhaps from western Asia Minor, where the "golden Pactolus" runs to the sea. Some, however, may have reached Troy from gold-rich Transylvania.

Gold is not the only metal that could have enticed merchants to the middle Danube and beyond. Deposits of cinnabar, the ore that yields mercury, are found near Vinca. Tin, important in bronze metallurgy, can be had in the Erz Mountains to the northwest in what is now Czechoslovakia. The journey from the Aegean to Vinca by way of the Vardar valley is not a difficult one. Traders from the south could also have sailed through the Dardanelles into the Black Sea and entered the Danube at its mouth. Still a third route is along the valley of the Maritsa River, through present-day Bulgaria.

Near Eastern merchants traveled great distances in those days, as is shown by the records of the dynasty founded by Sargon of Akkad soon after 2400 B.C. Sargon himself conquered Syria and appears to have campaigned far into eastern Asia Minor. In the opposite direction Akkadian merchants sailed the length of the Persian Gulf and beyond to trade with the remote civilization of the Indus valley. Romania is no farther, as the crow flies, from Mesopotamia than the Indus is. Even the distances of the two voyages—to Vinca from some port in Syria by way of the Danube, and to the Indus from the head of the Persian Gulf—are roughly comparable. In my opinion it is within the context of some such trade contact that the Tartaria tablets and their analogies with the early writing of Sumer and Crete can best be explained.

The ritual setting in which the Tartaria tablets were found provides a second possible context. It is just barely conceivable that magicians or priests of the Vinca culture were familiar with the art of writing, but even such familiarity is not necessary to the hypothesis. The culture's relatively elaborate ritual equipment seems to be of Near Eastern derivation. The furnishings include little three- and four-footed clay altars and an abundance of figurines such as the ones found at Tartaria. Both the altars and the figurines have analogies in the Aegean world to the south. A large ritual jar from an early level at Vinca is incised with a design that seems to represent the façade of a shrine; it is comparable to the shrine façades depicted on Sumerian seals of the Jemdet Nasr period and later. One can imagine archaic Sumerian writing as a part of some religious complex that eventually reached the Balkans from the Near East.

There is even a kind of backward precedent for such an event. Twice in later history systems of writing reached this part of Europe in the train of an imported religion. The first time, in the fourth century A.D., a Gothic bishop, Ulfilas, invented an alphabet so that his barbarous tribesmen could read the Bible in their own language. The second time, in the ninth century A.D., two Greek missionaries, Cyril and Methodius, invented the alphabet that won the Slavs of Moravia and Bohemia to Christianity. It is not impossible that missionaries of an even older religion carried the first example of writing to the Balkans thousands of years earlier.

But do the Tartaria tablets actually bear writing? Probably not. The tablets appear to be of local clay, which favors their having been made on the spot and not imported. The close resemblance of their signs to Sumerian ones, however, favors their having been copied from some other document available to the copyist on the spot. It seems quite possible that they are merely an uncomprehending imitation of more civilized peoples' written records. Certainly the language in which they are written, if it is one, is unknown. Perhaps the Tartaria tablets are nothing more than a pretense by some unlettered barbarian to command the magic embodied in an art he had witnessed but did not understand.

HUMAN FACE decorates a pot lid unearthed from the stratum at Troy that holds the remains of the city's second settlement. Other affinities between the pottery of the Vinca culture and of Troy include pots with similar shapes, polished surfaces and incised decorations.

24

STONEHENGE

JACQUETTA HAWKES
June 1953

THE GREAT prehistoric sanctuary of Stonehenge stands among the sweeping curves of the chalk downland of Salisbury Plain. Not very many miles away on a more northern stretch of the Wiltshire downs is Avebury—another most remarkable though less famous stone circle. Around both Avebury and Stonehenge cluster vast numbers of burial mounds, many of them the graves of wealthy Bronze Age chieftains whose presence there is proof of the fame and sanctity of these circles in ancient times.

The architecture of Stonehenge is arresting in its strangeness. Nowhere in the world is there anything quite comparable to this temple, built not of masonry but of colossal rectangular blocks of stone. Plainly it is the handiwork of a

people more barbaric than any of historic times, yet the careful shaping of the huge monoliths, the use of horizontal lintel stones, and above all the coherence of the whole as a work of architecture set it far above the usual megalithic building of prehistoric western Europe.

It is no wonder, then, that for the past thousand years Stonehenge has been so famous as to attract countless visitors and speculation of every kind. Among the many famous men who went there were Inigo Jones, Samuel Pepys, John Evelyn and William Wordsworth—indeed Wordsworth has enriched its literature with poetry of the first rank. James I knew it and was curious about its origin; Charles II, when he was sheltering at nearby Amesbury after the battle of

Worcester, spent a day there counting and measuring the stones to pass the time and forget his anxieties.

Today more than ever Stonehenge attracts its visitors. Summer tourists go there in thousands, leaving buses and cars to buy tickets at a Ministry of Works kiosk and approaching this holy place of their forebears along a path flanked by neat waste-paper baskets. Even in these conditions, once inside the circle visitors surrender to the power of its stones. In spite of our familiarity with architecture on a vastly greater scale, there is something about these massive, weather-beaten monoliths which awes modern men with thoughts of a savage, primitive, yet mightily aspiring world.

We know that immediately after the Norman Conquest Stonehenge was rec-

HEEL STONE is seen from within the circles of Stonehenge. Sir Norman Lockyer tried to date the monument by computing that on Midsummer Day (June 24) in 1680 B.C. the sun rose directly over the Heel Stone.

ognized as one of the wonders of Britain. The fanciful 12th-century historian Geoffrey of Monmouth suggested that the stones had been fetched to Salisbury Plain from Ireland by the wizard Merlin in the days of Ambrosius, the uncle of King Arthur. Subsequently, he said, the circles were used as the burial place of Ambrosius and his brother, Uther Pendragon, Arthur's father.

This tale was believed all through medieval times and was repeated with variations by writers in Latin, French and English. By the 16th-century Renaissance scholarship was harshly and sometimes mockingly questioning Geoffrey of Monmouth and the whole glorious but improbable Arthurian legend. But the new scholars and antiquaries hardly knew whom to put in Merlin's place as the founder of Stonehenge. During the 16th, 17th and 18th centuries this baffling inheritance from the past was attributed to the Romans, Danes, Phoenicians and Druids. Most of these theorists recognized it as a temple, but one school of thought (the Danish) identified it as a crowning place of kings.

TODAY we are inclined to smile at all these notions; we can supply dates and attach archaeological labels that look convincing enough. The truth is, however, that we still have not explained the unique architecture of Stonehenge. Stone circles are a special feature of prehistoric Britain. They are found all the way from the south of England to the extreme north of Scotland, where there are fine examples in the Orkneys. Some of them are circles of free-standing stones; others are enclosed by a circular bank and ditch. These circles are all assumed to be holy places, and all can be said to have some relationship with Stonehenge. But how inferior they are! Even Avebury cannot compare with the architectural grandeur of Stonehenge.

It is not surprising that Avebury and Stonehenge, the two most imposing circles in Britain, should both be situated on the Wiltshire downs. As geographers have often pointed out, this region forms the hub of the uplands system of southern England, and it was on these uplands that prehistoric settlement was most strongly concentrated. Throughout almost the whole of prehistoric times the English lowlands were made largely uninhabitable and impassable by the heavy growth of oak forest. The early farmers sought the chalk and limestone hills, where the thin, light soil could readily be cleared to improve pasturage and make room for their small grain plots.

On the broad chalk plateau of Salisbury Plain and the adjacent Marlborough Downs many lines of hills converge—the Cotswolds and their northern prolongation up to Yorkshire, the Chilterns, North and South Downs, Dorset Downs and Mendips. The plateau there-

fore early achieved the dominance usual to centers of communication. Not only were the pastoral tribesmen of this area sufficiently prosperous to be able to afford the prodigious expenditure of labor needed to build Stonehenge and Avebury, but they were able to build them in places accessible to the whole of England south of the Pennines. They may have been able to draw labor or tribute from such a wide area, but whether or not this was the case we can be reasonably confident that the sanctuaries served as rallying points. At the most important seasonal festivals tribesmen must surely have traveled to them along the ridgeways of all the radiating hills. There is interesting evidence for such a gathering of peoples in the occurrence of grave goods of a kind characteristic of the north of England in at least one of the barrow burials lying close to Stonehenge.

LIKE MANY Gothic cathedrals, Stonehenge is a composite structure in which feature was added to feature through the centuries. This structure includes several important parts in addition to the circles of standing stones which are what most people mean when they speak of Stonehenge. Before going on to discuss the history of the monument it will be well first to describe its parts [see diagram on page 224].

To the north of the sanctuary, stretches the great length of the Cursus, a very narrow embanked enclosure some 1¾ miles long. It owes its odd name to the 18th-century antiquary William Stukeley, who liked to fancy that it served as a course for chariot racing. It is easy to laugh at Stukeley's fantasy, but the actual purpose of this and the few other enclosures of the kind in southern England remains unexplained. What is of particular interest for an understanding of Stonehenge itself lies in a recent discovery made at the west end of the Cursus, at the point where the side banks appear to terminate against a long burial mound. In this area excavation and field survey discovered a strong concentration of chippings from the Blue Stones which now form a part of the sanctuary itself. It has therefore been suggested that these stones, known from other evidence to have been present in the area before they were erected in their present sockets, originally stood here at the west end of the Cursus.

The other important outlying earthwork associated with Stonehenge is the Avenue, which can be assumed to have been the main ceremonial approach to the sanctuary. It consists of two parallel lines of bank and ditch about 70 feet apart which, from the northeast side of the circles, run almost dead straight for 1,800 feet, then swing eastward and curve gradually toward the River Avon. The banks and ditches are now so nearly

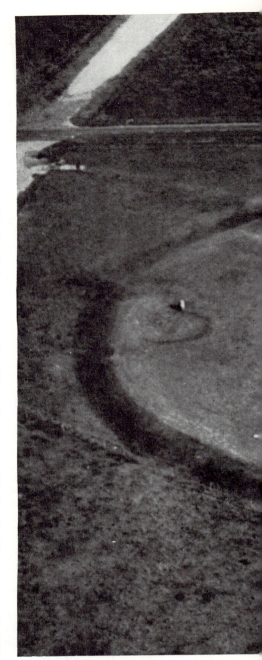

AERIAL VIEW of the monument shows how its stones are encircled

level as to be clearly visible only from the air.

A circular embankment about 320 feet in diameter encloses the sanctuary itself. Such an enclosing bank and ditch is the feature which is held to distinguish a "henge" from an ordinary freestanding stone circle. Immediately inside the bank is a ring of pits, named the Aubrey Holes after their 17th-century discoverer. They are 56 in number and all roughly circular. Cremation burials, without urns and normally without grave goods, were found in many Aubrey Holes and also in a quadrant of the ditch and bank.

Between the Aubrey Holes and the

by a bank and a ditch. The small white circles within the bank mark those Aubrey Holes which have been excavated. At the upper right is the Avenue, which runs straight for 1,800 feet and then curves toward the Avon.

stone circles are two more rings of pits, long known to archaeology as the Y and Z Holes; the individual pits are oval and about six feet long.

AFTER THIS account of the earthworks and ceremonial pits associated with the monument, we can leave these painfully unspectacular but historically important features and approach the stones themselves. Those that first catch the attention are the immense sarsens, great monoliths of sandstone. The nearest place from which blocks of this size could have been obtained apparently is the Avebury region, miles away, and the transport of the some 80

sarsens at Stonehenge, running up to 30 feet in length and weighing an average of 28 tons each, was a prodigious effort, especially as the journey necessitated the crossing of a broad, soft-bottomed and overgrown valley. Presumably they were dragged on rollers by men hauling on rawhide ropes.

The sarsen architecture of Stonehenge has two parts: an outer circle about 100 feet in diameter and an inner horseshoe formed of five gateways. The circle originally had 30 columns, united by a continuous lintel of smaller blocks laid over their tops. The stones are all roughly squared, and the lintel stones are secured onto the uprights by tenons and

sockets, and to one another by mortise joints. The chopping out of two tenons on the top of each upright and of the rails of the mortise joints is a remarkable achievement for masons working only with clumsy stone mauls. The largest sarsens of all are found in the inner horseshoe, which measures 44 feet across and 50 feet along the axial line. Its colossal central gateway is more than 25 feet high.

THE SARSEN peristyle and horseshoe setting astound us by their size and the unparalleled precision of their masonry; they please the eye, too, by their soft gray color and the richness of texture produced by the weathering of the sandstone. Yet it is the other element of this extraordinary monument that can claim the most fascinating and dramatic history. The plan of the outer circle and horseshoe of sarsens is repeated on a smaller scale by a circle and horseshoe of the so-called Blue Stones. These stones are very much smaller and they lack the architectural refinement of lintels. What is so astonishing about them is that they were made from rocks (mainly dolerites and rhyolites) which are found together only in the Presely Mountains in the extreme west of Wales.

It is equally astonishing whether one thinks of the immense physical difficulties of their transport from Wales to southern England or of the sanctity which must have resided in them to prompt prehistoric men to undertake such a feat.

The question of the route by which the stones were carried has been much disputed. Perhaps the most satisfactory view is that they came by sea (probably from Milford Haven in the west of Wales) to the mouth of the Bristol Avon and were then conveyed across Somerset and Wiltshire by a series of rivers

close enough together to require only short portages. This seems the easiest route—but even so the distance involved is well over 300 miles. Across the innermost tip of the Blue Stone horseshoe lies a single so-called Altar Stone. This supposed Altar Stone, which in fact may formerly have stood upright, is made of a variety of sandstone found near Milford Haven.

THE layout of the complicated sanctuary at once suggests different periods of construction for its parts. The enclosing embankment and the Aubrey

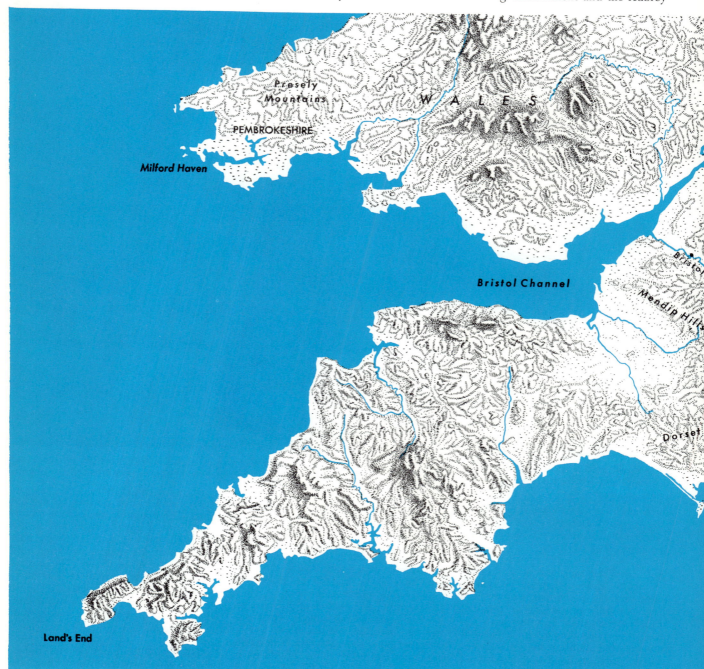

RELIEF MAP of southern England and Wales shows the geography which influenced the location of Stonehenge. When the monument was built, the English lowlands were covered with a thick oak forest; the early

Holes have one common center, while the stone structure is very precisely centered on a different point, a foot or two from the center of the earthwork. The axis of the stone complex as marked by the horseshoes falls exactly along the center line of the Avenue but considerably to one side of the entrance causeway through the earthwork. As for the Y and Z Holes, they are set in irregular arcs as though the distances had been measured not from a true center but by estimation from the outer sarsen circle.

Thus the plan suggests that the enclosure and Aubrey Holes are of one age,

the stone structure and the Avenue of a second, and the Y and Z Holes of a third. Excavation and analysis of many kinds have proved this division to be correct, and furthermore that this order in fact represents their correct chronological sequence. They have also shown that the Cursus belongs to the earliest period, being approximately contemporary with the enclosure and Aubrey Holes.

ALTHOUGH many difficulties and uncertainties still remain, years of digging and research have at last made it possible to give a coherent account of

the long history of Stonehenge. The first building period is now generally recognized as belonging to a late neolithic culture. These tribesmen dug the long entrenchments of the Cursus, the enclosure ditch with its single entrance and the ritual pits within. Just before or after the making of these very humble earthworks they transported the Blue Stones and Altar Stone from Wales. As these stones must already have been imbued with a most compelling religious value, it can be assumed that they had formed part of a sacred monument in Wales. They were set up at some spot

farmers thus sought the thinly covered chalk and limestone hills of Wiltshire. Some of the stones for the

monument came from the Presely Mountains in Wales by way of the Bristol Channel or around Land's End.

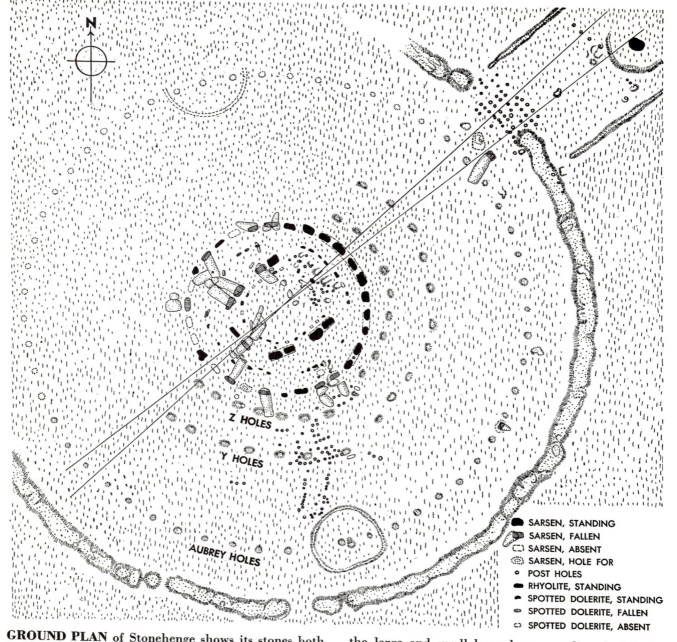

GROUND PLAN of Stonehenge shows its stones both in their present and original positions. The axes of both the large and small horseshoes are aligned with the Avenue, but the main entrance to the enclosure is not.

which may or may not have been at the western end of the Cursus.

During this earliest phase the neolithic peoples were already using the monument for cremation burials—a practice which seems to have continued unbroken into the second phase.

This first Stonehenge has been dated by British archaeologists as belonging to the centuries immediately after 2000 B.C. It was exceedingly gratifying to them to have their historical findings confirmed recently by radiocarbon dating of a piece of charcoal taken from one of the Aubrey Holes, which gave a date of about 1845 B.C., with a possible margin of error of 275 years.

The second period of Stonehenge,

the period of its greatness, appears to have followed upon the first with no greater break than is implied between the Romanesque and Gothic phases of a cathedral. The enormous sarsen blocks were dragged from the Marlborough Downs, given their final shaping with stone mauls and set in position; the Blue Stone monument was dismantled and its pieces reassembled to enhance the sanctity of the new building. At much the same time the Avenue was laid out as a ceremonial way. Cremation burials continued to be made inside the sacred area, while outside it the wealthy and powerful men and women of the tribe were buried with their gold, their scepters of office and other precious posses-

sions below the barrows which still ride so majestically upon many of the neighboring downs.

For the exact period and cultural background of the men of genius who designed this second Stonehenge there is no direct evidence. Certain elements which Stonehenge has in common with the relevant phase at Avebury suggest that this, like the more northern sanctuary, was built by beaker-using peoples who began to invade and settle in Britain in about 1800 B.C. On the other hand, it has been very tempting to assume that the building was done by the people of the Bronze Age Wessex culture, whose leaders lie buried in the richest of the associated barrow graves, and in whose time (about 1450 B.C.) the power and prosperity of the Salisbury Plain region was at its height.

AS FOR the uses for which this great building was raised, there is no possibility of doubting that it was a sacred place, and little need, except for the excessively cautious or scholastic, to refrain from calling it a temple. There is no question, either, that its orientation was dictated by the position of the midsummer sunrise. The axis of the second Stonehenge points to the spot where the sun would have risen at the summer solstice during the first half of the second millennium before Christ.

If in its second phase the monument reached its glory, in its third phase it must have presented a melancholy picture of decay. It would hardly be possible to claim anything better for a period represented by the Y and Z Holes, and possibly by a single inhumed burial! It is not known for what purpose these Y and Z Holes were dug, for they appear never to have held either posts or standing stones.

That they were dug after the stone circle was already tumbling into decay is clearly shown by at least one piece of evidence. One of the big sarsens of the outer stone circle has fallen across the Z circle, and there is no hole beneath the stone, although the spacing of the Z Holes indicates that one should have been there. It seems plain enough that it could not be dug because the stone already blocked the way.

Pieces of pottery found in the pits suggest that the Y and Z Holes date from the Celtic Iron Age, probably from about the second century B.C. If this is so, it is more than likely that they represent a very limited attempt to restore the use of the sanctuary after a long period of decay covering all the latter part of the Bronze Age. This Iron Age revival makes it permissible to say that perhaps by good luck Stukeley may not have been altogether wrong when he spread the idea, still too widely held, that Stonehenge was the handiwork of the Celtic priesthood of the Druids. Build it they most certainly did not, but they may conceivably have officiated there before the ancient sanctuary was abandoned and left to turn into a noble ruin.

AS WE have seen, the history of Stonehenge did not end with its abandonment. If we take a unified view of history, Stonehenge is no less important as a subject for countless chroniclers and many poets, as a place visited by Pepys and where Charles II whiled away an afternoon after the battle of Worcester, than it is as the greatest sanctuary of prehistoric Europe. Certainly we can say that if in the Bronze Age it was known throughout Britain, today it is famous all around the world.

VARIOUS ASPECTS of Stonehenge are shown by these photographs. The monument is seen from the east (*top*), southeast (*middle*) and northwest.

25

PREHISTORIC SWISS LAKE DWELLERS

HANSJÜRGEN MÜLLER-BECK
December 1961

Nearly everyone has heard about the lake dwellers of prehistoric Switzerland, who are said to have built their houses on stilts out over the water. There they were, in the land of the Alps, living like South Sea Islanders!

One man is primarily responsible for this rather romantic idea. In 1854 Ferdinand Keller, a reputable Swiss archaeologist, reported on a field of upright wooden pilings extending a few inches above the shore of the Lake of Zurich and exposed to view by a fall in the water level. Ethnologists had recently described whole villages in the Pacific islands that were built over water, the houses standing on platforms supported by logs driven into the water bed. With this image in mind, Keller proceeded to enlarge on the Zurich pilings. In prehistoric times, he wrote, Switzerland had been inhabited by people who lived in villages built on platforms over lakes [*see top illustration on opposite page*]. The statement found such immediate and widespread support that it was passed on virtually unaltered for nearly 100 years, not only in popular books on archaeology but in professional works as well. Tourists visiting southern Germany can still explore a life-size reconstruction of a pile dwelling that gives them a vivid and "authentic" view of this peculiar culture.

Nonetheless there is increasing evidence that Keller was wrong and that his less well-known colleague, Albert Jahn, was closer to the truth. Four years before Keller published his views Jahn had written about another pile field, this one a few yards off the shore of the Lake of Bienne and completely submerged beneath its waters. Like Keller, Jahn believed that the pilings had once served as part of a settlement. In Jahn's opinion, however, they had provided foundations for houses standing on the ground. The lake, he suggested, had advanced in the intervening centuries; where there now was water there had once been shore.

But Keller's hypothesis was not only more attractive; it also seemed to be supported by an abundance of evidence. Everyone interested in archaeology and ethnology was familiar with the pictures of South Sea island villages in travel books. What was more natural than to assume that prehistoric people should have lived like contemporary preliterate ones? Pile fields were discovered in great numbers as a result of the irrigation projects carried out in Switzerland between 1860 and 1880. Keller's pile field on the shore was an exception; in virtually every other case the upright logs were found in areas previously covered by lake water.

Keller's hypothesis was in fact just as speculative as Jahn's. But speculation was about all that archaeology could offer at the time. The methods of geological investigation then in use could not accurately determine dates for the construction of the pile fields. No one knew how to read the evidence in the layers of soil, lake sediment and rubble in which the piles stood. Such "culture layers" usually represent the floors of ancient dwellings; in Keller's interpretation they were made up of the refuse thrown into the lake from the platforms of the pile dwellings. But the techniques of archaeology did not yet allow detailed examination of the pile fields without such disturbance of the evidence they contained as to render almost worthless any judgment that might be made. Not until the 1920's, when systematic excavations were undertaken in a group of pile fields in southwestern Germany, did it become possible to make a genuinely scientific appraisal of the situation.

From that time on the Keller hypothesis was thrown open to serious question, and the "pile-dwelling problem," as it is called, became the subject of lively debate among archaeologists. As techniques of investigation were refined, it became clear that Jahn's view conformed far better to the facts than Keller's. By now it is widely agreed that the pile dwellers of prehistory lived on the shores of lakes, not on platforms over their waters.

My own concern with the pile-dwelling problem dates back to 1957, when, under the auspices of the Bern Historical Museum, I began excavations on the shores of the Lake of Burgäschi, in the Swiss midlands. This is a small lake, with a diameter of only about a third of a mile. Nevertheless, four separate and distinct Neolithic settlements have been found on its shores. One, excavated in the 19th century, was so badly disrupted that its archaeological value was completely destroyed. Two others have been only partially excavated in more recent times. The fourth, on the south shore of the lake, was the object of our investigation. We have studied it in detail and, although a final report of the findings will not be completed until 1963, the major outlines are clear. Our work has served two important purposes. It has helped to fill in the picture of Neolithic life in Europe north of the Alps and it has contributed significantly to a solution of the pile-dwelling problem.

Our first view of the south site was of a reedy shore behind which, at a distance of from five to 10 yards, begins the growth of bushes and trees that gradually deepens into true forest. A few piles protrude from the lake bed near the shore, but none reach as high as the sur-

PREHISTORIC SWISS PILE DWELLINGS were thought to have stood on platforms over lakes, like villages in certain Pacific islands. This drawing is based on a reconstruction that was proposed in 1854 by Ferdinand Keller, who originated the notion.

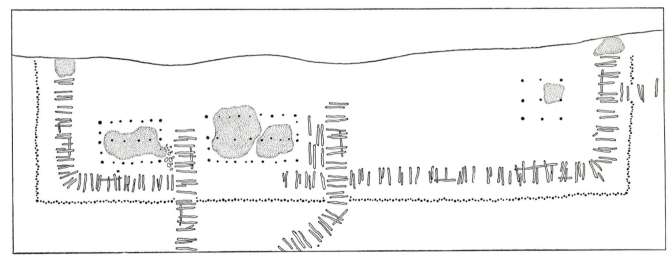

PILES AT BURGÄSCHI, found on lake shore, are shown as dots on this schematic representation of the top layer of the excavation. Shapes with irregular outlines are mounds of loam and rubble. Strips are remains of corduroy log road of the settlement.

PILE DWELLINGS at excavation site stood on the lake shore, as this reconstruction shows. Piles were driven into the ground to support houses and roads of the settlement. Pile dwellings here, among the most primitive excavated, date from Neolithic period.

face of the water. Nor are any visible along the beach; all are hidden beneath the layers of topsoil and lake sediments that have been laid down during the thousands of years since the area was occupied. Under these layers we found piles in profusion, more than 3,000 of them. Most are the trunks of alder, ash and young oak trees, and they measure from about three to seven and a half feet in length and from five to six inches in diameter. Originally set in the ground in a vertical position, they are now tilted at an angle, with their upper ends pointing out toward the lake. The logs that formed the roads of the settlement are still lying in the horizontal position in which they were originally placed. In addition to the piles, our excavations revealed parts of the walls and roofs of buildings and the mounds of loam, branches and rubble that served as their floors. What is more, we have uncovered artifacts and other remains that have helped us visualize the culture of the people.

Radiocarbon measurements show that the pile dwellers lived at the south site in the first quarter of the third millennium B.C. and remained there approximately 100 years. When they arrived, they found a broad and treeless strip of land that was ideal for cultivation. The lake, of moderate size when it was formed in the last ice age, had been gradually retreating, leaving on its shores mollusk shells and the deposits of carbon and lime that form around the roots of water plants. The soil cover was still too light to permit trees to take root and grow, but it was quite heavy enough for the demands of primitive agriculture, and its mineral-rich substratum was a guarantee of fertility.

If this stretch of virgin land was ideal for farming, it had serious drawbacks as a living place. The subsoil was wet and far too weak to hold the weight of houses. Structures built on it would have sagged and tilted within a short time if the builders had not found ways to secure the foundations. To make floors for their houses the settlers employed the older mesolithic technique of putting down layers of rubble, branches and soft earth, which they pounded into a smooth, firm surface. They then secured the underpinning of these floors by driving piles through the sediment down to the underlying gravel of bedrock.

Only a small fraction of the upright logs we uncovered at Burgäschi had formed part of the framework of the rectangular houses. By far the greatest number were anchor posts, driven into the ground to provide a firm base for the houses, for their loam floors and for the corduroy log roads of the settlement. But the anchor posts that were sunk when the settlers first arrived do not seem to have been adequate to support the community for the entire span of its occupancy. Whether the lake level rose with the passage of time or whether the buildings gradually sank into the wet ground despite the anchor posts is not known. In any event, it is clear that the settlement was often in need of repair. The floors sank in the middle as the earth beneath them gave way. For a while they could be leveled by the addition of new layers of rubble, branches and loam, and for as long as this expedient served, the houses were safe. But eventually more drastic action became necessary and the entire settlement had to be moved a few feet back from the lake, onto drier land. Each time the move was made, new anchor posts were sunk to support the new constructions. The piles that represent building foundations are disposed in overlapping layers, one behind and beneath another, in much the same manner as roofing tiles. Each layer is evidence of a new move back from the shore.

It was from the last layer, closest to the surface and consequently easiest to distinguish from the others, that we were able to reconstruct the appearance of the settlement during its final stage [*see middle and bottom illustrations on preceding page*]. At that time the entire settlement measured about 50 yards long by 10 yards wide. Among the piles we found were those that represented the remains of the palisade fence that enclosed this area on all but its lake side. Both outside and inside the settlement were a number of piles that had served as anchor posts. These supported two corduroy log roads, the remains of which we also found. The roads ran through two openings in the fence on the inland side and branched to lead to the fronts of the houses and to traverse the inner boundaries of the settlement. The fence had still a third opening, on the narrow side of the settlement near the shore. The road through this opening was only lightly reinforced, secured by fewer anchor pilings than the others.

Inside the settlement were three struc-

BURGÄSCHI is shown as black dot on this map of Switzerland. Lake of Zurich (*upper right*) is site of early discovery leading to idea that pile dwellings were built over lakes.

EXCAVATION AT SOUTH SITE revealed loam floors of houses and piles supporting them. Seen here is part of the floor of the larger house. Four-meter rule shows its size. Light area around floor is chalk, which lies immediately under the culture layer.

WOODEN HOE was found resting on chalk layer after excavation of the culture layer. The wet subsoil of the lake shore at Burgäschi acted as a barrier to air and so preserved logs and wooden implements of the settlement in good condition for more than 4,000 years.

tures. One, on the eastern side, was very small. There is no evidence that it had walls; only posts seem to have supported its roof. From this fact and from the fact that its loam floor was rather thin, we deduce that it was not used as a dwelling but for some other purpose. It may have been a granary, a working place or possibly an enclosure for small domestic animals.

The two larger structures were obviously dwelling places. The roof of the smaller of them was partially preserved, as were parts of the walls of both and the logs that served as their framework. This evidence makes the structure of the houses clear. They had pointed gable roofs, made of grass and reed. The unplastered walls were made of wicker-work and well-finished board about half an inch thick. On each of the thick loam floors was a fireplace, the position of which seems to have been changed several times. The doors of the houses faced away from the prevailing wind and gave on the corduroy roads that led outside the settlement. Since the walls were no more than three feet high, the houses must have been close and dark. But they were adequate as shelters against the night and bad weather.

The construction of the houses thus

IMPLEMENTS found at Burgäschi, seen here about half-size, showed differences in care of workmanship that were probably intentional. The arrow (*a*), with a wooden shaft and a

combined common primitive techniques with an innovation dictated by the peculiarities of the lakeside terrain. As far back as 5000 B.C. men were using branches and loam to form a thick flooring for the crude, dome-shaped huts they built on the shores of lakes. By 4000 B.C. the inhabitants of southern

Europe knew how to construct a rectangular house with a gabled roof and a framework of logs driven into the ground. The people who lived at the south site combined these two old principles and so produced a new kind of structure. Their gabled houses had log frames and loam floors and were secured by pilings driven deep into the ground.

This principle of supporting houses on pilings is still in use in coastal towns all over the world. One of its earliest known expressions is to be found at our excavation. The settlements that date from later times give evidence for the evolution of more refined techniques [*see illustration at bottom of these two pages*]. The settlement at the south site is primitive even in relation to its own period. In other parts of Europe fixed flooring was

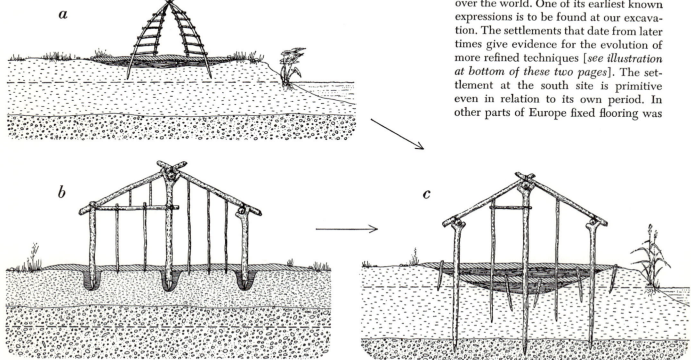

EVOLUTION OF SWISS PILE DWELLINGS is outlined in these drawings. In 5000 B.C. floors of mound-shaped lake-shore huts were reinforced with loam and rubble (*a*). By 4000 B.C. gabled rec-

tangular houses with framework of posts driven into the ground were built in southern Europe (*b*). At Burgäschi, occupied approximately 1,000 years later, these techniques were combined to

stone head, is the first such weapon discovered at a Neolithic site in Switzerland. The bone blade set in unworked wood (b) is highly

polished. The cylindrical vessel (c) is made of well-finished wood. The ax (d) has a stone blade and a broken wooden shaft.

already in use. By the time of the Copper Age and the Bronze Age the pile dwellers of Switzerland knew of it too. By then they also had metal tools with which to work wood. Their lake-shore settlements were constructed with wooden floors and supported by piles driven into the earth at one end and at the other into wooden plates, called ground plates, that served as the base for the flooring.

It is even possible that in time the pile dwellers learned to raise their houses slightly above the ground, as houses are today elevated in coastal communities in order to prevent the floor boards from rotting quickly. Since the ground level at different sites dating from the Copper Age and Bronze Age has not yet been fixed, it has not been determined

whether or not the more sophisticated pile dwellings elsewhere in Switzerland really reflect this refinement. Such a construction, if it was used, may sound reminiscent of the Keller hypothesis. Actually it has nothing to do with it. Keller had in mind entire settlements built on platforms over lakes. The present view is that the pile dwellers lived on the shores of lakes in houses with foundations reinforced by pilings.

The sealed, wet layers of clay, loam and lake sediments that preserved the piles at the south site also preserved other evidence of the life and culture of its people. Within the boundaries of the settlement was a layer of buried rubble, and scattered profusely through this culture layer were artifacts and objects of all kinds. There were the bones of ani-

mals, more than 80 per cent of them the bones of such wild species as deer, aurochs, boar, fox, beaver and bear. The remainder represent the remains of domesticated species such as pig, goat, sheep and dog. From this it is clear that although the settlers were stockbreeders, the hunting tradition was still strong. There were also flax and grains of cereal, as well as hazelnuts, berry seeds and mushrooms. This again is evidence that, whereas the settlers knew how to raise crops, they still obtained a good part of their food supply by the more primitive methods of gathering.

In these respects the people here were less advanced than contemporaneous peoples in Switzerland and other sections of Europe north of the Alps who

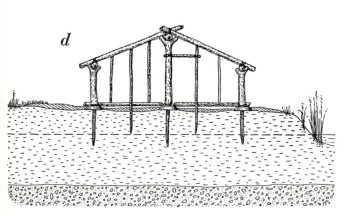

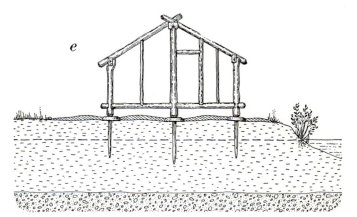

produce gabled rectangular houses with loam floors supported by underground pilings (c). By about 2000 B.C. wooden floors were in use and lake-shore houses were supported by pilings driven into

the ground through wooden plates beneath the floors (d). It is possible that in later times pile dwellings may have been elevated a little above the ground, as they are in coastal towns today (e).

were joined with them in the same pottery tradition. Our work uncovered hundreds of crudely shaped, unornamented ceramic pots of a type called Cortaillod, after the site on the Lake of Neuchâtel where they were first found. Other people who made this ware were primarily farmers and stockbreeders; the hunting and gathering component of their culture was far less important.

We uncovered many other artifacts: stone hatchets and knife blades, flint arrowheads, bone chisels and awls, harpoons and drinking cups made of deer horn. Among the most interesting of our finds were wooden implements, preserved for more than 4,000 years in the wet, airless ground. There were handles of hatchets, knives and sickles; clubs, mallets, short lances and drills used to make fire. There was also the shaft of an arrow with a stone arrowhead still fixed on it.

Perhaps the most interesting find was a string of copper beads, which had been placed near the wall of the smaller of the two houses. The beads, graduated in size and strung on thin cord, were made of a material rare in this part of Europe during the Neolithic period. Copper ore was commonly found much farther south, east and west. The beads are a strong argument for the beginning of trade that was to link the hinterlands of the Alps with the high civilizations of the Mediterranean.

We found some human teeth but no human bone at all. This is somewhat unusual for an agricultural Neolithic settlement, where archaeologists generally recover both the skeletons of buried dead and isolated bones often considered to be evidences of cannibalism. Our failure to find any human bone is another indication of the strength of the hunting tradition among these people. Hunters are rarely cannibals, and they seldom bury their dead. They leave the bodies in the open air, where scavenging and decomposition cause all traces of them to disappear.

From the size of the settlement and from what we know about the size of hunting groups we deduce that the entire community at the south site consisted of no more than two or three families, perhaps three generations in lineal descent. There may have been as many as 40 people; the number of animal bones we found suggests that the food supply was adequate for a group of this size. But it is more likely that the total population was between 20 and 30.

In such small groups social organization is generally loose, and the evidence suggests that the members of this community lived together on a basis of equality, with people coming and going as they chose. The separate entrances in the fence that surrounded the settlement and the separate roads to the houses within it would not have been found in a larger community, where relatively tight regulations usually govern the behavior of its members.

Yet such tight social organization was already operative in many parts of the world. The great temples and pyramids of Egypt are contemporaneous with the tiny settlement we excavated. Beyond the Alps and across the Mediterranean a complex culture was reaching a zenith at the same time that the modest culture of the pile dwellers was beginning to emerge. Switzerland, in a sense, was a backwater, but it was a corner of the world in which people could enjoy social individuality, a quality of life that has not been suppressed in this part of Europe even for a short time up to the present day.

The singular innovation in engineering that gives the pile dwellers their name was to provide the stuff of scientific controversy more than four millennia later on. That controversy has given impetus to fruitful investigation into the prehistory of Europe.

CLAY POTS were found at Burgäschi by the hundreds. All were crudely shaped and undecorated. Such ware, called Cortaillod, is the most common type found at excavations of Neolithic sites in Switzerland.

COPPER BEADS found at Burgäschi indicate the beginnings of trade with southwestern Europe. Copper ore was very rare in sections north of the Alps during the Neolithic period.

26

FROZEN TOMBS OF THE SCYTHIANS

M. I. ARTAMONOV
May 1965

Judging by the remains of ancient cultures, one might suppose that the material creations of prehistoric men were limited to objects made of stone, clay, bone and a few metals such as copper, gold and iron. Archaeologists are of course aware that this is a false impression, attributable to the fact that nature is hostile to the preservation of organic materials. Normally anything made of wood, leather, cloth or the like cannot long survive exposure to the disintegrating effects of weather or burial. This circumstance has caused a certain distortion of our view of the everyday life and activities of peoples of the distant past.

Occasionally archaeologists have been fortunate enough to discover ancient settlements at sites where their contents have been preserved by conditions of permanent wetness or permanent dryness—for example in the lake bottoms and peat bogs of Switzerland, in the marshes of the northwestern U.S.S.R. and in the deserts of Egypt. These rare finds give us quite a different picture of ancient life. As if a black-and-white photograph were suddenly rendered in color to reveal a richness of detail not previously visible, they bring to light an astonishing profusion of garments, furnishings and other creations in wood, fur, leather and fiber. In short, they show that the trappings of life in prehistoric civilizations included many of the materials we consider modern.

In central Siberia, a land whose prehistory has been almost completely unknown, Soviet archaeologists have in recent years uncovered the remains of an ancient people kept remarkably intact by still another means of preservation: refrigeration. The find consists of a number of burial mounds high in the Altai Mountains on the border between Siberia and Outer Mongolia. Through an accident of their construction these graves have been frozen virtually since they were made more than 2,000 years ago. In each of the mounds the burial chambers were covered with a layer of massive boulders. This layer was not airtight, and the burial chambers were soon filled with freezing air during the cold Altai winter. Because cold air is heavier than warm, the frigid air below the boulders was not penetrated by warm air during the short Altai summers; only still colder, denser air could settle into the chambers. Thus the graves became natural refrigerators. Here, in these chambers of eternal frost, the bodies of ancient chieftains, with their horses, clothing and varied possessions, have been preserved from decay.

The Altai finds have opened up a significant ancient culture. These buried horsemen belonged to one of the great tribes of "barbarians"—nomads who roamed the steppes of Eurasia in the time of ancient Greece and Persia and were called by ancient writers the Scythians. Little has been known about the Scythians—if we may call them that —of central Asia. Now the graves in the Altai Mountains show that these remote and nearly forgotten people were in surprisingly close contact with the cultures of Greece, Iran and China. What is more, the artifacts from these graves reveal that the people who made them had an unexpected sophistication and creativeness in art.

Let us note first that there has been much speculation about the origins and migrations of the Eurasian tribes. Whatever their origin, throughout the first millennium B.C. these peoples hovered at the entire northern frontier of the established civilizations of Greece and western Asia, ranging the steppes from the Black Sea all the way to China. They traded with the Greeks and Iranians when they had to and raided their cities when they could. But the wandering tribes of the steppes also developed a common way of life of their own, with the same kind of economy (mainly pastoral) and common cultural characteristics. This was the culture described by ancient writers as "Scythian."

Herodotus and other Greek writers give something of a picture of the life of the Scythians, based mainly on the tribes living in contact with Greek colonists on the northern shore of the Black Sea. The Greek accounts, however, are inconsistent and become vaguer as they reach further into the continent of Asia beyond the northern shore of the Black Sea, until finally they fade off into pure legend. They picture central Asia as inhabited by a series of fabulous baldheaded creatures: the Argippaei, the one-eyed Arimaspi and the gold-guarding griffins (beings with the head of an eagle and the body of a lion).

It remained for modern archaeologists to reconstruct a clearer and more accurate account of the Scythians. Excavations of ancient Scythian burial mounds near the Black Sea, beginning in the 19th century, have turned up an extraordinary collection of objects that are considered to be among the greatest treasures of the State Hermitage Museum in Leningrad. Unfortunately most of these graves, like burials elsewhere, had been plundered by treasure hunters before archaeological workers found them. Nevertheless, the archaeologists recovered many remarkable pieces, fashioned in gold, silver, bronze and ceramic materials. Some of these objects had been produced by craftsmen of Greece and Asia Minor, but most were the work of Scythian artists. They were distinguished by their depiction of animal forms—the so-called "animal style" now

ALTAI MOUNTAIN REGION of Siberia (*color*) lies near the boundary between Mongolia and Chinese Turkestan. The Scythian treasures in Siberia first came to light in the 18th century, when some 200 pieces of gold sculpture were sent to Peter the Great.

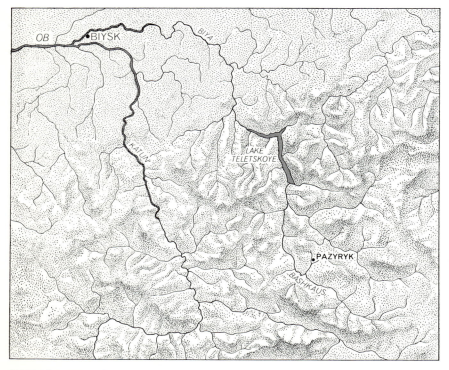

RICHEST ALTAI SITE is the highland valley of Pazyryk, south of Lake Teletskoye. Six Scythian tombs in the area were excavated by Soviet archaeologists between 1947 and 1949.

famous as a trademark of Scythian art.

The study of these treasures by scholars at the Hermitage has steadily added to our knowledge of the Scythians and their easterly cousins. For example, for a long time the collection has included a most unusual group of finds from Scythian graves in western Siberia. These objects were extracted from burial mounds by gold hunters around the end of the 17th century and found their way into the possession of Peter I ("Peter the Great"). The more than 200 assorted gold items include plates with extraordinary pictures of fighting beasts and other animals in the distinctive Scythian animal style; they differ from the objects found near the Black Sea only in that they show Iranian rather than Greek influence and picture local animal life of the Siberian region.

It is against this background that we can now place the discoveries in the Altai Mountains, part of the region that the Greek historians supposed to be populated by one-eyed men and griffins. Strangely enough, objects of the Altai type have been known for more than a century and a half, but their significance was not realized until fairly recently. Around the beginning of the 19th century an engineer in the Altai area named P. K. Frolov collected from various sources a number of local art objects of bronze, bone and wood. Some of them were particularly notable wood carvings; all were executed in the typically Scythian animal style. No doubt Frolov realized that the objects were old, but there is no indication that he connected them with the distant past. Then in the 1860's an archaeologist, V. V. Radlov, excavated two big burial mounds in the same region. Among his finds in these mounds were some fur garments in excellent condition and some carved wood like the items in Frolov's collection. Apparently it did not occur to Radlov or anyone else to wonder how it was that these things were so well preserved; at any rate, no effort was made to follow up the discoveries by searching for other graves.

The present scientific interest in digging up the past of the Altai area began in 1927. In that year a Soviet archaeologist, M. P. Gryaznov, went to work on a stone mound in the vicinity of Shiba in the Altai Mountains. In it he found objects of metal, wood and bone like those in the Frolov and Radlov collections. This time the discoveries inspired a systematic and carefully scientific investigation of similar mounds in the region. In 1929 S. I. Rudenko opened a large boulder-roofed mound in the Pazyryk valley, which was to become celebrated for the richness of archaeological finds in it. World War II interrupted Rudenko's work, but he returned to the Pazyryk valley in 1947 and soon excavated six more mounds there. He went on to uncover two others at Bash Adar and two at Tuekte. All these graves were protected by the perpetual frost and their contents were remarkably well preserved. Several other mounds with shallower layers of boulders have also been excavated in the same region; in these the burials had suffered further decay.

The archaeologists found the big, stone-roofed graves partly filled with layers of ice. In the process of excavating them the ice had to be melted bit by

bit with boiling water and bailed out. When the diggers finally cleared and examined the burial chambers, they found that every one had been thoroughly looted by plunderers many centuries before. There was clear evidence of the manner and extent of the lootings, and certain clues allow us to guess even the approximate time they took place.

As an example of the construction of the burial mounds, let us take those of the Pazyryk type [see illustrations below]. The builders first dug a rectangular pit approximately 15 feet deep and some 25 feet on a side. In this excavation they erected a wood framework, leaving a space between the frame and the earth wall on the north side large enough to receive the dead chieftain's horses, which were slaughtered in the

funeral rites; from five to 22 horses were found in this space in the Pazyryk graves. Inside the first framework the grave builders usually constructed a second, filling the space between the two with earth or stone. The inner structure enclosed the burial chamber itself, which was a shallow room no more than five feet high with a board floor and walls and ceiling, all covered with a thick layer of felt. The body of the dead man, sometimes with that of his wife or concubine, was placed in a single large coffin made of the hollow trunk of a larch tree. (Occasionally two smaller coffins were found in a grave.) The coffin was covered with carved figures of animals or with designs cut out of leather or birch bark [see bottom illustration on next page]. In the cham-

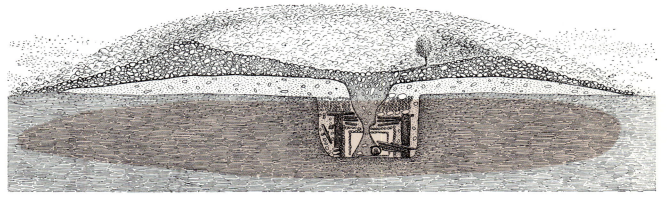

PAZYRYK TOMB, shown in cross section, was built of wood at the bottom of a pit 15 feet deep. A thick layer of logs over the roof of the chamber served to fill the pit up to the original level of the ground, after which the earth from the excavation was used to make a low, wide mound. The Scythians then carted large numbers

of boulders to the site and piled them high on the earth mound. The empty spaces between the boulders collected chill winter air that did not reheat during the brief summer. Eventually the earth below the mound became frozen (color) and the contents of the tomb were thus preserved. This is mound No. 5 at Pazyryk.

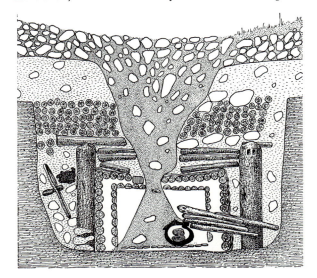

UNDERGROUND STRUCTURE consists of a heavy wood frame within which was built a double-walled burial chamber where the coffin and household goods were placed. Horses were sacrificed and piled along the north side of the pit. Every burial chamber at Pazyryk was looted by robbers, who dug down to the layer of logs and then chopped their way inside (note the disturbed area).

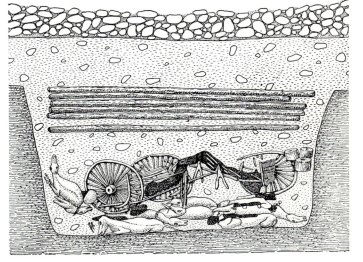

HORSE SACRIFICE at mound No. 5 included the wheels and the frame of a four-horse carriage, as well as saddles, harness and other trappings. Mares evidently were seldom ridden or driven; all the slain horses were geldings. Because the ancient looters did not usually dig up the horse sacrifices modern archaeologists have found many of the finest Scythian artifacts among these burials.

236

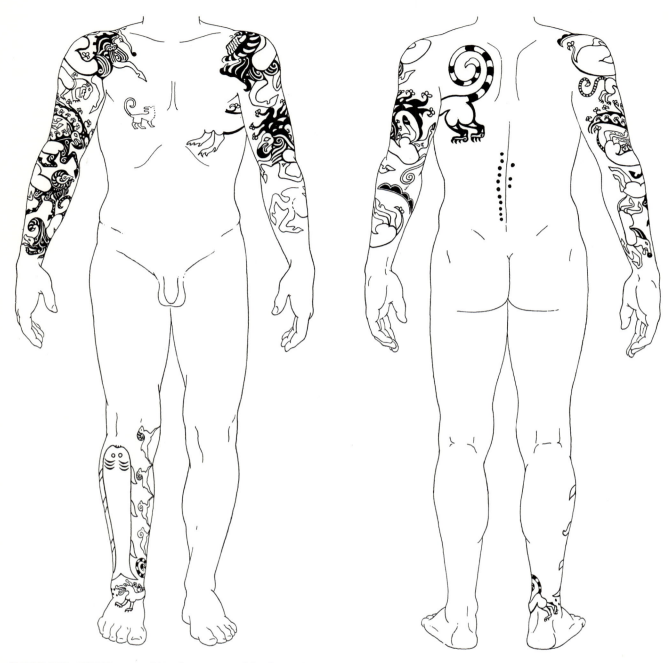

TATTOOED CHIEF, most of his skin preserved by the freezing temperature of mound No. 2 at Pazyryk, had both arms and one leg decorated with designs in the celebrated "animal style" of the Scythians. The figures were formed by first pricking the skin and then rubbing in soot. The various carnivores portrayed seem to be mythical felines; the herbivores (*for example the row of mountain sheep on the leg*) are more realistically rendered. The chief's head was scalped and crushed, suggesting death in battle.

ANIMAL STYLE in Scythian art is further exemplified by this quartet of wildcats incised on a coffin made from the trunk of a larch tree. Other tree-trunk coffins in Altai tombs display carvings of deer, mountain sheep, moose, and even roosters arrayed in rows.

ber with the dead were placed various funeral goods—low tables with carved legs, wooden stools, dishes containing food and so on. The chamber was then roofed with several layers of bark and logs. On this was heaped the soil from the excavation, topped by a stone platform some 120 to 150 feet in diameter. The entire mound sometimes rose as high as 13 or 14 feet above ground level.

All the burial mounds discovered in the Altai region had been broken into by plunderers in exactly the same way, evidently by men who knew their construction quite well. The looters first dug a shaft into the mound to the timbered ceiling of the burial chamber, then cut a hole in the ceiling large enough for a man to lower himself through it into the room. They generally took everything of value that was not too heavy to move. They seldom bothered, however, to dig into the space where the horses were buried, because it was too difficult to search through the stones and earth heaped on them and nothing very valuable was interred with them.

It appears that the robbers must have looted these graves some considerable time after they were built—a time probably measured in generations. In the first place, their digging operations were done quite openly, which indicates that there were no living relatives of the dead on hand to stop them. A second clue is presented by the peculiar stratification of the ice in several of the burial chambers. In each case the bottom layer was made up of clean ice in which the archaeologists found funeral objects still embedded. This ice must have formed from moisture wrung by the cold from the thin, dry mountain air. That it took some time for the ice to form can be deduced from the fact that sacrificial meats left at the time of burial had rotted away, leaving only bones, before the burial chamber chilled and the ice accumulated. Above this layer of clean ice the archaeologists found a mass of ice containing dirt and rubbish, which was washed into the chamber by ground water leaking through the hole in the ceiling by which the looters made their entry.

All of this indicates a substantial lapse of time between the burials and the plundering of the graves. On the other hand, the timbers through which the robbers hacked their way into the graves give evidence that they had been cut by primitive metal axes, which means that the robberies must have

occurred long ago. In all probability the looters were Turks who invaded the Altai Mountains sometime after the third century B.C.

The ransacked burial chambers were in great disorder, with the bodies of the dead scattered about, their clothing stripped off and their extremities sometimes amputated, evidently so that the thieves could remove necklaces and other ornaments. In one grave, for example, both the man and the woman were beheaded by the looters, and from the woman's body both feet, one leg and the right hand were cut off. The felt coverings were torn from the walls of the chamber, apparently in order to remove the copper nails that had suspended them.

No doubt what the archaeologists

have found in the Altai graves is only a small part of their original contents. Nevertheless, even the plundered remains make up a picture incomparably more detailed and more revealing than other graves have yielded, thanks to the permanent frost that preserved these remains.

The bodies of the dead, in the first place, were in remarkable condition, with even the hair and skin still in a good state of preservation. They had been carefully embalmed. The brains, internal organs and sections of muscle had been removed, and to maintain the shape of the body the corpses had been stuffed with grass or hair and the skin was then sewed up with threads made of hair or tendons. One man's skin was covered with tattoos of animals in the

PREDATORS IN ACTION are typical subjects of Scythian art. Both figures are cut from leather; the griffin seizing a moose (top) is repeated 20 times along the border of a hide rug from mound No. 2 at Pazyryk. The tiger or leopard striking down a mountain sheep (bottom) decorates a saddle; it is also from mound No. 2. The most common predators are felines; the figures are distinctively Scythian but the theme was derived from Persia.

PHEASANTS were embroidered in silk on a saddlecloth found at Pazyryk mound No. 5. Both the use of silk and the style of the figures strongly suggest a Chinese origin.

HEADDRESS for a horse, from mound No. 2, combines a mountain sheep's head and a bird. Such objects were not special funeral wares; they show clear signs of daily use.

typical style of Scythian decoration [*see top illustration on page 236*]. All the corpses had had their heads either partly or entirely shaved, but before their burial hair had been attached artificially to the heads of the women and beards to the faces of the men.

Enough scraps and remnants of clothing were found in the graves to give a fairly good idea of the people's wearing apparel. All the clothing was made of leather, fur or felt, except for some shirts that were woven of hemp or a hemplike fiber. Apparently wool was not used for clothing (although, as we shall see, a woolen rug was one of the items found in the Altai remains). The men wore narrow trousers made of many pieces of chamois-like leather, felt stockings, high boots with soft soles, and a spacious, capelike tunic with long, decorated sleeves. Their headgear was a felt hat with leather-covered earflaps or a peaked felt cap. The women's garments included a similar tunic, with a bib worn over the chest, and felt stockings. They wore dress boots made of leopard fur and elaborately embroidered with beads even on the soles—obviously not practical for walking but clearly suggesting that the women must have been in the habit of sitting cross-legged so that the soles of their boots showed. Their headwear, then as now, was more varied than the men's. One woman had a kind of cap topped with a crown of jagged teeth; another wore a little cap of carved wood attached to a complicated coiffure. Several belts were found, one of them decorated with silver plaques.

Although the looters had stripped practically every piece of jewelry from the graves, a few small items that escaped their notice remain as samples of the rich adornment that must have been buried with the bodies. The Altai Mountains have always been famous as a gold-mining area. In the pillaged remains of the graves the archaeologists recovered only one example of solid gold jewelry—a pair of finely wrought earrings. They also found some gold-covered fragments of a necklace (with representations of griffins!), a few gilded bronze plaques bearing animal figures, which were sewed on clothing, and a small quantity of beads, some of them made of turquoise. There were a few toilet articles, including a comb of horn and three mirrors—one made of bronze, one of silver with a long horn handle and one of a white metal, a kind of Chinese zinc.

Very few weapons were found in the graves. There were fragments, however, which showed that weapons were deposited originally in the burials—pieces of pikestaffs from which the looters had removed the bronze heads, remains of shields made of wooden frames covered with leather (and one made of wood carved to look like leather) and fragments of a short iron sword and a dagger.

Among the more or less intact items of domestic goods were wooden tables, wooden serving dishes with little feet, wooden headboards for beds, wooden and pottery plates, felt mats and a stone lamp. There were bags, flasks, purses and cases made of leather, sacks made of fur and rugs and shawls made of felt and leather. There were also some musical instruments—drums made of horn and an instrument like a harp. One particularly interesting apparatus was a kind of cone-shaped miniature tent, covered with a felt or leather rug, standing over a copper censer. Hemp seeds found on the spot suggest that this contrivance was a special enclosure that could be filled with narcotic smoke from the burning seeds. The use of other drugs was also indicated by the presence of horn containers, in one of which was a small wooden spoon such as is still commonly used with snuff-boxes in central Asia.

It is in the horse burials that the archaeologists have unearthed the most complete and best-preserved picture of the materials and art of the people who built these mounds. As already noted, the plunderers scarcely touched the part of the mound where the horses were buried. Furthermore, this section too was protected by the frost. The horses were found in excellent condition, and so were the accouterments interred with them.

The animals were a mixed collection —some large and of high breeding, others just run-of-the-herd. Almost all were riding horses, and they were all geldings between two and 20 years old. All had their manes clipped and their tails bobbed; some of the tails were plaited and smartly tied in a knot. Before burial with their master each had been killed by an ax blow on the head.

Some of the horses still wore blankets of felt and had leather covers over their tails, but most of the trappings had been removed and merely piled in the grave with the animals. These trappings are in every way remarkable. Each saddle consists of two pillows, stuffed with deer hair or grass and sewed together, combined with a saddlecloth, a girth and a strap passing under the horse's tail. The saddle and saddlecloth are decorated in almost unbelievably elaborate fashion: they are covered with cutouts of colored felt or leather depicting fights between wild animals, with details in colored thread and insets of beaten gold or tin. The saddle and bridle are also festooned with pendants carved out of leather or wood in a great variety of designs. Many of these beautiful and intricate carvings were covered with thin sheets of gold or tin and were found intact. Signs of wear and of repairs show that the gilded equipage was not mere funeral decoration but the regular gear that riders used on their mounts.

This was not all: the horses also wore, even on ordinary occasions, a still more spectacular item of dress in the form of a decorated slipcover, or mask, over the head. One of those found on a horse's head in the Altai graves had two large antlers attached to the top and a picture of a tiger outlined in fur along the muzzle. Another mask depicted a tiger attacking a winged griffin with tooth and claw. A third had a sculptured mountain sheep's head, and on the sheep's neck stood a big bird stretching its wings [see bottom illustration on opposite page].

In one of the burial mounds at Pazyryk (the fifth one excavated) two most unusual rugs were found buried with the horses. One is of woven wool, and it has the distinction of being the oldest known article in the world made of wool fiber. Measuring six by six and a half feet, it is woven in many colors and in an incredibly complicated fashion: in an area of 100 square centimeters (about 15½ square inches) 3,600 knots can be counted. The central panel of the rug contains a pattern consisting of four-pointed stars, and its wide border has figures of griffins, spotted deer and horsemen. The other rug is made of felt, with designs applied in color. The main feature is a frieze with a repeated composition representing a horseman with a flying cloak [see the illustration on page 240] before a goddess who sits on a throne and holds a plant in her hand. In its theme and its technique this rug is strongly reminiscent of the Greco-Scythian art in the Black Sea region.

The materials found with the horses tell us something about the technology, as well as the art, of the ancient Altai horsemen. Along with the horses were found parts of primitive wagons. The wheels were of solid wood, cut from the trunks of larch trees. Judging by

USE OF NARCOTICS by the Scythians is evidenced by these objects from mound No. 2. The stoollike device is a censer for burning hemp; the pot contained hemp seeds. The six sticks formed the frame of an 18-inch-high tent in which the hemp smoke was collected.

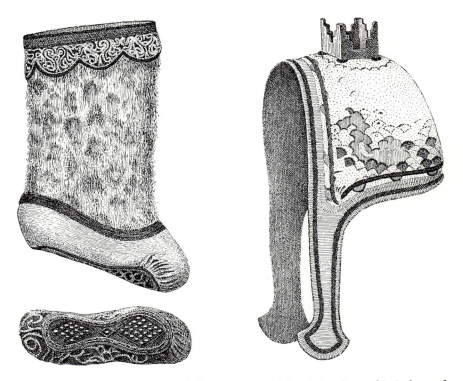

HAT AND BOOTS found at Pazyryk demonstrate a high level of craftsmanship in furs and skins. The crested hat is a man's, the fur boot a woman's. The sole of a second boot (bottom left) is embroidered with glass beads and pyrite crystals; it was obviously not for walking.

SCYTHIAN HORSEMAN, with flying cloak and bold moustache, is one of two figures used repeatedly to decorate the largest piece of cloth found in the frozen burial chambers in the Pazyryk valley of the Altai Mountains. Made of felt, the cloth was probably used as a rug. The preserved portion measures 15 by 21 feet; horse and rider occupy 16 square feet. The tombs were built about 300 B.C.

the signs of heavy wear in the axle holes, it appears that these wagons were used to drag up the boulders for the barrows and were then thrown into the pit when it was filled in. The fifth Pazyryk mound yielded up pieces of a much more complex wagon—evidently a kind of coach with four large, spoked wheels and a body consisting of latticed sides and a flat roof [see illustration at bottom right on page 235]. The shaft's yoke and traces show that the coach was pulled by four horses.

I have given only a quick survey of the finds in the Altai burial mounds; they make up a large collection that has been described in full detail in archaeological journals. We now ask: Who were these people—these artistic "barbarians" who lived in the Altai Mountains well over 2,000 years ago?

It can be said at once that they were clearly of Iranian origin. The woolen rug found in the fifth Pazyryk mound and many of the other objects can definitely be identified as Iranian in style. Beyond this, the obvious Black Sea influence and the general features that run through all the artifacts, particularly the familiar animal style, place the group within the overall Scythian culture that prevailed among the tribes of Eurasia.

At the same time the Altai remains also show a close contact with China. Although most of the individuals buried in the graves are of European stock, some are plainly Mongoloid. Moreover, some of the objects—such as a mirror and a saddlecloth with fine silk embroidery—are Chinese in origin [see top illustration on page 238]. There is every indication, indeed, that the Altai area was a meeting place between the Scythian nomads and ancient China. Here, it seems, was one of the ultimate extensions of the great Indo-European migration that stopped at China's doorstep.

Chinese documents of the third and second centuries B.C. tell of an Indo-European people in this region whom they call the Yueh-chih. In all probability these were the same people who built at least some of the Altai burial mounds. The Yueh-chih transmitted the Scythian art style to the Huns of Mongolia and northern China. Eventually they were dislodged from the region and driven westward by the Huns or the Turks.

Estimates of the dates of the Altai graves differ rather widely. From comparisons of the tree-growth rings in the excellently preserved timbers of the burial mounds it has been possible to judge the relative ages of the mounds pretty well. Apparently the difference between the oldest (the first mound at Tuekte) and the most recent (the fifth mound at Pazyryk) is about 200 years. We can be fairly confident about the accuracy of this relative chronology, because the tree-ring results agree with carbon-14 analyses of the wood, but the absolute dates are much more uncertain. The margin of error in the carbon-14 absolute dating is plus or minus 130 years, and the estimates of various authorities on the dates of the individual mounds range all the way from the seventh century B.C. to the first century of our era. The seventh-century date seems to me unlikely. The oldest examples of the Scythian animal style found in Iran and in the Black Sea area go back no further than the end of the seventh century B.C., and it is not to be expected that the style would have appeared earlier in a region near the extreme limit of the nomadic migrations; there is no basis whatever for supposing that the style originated in Siberia rather than at the fountainheads of Scythian culture near ancient Greece and Iran. The most probable dates for the burial mounds in the Altai Mountains are between the fifth (or at the earliest the sixth) and the third centuries B.C. The artistic styles in the Pazyryk mounds, for example, seem closely similar to those found in Iranian burials near the Black Sea (at Semibratny), which date from the fifth and fourth centuries B.C. Like the Semibratny burials, the successive Pazyryk graves show a gradual evolution of the animal style from realistic, three-dimensional forms to stylized, ornamental designs. This no doubt was a delayed but parallel reflection of the Black Sea development.

In any case, we are deeply indebted to the intervention of nature that preserved for us, in the frozen graves of the Altai Mountains, examples of ancient Scythian art in a great variety of materials that elsewhere have been effaced by the destructive processes of time. The Altai remains demonstrate clearly that art has been important to man in all times and among all peoples. Even in the so-called barbaric state man has enriched his life, from the cradle to the grave, with artistic creations. In every culture and age art has served not only to fulfill his aesthetic needs but also to shape his ideological concepts within the framework of his environment, his economy and his social relations.

SUMMIT OF CITY MOUND at Kültepe, which rises more than 60 feet above the level of the surrounding plain, is the open, treeless area in the bottom half of this photograph. The piles of rubble at the perimeter (*left center*) were left by early excavators who mistook the mound for the source of Assyrian cuneiform tablets. A recent excavation can be seen in progress in the foreground.

PRE-HITTITE ARTIFACTS found in the vicinity of Kültepe are characteristic of the indigenous art at the time of the Assyrian colonization of Anatolia. The three gold objects are a bowl, a cere- monial headdress and an ornamental pendant about four inches long. The pitcher (*left*), animal forms (*center*) and fruitstand (*right*) are all made of polished clay. Objects are not in same scale.

27

AN ASSYRIAN TRADING OUTPOST

TAHSIN ÖZGÜÇ
February 1963

Students of the ancient world once tended to think of each civilization as an isolated entity, a network of agricultural communities and administrative cities tied together by common cultural and political institutions and perhaps by rudimentary trade or some special common need such as an irrigation system. Sumer, Egypt, Assyria and the rest were conceived of as existing contemporaneously but more or less independently, or as succeeding each other in cycles of conquest or rebellion. In recent years a great deal of archaeological evidence has accumulated to show that this conception was incorrect, that man of the ancient civilizations was to a surprising degree a traveler and trader, and that civilizations influenced one another across deserts, mountains and seas. Most of the evidence has necessarily been indirect. Archaeologists investigating a site have found raw material that must have come from a distant place, an artifact of unmistakably foreign manufacture, a written reference to far-off peoples or a clear case of alien influence in indigenous works of art.

The site in central Turkey that my colleagues and I have been excavating for the past 14 years has provided more explicit and detailed evidence for such an interrelation of two ancient civilizations. What we have been studying is a commercial "colony," a foreign outpost in the central Anatolian city of Kanesh. Here, for 200 years from 1950 B.C. to 1750, two peoples with different languages and cultures lived together in a mutually advantageous commercial symbiosis. The local people were the native Hatti of Anatolia; the foreigners were Assyrian traders and businessmen from the plains of Mesopotamia far to the south. Their homes and artifacts and above all the thousands of clay tablets on which they recorded every detail of

their personal and business lives are providing us with a detailed picture of the complex politico-economic ties by which the Assyrians of Kanesh were linked to their homeland and to the local people and rulers.

The Assyrian colony in Kanesh was the culmination of many centuries of trade development. Since the plain of the Tigris and Euphrates is conspicuously deficient in mineral resources, the Mesopotamian cities were dependent from the beginning on imports for their metals. There are indications that as early as 3500 B.C. trade expeditions from the southernmost cities of Sumer were obtaining copper from the mountains of Urartu and central Anatolia, more than 1,000 miles to the north. A half-legendary text dating from a later period recalls a punitive expedition led by King Sargon the Great of Akkad against the Anatolian city of Purushanda, in the area of the "silver mountains," where the natives had been molesting itinerant Akkadian merchants. By the turn of the second millennium B.C. extensive foreign trade had become established as one of the primary features of Mesopotamian culture, and the most enterprising and successful businessmen of this period were the Assyrians.

Instead of relying on occasional expeditions, the Assyrians assured themselves of an adequate and dependable flow of raw materials by setting up permanent trade colonies at key locations throughout the principal ore-producing districts of central and eastern Anatolia. Regularly scheduled donkey caravans traveling over fixed trade routes connected these colonial outposts to the Assyrian capital of Assur [*see map on next two pages*]. Nine such colonies, or *karums,* are known to have existed in major cities of the indigenous Hatti between 1950 B.C. and 1750. Of eight of

these colonies only the names remain; their locations have not been discovered. Kanesh, the one colony that has been found, was the largest and was the controlling center of the whole network. The relation between the Assyrians and the Hatti and their rulers was for the most part harmonious. It was the rise to power of a new Indo-European ethnic group, the Hittites, that eventually put an end to the period of Assyrian colonization. But the Assyrians had left their mark. During their stay the indigenous Anatolian culture had become mixed with that of Mesopotamia. The amalgam became the basis of the ascendant Hittite civilization.

It is a curious fact that scholars knew a little about Kanesh and even suspected it was an Assyrian trading center long before Kanesh itself was uncovered. In 1881 clay tablets bearing Assyrian cuneiform inscriptions began to turn up in the shops of antique dealers in the modern Turkish city of Kayseri, 13 miles southwest of the site of Kanesh. They found a ready market among interested philologists and archaeologists, who could learn only that the tablets had been found by natives of the small village of Karahüyük. The village was near an ancient site known simply as Kültepe, or "ash mound": a hill rising more than 60 feet from the surrounding plain and covered by charred remains. When the French explorer Ernest Chantre undertook the first excavations of the mound in 1893, the villagers were unhelpfully reticent, and Chantre could not find the source of the tablets. Neither could a succession of scholars who followed him, until, in 1925, the Czech scholar Bedřich Hrozný had better luck. A friendly cook for his archaeological field party suggested that he look not on the mound but about 100 yards to the northeast. Hrozný dug there and came on the Assyrian merchants' quarter, the *karum* of Kanesh.

It is in the *karum* that our research under the auspices of the Turkish Historical Society and the Turkish Government's Department of Antiquities has been concentrated since 1948. We have found many thousands of clay tablets, and as we slowly decipher their wedge-shaped cuneiform characters the operations of the Assyrian trading system and the life of Kanesh emerge with increasing clarity.

The principal exports from Anatolia were, of course, metals. Gold, silver and precious stones made up most of the shipments to the markets of Assur. The Assyrians also traded locally in Anatolian copper, which the natives alloyed with tin to make bronze. Large quantities of tin, which was not available anywhere in Anatolia, constituted about 50 per cent of the imports. The Assyrians presumably obtained tin from some-

where in the Zagros Mountains east of Assyria, but their exact source of supply is not known. Textiles and clothing were the other major imports to Anatolia. In addition the Assyrians carried on a brisk local trade in hides, fleece, wool and rugs.

The trade was conducted both by direct barter and by exchange of currency. Gold was the principal capital of the commercial firms at Assur and was sometimes used as money, but silver provided the primary currency for trade with the natives. Both gold and silver were mined extensively in Anatolia, refined at the mines and shipped back to Assur. Within the native economy, on the other hand, copper was the medium of exchange.

The Assyrian merchants applied different terms in their dealings with the local people and among themselves. To their fellow merchants they extended credit more freely and at lower interest rates. In their transactions with the na-

tives they generally preferred cash payment, and when they made loans to Anatolians it was at a higher rate and for a shorter term. Imported manufactures sold in Anatolia at a 100 per cent markup on their price in Assur. The institution of collateral played an important role in trading contracts. A debt might be secured by every item of a man's property—including his wife and children.

As was their practice throughout Anatolia, the Assyrians did not attempt to interfere in any way with local politics. They managed their commercial activities and settled disputes among themselves through their own Assyrian institutions: local councils made up of officials appointed from Assur and other members elected by resident Assyrian traders for specific terms of office. Where commerce impinged on local politics their councils negotiated treaties or other agreements with the local princes.

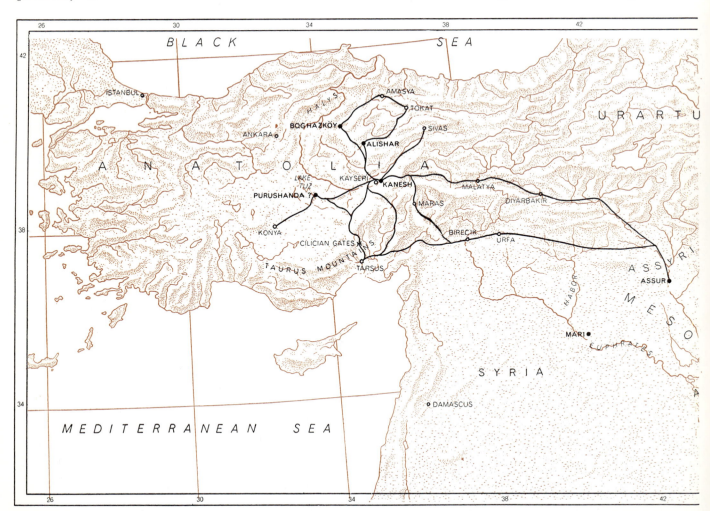

PRINCIPAL TRADE ROUTES traversed by the Assyrian merchants originated at Assur in northern Mesopotamia and terminated at the central Anatolian city of Kanesh. The northern route followed the upper Tigris River Valley and entered Kanesh from the east. The southern route skirted the edge of the North Syrian desert and ascended the Anatolian Plateau from three different

The dependence of the councils on the home government at Assur was effected by making them all subject to the *karum* at Kanesh, which was in turn directly connected to Assur, or, as it is usually referred to in the tablets, "the City."

Most of the major Anatolian cities of the period were ruled by local princes and princesses and were entirely autonomous. The Assyrian merchants paid taxes to the local prince on imports, exports and sales. In return the prince guaranteed the trade caravans safe passage through his territory. In the event of any change in local government, such as the accession of a new prince to the throne, an oath of confidence was asked from the council of the *karum*. The prince also acted as an arbitrator in cases of conflict between the Assyrians and his native subjects. For a certain fee the prince would provide storage space for merchandise in the cellar of his palace. We have found such cellar warehouses in both of the two palaces so far exca-

vated on the Kültepe mound. In addition to his regular fee the prince also had the first option to buy any of the latest imports from Assur.

Most of the documents unearthed from the *karum* at Kanesh are of a purely commercial nature. They include business letters, contracts, bills of lading, memoranda about purchases and sales, and deeds between Assyrian traders. The local princes and even some of the common people learned to use the Assyrian script. We have found letters from one native to another, legal documents, lists of palace staffs and documents bearing on family relations that teach us something about the Hatti administrative system and civilization. In some cases the mention of proper names—local gods, people and places—provides a clue to the unwritten local language of the time.

More than most archaeological finds, some of the tablets give vivid insights into personal lives. One letter from a woman at home in Assur to her trader husband in Kanesh complains about her mother-in-law. Another woman left behind in Assyria writes to bemoan the fact that she does not have enough money to buy a sacrifice to a god. And we have one letter, apparently never dispatched, in which a woman whose mother-in-law is dying asks her sister-in-law to come to Kanesh to help. Encountered among vast stacks of commercial documents, these letters cut sharply through the centuries and remind one of the human beings behind the clay tablets and pottery shards.

The first Assyrian traders settled at Kanesh in about 1950 B.C. They established residence in a section of the city that lay like a crescent around the northeastern rim of the central mound, and it was this area that became the Assyrian *karum*. It is some 1,000 yards long, 700 yards wide and only a couple of yards above the level of the plain. Whereas the central city was populated from the Early Bronze Age until the end of the Roman era in the fourth century A.D., the *karum* was inhabited for but a short period of time. Only four distinct building levels are to be found there, the total thickness of which, from virgin soil to the floor of the latest level, is just under 28 feet. The two lowest levels, designated III and IV, antedate the Assyrian colonization and no written documents have yet been found there. It is Level II that introduces the documented historical era and the Assyrians, and it is here that we have unearthed the ma-

jority of the tablets—more than 14,000 of them.

The city of this era was divided into various quarters by squares and streets wide enough to allow the passage of carts. The residences of the Assyrian merchants were concentrated in the center and northern section of the *karum*, with local Anatolians in the southern part. Apparently the Assyrians preferred to stick together, but the boundaries between quarters were not distinct. The shops of craftsmen were grouped at the center of the community. We have found two-room buildings containing large amounts of crockery and kitchen equipment; these may have been restaurants. Other small buildings open to the street and outfitted with stone or wooden shelves seem to have been shops of some kind, but we do not yet know what they contained. Most of the residences were two stories high and had three or four rooms on each floor, grouped around a covered courtyard. In many cases small rooms filled with tablets and separated from the living quarters appear to have served as offices.

Unfortunately for the inhabitants but fortunately for the archaeologist, the history of Level II ended with a disastrous fire. The inhabitants departed in a hurry, leaving behind them the contents of their houses and workshops. Whatever resisted the flames remains to this day substantially as it was abandoned. The site was uninhabited for between 30 and 60 years, after which a new city was built on the ruins, apparently by a new generation of Assyrian merchants. The new city is designated I*b* to distinguish it from a slightly later, non-Assyrian level, I*a*. The houses of I*b* were larger and individual rooms were more spacious. Although we have found less evidence of business activity in the form of cuneiform records (only some 80 tablets have been unearthed so far), Level I*b* apparently represents a city at least as prosperous as its predecessor. Whereas the walls of houses in the earlier city had been built of mud brick on wooden frames, stone-wall construction now became more popular. The Assyrian merchants were still influential in the I*b* city, but more of the native merchants in the southern part of the city now lived in houses as large and well designed as those of the colonists.

The artifacts found in Levels II and I*b* reflect the remarkable degree to which the Assyrian colonists adopted the culture of their Hatti neighbors. Except for the clay tablets, with their cuneiform script and distinctly Meso-

directions. **Auxiliary routes connected all the major trade centers of Anatolia to Kanesh. Open circles indicate modern cities.**

potamian cylinder-seal impressions, all the artifacts of these levels are in the native style. If the tablets and their sealed envelopes had not been found, in fact, we might never have suspected the existence of the merchant colony.

It was during the colonial period that the ceramic art reached its highest de-

velopment in Anatolia. Some of the pottery was richly decorated, but the finest pieces depended for their beauty on purity of line and burnished monochrome finishes. Human and animal figures, drinking cups and small cosmetic boxes molded in the form of animals rank among the masterpieces of their kind.

The clay envelopes in which cuneiform tablets were enclosed were sealed with elaborate impressions made by carved stone cylinder seals [see bottom illustration on page 247]. The natives took over this ancient Mesopotamian device and developed it in their own distinctive style. In the locally made seals

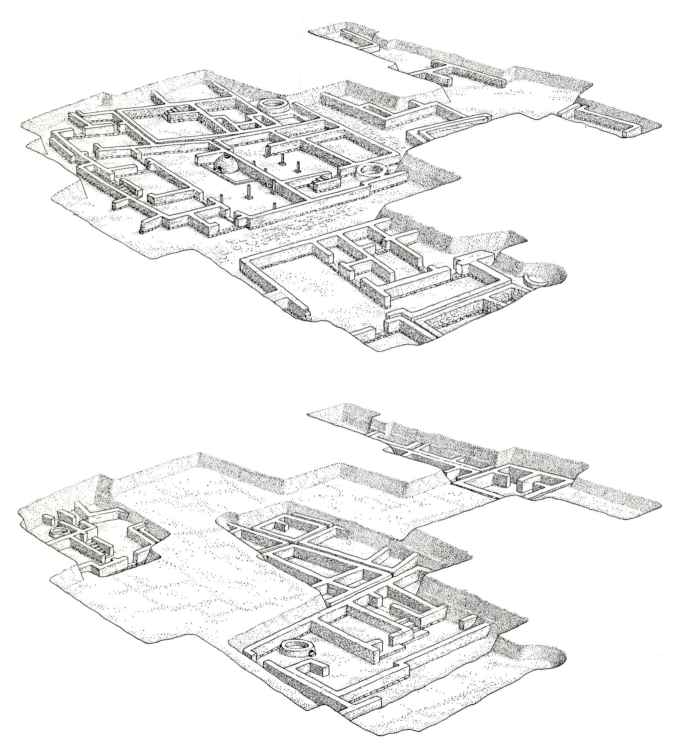

KARUM OF KANESH had four distinct building levels, two of which are shown in this schematic drawing of an excavation at the site. The houses of the earlier Level II (bottom), the settlement in which most of the clay tablets were found, were largely of mudbrick construction. Those of the later Level Ib (top) were more spacious and closer together, and many of them had stone walls.

BRONZE DAGGER from the mound of Kanesh bears the Assyrian words "Palace of Anitta, the King." Anitta ruled in the region toward the end of the Assyrian colonial period.

ivory. Both materials are native to North Syria. The ivory statuette is remarkably similar to the figures of naked goddesses discovered at Mari in North Syria and must have been an import from that area. Both of these figurines were found in the grave of a foreign merchant. They are in sharp contrast to the majority of the religious figures uncovered in Level I*b*, which are in the native style. Most of these are lead plaques showing the principal Anatolian goddess, with or without her family, in low relief. We have also found the stone molds from which the plaques were cast.

During the time when Level I*b* was occupied, major changes were taking place in Anatolia. Regional kings arose and began to extend their control over the feudal domains of the local princes. One of the rulers was Anitta, whose name appears on a bronze dagger unearthed in the remains of a palace on the mound of Kanesh. Anitta was king of the city of Kussara and apparently held dominion over Kanesh. Shortly after the reign of Anitta, during the first half of the 18th century B.C., invaders from the north—presumably Hittites—attacked and burned both the central city and the Level I*b* karum. Although a small city was built on the ruins and left its remains as level I*a* in the *karum* area, the fire marked the end of the Assyrian colony. With the consolidation of political power in the Hittite Old Kingdom, the immediate Assyrian influence in Anatolia was at an end.

The influence of Assyria in Anatolia nonetheless persisted. For more than a century the Anatolians had been in direct contact with the advanced culture of Mesopotamia, with a written lan-

processions of gods and scenes of the hunt and of battle are prominent; many of these themes were later developed into primary motifs of Hittite art.

Although the resident Assyrians apparently had little effect on Anatolian art forms aside from the cylinder seals, we have found a strong North Syrian influence, particularly in metal objects, pottery and small statues. Evidence of this influence is found in both imports and imitative native products. One of the most interesting imports is a hollow-shafted adz that is distinctly foreign to Anatolia and must have been brought in from the area of the Habor River [*see* map on pages 244 and 245]. This tool and many other metal objects found in specific strata at Kanesh and at Syrian sites

are useful for establishing archaeological synchronism. In both levels of the *karum* we have found clothing pins, axes, daggers and spearheads fashioned in bronze, silver or gold. None of these objects has been excavated at levels dating from either before or after the Assyrian colonization. The fact that they are not Assyrian but North Syrian indicates that the Kanesh *karum* maintained close relations not only with Assur but also with other neighboring lands. Some of them may not have been important items of trade but merely the personal effects of itinerant merchants passing through Kanesh.

Among the figurines of gods and goddesses, we have found two that are in a style alien to Anatolia. One is made of a glazed pottery and the other of

CYLINDER SEAL is shown at the right. At the left is its impress, made by rolling it over wet clay. Cylinder seals were characteristic Mesopotamian devices and were introduced into Anatolia by the Assyrians. This particular seal probably came from North Syria.

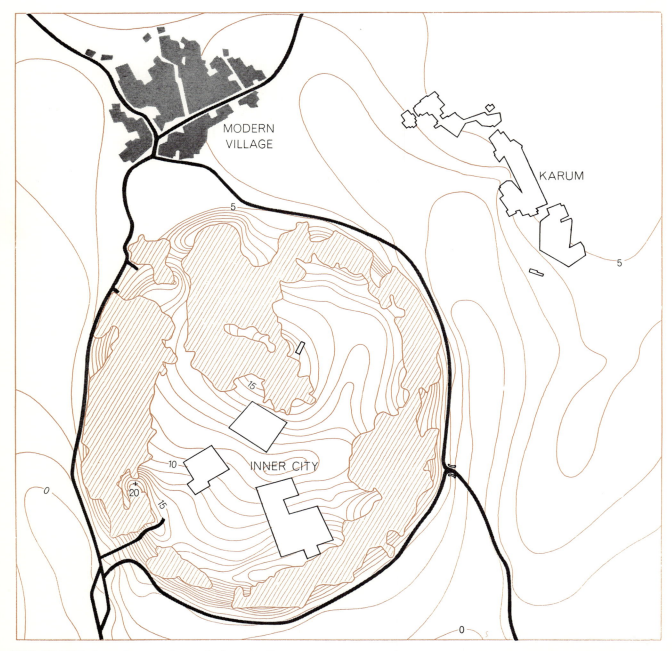

MAP OF SITE shows the central mound where the Hatti city of Kanesh was located and the outlying *karum* of the Assyrian merchants. The diagonally hatched areas around the perimeter of the mound were excavated by early archaeologists. The author's excavations on the mound and in the *karum* are outlined in black. Contour intervals are indicated in meters above the level of the plain.

CLAY TABLETS were often stored in large earthenware jars like this one, photographed as it was uncovered in the house of a merchant in Level II. The foot rule indicates scale.

guage and with a highly organized commercial system. Assyrian scribes served in the palaces of the Anatolian kings, and some of the local people learned enough of the written language to use it for commercial, legal and administrative purposes. The upper classes in particular came under the broadening influence of the Assyrians. They acquired a taste for the fashions and luxuries of Babylon and picked up administrative techniques and business acumen. Perhaps most important of all, this provincial people acquired from the Assyrians a sense of empire that later expressed itself in the powerful Hittite civilization, which dominated Asia Minor in the centuries that followed.

CLAY ENVELOPES in which the tablets were enclosed to be filed or dispatched were sealed with the writer's personal design, applied with a cylinder seal. Such a design is seen at the top of this envelope. The writing below may be an address or a summary of contents.

BIBLIOGRAPHIES

I PALEOLITHIC HUNTERS AND GATHERERS

1. The Idea of Man's Antiquity

A HUNDRED YEARS OF ANTHROPOLOGY. Thomas Kenneth Penniman. Duckworth & Co., Ltd., 1952.

THE TESTIMONY OF THE SPADE. Geoffrey Bibby. Alfred A. Knopf, 1956.

2. Evolution of Paleolithic Art

L'ARTE DELL'ANTICA ETA DELLA PIETRA. P. Graziozi. Sansoni, 1956

QUATRE CENTS SIÈCLES D'ART PARIÉTAL: LES CAVERNES ORNÉES DE L'ÂGE DU RENNE. Abbé Henri Breuil. Centre d'Études et de Documentation préhistorique, 1952.

LES RELIGIONS DE LA PRÉHISTOIRE (PALÉOLITHIQUE). André Leroi-Gourhan. *Mythes et religions: Vol. LI.* Presses Universitaires de France, 1964.

LA SIGNIFICATION DE L'ART RUPESTRE PALÉOLITHIQUE. A. Laming-Emperaire. Picard, 1962.

TREASURES OF PREHISTORIC ART. André Leroi-Gourhan. Harry N. Abrams, Inc., 1967.

3. The Solutrean Culture

LAUGERIE-HAUTE PRÈS DES EYZIES (DORDOGNE). Denis and Élie Peyrony in *Archives de L'Institut de Paléontologie Humaine,* Mémoire 19; June, 1938.

RADIOCARBON DATES AND UPPER PALAEOLITHIC ARCHAEOLOGY IN CENTRAL AND WESTERN EUROPE. Hallam L. Movius, Jr., in *Current Anthropology,* Vol. 1, Nos. 5–6, pages 355–375; November, 1960.

RELIQUIAE AQUITANICAE; BEING CONTRIBUTIONS TO THE ARCHAEOLOGY AND PALAEONTOLOGY OF PÉRIGORD AND THE ADJOINING PROVINCES OF SOUTHERN FRANCE. Edouard Lartet and Henry Christy. Williams & Norgate, 1875.

4. A Paleolithic Camp at Nice

LES NIVEAUX QUATERNAIRES MARINS DES ALPES-MARITIMES: CORRÉLATIONS AVEC LES INDUSTRIES PRÉHISTORIQUE. Henry de Lumley in *Compte rendu sommaire des Séances de la Société Géologique de France,* Vol. 5, 7th Series, pages 163–164; 1963.

LES FOUILLES DE TERRA AMATA À NICE: PREMIERS RÉSULTATS. H. de Lumley in *Bulletin du Musée d'Anthropologie préhistorique de Monaco,* No. 13, pages 29–51; 1966.

5. Shanidar Cave

A PALEOLITHIC SITE IN THE ZAGROS MOUNTAINS OF NORTHERN IRAQ. REPORT ON A SOUNDING AT SHANIDAR CAVE (PART I). R. S. Solecki in *Sumer,* Vol. 8, No. 2, pages 127–192; 1952.

A PALEOLITHIC SITE IN THE ZAGROS MOUNTAINS OF NORTHERN IRAQ. REPORT ON A SOUNDING AT SHANIDAR CAVE (PART II). R. S. Solecki in *Sumer,* Vol. 9, No. 1, pages 60–105; 1953.

THE SEVEN CAVES: ARCHAEOLOGICAL EXPLORATIONS IN THE MIDDLE EAST. Carleton S. Coon. Alfred A. Knopf, 1957.

SHANIDAR CAVE, A PALEOLITHIC SITE IN NORTHERN IRAQ. Ralph S. Solecki in *Annual Report of the Board of Regents of the Smithsonian Institution,* pages 389–425; 1954.

THE SHANIDAR CAVE SOUNDING, 1953 SEASON, WITH NOTES CONCERNING THE DISCOVERY OF THE FIRST PALEOLITHIC SKELETON IN IRAQ. R. S. Solecki in *Sumer,* Vol. 9, No. 2, pages 229–232; 1953.

6. Isimila: A Paleolithic Site in Africa

EARLY MAN IN AFRICA. J. Desmond Clark in *Scientific American,* Vol. 199, No. 1, pages 77–83; July, 1958.

HUMAN ECOLOGY DURING THE PLEISTOCENE AND
LATER TIMES IN AFRICA SOUTH OF THE SAHARA.
J. Desmond Clark in *Current Anthropology*, Vol.
1, No. 4, pages 307–324; July, 1960.

TOOLS AND HUMAN EVOLUTION. Sherwood L. Wash-
burn in *Scientific American*, Vol. 203, No. 3, pages
63–75; September, 1960.

II   NEOLITHIC VILLAGERS AND FARMERS

7. From Cave to Village

REPORT OF ROBERT J. BRAIDWOOD ON WORK IN
NORTHERN IRAQ. *American Journal of Archaeology*, Vol. 56, No. 1, pages 47–49; January, 1952.

8. The Agricultural Revolution

ANIMAL DOMESTICATION IN THE PREHISTORIC NEAR
EAST. Charles A. Reed in *Science*, Vol. 130, No.
3,389, pages 1,629–1,639; December 11, 1959.

DOMESTICATION OF FOOD PLANTS IN THE OLD WORLD.
Hans Helbaek in *Science*, Vol. 130, No. 3,372,
pages 365–372; August 14, 1959.

NEAR EASTERN PREHISTORY. Robert J. Braidwood
in *Science*, Vol. 127, No. 3,312, pages 1,419–
1,430; June 20, 1958.

PREHISTORIC INVESTIGATIONS IN IRAQI KURDISTAN.
Robert J. Braidwood and Bruce Howe in *Studies
in Ancient Civilization*, No. 31. University of
Chicago Press. 1960.

9. Obsidian and the Origins of Trade

OBSIDIAN AND EARLY CULTURAL CONTACT IN THE
NEAR EAST. Colin Renfrew, J. E. Dixon and J. R.
Cann in *Proceedings of the Prehistoric Society
for 1966*, New Series, Vol. 32, No. 2, pages 30–
72; December, 1966.

OBSIDIAN IN THE AEGEAN. Colin Renfrew, J. R. Cann
and J. E. Dixon in *The Annual of the British
School at Athens*, No. 60, pages 225–242; 1965.

10. Ancient Jericho

JERICHO GIVES UP ITS SECRETS. Kathleen M. Kenyon
and A. Douglas Tushingham in *The National
Geographic Magazine*, Vol. CIV, No. 6 pages 853–
870; December, 1953.

11. An Early Neolithic Village in Greece

THE DAWN OF CIVILIZATION: THE FIRST WORLD
SURVEY OF HUMAN CULTURE IN EARLY TIMES.
Edited by Stuart Piggott. McGraw-Hill Book
Company, 1961.

EXCAVATIONS AT THE EARLY NEOLITHIC SITE AT
NEA NIKOMEDEIA, GREEK MACEDONIA (1961
SEASON). Robert J. Rodden *et al.* in *Proceedings
of the Prehistoric Society for 1962*, New Series,
Vol. XXVIII, pages 267–288, 1962.

THE SCIENCE AND HISTORY OF DOMESTIC ANIMALS.
Wolf Heere in *Science in Archaeology*, edited by
Don Brothwell and Eric Higgs. Thames and Hud-
son, 1963

12. A Hunters' Village in Neolithic Turkey

A METHOD OF CALCULATING THE DIETARY PER-
CENTAGE OF VARIOUS FOOD ANIMALS UTILIZED
BY ABORIGINAL PEOPLES. Theodore E. White
in *American Antiquity*, Vol. 18, No. 4, pages 396–
398; April, 1953

PREHISTORIC FAUNA FROM SHANIDAR, IRAQ. Dexter
Perkins, Jr., in *Science*, Vol. 144, No. 3626, pages
1,565–1,566; June 26, 1964.

SUBERDE EXCAVATIONS, 1964. Jacques Bordaz in
*Anatolian Studies: Journal of the British Institute
of Archaeology at Ankara*, Vol. 15, pages 30–32;
1965.

SUBERDE. Jacques Bordaz in *Anatolian Studies:
Journal of the British Institute of Archaeology at
Ankara*, Vol. 16, pages 32–33; 1966.

13. An Early Farming Village in Turkey

PREHISTORIC MEN. Robert J. Braidwood. Scott, Fores-
man and Company, 1967.

NATURAL ENVIRONMENT OF EARLY FOOD PRODUC-
TION NORTH OF MESOPOTAMIA. H. E. Wright, Jr.,
in *Science*, Vol. 161, No. 3839, pages 334–339;
July 26, 1968.

14. A Neolithic City in Turkey

ANATOLIA BEFORE C. 4000 B.C. AND C. 2300–1750 B.C.
James Mellaart in *Cambridge Ancient History
Fascicle No. 20*. Cambridge University Press,
1964.

THE BEGINNINGS OF MURAL PAINTING. James Mellaart
in *Archaeology*, Vol. 15, No. 1, pages 2–12; Spring,
1962.

DEITIES AND SHRINES OF NEOLITHIC ANATOLIA:
EXCAVATIONS AT ÇATAL HÜYÜK, 1962. James
Mellaart in *Archaeology*, Vol. 16, No. 1, pages
29–38; Spring, 1963.

III BRONZE AGE CITIES AND CIVILIZATIONS

15. The Origin of Cities

LA CITÉ-TEMPLE SUMÉRIENNE. A. Falkenstein in *Cahiers D'Histoire Mondiale*, Vol. I, No. 4, pages 784–814; April, 1954.

CITY INVINCIBLE: A SYMPOSIUM ON URBANIZATION AND CULTURAL DEVELOPMENT IN THE ANCIENT NEAR EAST. Oriental Institute Special Publication, 1960.

EARLY POLITICAL DEVELOPMENT IN MESOPOTAMIA. Thorkild Jacobsen in *Zeitschrift für Assyriologie und Vorderasiatische Archäologie*, Vol. 52, No. 18, pages 91–140; August, 1957.

THE PREINDUSTRIAL CITY. Gideon Sjoberg in *American Journal of Sociology*, Vol. I, No. 5, pages 438–445; March, 1955.

WHAT HAPPENED IN HISTORY. V. Gordon Childe. Penguin Books, Inc., 1946.

16. The Sumerians

ANCIENT NEAR EASTERN TEXTS RELATING TO THE OLD TESTAMENT. Edited by James B. Pritchard. Princeton University Press, 1950.

THE ART AND ARCHITECTURE OF THE ANCIENT ORIENT. Henri Frankfort. Penguin Books, 1954.

THE BIRTH OF CIVILIZATION IN THE NEAR EAST. Henri Frankfort. Indiana University Press, 1951.

THE INTELLECTUAL ADVENTURE OF ANCIENT MAN. H. and H. A. Frankfort, John A. Wilson, Thorkild Jacobsen and William A. Irwin. The University of Chicago Press, 1946.

SUMERIAN MYTHOLOGY: A STUDY OF SPIRITUAL AND LITERARY ACHIEVEMENT IN THE THIRD MILLENNIUM B.C. S. N. Kramer. The American Philosophical Society, 1944.

FROM THE TABLETS OF SUMER: TWENTY-FIVE FIRSTS IN MAN'S RECORDED HISTORY. Samuel Noah Kramer. The Falcon's Wing Press, 1956.

17. The Decline of the Harappans

THE CAMBRIDGE HISTORY OF INDIA: THE INDUS CIVILIZATION. Sir Mortimer Wheeler. Cambridge University Press, 1953.

CIVILIZATION AND FLOODS IN THE INDUS VALLEY. George F. Dales in *Expedition*, Vol. 7, No. 4, pages 10–19; Summer, 1965.

THE END OF THE ANCIENT CITIES OF THE INDUS. Robert L. Raikes in *American Anthropologist*, Vol. 66, No. 2, pages 284–299; April, 1964.

THE MOHENJO-DARO FLOODS. Robert L. Raikes in *Antiquity*, Vol. 39, No. 155, pages 196–203; September, 1965.

18. A Forgotten Civilization in the Persian Gulf

ANCIENT ARABIA: EXPLORATIONS IN HASA, 1940–1941. P. B. Cornwall in *The Geographical Journal*, Vol. CVII, pages 28–50; January-June, 1946.

BAHREIN AND HEMAMIEH. Ernest Mackay, Lankester Harding and Flinders Petrie. British School of Archaeology in Egypt, No. 47; 1929.

THE SEAFARING MERCHANTS OF UR. A. L. Oppenheim in *Journal of the American Oriental Society*, Vol. 74, pages 6–17; 1954.

NEW INVESTIGATIONS AT MOHENJO-DARO. George F. Dales in *Archaeology*, Vol. 18, No. 2, pages 145–150; Summer, 1965.

19. An Early City in Iran

THE SUMERIANS: THEIR HISTORY, CULTURE, AND CHARACTER. Samuel Noah Kramer. The University of Chicago Press, 1963.

THE INDUS CIVILIZATION. Sir Mortimer Wheeler. Cambridge University Press, 1968.

EXCAVATIONS AT TEPE YAHYĀ, SOUTHEASTERN IRAN, 1967–1969. C. C. Lamberg-Karlovsky in *Bulletin of the American Journal of Prehistoric Research*, No. 27. Peabody Museum, Harvard University, 1970.

THE PROTO-ELAMITE SETTLEMENT AT TEPE YAHYĀ. C. C. Lamberg-Karlovsky in *Iran*, Vol. 9, 1971.

20. The Tombs of the First Pharaohs

GREAT TOMBS OF THE FIRST DYNASTY: EXCAVATIONS AT SAQQARA. Walter B. Emery. Vol. I, Government Press, 1949; Vol. II, Oxford University Press, 1954.

IV RECENT PERSPECTIVES AND PROBLEMS

21. Radiocarbon Dating

RADIOCARBON DATING. Willard F. Libby. University of Chicago Press, 1952.

22. Carbon 14 and the Prehistory of Europe

COLONIALISM AND MEGALITHISMUS. Colin Renfrew

in *Antiquity*, Vol. 41, No. 164, pages 276–288; December, 1967.
THE AUTONOMY OF THE SOUTH-EAST EUROPEAN COPPER AGE. Colin Renfrew in *Proceedings of the Prehistoric Society*, Vol. 35, pages 12–47; 1969.
NOBEL SYMPOSIUM 12: RADIOCARBON VARIATIONS AND ABSOLUTE CHRONOLOGY. Edited by Ingrid U. Olsson. John Wiley & Sons, Inc., 1970.
THE TREE-RING CALIBRATION OF RADIOCARBON: AN ARCHAEOLOGICAL EVALUATION. Colin Renfrew in *Proceedings of the Prehistoric Society*, Vol. 36, pages 280–311; 1970.

23. The Tartaria Tablets

CHRONOLOGY OF THE NEOLITHIC IN TRANSYLVANIA IN THE LIGHT OF THE TARTARIA SETTLEMENT'S STRATIGRAPHY. N. Vlassa in *Dacia*, Vol. 7, pages 485–494; 1963.
UNE CIVILISATION ÉGÉO-ORIENTALE SUR LE MOYEN DANUBE. Vladislav Popovitch in *Revue Archéologique*, Tome II, pages 1–56; July-September, 1965.
THE TARTARIA TABLETS. M. S. F. Hood in *Antiquity*, Vol. 41, No. 162, pages 99–113; June, 1967.
THE TARTARIA TABLETS: A CHRONOLOGICAL ISSUE. Evžen Neustupný in *Antiquity*, Vol. 42, No. 165, pages 32–35; March, 1968.

24. Stonehenge

THE AGE OF STONEHENGE. E. Herbert Stone in *The Nineteenth Century and After*, Vol. 95, pages 97–105; January-June, 1924.

25. Prehistoric Swiss Lake Dwellers

DIE AUSGRABUNGEN IN DER SPÄTBRONZEZEITLICHEN UFERSIEDLUNG ZUG-SUMPF. Josef Speck in *Das Pfahlbau-problem*, edited by W. U. Guyan et al., pages 275–334. Birkhäuser, 1955.
PFAHLBAUSTUDIEN. Emil Vogt in *Das Pfahlbau-problem*, edited by W. U. Guyan et al., pages 119–219. Birkhäuser, 1955.
REVIEW OF DAS PFAHLBAUPROBLEM. H.-G. Bandi in *Bonner Jahrbücher*, No. 155–156, Part II, pages 623–631; 1955–1956.

26. Frozen Tombs of the Scythians

CULTURE OF THE PEOPLE OF THE ALTAI HIGHLANDS IN THE SCYTHIAN PERIOD. S. I. Rudenko, 1953. (In Russian.)
CULTURE OF THE PEOPLE OF CENTRAL ALTAI IN THE SCYTHIAN PERIOD. S. I. Rudenko, 1960. (In Russian.)
HORSES OF THE PAZYRYKSK BURIAL MOUNDS. V. O. Vitt in *Soviet Archeology*, 1952. (In Russian.)
MATERIALS ON THE ARCHEOLOGY OF SIBERIA: EXCAVATIONS OF ACADEMICIAN V. V. RADLOV IN 1865. A. A. Zakharov in *Treatises of the State Historical Museum: Vol. I*, 1926. (In Russian.)
RELATIVE CHRONOLOGY OF THE PAZYRYKSK BURIAL MOUNDS. I. M. Zamotorin in *Soviet Archeology*, No. 1, 1959. (In Russian.)

27. An Assyrian Trading Outpost

EARLY ANATOLIA. Seton Lloyd. A Pelican Book, 1956.
INSCRIPTIONS FROM ALISHAR AND VICINITY. Ignace J. Gelb in *Oriental Institute Publications*, Vol. XXVII. University of Chicago Press, 1935.
NEW FINDS IN THE "KARUM" OF KANESH. Tahsin Özgüç in *The Illustrated London News*, Vol. 219, No. 5868, pages 544–547; October 6, 1951.
SOME ASPECTS OF COMMERCIAL LIFE IN ASSYRIA AND ASIA MINOR IN THE NINETEENTH PRE-CHRISTIAN CENTURY. Julius Lewy in *Journal of the American Oriental Society*, Vol. 78, No. 2, pages 89–101; June, 1958.
WHERE THE ASSYRIANS BUILT A COMMERCIAL EMPIRE IN SECOND-MILLENNIUM ANATOLIA: EXCAVATING THE "KARUM" OF KANES. Tahsin Özgüç in *The Illustrated London News*, Vol. 216, No. 5778, pages 68–71; January 14, 1950.

INDEX